Augmented Reality and the Future of Education Technology

Rashmi Aggarwal
Chitkara University, India

Prachi Gupta
Chitkara University, India

Satinder Singh
USB, Chandigarh University, India

Rajni Bala
Chitkara Business School, Chitkara University, India

A volume in the Advances in Educational Technologies and Instructional Design (AETID) Book Series

Published in the United States of America by
IGI Global
Information Science Reference (an imprint of IGI Global)
701 E. Chocolate Avenue
Hershey PA, USA 17033
Tel: 717-533-8845
Fax: 717-533-8661
E-mail: cust@igi-global.com
Web site: http://www.igi-global.com

Copyright © 2024 by IGI Global. All rights reserved. No part of this publication may be reproduced, stored or distributed in any form or by any means, electronic or mechanical, including photocopying, without written permission from the publisher.
Product or company names used in this set are for identification purposes only. Inclusion of the names of the products or companies does not indicate a claim of ownership by IGI Global of the trademark or registered trademark.

Library of Congress Cataloging-in-Publication Data

Names: Aggarwal, Rashmi, 1974- editor. | Gupta, Prachi, 1970- editor. | Singh, Satinder, 1988- editor. | Bala, Rajni, 1984- editor.
Title: Augmented reality and the future of education technology / Edited by Rashmi Aggarwal, Prachi Gupta, Satinder Singh, Rajni Bala.
Description: Hershey, PA : Information Science Reference, [2024] | Includes bibliographical references and index. | Summary: "This book investigates the transformative power of technology in education. It investigates the various ways in which these technologies are employed in education today, as well as the difficulties and opportunities they provide"-- Provided by publisher.
Identifiers: LCCN 2024010190 (print) | LCCN 2024010191 (ebook) | ISBN 9798369330159 (hardcover) | ISBN 9798369345085 (paperback) | ISBN 9798369330166 (ebook)
Subjects: LCSH: Education--Effect of technological innovations on. | Augmented reality in education. | Educational technology.
Classification: LCC LB1028.3 .A92 2024 (print) | LCC LB1028.3 (ebook) | DDC 371.33--dc23/eng/20240306
LC record available at https://lccn.loc.gov/2024010190
LC ebook record available at https://lccn.loc.gov/2024010191

This book is published in the IGI Global book series Advances in Educational Technologies and Instructional Design (AETID) (ISSN: 2326-8905; eISSN: 2326-8913)

British Cataloguing in Publication Data
A Cataloguing in Publication record for this book is available from the British Library.
All work contributed to this book is new, previously-unpublished material.
The views expressed in this book are those of the authors, but not necessarily of the publisher.
For electronic access to this publication, please contact: eresources@igi-global.com.

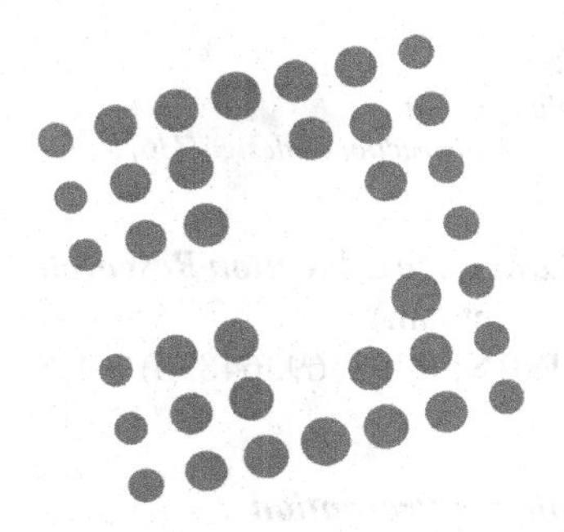

Advances in Educational Technologies and Instructional Design (AETID) Book Series

Lawrence A. Tomei
Robert Morris University, USA

ISSN:2326-8905
EISSN:2326-8913

MISSION

Education has undergone, and continues to undergo, immense changes in the way it is enacted and distributed to both child and adult learners. In modern education, the traditional classroom learning experience has evolved to include technological resources and to provide online classroom opportunities to students of all ages regardless of their geographical locations. From distance education, Massive-Open-Online-Courses (MOOCs), and electronic tablets in the classroom, technology is now an integral part of learning and is also affecting the way educators communicate information to students.

The **Advances in Educational Technologies & Instructional Design (AETID) Book Series** explores new research and theories for facilitating learning and improving educational performance utilizing technological processes and resources. The series examines technologies that can be integrated into K-12 classrooms to improve skills and learning abilities in all subjects including STEM education and language learning. Additionally, it studies the emergence of fully online classrooms for young and adult learners alike, and the communication and accountability challenges that can arise. Trending topics that are covered include adaptive learning, game-based learning, virtual school environments, and social media effects. School administrators, educators, academicians, researchers, and students will find this series to be an excellent resource for the effective design and implementation of learning technologies in their classes.

COVERAGE

- K-12 Educational Technologies
- Virtual School Environments
- E-Learning
- Digital Divide in Education
- Adaptive Learning
- Game-Based Learning
- Social Media Effects on Education
- Online Media in Classrooms
- Classroom Response Systems
- Higher Education Technologies

IGI Global is currently accepting manuscripts for publication within this series. To submit a proposal for a volume in this series, please contact our Acquisition Editors at Acquisitions@igi-global.com or visit: http://www.igi-global.com/publish/.

The Advances in Educational Technologies and Instructional Design (AETID) Book Series (ISSN 2326-8905) is published by IGI Global, 701 E. Chocolate Avenue, Hershey, PA 17033-1240, USA, www.igi-global.com. This series is composed of titles available for purchase individually; each title is edited to be contextually exclusive from any other title within the series. For pricing and ordering information please visit http://www.igi-global.com/book-series/advances-educational-technologies-instructional-design/73678. Postmaster: Send all address changes to above address. Copyright © 2024 IGI Global. All rights, including translation in other languages reserved by the publisher. No part of this series may be reproduced or used in any form or by any means – graphics, electronic, or mechanical, including photocopying, recording, taping, or information and retrieval systems – without written permission from the publisher, except for non commercial, educational use, including classroom teaching purposes. The views expressed in this series are those of the authors, but not necessarily of IGI Global.

Titles in this Series

For a list of additional titles in this series, please visit:
http://www.igi-global.com/book-series/advances-educational-technologies-instructional-design/73678

Considerations and Techniques for Applied Linguistics and Language Education Research
Hung Phu Bui (University of Economics, Ho Chi Minh City, Vietnam)
Information Science Reference • © 2024 • 241pp • H/C (ISBN: 9798369364826) • US $245.00

Comprehensive Sexuality Education for Gender-Based Violence Prevention
Mariana Buenestado-Fernández (University of Cantabria, Spain) Azahara Jiménez-Millán (University of Córdoba, Spain) and Francisco Javier Palacios-Hidalgo (University of Córdoba, Spain)
Information Science Reference • © 2024 • 342pp • H/C (ISBN: 9798369320532) • US $245.00

Enhancing Curricula with Service Learning Models
Sharon Valarmathi (Christ University, India) Jacqueline Kareem (Christ University, India) Veerta Tantia (Christ University, India) Kishore Selva Babu (Christ University, India) and Patrick Jude Lucas (Christ University, India)
Information Science Reference • © 2024 • 328pp • H/C (ISBN: 9798369359334) • US $265.00

Encouraging Transnational Learning Through Virtual Exchange in Global Teacher Education
Alina Slapac (University of Missouri-St. Louis, USA) and Cristina A. Huertas-Abril (University of Córdoba, Spain)
Information Science Reference • © 2024 • 424pp • H/C (ISBN: 9781668478134) • US $215.00

Utilizing Visuals and Information Technology in Mathematics Classrooms
Hiroto Namihira (Otsuma Women's University, Japan)
Information Science Reference • © 2024 • 264pp • H/C (ISBN: 9781668499870) • US $220.00

701 East Chocolate Avenue, Hershey, PA 17033, USA
Tel: 717-533-8845 x100 • Fax: 717-533-8661
E-Mail: cust@igi-global.com • www.igi-global.com

Table of Contents

Preface xvi

Chapter 1
Augmenting Reality (AR) and Its Use Cases: Exploring the Game Changing Potential of Technology 1
Kumar Shalender, Chitkara Business School, Chitkara University, Punjab, India
Babita Singla, Chitkara Business School, Chitkara University, Punjab, India

Chapter 2
Awareness Towards Augmented Reality Learning Tools for Quality Assurance in Higher Education for the Holistic Development of Students 11
Amandeep Kaur, Chitkara Business School, Chitkara University, India

Chapter 3
Enhancing Postgraduate Education in India: A Qualitative Exploration of Innovative Pedagogies and Curriculum Frameworks 19
Neena Omprakash Nanda, Vivekanand Education Society's Institute of Management Studies and Research, India
Geetanjali Pinto, SIES School of Business Studies, India
Bhavna Raina, Vivekanand Education Society's Institute of Management Studies and Research, India

Chapter 4
Exploring Teacher Use of Augmented Reality (AR) and Virtual Reality (VR) in South Africa and Turkey 40
Huseyin Kocasarac, Ministry of Education, Ankara, Turkey
Handson Fingi Mlotshwa, Matthew Goniwe School of Leadership and Governance, South Africa

Chapter 5
Fostering Academic Honesty for E-Content 56
Shefali Saluja, Chitkara Business School, Chitkara University, India
Amandeep Singh, Chitkara Business School, Chitkara University, India
Sandhir Sharma, Chitkara Business School, Chitkara University, India

Chapter 6
Immersive Innovations: Exploring the Use of Virtual and Augmented Reality in Educational Institutions 66
Sabyasachi Pramanik, Haldia Institute of Technology, India

Chapter 7
Immersive Learning: Navigating the Future With Virtual and Augmented Reality in Education 86
Garima Arora, Maharishi Markandeshwar University (deemed), India
Vinod Kumar, Maharishi Markandeshwar University (deemed), India
Ankur Mangla, Maharishi Markandeshwar University (deemed), India
Rajit Verma, Maharishi Markandeshwar University (deemed), India

Chapter 8
Influence of Virtual Reality as a Tool to Revolutionize Industry Education 108
Tanushree Thakur, Chitkara University, India
Shraddha Bhatia, Chitkara University, India
Gurpreet Kaur, Manav Rachna University, India

Chapter 9
Leveraging Minecraft for Enhanced Spatial Perception and Academic Achievement 122
Şevket Huntürk Acar, Sinop University, Turkey
Hülya Karaçalı Taze, Sinop University, Turkey
Tugra Karademir Coşkun, Sinop University, Turkey

Chapter 10
Navigating the Complexities of Academic Integrity in E-Learning: Challenges and Strategies 157
Rajni Bala, Chitkara Business School, Chitkara University, Punjab, India
Prachi Gupta, Chitkara Business School, Chitkara University, Punjab, India

Chapter 11
Pedagogical Transformation: Integrating Innovative Approaches in Teaching 168
Yogita Rawat, ITM Business School, India
Prachi Yadav, ITM Business School, India

Chapter 12
Powerful AI in Social Science Research 188
Satinder Singh, Chitkara University, India
Rashmi Aggarwal, Chitkara University, India

Chapter 13
Revolutionizing Education: The Transformative Power of EdTech 196
Shivangi Shukla Bhavsar, Narayana Business School, India
Yogi Agravat, Narayana Business School, India
Imroz Mansuri, Narayana Business School, India

Chapter 14
Role of Metaverse in the Education Sector 215
Priya Jindal, Chitkara Business School, Chitkara University, Punjab, India
Ansh Jindal, Chitkara Business School, Chitkara University, Punjab, India
Deepa Sharma, Maharishi Markandeshwar University (deemed), Ambala, India

Chapter 15
Unlocking the Future: The Role of Digital Learning Materials in Fostering 21st-Century Skills Among University Students 229
Tugra Karademir Coşkun, Sinop University, Turkey

Compilation of References 253

About the Contributors 290

Index 295

Detailed Table of Contents

Preface..xvi

Chapter 1
Augmenting Reality (AR) and Its Use Cases: Exploring the Game Changing Potential of Technology 1
Kumar Shalender, Chitkara Business School, Chitkara University, Punjab, India
Babita Singla, Chitkara Business School, Chitkara University, Punjab, India

Augmented reality (AR) is fast finding favour among stakeholders across industrial sectors, and this research aims to explore the potential of the technology through its use cases. With the help of real-world cases, the chapter deeply dives into the applications of AR across different industries and analyses how the technology can prove beneficial for stakeholders operating in different businesses. The study also proposes a conceptual framework that can help adopt the technology in the future by highlighting the importance of academics, industry, and policymakers for ensuring the widespread adoption of the technology. The study is significant because it offers wide-ranging implications for players and can prove instrumental in helping AR spread its wings far and wide across different businesses and industry verticals.

Chapter 2
Awareness Towards Augmented Reality Learning Tools for Quality Assurance in Higher Education for the Holistic Development of Students.........11
Amandeep Kaur, Chitkara Business School, Chitkara University, India

The chapter proposes to bring forth the need for holistic development of the students which relies on the quality standards of the educational organisations imparting education. Academic organisations need to be well versed with augmented reality-based learning technologies for imparting class communicative and professional skills. A theoretical approach to the study of awareness towards augmented reality based tools for quality assurance in higher education for holistic development of students has been adopted. Extensive study of literature and previous practices has been carried out with respect to use of AR tools for quality assurance in higher education. Content analysis has been used as a research tool for the study. A thorough and in-depth literature review has been referred for studying the awareness towards AR-based quality assurance in higher education for holistic development of students. There is a need to generate more awareness towards AR-based quality assurance tools in higher education for holistic development of students. There is a race of competitiveness for business reasons which can be constructively moulded towards the real growth of the students by enhancing the quality of the education imparted. By using content analysis, an in-depth and systematized analysis of contents was done to bring forth the need of real quality assurance in higher education for holistic development and growth of its students.

Chapter 3
Enhancing Postgraduate Education in India: A Qualitative Exploration of Innovative Pedagogies and Curriculum Frameworks 19
Neena Omprakash Nanda, Vivekanand Education Society's Institute of Management Studies and Research, India
Geetanjali Pinto, SIES School of Business Studies, India
Bhavna Raina, Vivekanand Education Society's Institute of Management Studies and Research, India

This chapter explores the imperative task of expanding the intellectual horizons of postgraduate students in India. It investigates various methodologies, pedagogical approaches, and educational strategies to address the challenges in traditional postgraduate education systems. Using qualitative methods, the chapter analyzes the integration of experiential learning, technology-enhanced education, collaborative projects, and real-world applications in the postgraduate curriculum. Drawing on the social cognitive theory by Albert Bandura, the research examines how observational learning and modeling influence postgraduate students. The findings aim to inform educational stakeholders about effective strategies for fostering a profound understanding among postgraduate students and preparing them for contemporary challenges. Overall, the chapter contributes to ongoing efforts to enhance the quality and relevance of higher education in India.

Chapter 4
Exploring Teacher Use of Augmented Reality (AR) and Virtual Reality (VR) in South Africa and Turkey 40
Huseyin Kocasarac, Ministry of Education, Ankara, Turkey
Handson Fingi Mlotshwa, Matthew Goniwe School of Leadership and Governance, South Africa

The purpose of this study was to explore the extent to which teachers in South Africa and Turkey are adopting and utilizing augmented reality (AR) and virtual reality

(VR) in teaching and learning. A case study design approach was utilized, and data was collected using a questionnaire using Google Forms. This study involved 29 teachers from both countries: 16 teachers from South Africa and 13 teachers from Turkey participated in a randomized sample. The results of the study reveal that 56% of South African teachers and 38% of Turkish teachers have explored the use of AR and VR in teaching and learning. Mathematics and science-oriented subjects were the most dominant in terms of the integration of AR and VR. The teachers who could not integrate were limited by the availability of digital resources in both countries.

Chapter 5
Fostering Academic Honesty for E-Content 56
Shefali Saluja, Chitkara Business School, Chitkara University, India
Amandeep Singh, Chitkara Business School, Chitkara University, India
Sandhir Sharma, Chitkara Business School, Chitkara University, India

Ensuring academic honesty is challenging in regular classrooms, but it is even more complex in online courses since the use of technology is fundamental to teaching and learning. The way content is presented to students in education has altered due to the internet. Due to the flexibility and convenience of receiving course materials via the internet, an increasing number of students are choosing to enroll in online courses nowadays. The behaviour of students, faculty, and staff is governed by the moral code or ethical policy of academia, which is known as academic honesty. This chapter identifies the thefts in e-learning and the ways to ensure ethics and governance in the development of online courses.

Chapter 6
Immersive Innovations: Exploring the Use of Virtual and Augmented Reality in Educational Institutions 66
Sabyasachi Pramanik, Haldia Institute of Technology, India

This chapter examines the transformative influence of immersive technology, namely virtual reality (VR) and augmented reality (AR), on higher education. The chapter illustrates the significant impact of VR and AR on education by tracing their evolutionary trajectory from their conceptual roots in the mid-20th century to their current implementations. Conventional lectures and textbooks are being replaced with immersive learning environments, leading to a transformation of traditional classroom paradigms. VR and AR enable students to immerse themselves in virtual environments, where they may engage with three-dimensional models, historical reenactments, and complex simulations. The chapter also explores the challenges and consequences associated with the integration of new technology, such as the need for specialized instruction and ensuring accessibility for all students.

Chapter 7
Immersive Learning: Navigating the Future With Virtual and Augmented Reality in Education..86
Garima Arora, Maharishi Markandeshwar University (deemed), India
Vinod Kumar, Maharishi Markandeshwar University (deemed), India
Ankur Mangla, Maharishi Markandeshwar University (deemed), India
Rajit Verma, Maharishi Markandeshwar University (deemed), India

Immersive learning and technology are instructional strategies that use cutting-edge technologies to create dynamic and captivating learning environments. With this combination, the learning environment should be more immersive and productive, increasing the impact and engagement of education. Virtual reality (VR) and augmented reality (AR) are such innovative technologies that increase opportunities in education. This chapter examined how AR and VR are used in education, particularly during the knowledge dissemination. These technologies offer both teachers and students novel platforms for teaching by providing interactive environments, immersives and simulations that have revolutionised the field of learning tactics. However, to meet the huge demand in education, these technologies are still at their growing stage and require more resources. The chapter also focuses on the differences, and educational benefits of AR and VR, as well as the possibilities for mobile learning environments and future applications of these technologies in education.

Chapter 8
Influence of Virtual Reality as a Tool to Revolutionize Industry Education.....108
Tanushree Thakur, Chitkara University, India
Shraddha Bhatia, Chitkara University, India
Gurpreet Kaur, Manav Rachna University, India

Virtual reality (VR) improves learning and ensures the engagement of students in grabbing effective and efficient knowledge and skills. A real and imaginary world is created, which helps a student to understand what is being taught by interacting with a virtual world. VR helps students to experience destinations from across the world without having to leave the classroom. Even though virtual reality has provided new teaching and learning models to meet the requirements of the learners in 21st century, it's not fully implemented. Therefore, the present study aims to review the literature pertaining to the application of virtual reality in the educational industry. Further, the study recommends ways to bring about revolution in the education industry by re-establishing new advanced education techniques which will help the students in gaining better understanding of concepts.

Chapter 9
Leveraging Minecraft for Enhanced Spatial Perception and Academic Achievement 122
Şevket Huntürk Acar, Sinop University, Turkey
Hülya Karaçalı Taze, Sinop University, Turkey
Tugra Karademir Coşkun, Sinop University, Turkey

This study aims to reveal the impact of using the digital game Minecraft: Education Edition in teaching geographical features in social studies on the achievement and spatial perception skills of 5th grade students. The research adopts a sequential explanatory mixed-method design. Quantitative data was collected using self-assessment and teacher assessment forms on spatial perception skills, and an achievement test developed by the researchers. Qualitative data was gathered through interviews. The study found that using Minecraft led to an increase in students' achievement and their skills in examining space. This study provides valuable insights for educators and curriculum developers, offering a potential pathway to enhance students' understanding of geographical concepts and spatial perception skills through interactive digital tools such as Minecraft: Education Edition in the future.

Chapter 10
Navigating the Complexities of Academic Integrity in E-Learning: Challenges and Strategies 157
Rajni Bala, Chitkara Business School, Chitkara University, Punjab, India
Prachi Gupta, Chitkara Business School, Chitkara University, Punjab, India

Learning has been transformed by e-learning, which makes it simpler to learn from any location. It can be challenging, tough, to make sure people are being truthful when they learn online. As it is very easy to get material online, people can engage in practices like copying from the internet and cheating in online tests. We need to come up with innovative strategies to fight cheating and maintain equitable education for all as technology advances. To guarantee that everyone adheres to the same standards of honesty, educational institutions require support and well-defined policies. The study investigates the driving force behind student involvement in academic dishonesty. The solutions and difficulties of upholding the academic integrity in online learning contexts are also covered in the study. This chapter discusses the factors responsible for students' involvement in academic dishonesty. The chapter also discusses strategies that educational institutions can adopt to maintain academic integrity.

Chapter 11
Pedagogical Transformation: Integrating Innovative Approaches in Teaching 168
Yogita Rawat, ITM Business School, India
Prachi Yadav, ITM Business School, India

Over time, education has transformed, requiring innovative pedagogical techniques to stay relevant. This chapter offers an array of research-based teaching strategies, providing educators with an overview of transformational pedagogy. It consists of fundamental pedagogical concepts and explores evolving trends like gamification, blended learning, storytelling, project-based learning, and experiential learning. Each approach is examined comprehensively, including theoretical foundations, their ability to foster critical thinking, collaborative learning impact, and overall influence on student development. Given the distinct advantages and disadvantages of each technique, educators must discern the most suitable for their classrooms to enhance student engagement and ensure inclusive learning opportunities. Ultimately, it serves as a guide for teachers seeking to innovate learning methods and empower every student to actively participate, thus preparing them for success in our constantly evolving world.

Chapter 12
Powerful AI in Social Science Research 188
Satinder Singh, Chitkara University, India
Rashmi Aggarwal, Chitkara University, India

The never-ending improvements in artificial intelligence models have been astonishing in each sphere of life, especially the business segments and academic research. Even though the involvement of AI in social and business environments has already raised many key concerns, academia and business world experts recommend safely deploying this next digital revolution. Several key aspects of AI can bring forth marvelous results. In this chapter, the authors advocate a safety model of AI which can not only speed up the research tools and technique but also open the broader window to achieve the research objectives with more depth and explanatory answers. This chapter's major contribution is exploring viable and secure solutions to use powerful AI models to improve and faster the social science research approaches.

Chapter 13
Revolutionizing Education: The Transformative Power of EdTech 196
Shivangi Shukla Bhavsar, Narayana Business School, India
Yogi Agravat, Narayana Business School, India
Imroz Mansuri, Narayana Business School, India

The incorporation of educational technology (EdTech) into modern educational practices has resulted in a paradigm change in teaching and learning approaches. This chapter explores the diverse landscape of EdTech tools and platforms, categorizing them into learning management systems (LMS), interactive learning tools (ILT), virtual and augmented reality (VR and AR) tools, massive open online courses (MOOCs), and other online learning platforms. It goes into EdTech's evolution, charting its historical development and emphasizing major milestones, as well as assessing its scope and significance in today's educational context. The chapter emphasizes how EdTech transforms education by increasing student engagement, interaction, and personalized learning experiences.

Chapter 14
Role of Metaverse in the Education Sector...215
Priya Jindal, Chitkara Business School, Chitkara University, Punjab, India
Ansh Jindal, Chitkara Business School, Chitkara University, Punjab, India
Deepa Sharma, Maharishi Markandeshwar University (deemed), Ambala, India

Education is widely regarded as a catalyst for transformation. Students are introduced to novel academic and research domains through the integration of technological advancements. The Metaverse inclusion in the education sector has marked a radical break with conventional teaching practices by introducing a new paradigm shift in classroom education. This chapter is about the examination of the possible role of the metaverse in the future of education. Metaverse platforms possess the ability to bridge the gap between the digital and physical worlds by providing students with a safe controlled and diverse interactive learning environment, which advances their interaction. The chapter also covered the educational difficulties brought about by the Metaverse, including protecting students from potential dangers and establishing standards to ensure a high-quality education that sets an example for the world at large.

Chapter 15
Unlocking the Future: The Role of Digital Learning Materials in Fostering 21st-Century Skills Among University Students 229
Tugra Karademir Coşkun, Sinop University, Turkey

In this study, the aim is to determine the effect of the digital learning material development process on university students' 21st-century competencies. Eighty-five university students voluntarily participated in the study, and the research was designed using a sequential exploratory design. Quantitative data were collected through achievement tests, while qualitative data were gathered using an interview form. Achievement tests were administered before and after an eight-week training program, and interviews were conducted at the end of the training sessions. Students were given various tasks during the training process. The obtained quantitative data were subjected to cluster analysis, while the qualitative data underwent content analysis. As a result of the cluster analysis, the group with a low achievement score from the two divided groups reported the development of 21st-century competencies in 12 themes, while the group with a high achievement score reported the development in 15 themes.

Compilation of References 253

About the Contributors 290

Index 295

Preface

Welcome to *Augmented Reality and the Future of Education Technology*. As editors, we are thrilled to present this edited reference book, which delves into the transformative power of technology in education, with a specific focus on augmented reality (AR) and its implications for the future of learning.

The rapid development of transformative technologies is reshaping the landscape of education. From classrooms to online platforms, these technologies are revolutionizing the way we teach, learn, and assess knowledge. They are not only challenging traditional educational paradigms but also opening up new possibilities for personalized and engaging learning experiences.

In this book, we explore the multifaceted impact of technology on education, examining both the opportunities and challenges it presents. We provide insights into how educators are integrating technology into their teaching practices, the digital mindset required for effective technology adoption, and the wealth of digital learning resources available to enhance educational experiences.

Our aim is to offer a comprehensive understanding of transformative technologies in education, focusing on key topics such as learning management systems, educational apps and software, virtual reality, artificial intelligence, and the metaverse. Through in-depth discussions and case studies, we explore how these technologies are reshaping pedagogy, student engagement, and organizational culture within educational institutions.

We hope this book serves as a valuable resource for educators, researchers, administrators, policymakers, and students interested in the intersection of technology and education. By embracing the potential of augmented reality and other transformative technologies, we can unlock new possibilities for learning and empower future generations to thrive in an increasingly digital world.

Chapter 1, "Augmenting Reality (AR) and Its Use: Cases Exploring Game Changing Potential of Technology," by Kumar Shalender and Babita Singla, provides an in-depth exploration of AR's applications across various industries. Through real-world case studies, the chapter analyzes how AR technology can benefit stakeholders in diverse business sectors, offering a conceptual framework for future adoption.

Chapter 2, "Awareness Towards Augmented Reality Learning Tools for Quality Assurance in Higher Education for Holistic Development of Students," by Amandeep Kaur, emphasizes the importance of holistic student development in educational institutions. The chapter advocates for the integration of AR-based learning technologies to enhance communication and professional skills, aligning with regulatory requirements while fostering overall youth development.

In Chapter 3, "Enhancing Postgraduate Education in India: A Qualitative Exploration of Innovative Pedagogies and Curriculum Frameworks," by Neena Nanda, Geetanjali Pinto, and Bhavna Raina, the focus shifts to postgraduate education in India. Through qualitative analysis, the chapter explores innovative pedagogical approaches and curriculum frameworks to address challenges in traditional postgraduate education systems, contributing to ongoing efforts to enhance higher education quality and relevance.

Chapter 4, "Exploring Teacher Use of Augmented Reality (AR) and Virtual Reality (VR) in South Africa and Turkey," by Huseyin Kocasarac and Handson Mlotshwa, investigates the adoption of AR and VR technologies by teachers in South Africa and Turkey. Through a case study approach, the chapter examines the extent of technology integration in teaching and learning, revealing insights into subject preferences and resource availability.

Continuing with Chapter 5, "Fostering Academic Honesty for E-Content," by Shefali Saluja, Amandeep Singh, and Sandhir Sharma, the focus shifts to ensuring academic integrity in online learning environments. The chapter identifies challenges in maintaining ethics and governance in e-learning, offering strategies to mitigate academic dishonesty and uphold integrity standards.

In Chapter 6, "Immersive Innovations: Exploring the Use of Virtual and Augmented Reality in Educational Institutions," by Sabyasachi Pramanik, the transformative impact of immersive technologies on higher education is examined. The chapter traces the evolution of VR and AR in education, highlighting their potential to revolutionize traditional classroom models while addressing challenges associated with technology integration.

In Chapter 7, "Immersive Learning: Navigating the Future With Virtual and Augmented Reality in Education," by Garima Arora, Vinod Kumar, Ankur Mangla, and Rajit Verma, further explores the use of AR and VR in education. The chapter discusses their role in creating interactive learning environments, enhancing student engagement, and paving the way for future applications in mobile learning.

In Chapter 8, "Influence of Virtual Reality as a Tool to Revolutionize Industry Education," by Tanushree Thakur, Shraddha Bhatia, and Gurpreet Kaur, the focus is on leveraging VR to transform industry education. The chapter reviews the application of VR in educational settings, proposing strategies to enhance learning outcomes and revolutionize educational practices.

Chapter 9, "Leveraging Minecraft for Enhanced Spatial Perception and Academic Achievement: Minecraft for Enhanced Spatial Perception and Academic Achievement," by Sevket Huntürk Acar, Hülya Karaçali Taze, and Tugra Karademir Coskun, investigates the impact of Minecraft: Education Edition on students' spatial perception skills and academic achievement. Through mixed-method research, the chapter offers valuable insights into using digital games for educational purposes.

Chapter 10, "Navigating the Complexities of Academic Integrity in E-Learning: Challenges and Strategies," by Rajni Bala and Prachi Gupta, addresses the complexities of maintaining academic integrity in online learning environments. The chapter examines factors driving academic dishonesty and proposes strategies to uphold integrity standards in e-learning contexts.

In Chapter 11, "Pedagogical Transformation- Integrating Innovative Approaches in Teaching," by Yogita Rawat and Prachi Yadav, innovative teaching strategies are explored to adapt to evolving educational paradigms. The chapter discusses gamification, blended learning, storytelling, project-based learning, and experiential learning, offering insights for educators seeking to enhance student engagement and learning outcomes.

Chapter 12, "Powerful AI in Social Science Research," by Satinder Singh and Rashmi Aggarwal, delves into the role of artificial intelligence (AI) in social science research. The chapter advocates for safe and ethical AI deployment, exploring how AI models can enhance research methodologies and provide deeper insights into social phenomena.

Chapter 13, "Revolutionizing Education: The Transformative Power of EdTech," by Shivangi Shukla Bhavsar, Yogi Agravat, and Imroz Mansuri, examines the transformative impact of educational technology (EdTech) on teaching and learning. The chapter traces the evolution of EdTech tools and platforms, highlighting their significance in increasing student engagement and personalized learning experiences.

In Chapter 14, "Role of Metaverse in the Education Sector," by Priya Jindal, Ansh Jindal, and Deepa Sharma, the role of the metaverse in education is explored. The chapter discusses the potential of metaverse platforms to create interactive learning environments, while addressing challenges and setting standards for high-quality education.

Finally, Chapter 15, "Unlocking the Future: The Role of Digital Learning Materials in Fostering 21st-Century Skills Among University Students," by Tugra Karademir Coskun, investigates the impact of digital learning materials on university students' 21st-century competencies. Through a mixed-method approach, the chapter offers insights into the development of student skills through digital learning materials.

Each chapter in this edited reference book contributes unique perspectives and insights into the transformative potential of augmented reality and other innovative technologies in education. We hope that this book serves as a valuable resource for educators, researchers, policymakers, and stakeholders striving to navigate the complex intersection of technology and education in the 21st century.

As editors of *Augmented Reality and the Future of Education Technology*, we are thrilled to present this comprehensive exploration of the transformative power of technology in education, with a specific focus on augmented reality (AR) and its implications for the future of learning.

The chapters included in this edited reference book provide valuable insights into the multifaceted impact of technology on education. From the exploration of AR's applications across various industries to the examination of innovative pedagogical approaches in postgraduate education, each chapter offers a unique perspective on how technology is reshaping the educational landscape.

We delve into topics such as the integration of AR and virtual reality (VR) in teaching practices, the importance of maintaining academic integrity in online learning environments, and the role of artificial intelligence (AI) in social science research. Through in-depth discussions and case studies, we explore how these technologies are revolutionizing pedagogy, student engagement, and organizational culture within educational institutions.

Each chapter contributes unique perspectives and insights into the transformative potential of augmented reality and other innovative technologies in education. We believe that this edited reference book will inspire further research and innovation in the field of education, paving the way for a more engaging, personalized, and effective learning experience for all.

Rashmi Aggarwal
Chitkara Business School, Chitkara University, India

Prachi Gupta
Chitkara Business School, Chitkara University, India

Satinder Singh
Chitkara Business School, Chitkara University, India

Rajni Bala
Chitkara Business School, Chitkara University, India

Chapter 1
Augmenting Reality (AR) and Its Use Cases:
Exploring the Game Changing Potential of Technology

Kumar Shalender
https://orcid.org/0000-0002-7269-7025
Chitkara Business School, Chitkara University, Punjab, India

Babita Singla
https://orcid.org/0000-0002-8861-6859
Chitkara Business School, Chitkara University, Punjab, India

ABSTRACT

Augmented reality (AR) is fast finding favour among stakeholders across industrial sectors, and this research aims to explore the potential of the technology through its use cases. With the help of real-world cases, the chapter deeply dives into the applications of AR across different industries and analyses how the technology can prove beneficial for stakeholders operating in different businesses. The study also proposes a conceptual framework that can help adopt the technology in the future by highlighting the importance of academics, industry, and policymakers for ensuring the widespread adoption of the technology. The study is significant because it offers wide-ranging implications for players and can prove instrumental in helping AR spread its wings far and wide across different businesses and industry verticals.

DOI: 10.4018/979-8-3693-3015-9.ch001

Copyright © 2024, IGI Global. Copying or distributing in print or electronic forms without written permission of IGI Global is prohibited.

1. INTRODUCTION

The influence of technology in every sphere of life is very much evident today. We are witnessing an exponential rise in technology integration across the industrial vectors with no sector remaining immune to the impact of the technology. Players across the industrial ecosystems have taken a proactive approach and are today using the technology to deliver better value, services, and facilities to their customers. From the use of information technology and artificial intelligence to simulation models and predictive analytics, businesses across the industrial sectors are at the forefront of using new technologies and innovations. Counted among the prominent technologies, augmented reality (AR) is proving a game changer thanks to its exceptional capabilities to enhance customer experiences. By simulating real-world conditions in an interactive and immersive way, AR has opened new ways of customer interactions across the globe (Aggarwal et. al. 2020). In the education sector alone, the use of AR/VR use is expected to reach $19.6 bn by the end of 2023 compared to the $9.3 bn size of the segment recorded in 2018. It is very clear from the growth numbers that going forward the use of AR will dominate across disciplines and will help businesses realise their true potential. The primary differentiator that AR brings to the table is the use of digital tools and technologies. Among the primary use cases of AR, the technology is finding prominence in the education and training domains. From converting textbooks into 3D models to simulating phenomena that are quite difficult to explain in the real world, AR is capable of doing it all. Quality of content can also be significantly enhanced with the use of AR and today we have a lot of AR applications in engineering, medical, and training aspects related to several industries. Many studies have found that the retention of aspirants increases significantly when learning happens through the use of AR. Especially in the domains where simulating real-world conditions is a challenging task, AR comes into the picture and allows educational institutes, universities, and training departments to help aspirants become skilled on difficult parameters of productivity and performance. Take, for instance, the Department of History and Archaeology. With the help of AR, both these departments can help students understand the ancient concepts in a more vivid, interactive, and immersive manner. AR can help faculty show students digital replicas of ancient civilizations and allow them to better understand the various civilizational heritages associated with the ancient communities. Similarly in the aviation and firefighting department, AR can be used for simulating real job situations, thereby saving a lot of cost and resources while allowing the trainers to keep new hires safe from the dangerous aspects of on-the-job training at the initial stage of their induction. Owing to all these benefits, it comes as no surprise that AR is on its way to dominate the education and training industry and with significant technology upgrades in the process, AR will change the very face of the training industry in the future. Against this specific background, this research explores the game-changing potential of AR in the education sector through its use cases. By looking into the practical applications of AR, the research gives the conceptual framework for enhancing the integration of technology in the education and training industry (Adamaska 2023). The framework takes into consideration the crucial role of stakeholders to ensure that the technology is implemented in a manner that bodes well for students, academicians, trainers, and the corporate sector among others. The conclusion section towards the end discusses the important implications of the study and offers guidelines for further strengthening the role of AR in the education and training sector.

2. AR IN EDUCATION SECTOR: POTENTIALLY TRANSFORMING USE CASES

2.1 Immersive Learning

AR comes with the unique capability of converting theoretical concepts into 3D, interactive visual diagrams that can take the learning experience of students to a whole new level. There are many tools and technologies in AR that can enhance the learning quotient and by helping faculty engage the learners effectively, AR can prove instrumental in strengthening the conceptual clarity among learners. AR applications can be conceptualized and developed for almost every discipline and the best part is that the technology is increasingly becoming more cost-effective and accessible owing to a wave of innovations in the domain (Al Badi et al. 2023). Take, for instance, the rising popularity of QuiverVision which is an AR-based colouring app. This app can present things in 3D form and allow students to use their digital versions to better understand their structure, use, and application. By combining both entertainment and educational aspects, this AR app is proving extremely beneficial for learners at the primary level of education. With the help of this app, learners can bring various images and their artistic impressions to life. This interactive feature makes this app different from the others and extremely efficient in imparting learning through fun. Another wonderful example of an AR app that is helping to develop conceptual clarity among learners is Arloon Chemistry. With the help of this app, students can rearrange the molecules and understand the subject at its basic level. With all these benefits, the AR integration drive at different levels of Education and Training is on the rise and expected to pick up the pace going forward (Kolo, 2021).

2.2 Space Training

Training the astronauts without actually sending them to space has become possible thanks to the technology of AR. It is fascinating to know that the leading space research agency NASA makes comprehensive use of AR for training its astronauts. With the help of AR technology, the space agency has simulated the space environment wherein trainees are trained on various aspects of exploration, observations, and analysis techniques. By mimicking the space environment, astronauts get a fair idea of the challenges, issues, and problems that they need to face while travelling to space. The various facets of the training techniques that can be helped by the AR include assembling and disassembly aircraft modules, exploring the lunar surfaces, analysing and maintaining the pressure inside the shuttle, and many more such things. The amount of savings that can be realised by using the AR technique in the space sector is enormously large. In addition to providing training, the AR tools can also help astronauts understand the complexity of the outer space environment by offering analysis on a host of parameters. As astronauts have to face many complex situations within the space shuttle, AR can help by offering the same conditions to technicians in a simulated environment, thereby allowing trainees to get hands-on training. In sum, the use of AR in the space industry is proving significantly beneficial and by offering these multiple benefits, AR tools and technologies are increasingly finding favour among astronauts across the globe (Shalender & Shankar 2023).

2.3 Medical Field

The scope of the application of AR in the medical field is very large and holistic. From training doctors to simulating surgeries and operations, AR is revolutionising training in the medical field. Considered an example of a popular AR app called Human Anatomy Atlas. This app is specifically built on the AR platform and is widely used to help physicians better understand human anatomy through various simulation models. Similarly, many AR apps are available today which help surgeons further hone their skills with the help of simulated environments and virtual human bodies (Mandal 2023). Touch Surgery is one of the fast-growing apps that help users excel in surgery by offering them virtual patients and letting them operate in a completely risk-free environment (Davenport & Kalakota 2019). Another important aspect of the AR apps that aid medical practitioners is the holistic database of videos and information that can be made available to practitioners. The latest information and databases help the medical fraternity to keep themselves updated with the latest happening in the field and hence offer the best services to target audiences (Shalender & Yadav 2019).

2.4 Defence Training

Counted among the most prominent applications of AR, the use of technology in the defence sector comes with multiple benefits. Especially when it comes to training newly inducted soldiers, AR technology can be extremely beneficial. By emulating the combat environment with the help of AR devices and technologies, the training of the inductees can be done without actually putting them in a risky environment. The training of the soldiers related to arms and ammunition can be accomplished in a simulated environment and these procedures can be replicated in other allied procedures to bring huge among of resource savings on the financial front (Shalimov, 2023). The AR technology is also proving crucially instrumental in offering cybersecurity training that is required to secure sensitive weaponry and missile technology in the war front (Kulshrestha et al. 2022). The use of AR Technology has also allowed the military across the globe to save on travel expenses that are associated with the training of soldiers related to special terrains. The important contribution that AR is making to the training of forces is well reflected in the use of Augmented Immersive Team Trainer (AITT) used by the US marine forces. The concept was tested by the country a few years back and since then, the marine forces have been consistently using AITT to derive effective results on various training parameters. In addition, the option of customising the terrain according to the requirement of specific training programs also makes AR a desirable technology among the forces (Shalender, 2023).

2.5 AR and Manufacturing Industry

AR has immense application potential in the manufacturing industry, especially in the processes and procedures where complex machinery is involved. Whether it is the training of manpower or robots, AR applications are proving their utilities in a big manner. People employed in production processes can accomplish difficult tasks with the help of AR screens where instructions can be given to the specific procedures. These instructions are displayed in an interactive manner that helps trainees complete their tasks without much difficulty (Manohar et al. 2020). AR screens are specifically becoming beneficial for the production of automobiles, scooters, EVs, and semiconductors among others. AR can also simulate the complex production environment to help trainers understand the basic procedures and processes involved in the complex manufacturing of specific products. The AR apps can be used in conjunction with 3D goggles to transmit and train employees on specific aspects of their job training. Siemens, a well-known German company, is now using AR technology to train its manpower in the welding process. Similarly, AR can prove instrumental in delivering superior training in assembly, lathing, machining, and other allied processes which are part of the manufacturing industry. The effectiveness of the training program can be augmented with the use of AR headsets which offer step-by-step instructions to trainees to complete the particular task as per the laid-out procedure (Ross, 2019). This contribution of AR in training employees can become helpful in filling the skill gap that continues to present challenges for the manufacturing industry. As per the study conducted by Deloitte in association with the manufacturing institutes in the year 2018, it has been found that by 2028, a total of 2.4 million positions in the production sector might remain vacant owing to a lack of skills among the present workforce. This huge gap in skills can be effectively bridged with the help of AR tools in the production industry (Sinha, 2021). Other important areas in the production discipline where the use of AR can prove crucial for enhancing efficiency include proactive maintenance, timely assembly, and reducing processing and operational errors.

2.6 AR in Retail Sector

Arguably, the most significant application of AR is in the retail Industry which has enormously benefited from the application of the technology in conjunction with virtual reality (VR). The combination of AR and VR has significantly uplifted the customer experience in the retail sector. From training new retail employees to enhancing their product knowledge and delivering superior customer services, AR is helping retail organisations stay on top of their game. AR and VR can come together and offer superior displays of products and services to the customers and also allow retailers to personalise the product as per the needs and preferences of the target market. AR tools also enhance the shopping experience and by allowing buyers to try clothes, virtually place furniture, and experience services, these can help the entire retail ecosystem to deliver greater experiences to the customers (Saxena, 2023). The IKEA Kreativ app is a wonderful example of how AR can be used to enhance the customer experience. The app allows customers to visualise the product in their house by creating a 3D replica by scanning the room with their smartphone. Similarly, AR tools and technologies have been built by several other companies including the likes of Toyota, Amazon, Flipkart, LG, etc. which allow potential buyers to virtually experience the things before actually buying them in the stores or ordering online. In addition, there are a host of AR tools that can be used to collect relevant data about the needs and preferences of the customers and these insights can be then used for delivering personalised experiences. Many retail stores have gone ahead and now using AR to gamify in-store shopping which has led to increased footfalls across their retail chains (Shaheen, 2021).

3. ADOPTION FRAMEWORK: AR IN EDUCATION AND TRAINING INDUSTRY

The education, training, and corporate sectors can benefit immensely from the adoption of AR tools and technologies. As demonstrated from the examples above, AR can significantly enhance the learning quotient of students while bringing efficient training to the doorsteps of many industries across the globe. To ensure that AR tools are made available and accessible to both the training and education sectors, there is a need to come up with a comprehensive plan involving stakeholders from across the education and training ecosystems. The collaboration between academia and industry is very important here as the desired levels of AR attainment can be accomplished only with a constructive and constant exchange of information between these stakeholders. Academicians and researchers can come up with novel theories that will facilitate the integration of AR while executives can focus on developing new use cases for AR adoption in the industry. By taking this mutually beneficial approach, AR adoption can be facilitated across both the education and training industries with partners in both ecosystems helping each other to develop, implement, analyse, and redefine AR tools and their application in different domains. This collaborative partnership will also help in enhancing the use cases of AR that can be developed in other industries (refer to Figure 1). Another important stakeholder that must collaborate with both academia and industry is policymakers whose participation in the adoption of AR tools will prove critically important for the sector. The laws and regulations related to the technology continue to evolve quite quickly and hence, it becomes challenging for the regulators to come up with a standardised policy framework for regulating technology tools. In such an environment, it becomes imperative for policymakers to remain in constant touch with both industry and academia so that favourable policies can be made for the sector.

A dedicated group of experts must be constituted that look specifically into the policy framework in the AR and VR segment. This should be followed by regular meetings between all the important partners enabling the exchange of information while keeping a closed tab on the new happenings in the field of technology. By bringing all these three stakeholders together, AR adoption in terms of its tools and technologies can be enhanced significantly. It is also essential that the viewpoint of different industrial sectors should also be taken into consideration and regular customer interactions must be conducted to know the needs and preferences of prospective buyers regarding AR. Many AR tools will need the customer's consent as they collect the data and information related to their shopping and purchase behaviour and hence policymakers have to give special attention to the data and information privacy issues related to the collection, dissemination, and analysis of the sensitive information.

Figure 1. AR Adoption Framework
Source: Authors' own conceptualisation

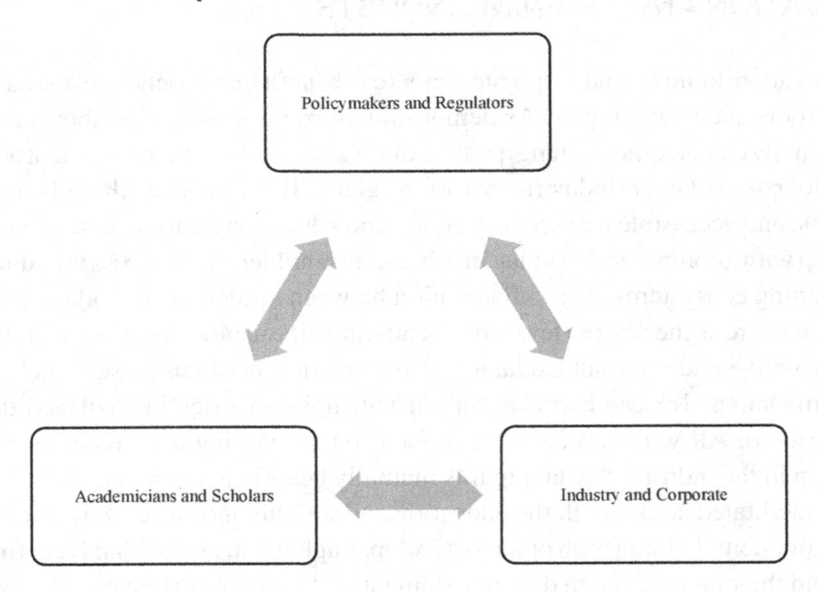

4. CONCLUSION AND DISCUSSION

AR tools are very useful in enhancing the utilities of businesses and values across the business verticals. From the education sector to different industrial segments, AR is proving beneficial for elevating the efficiency and effectiveness of several businesses operating in different verticals. Many experts believe that AR can change the entire scenario of the education and training industry going forward and to realise this dream, it's equally important to offer an adoption framework to help AR enhance its utility among the potential segments. The conceptual framework discussed in this chapter is a step in that direction and by consolidating the contribution of all three stakeholders, the title takes a holistic approach to encourage the use of AR in the industries and education domain. The growing interest of businesses across product categories is also encouraging the corporate sector to adopt AR tools to deliver more benefits to end customers. While many industries in the examples cited above have already gone ahead with the integration of AR tools, others are also going for more focused integration of the technology in the coming years. The multiple benefits associated with AR include offering more engaging and interactive experiences which are more cost-effective and affordable. The safety and security of the training procedures offered by the simulated environment using different kinds of AR tools are among the significant benefits of the technology. The capability of these tools to offer training opportunities using the simulated environment comes across as a huge cost and resource savings for organisations. Thanks to all the benefits, AR is finding favour among all spheres of life. To continue with this wave of adoption, it becomes important that holistic policy should be drafted related to the adoption of AR in both education and the corporate sector. The fundamental aspects of the technology and the emerging challenges related to data use and privacy must be addressed in this policy and accordingly, guidelines should be issued to all stakeholders for the successful adoption and integration of AR in their policies and procedures. The research has significant implications and can help the industry discover new use cases for AR and implement the technology to achieve significant benefits in the allied areas of performance. It is also essential to know that the coming together of people from different spheres of life belonging to the field of Academics, industry, and policymaking is very much desirable at this crucial juncture. The time has been ripe for the integration of AR and by using the technology to achieve elevated business performance, can be made for the technology among the shareholders of the company. AR has got the ability to comprehensively change the business scenarios across the different industries and by using the technology in the right spirit, the upcoming business can be able to build and scale their fortunes at a much faster pace than their contemporaries.

REFERENCES

Adamska, I. (2023). Practical examples of AR in education. Available at https://nsflow.com/blog/examples-of-ar-in-education

Aggarwal, A., Chand, P. K., Jhamb, D., & Mittal, A. (2020). Leader–Member Exchange, Work Engagement, and Psychological Withdrawal Behavior: The Mediating Role of Psychological Empowerment. *Frontiers in Psychology*, *11*(423), 423. Advance online publication. doi:10.3389/fpsyg.2020.00423 PMID:32296361

Al Badi, F. K., Alhosani, K. A., Jabeen, F., Stachowicz-Stanusch, A., Shehzad, N., & Amann, W. (2022). Challenges of AI Adoption in the UAE Healthcare. *Vision (Basel)*, *26*(2), 193–207. doi:10.1177/0972262920988398

Davenport, T., & Kalakota, R. (2019). The potential for artificial intelligence in healthcare. *Future Healthcare Journal*, *6*(2), 94–98. doi:10.7861/futurehosp.6-2-94 PMID:31363513

Kolo, K. (2021). 9 AR Platforms Bring Augmented Reality Content in the Classroom. Available at https://www.thevrara.com/blog2/2021/10/26/9-desktop-ar-platforms-to-bring-ar-content-in-the-classroom

Kulshrestha, D., Tiwari, M. K., Shalender, K., & Sharma, S. (2022). Consumer Acatalepsy Towards Buying Behaviour for Need-Based Goods for Sustainability During the COVID-19 Pandemic. *Indian Journal of Marketing*, *52*(10), 50–63. doi:10.17010/ijom/2022/v52/i10/172347

Mandal, A. (2023). How surgeons are using AI to diagnose a brain tumour. Available at: https://www.financialexpress.com/healthcare/news-healthcare/how-surgeons-are-using-ai-to-diagnose-brain-tumor-bkg/3271108/

Manohar, S., Mittal, A., & Marwah, S. (2020). Service innovation, corporate reputation and word-of-mouth in the banking sector: A test on multigroup-moderated mediation effect. *Benchmarking*, *27*(1), 406–429. doi:10.1108/BIJ-05-2019-0217

Ross, T. (2019). Top 10 Augmented Reality Tools for the Classroom. Available at https://www.ebsco.com/blogs/ebscopost/top-10-augmented-reality-tools-classroom

Saxena, K. (2023). Future Prospects of Augmented Reality in the Education Industry. Available at https://www.codingninjas.com/studio/library/augmented-reality-in-education-industry

Shaheen, M. Y. (2021). Applications of Artificial Intelligence (AI) in healthcare. *RE:view*. Advance online publication. doi:10.14293/S2199-1006.1.SOR-.PPVRY8K.v1

Shalender, K. (2023). *Skill development for society 5.0: A focus on the new-age skilling process. Innovations and Sustainability in Society 5.0*. Nova Science Publisher.

Shalender, K., & Shankar, S. (2023). *Building Innovation Culture for the Automobile Industry: Insights from the Indian Passenger Vehicle Market. Constructive Discontent in Execution*. Apple Academic Press.

Shalender, K., & Yadav, R. K. (2019). Strategic Flexibility, Manager Personality, and Firm Performance: The Case of Indian Automobile Industry. *Global Journal of Flexible Systems Managment*, *20*(1), 77–90. doi:10.1007/s40171-018-0204-x

Shalimov, A. (2023). Augmented reality in education: How to apply it to your EdTech Business. Available at https://easternpeak.com/blog/augmented-reality-in-education/

Sinha, S. (2021). Augmented Reality (AR) In Education: A Staggering Insight Into The Future. Available at https://elearningindustry.com/augmented-reality-in-education-staggering-insight-into-future

Chapter 2
Awareness Towards Augmented Reality Learning Tools for Quality Assurance in Higher Education for the Holistic Development of Students

Amandeep Kaur
Chitkara Business School, Chitkara University, India

ABSTRACT

The chapter proposes to bring forth the need for holistic development of the students which relies on the quality standards of the educational organisations imparting education. Academic organisations need to be well versed with augmented reality-based learning technologies for imparting class communicative and professional skills. A theoretical approach to the study of awareness towards augmented reality based tools for quality assurance in higher education for holistic development of students has been adopted. Extensive study of literature and previous practices has been carried out with respect to use of AR tools for quality assurance in higher education. Content analysis has been used as a research tool for the study. A thorough and in-depth literature review has been referred for studying the awareness towards AR-based quality assurance in higher education for holistic development of students. There is a need to generate more awareness towards AR-based quality assurance tools in higher education for holistic development of students. There is a race of

DOI: 10.4018/979-8-3693-3015-9.ch002

Copyright © 2024, IGI Global. Copying or distributing in print or electronic forms without written permission of IGI Global is prohibited.

competitiveness for business reasons which can be constructively moulded towards the real growth of the students by enhancing the quality of the education imparted. By using content analysis, an in-depth and systematized analysis of contents was done to bring forth the need of real quality assurance in higher education for holistic development and growth of its students.

INTRODUCTION

Higher education has to render qualitative performance which requires consensual and directional efforts. Advancements in technology are happening at an accelerating pace. The impact of accelerating advancement is in every sector. Education sector is facing the challenge of easing up of the lessons and making them interesting at the same time. With the aid of augmented reality based tools, delivery of quality content accompanied with easy grasping by the students is possible. Furthermore, higher education is also facing increased pressure for advancement from regulatory bodies. So, there is a dire need for development of generic educational model in academics. Augmented reality is an interactive experience which merges the digitally generated information with the real world. Use of AR based technology tools in teaching facilitates faster, interesting, reality based and in depth learning of contents. But at the same time there is a need to realise that true quality standards of higher education institutions rely on the awareness, use and promotion of AR tools to enhance the real learning of its students. AR based tools would help in developing an environment of experience based learning thereby providing opportunities to get more familiarity with subjects like sciences, social sciences and languages. Furthermore, Use of AR based tools helps in delivering knowledge via digital storytelling and games for enhanced learning. For fostering a culture of divergent thinking amongst its students there is a need for generation of awareness and development of digital literacy amongst the students. AR tools have an inbuilt capability of enhancing learning and learning outcome by involving multiple sensory organs and by reducing the load on our cognitive senses. Though it is challenging that faculty member, administration, higher authorities and students all have to be at par in learning and application of AR tools but it's a promising and effective tool for enriched results.

LITERATURE REVIEW

The performance of the education sector can be improved to a greater extent by bringing modernisation in the education system. Maximum use of AR is prevalent in mobile applications and AR can work without hardware. Since majority of teens have an access to smart phones so education can turn more accessible and interactive. (Kamińska et al 2023). The use of AR based tools significantly enhanced the performance of students in the subject of sciences, (Kalemkuş, J. & Kalemkuş, F. 2023). The use of AR bot has added to enhanced involvement and enjoyable learning with respect to algorithm designing amongst the students. (Yang et al 2023). Quality controllers reflect significant association with effectiveness in performance. (Seyfried & Pohlenz 2020). A Wide participation of students and teachers is contributing constructively in forming of quality assurance practices in Chinese universities. (Zhang et al 2022).There is a need for development of a quality culture. There is further a need for quality enhancement in the curriculum development and enhancements (Lucander & Christersson 2020). For the holistic development of the curriculum, there is a dire need of quality enhancement as the ratings of its students and the faculty members, research paper published and reviewed by staff and students, their access to E resource content for quality work are all vital aspects (Kobets et al., 2021). With increased challenges of globalisation in higher education, quality assurance is turning equally challenging. (Williams & Harvey, 2015). Accreditation is a mean to evaluate and reflect the true quality of educational institutions and their curriculums. Accreditations are constructively contributing towards the quality enhancement by checking the standards designed and laid are being complied by the higher education sector and its organisations. (Ibrahim, 2014). Increased involvement of educationists and researchers with respect to opportunities and growth perspectives attached with AR demands curriculum enrichment there by ensuring sustainable practices in the long run (Sviridova et al 2023). Economic advancement of a country is to great extent dependent upon the volume and quality of volume possessed by its people.

Thus every country's higher education sector must aspire for quality maintenance and adherence to the same. At the same time Accreditation also brings uniformity amongst professionals and educational organisations at the time. Collaborative support of authorities, higher education organisations working well aligned with AR tools is a prerequisite for effective assurance.

OBJECTIVE OF THE STUDY

1. To study Awareness of educational organisations towards the use of AR tools as an aid towards Quality Assurance in Higher Education.
2. To study contribution of Quality Education for holistic development of students in Higher Education.

AWARENESS OF EDUCATIONAL ORGANISATIONS TOWARDS THE USE OF AR TOOLS AS AN AID TOWARDS QUALITY ASSURANCE IN HIGHER EDUCATION

A study in Malaysia brought forward a significant awareness towards use of AR applications in the education sector and further proposed AR tools as significant contributors towards learning of teachers and students. (Wei et al., 2021). A study further recommended an e-learning application on grounds of awareness and expanded learning base needs. (Neffati et al., 2021). In an artificial environment it is difficult to imagine the real environment and its variables so, AI tools aid in adding to the perception of the educators and the students. (Tashko & Elena 2015). Apart from awareness there is a need of understanding the expectations of the users for wider utility and application of AR based systems. Dalim et al. (2017).There are innumerable merits attached with AR technologies for higher education sector. (Akçayır & Akçayır 2017). To be cautious in quality enhancement and overall development of students' universities need to facilitate and foster adoption of AR tools as they played a constructive role in covid pandemic where things turned standstill but the education sector continued with its operations under dire circumstances due to the aid of technology. (Mittal et al., 2022). AI tools have added to the independent learning and is helping in fostering the interest of the audiences in learning and developing with the aid of technology and thereby replacing the traditional textbooks and equipment's. (Gurevych et al., 2021). Use of AR based tools in education have brought a technological advancement, ease and interest of students and the educators in replacing pens and notebooks with e-books, software's and presentations which on one hand added to the quality education and on the other hand aids in development of a research inclination amongst the students and the educators.(Haleem et al., 2022). For long term development and ease of delivering quality content, educators themselves need to be well versed with disruptive technologies. (Wawak et al., 2023).

One of the vital components is imparting of qualitative education for sustainable development as per United Nations agenda 2030. AR tools are emerging as a contributory medium towards inclusive development of education sector. For enhancing efficiency in a qualitative way apart from the availability of information, its application at an appropriate time and place has a role to play. Apart from the ease of its use and awareness, there is a need to work towards a quicker adoption attitude towards AR and its tools.

CONTRIBUTION OF QUALITY EDUCATION FOR HOLISTIC DEVELOPMENT OF STUDENTS IN HIGHER EDUCATION

Idea of Holistic development is a route towards sustainable development. So, relating educational objectives to sustainability in itself is a quality parameter. (Spychalski et al 2023). A harmonised and uniform reform in the entire education sector worldwide would be constructive in materialisation of a quality plan.(Srikanthan & Dalrymple2002).The idea behind holistic development is a balanced growth covering all aspects for wholesome development as physical, mental, aesthetic, spiritual and emotional as well. Holistic development is going to be long term with both internal and external personality enhancement. It's a drive with a genuine and generous concern towards the holistic growth. (Mahmoudi et al., 2012).

Holistic development is a way towards self-improvement. It is a route for the development of critical learners which would automatically improve the learning environment and the level of students and teachers respectively. Kelly's Personal Construct Theory further supports the holistic learning as a route to development of critical learners (Patel et al., 2003). Continuous self-assessments can be productive in quality enhancement. (Ibrahim 2014).This study proposed AR based optical simulations for advanced growth of students. (Neffati et al., 2021). A study brought forward that AR technology plays a constructive role in enhancing the exploring skills of the students and thereby enhances motivational level of its students. Further an amalgam of digital and physical objects aids in enhanced development of various skills as critical thinking, analytical and communicative. (Akçayır & Akçayır, 2017). A positive perception towards utility derived from the smartphones is linked to its adoption rate. (Mittal et al., 2020). By being aware and inclined towards AR tools and the utility attached with them, with respect to enhanced competitive spirits, responsiveness rate and improved outcome is going to benefit manifolds in times to come.

CONCLUSION

Though AR based learning is interactive but at the same time it brings along numerous challenges. Students may get exposed to large amount of data and information with the use of multiple AR enabled devices which may lead to information overload. Faculty members may face challenges pedagogical or technological in impart of contents. At the same time Universities in higher education have to work rigorously towards delivering of quality education for which aid of augmented reality based tools cannot be compromised. Imparting of Quality education for holistic development is utmost. At the same time it would be constructive in meeting the agenda of SDG

2030.Furthermore it would aid in skill development and enhancement for professional growth too. Thus, AI based learning tools would assist in quality assurance in the educational curriculum and in the holistic growth of educators and students.

REFERENCES

Akçayır, M., & Akçayır, G. (2017). Advantages and challenges associated with augmented reality for education: A systematic review of the literature. *Educational Research Review*, *20*, 1–11. doi:10.1016/j.edurev.2016.11.002

Dalim, C. S. C., Kolivand, H., Kadhim, H., Sunar, M. S., & Billinghurst, M. (2017). Factors influencing the acceptance of augmented reality in education: A review of the literature. *Journal of Computational Science*, *13*(11), 581–589. doi:10.3844/jcssp.2017.581.589

Gurevych, R., Silveistr, A., Mokliuk, M., Shaposhnikova, I., Gordiichuk, G., & Saiapina, S. (2021). Using augmented reality technology in higher education institutions. *Postmodern Openings*, *12*(2), 109–132. doi:10.18662/po/12.2/299

Haleem, A., Javaid, M., Qadri, M. A., & Suman, R. (2022). Understanding the role of digital technologies in education: A review. *Sustainable Operations and Computers*, *3*, 275–285. doi:10.1016/j.susoc.2022.05.004

Ibrahim, H. A. H. (2014). Quality assurance and accreditation in education. *Open Journal of Education*, *2*(2), 106–110. doi:10.12966/oje.06.06.2014

Kalemkuş, J., & Kalemkuş, F. (2023). Effect of the use of augmented reality applications on academic achievement of student in science education: Meta analysis review. *Interactive Learning Environments*, *31*(9), 6017–6034. doi:10.1080/10494820.2022.2027458

Kamińska, D., Zwoliński, G., Laska-Leśniewicz, A., Raposo, R., Vairinhos, M., Pereira, E., Urem, F., Ljubić Hinić, M., Haamer, R. E., & Anbarjafari, G. (2023). Augmented reality: Current and new trends in education. *Electronics (Basel)*, *12*(16), 3531. doi:10.3390/electronics12163531

Kobets, V., Liubchenko, V., Popovych, I., & Koval, S. (2021). Institutional Aspects of Integrated Quality Assurance of Engineering Study Programs at HEI Using ICT. In *Design, Simulation, Manufacturing: The Innovation Exchange* (pp. 301–310). Springer International Publishing. doi:10.1007/978-3-030-77719-7_30

Lucander, H., & Christersson, C. (2020). Engagement for quality development in higher education: A process for quality assurance of assessment. *Quality in Higher Education*, *26*(2), 135–155. doi:10.1080/13538322.2020.1761008

Mahmoudi, S., Jafari, E., Nasrabadi, H. A., & Liaghatdar, M. J. (2012). Holistic education: An approach *for 21 century. International Education Studies*, *5*(2), 178–186. doi:10.5539/ies.v5n3p178

Mittal, A., Aggarwal, A., & Mittal, R. (2020). Predicting university students' adoption of mobile news applications: The role of perceived hedonic value and news motivation. *International Journal of E-Services and Mobile Applications*, *12*(4), 42–59. doi:10.4018/IJESMA.2020100103

Mittal, A., Mantri, A., Tandon, U., & Dwivedi, Y. K. (2022). A unified perspective on the adoption of online teaching in higher education during the COVID-19 pandemic. *Information Discovery and Delivery*, *50*(2), 117–132. doi:10.1108/IDD-09-2020-0114

Neffati, O. S., Setiawan, R., Jayanthi, P., Vanithamani, S., Sharma, D. K., Regin, R., ... Sengan, S. (2021). An educational tool for enhanced mobile e-Learning for technical higher education using mobile devices for augmented reality. *Microprocessors and Microsystems*, *83*, 104030. doi:10.1016/j.micpro.2021.104030

Patel, N. V. (2003). A holistic approach to learning and teaching interaction: Factors in the development of critical learners. *International Journal of Educational Management*, *17*(6), 272–284. doi:10.1108/09513540310487604

Seyfried, M., & Pohlenz, P. (2020). Assessing quality assurance in higher education: quality managers' perceptions of effectiveness. Academic Press.

Spychalski, B. (2023). Holistic Education for Sustainable Development: A Study of Shaping the Pro-Quality Attitude of Students in the Polish Educational System. *Sustainability (Basel)*, *15*(10), 8073. doi:10.3390/su15108073

Srikanthan, G., & Dalrymple, J. F. (2002). Developing a holistic model for quality in higher education. *Quality in Higher Education*, *8*(3), 215–224. doi:10.1080/1353832022000031656

Sviridova, E., Yastrebova, E., Bakirova, G., & Rebrina, F. (2023, October). Immersive technologies as an innovative tool to increase academic success and motivation in higher education. [). Frontiers.]. *Frontiers in Education*, *8*, 1192760. doi:10.3389/feduc.2023.1192760

Tashko, R., & Elena, R. (2015). Augmented reality as a teaching tool in higher education. *International Journal of Cognitive Research in Science. Engineering and Education*, *3*(1), 7–15.

Wawak, S., Teixeira Domingues, J. P., & Sampaio, P. (2023). Quality 4.0 in higher education: Reinventing academic-industry-government collaboration during disruptive times. *The TQM Journal*. Advance online publication. doi:10.1108/TQM-07-2023-0219

Wei, C. Y., Kuah, Y. C., Ng, C. P., & Lau, W. K. (2021). Augmented Reality (AR) as an enhancement teaching tool: Are educators ready for it? *Contemporary Educational Technology*, *13*(3), ep303. doi:10.30935/cedtech/10866

Williams, J., & Harvey, L. (2015). Quality assurance in higher education. The Palgrave international handbook of higher education policy and governance, 506-525.

Yang, F. C. O., Lai, H. M., & Wang, Y. W. (2023). Effect of augmented reality-based virtual educational robotics on programming students' enjoyment of learning, computational thinking skills, and academic achievement. *Computers & Education*, *195*, 104721. doi:10.1016/j.compedu.2022.104721

Zhang, R., Zhou, J., Hai, T., Zhang, S., Iwendi, M., Biamba, C., & Anumbe, N. (2022). Quality assurance awareness in higher education in China: big data challenges. *Journal of Cloud Computing, 11*(1), 1-9.

Chapter 3
Enhancing Postgraduate Education in India:
A Qualitative Exploration of Innovative Pedagogies and Curriculum Frameworks

Neena Omprakash Nanda
https://orcid.org/0000-0002-5290-2036
Vivekanand Education Society's Institute of Management Studies and Research, India

Geetanjali Pinto
https://orcid.org/0000-0001-5832-7100
SIES School of Business Studies, India

Bhavna Raina
https://orcid.org/0000-0002-7635-8741
Vivekanand Education Society's Institute of Management Studies and Research, India

ABSTRACT

This chapter explores the imperative task of expanding the intellectual horizons of postgraduate students in India. It investigates various methodologies, pedagogical approaches, and educational strategies to address the challenges in traditional postgraduate education systems. Using qualitative methods, the chapter analyzes the integration of experiential learning, technology-enhanced education, collaborative projects, and real-world applications in the postgraduate curriculum. Drawing on the social cognitive theory by Albert Bandura, the research examines how observational learning and modeling influence postgraduate students. The findings

DOI: 10.4018/979-8-3693-3015-9.ch003

Copyright © 2024, IGI Global. Copying or distributing in print or electronic forms without written permission of IGI Global is prohibited.

aim to inform educational stakeholders about effective strategies for fostering a profound understanding among postgraduate students and preparing them for contemporary challenges. Overall, the chapter contributes to ongoing efforts to enhance the quality and relevance of higher education in India.

1. INTRODUCTION

According to World Bank "Higher Education is instrumental in fostering growth, reducing poverty and boosting shared prosperity. It benefits not just the individual, but the entire education system". Owing to double disruption caused by Industrial Revolution 4.0 (IR4.0) and COVID-19, there is a need to reshape the work and skills needed across industries and marketplaces. More than 85 million jobs are expected to be displaced by the IR4.0, and 40% of the core skills will change for the employees by 2025 (World Economic Forum, 2020). There is a growing feeling among jobseekers and job-providers that present prospects lack core skills. To close this gap, there is a need for a comprehensive strategy from the government as well as from enterprises and higher education institutions. For this purpose, higher education institutions are undergoing a change in their teaching–learning practices, with the core goal of giving students the necessary skills and competencies to succeed in a complex and uncertain society (Ragavan et al., 2021).

The qualitative study on the Qualitative Exploration of Innovative Pedagogies and Curricular Frameworks by use of Social Cognitive Theory (SCT) components on postgraduate students promises significant benefits to the field of education. By delving into observational learning, social and cultural factors, hands-on experiences, technology, and teaching methods, the research aims to deepen our comprehension of how these elements collectively shape the learning experiences of postgraduate students. Such insights can be instrumental in tailoring educational practices to the unique needs of postgraduate learners, fostering a more engaging and effective learning environment. This study also has the potential to guide educators in promoting positive behaviours and engagement among postgraduate students, contributing to the creation of more interactive and inclusive learning environments.

Moreover, by exploring the impact of technology within the SCT framework, the research can inform strategic technology integration that enhances, rather than detracts from, postgraduate learning experiences. This study also finds that by incorporating SCT into higher education, educators can create engaging, motivating, and collaborative learning environments that promote self-efficacy, behavioural capability, and other key components of SCT. This can lead to better learning outcomes and a more positive educational experience for students. Additionally, findings related to hands-on learning experiences can inform curriculum design, allowing for the incorporation of experiential learning opportunities aligned with SCT principles. In summary, the research endeavours to provide valuable insights that have the potential to positively transform the landscape of postgraduate education, benefiting both students and educators alike.

The rest of the study is organised as follows: Section 2 underpins the theoretical background and conceptual framework based on which this study is performed. Section 3 provides a detailed review of the literature based on which enables us to identify the research questions and objectives of the study. The data and methodology are provided in the section 4 followed by analysis of the results in section 5. The last section concludes the paper and also provides scope for future work.

2. THEORETICAL BACKGROUND AND CONCEPTUAL FRAMEWORK

2.1 Higher Education in India

To understand higher landscape in India the All-India Survey of Higher Education (AISHE) 2020-21 has highlighted positive developments as well as areas that deserve attention to ensure continued progress. The positive developments are in area of university growth totalling to 1,113 universities in 2020-21. There are 17 Universities exclusively for women as compared to 11 in 2014-15. The number of colleges has increased by 1453 during 2020-21, to 43,796 in 2020-21 from 42,343 in 2019-20. The Number of colleges per lakh eligible population (population in the age-group 18-23 years) in the country is 31. It was 27 in 2014-15. The annual rate of increase in enrolment has also shown an improvement over the years. The increase in enrolment in 2020-21 over 2019-20 is 7.4%, which was 3% during 2019- 20 and 2.7% during 2018-19. Further, overall increase in enrolment since 2014-15 is 20.9%. In the year 2020-21, Gross Enrollment Ratio (GER) in 2020-21 over 2019-20 has increased by 1.7 as per 2011 projection, which is highest ever increase in GER.

Further the survey also reveals that about 78.09% of the students are enrolled in undergraduate level courses and remaining 11.5% are enrolled in postgraduate level courses. Number of teachers has increased by 47,914 in 2020-21 over 2019-20. For Regular Mode Pupil Teacher Ratio (PTR) in Universities and Colleges is 24 whereas PTR for Universities and its Constituent Units, in regular mode, is 19. The National Education Policy -2020 (NEP, 2020) envisions an India centred education system that contributes directly to transforming our nation sustainably into an equitable and vibrant knowledge society by providing high quality education to all. In this new system, Higher Education Institutions (HEIs) faculty members are considered as collaborators and guide of educating students to make them as innovators & creative thinkers. Teaching-learning method mainly focuses on classroom training, fieldwork, and research projects. Pedagogy in HEIs to focus on communication, presentation, discussion, debate, research, analysis, and interdisciplinary thinking and Student-Centred teaching & learning process instead of Teacher centred teaching model. Keeping this is in perspective and realizing that students are the most important stakeholders of higher education system it becomes critical to understand the student perspective in Enhancing Postgraduate Education in India in terms of Pedagogies and Curricular Frameworks.

2.2 Social Cognitive Theory (SCT) and Dynamics of Higher Education

Social Cognitive Theory (SCT) is a learning theory that posits that learning occurs in a social context with a dynamic and reciprocal interaction of the person, behavior, and environment.

The paper by Bowden et al., (2021) highlights effective teaching methods, curriculum design, and strategies for policymakers in postgraduate education. However, the paper suggests that there is potential to delve deeper into student perspectives by conducting surveys or interviews with postgraduate students. This approach could provide valuable insights into their preferences, challenges, and experiences in different educational settings. The search results provide further information on the use of Social Cognitive Theory (SCT) in educational research. For example, one study used SCT to guide a qualitative study on knowledge gaps in school health education (Sohail, 2020). Another study integrated SCT with the Technology Acceptance Model (TAM) to explore the impact of mobile learning in art education (Almaiah et al., 2021). Additionally, SCT has been used to explore the impact of social and cultural factors on learning (Grusec, 1992) and to develop a new pedagogical framework for enhancing self-regulation and social interactions in learning (Abdullah et al., 2017). Overall, the research gap identified in the paper by Bowden et al., (2021) suggests that there is a need for more research on student perspectives in postgraduate education, particularly in relation to SCT. This approach could provide valuable insights into the complex dynamics influencing individual learning and behavior in the postgraduate educational context.

In summary, within Bandura's SCT, observation and modeling are central to the process of learning and behavior change, while social and cultural factors are integral to understanding the influence of the environment on individual behaviours. Figure 1 illustrates the interconnected nature of these components, showcasing how each element contributes to and influences the others within the framework of Social Cognitive Theory with respect to post graduate education.

Figure 1. Mapping Postgraduate Education Experiences: A Framework Aligned with Social Cognitive Theory

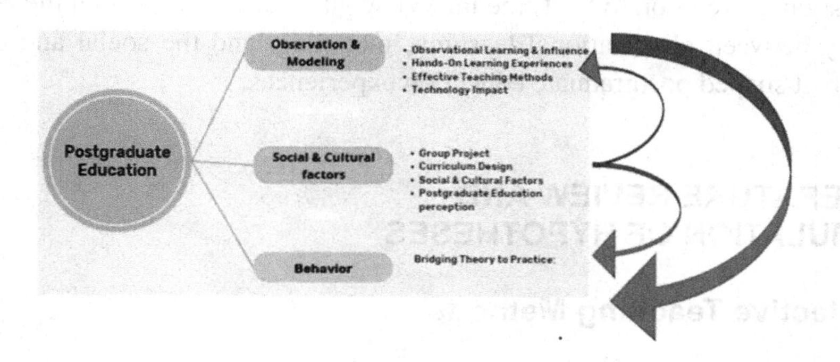

According to Bandura (1986), social cognitive theory emphasizes observation and modelling are fundamental concepts that influence behavior and learning. Here's how these concepts are defined within the theory:

Observation and Modelling

Observational Learning: This refers to the process of learning through observing others. Individuals acquire new behaviors and knowledge by paying attention to the actions and experiences of others.

Modelling: Modelling involves imitating the behavior of others. It is a key mechanism through which observational learning occurs. Individuals may choose to replicate behavior that has been observed and modeled by others. (Bandura,1986)

Social and Cultural Factors

SCT describes the influence of individual experiences, the actions of others, and environmental factors on behavior. Social and cultural factors play a significant role in shaping individual health behaviors within the framework of SCT (Hardin & Greer, 2009).

Behavior:

SCT emphasizes the role of observational learning and modeling in shaping behavior. Individuals learn and adopt new behaviors through the process of observing others and modeling their actions.

Based on above the following interview guide was created to enquire about the presence of various components of SCT in current education system. By framing the questions in relation to SCT, the interview guide aimed to unravel the nuanced interplay between observational learning, modeling, and the social and cultural factors that shaped postgraduate education experiences.

3. LITERATURE REVIEW AND FORMULATION OF HYPOTHESES

3.1 Effective Teaching Methods

Literature has denominated certain abilities as "21st-century skills" (Buckingham Shum and Deakin Crick, 2016; Liesa-Orús et al., 2020). Particularly, in business education, students must get specific training to make informed decisions that influence complex systems with thousands of factors interacting with each other (Kutz et al., 2016). Partnership for 21st Century Skills (P21, 2007) Organization for Economic Co-operation and Development; United Nations Educational, Scientific and Cultural Organization; and Assessment and Teaching of the 21st Century Skills (ATC21S), have presented numerous proposals regarding 21st-century skills. They all concur that each student's learning should be centred on developing 21st-century abilities. Problem-solving, critical thinking, decision-making, cooperation and invention are just a few of the few yet vital abilities that were highlighted by the ATC21S (Binkley et al., 2012).

Further, Javed et al. (2019) includes critical thinking, problem-solving, creativity, people management and coordination among the top 10 skills. For professionals and citizens of the 21st century, ethics- related skills and abilities are crucial. Globalization, multiculturalism, and the development in information & communication technology (ICT) use, provide ethical issues. This dimension is related to the skills of accountability, decision-making and critical thinking (Ananiadou and Claro, 2009). To increase students' employability, which is defined as "the likelihood of students to acquire a job" (Harvey, 2001), it is important for them to gain the necessary knowledge, skills, and attitude (Harvey, 2001; Hillage and Pollard, 1999). In the current educational environment, entrepreneurship education – which instructs students on how to launch new businesses – is gaining increased momentum (Holzmann et al., 2018; Melnikova et al., 2017; Zhang, 2017).

Sustainability is yet another important issue that needs to be addressed (van der Aalst et al., 2010). The sustainability attitude, particularly regarding economic, environmental and social challenges, has aided and supported the development of talents (Fabricatore and Lopez, 2012). Business education must help students transition to the 21st-century workforce by giving them real-world experience, ensuring the development of certain business abilities, thus increasing their self-confidence. One of the objectives of higher education is to improve the ability of students to apply knowledge and solve everyday problems that are close to their professions. It is not enough to ensure that they gain the required knowledge, it is also necessary to provide them with opportunities to deploy skills in real contexts (Huang & Jiang, 2020; Kalyuga et al., 2010).

Higher education must respond to the changing demands of today's world. To accomplish this, it needs to modify the core of the educational process: the teaching and learning process (Bridgstock,2016; Jollands, 2015; Mitchell, & Rost-Banik, 2020). Experiential learning is a process that enables students to learn through 'doing', 'learning while experiencing', and learning through 'hands on practice' and 'reflection' (Fry et al., 2015). It is a powerful tool for making that change in higher education (Miettinen, 2000). This methodology allows students to transfer what they have learned in class to authentic situations (Guo et al., 2016), achieving an in-depth understanding of the contents (Baker et al., 2005; Kayes et al., 2005). This way of learning implies providing the student with greater autonomy and responsibility, involving them personally with their learning process and the context in which it takes place. Also, emphasize learning flexibility to encompass all learning modes for full cycle learning, developing students' meta-learning capabilities and adaptive learning (Kolb, & Kolb, 2017).

Moreover, experiential learning helps students to establish connections between experience and theory (Earnest et al., 2016; Romero, 2010), facilitating the transition between undergraduate education and the world of work (Friedman, & Goldbaum, 2016). Butler et al. (2019) describes this link by stating that Experiential Learning (EL) enables students to participate in a tangible experience, reproduce that experience and other evidence, cultivate theories in line with experiences and apply the acquired skills in a new work situation. A study conducted by Abdullah et al. (2019) in the context of Malesia revealed that the use of EL in Vocational Educational Training (VET) empowered students to acquire skills. The results further showed that "learning outcomes have a practical influence on the student's applying skills in a new environment" (Abdullah et al., 2019, p. 8). These findings suggest that the application of ELT in VET yields good results in the process and outcome of learning, which are real-world skills. In the context of skills development for youths, Lantu et al. (2022) assessed the role of ELT in improving entrepreneurial training programmes. The findings showed that the application of EL improved the effectiveness of the entrepreneurial training programmes by helping the students to start owning small businesses. EL improved the effectiveness of entrepreneurial skills training because the students experienced working in a real business setting (Lantu et al., 2022). The students admitted that the programme effectively improved their entrepreneurial skills to start their businesses. The study concludes that the skills development programme also "prepared the students to enter the workplace and produce qualified human capital to meet industry needs" (Lantu et al., 2022, p. 122).

Today, a variety of digital technologies are used in classrooms for various purposes including communication, coursework, information storage and research. In some cases, the institution selects the technologies to be used (e.g. e-mail system, learning management system (LMS)), in other cases, it is the instructor or students (e.g. presentation software, web-based applications). In a study published by Kozma (2003) examined 174 case studies from 28 countries of innovative pedagogical practices. In this study, Kozma found that students and instructors use technology tools for purposes such as searching for information, designing products, publishing findings and teachers use technology for instructional purposes including presenting instructional content, monitoring student progress. In more recent studies, the types of and purposes for technologies used in classrooms have expanded significantly (Buchanan et al., 2013; Fichten et al., 2015; Venkatesh et al., 2016). Some of the different types of technology used in classrooms for instructional purposes include the internet, e-mail, course/LMSs (e.g. Blackboard, Moodle), word processing, blogs and wikis, social media (e.g. Facebook, Twitter), presentation software (e.g. PowerPoint, Prezi), online audio and video, cloud and web based applications (e.g. Google Drive), virtual and augmented reality software and devices, tablet and SmartPhone apps, interactive devices(e.g. clickers) and interactive whiteboards (e.g. SmartBoard) (Buchanan et al., 2013; Fichtenet al., 2015; Venkatesh et al., 2016).

As technology has become increasingly integrated in the lives of young people (Ofcom, 2017), a constant demand is placed upon them to interact with changing technologies for communication, transaction, pleasure etc. (Office of Education Technology, 2017). It is undeniable that access to social media, gaming technology and "on demand" entertainment platforms have fundamentally altered the broader context of human/technology interaction. As this technological environment has (and continues to evolve) it must be acknowledged that learners will have an expectation that support for learning will be available through a technology-driven media. Against these wider social "backdrops" there is therefore, a clear role for technology enhanced learning within the academic context. These in turn may take a number of formats such as problem solving through such encounters as game platforms, acquisition of information (knowledge and skill acquisition) and media platforms such as "YouTube" (Lewis, 2019). For many students today, their initial and continued engagement within higher education is often shaped by their experiences of teaching and learning within the first year of their programme of study (Lewis, 2019).

However, there is often a mismatch between students´ expectations and their training. In general, they want more practical activities and abilities´ training, and instead, they receive mainly theoretical and scientific knowledge (Goedeke & Gibson, 2011; Green et al., 2017). Higher education has to respond to the changing demands of today's world. To accomplish this, it needs to modify the core of the educational process: the teaching and learning process (Bridgstock,2016; Jollands, 2015; Mitchell, & Rost-Banik, 2020). Though skills shortages and skills mismatches are not new in the academic debates, their severity has increased in some countries along with the economic growth in recent years. For instance, many Asian countries have been suffering from a shortage of skilled workers (United Nations, 2020). The reason is that the training delivery and learning approaches are practice-oriented to develop job-related skills and directed to the real world of work (Eicker et al., 2016; Lolwana, 2016).

3.2 Research Questions

RQ1. How do observational learning, modelling, social and cultural factors, hands-on learning experiences, technology, and teaching methods collectively influence the learning experiences and behaviours of postgraduate students within the framework of Social Cognitive Theory?

RQ2. In what ways do postgraduate students perceive and navigate the interplay between hands-on learning experiences, technology, and teaching methods within the context of Social Cognitive Theory, and how does this impact their overall educational journey?

3.3 Research Objectives

- To explore the influence of observational learning and modelling on postgraduate students' learning experiences and behaviour.
- To understand the impact of social and cultural factors on postgraduate students' learning experiences and educational strategies.
- To examine the role of hands-on learning experiences, technology, and effective teaching methods in postgraduate education within the framework of SCT.

4. METHODOLOGY

4.1 Data

Students from higher education institutes were interviewed with standardised questionnaire. The main source of data was students studying in higher education institutes in Mumbai. Data through detailed questionnaire was collected from 10 students in higher educational institutes in India.

4.2 Variables

Each question in the interview guide was designed to explore aspects of postgraduate education in connection with the Social Cognitive Theory (SCT) by Albert Bandura. SCT emphasizes observational learning, modelling, and the impact of social and cultural factors on individual learning and behavior. The questions were tailored to gather insights from participants that aligned with key principles of SCT, providing a lens through which to understand the complex dynamics of postgraduate education.

1. Curriculum Challenges: Understanding the challenges in the postgraduate curriculum through SCT involved exploring how observational learning and modelling impacted individuals' perceptions of the curriculum. By asking about specific challenges faced, the aim was to uncover how observational learning influenced students' views on the curriculum and how they modelled their behaviors based on these observations.

2. Holistic Education and Scope Expansion: SCT suggests that learning extends beyond individual experiences to encompass observational learning from others. Questions about holistic education aimed to reveal how participants perceived and modelled their understanding of education beyond academics, considering the influence of social factors on their broader educational perspectives.

3. Experiential Learning: SCT underscores the importance of hands-on experiences and observational learning. Questions about hands-on learning experiences explored how participants engaged with and modelled their behaviors based on practical experiences, aligning with the SCT's emphasis on learning through observation and participation.

4. Technology-Enhanced Education: SCT acknowledges the role of technology in observational learning. Questions about the use of technology aimed to understand how participants observed and modelled behaviors influenced by technology in the educational context.

5. Collaborative Projects: SCT emphasizes the influence of social factors on learning. Questions about group projects explored how collaborative efforts shaped

individuals' learning experiences, aligning with SCT principles that highlight the impact of social interactions on observational learning and behavior modelling.

6. Real-World Applications: SCT underscores the application of knowledge in real-life contexts. Questions about applying theoretical knowledge aimed to uncover how participants observed, modelled, and applied learned behaviors in practical situations, aligning with SCT's emphasis on the integration of observational learning into real-world scenarios.

7. Effective Teaching Methods: SCT suggests that individuals learn through observing effective models. Questions about preferred teaching approaches explored how participants perceived effective teaching methods and modelled their learning behaviors based on observed teaching practices.

8. Curriculum Design: SCT emphasizes the impact of environmental factors on learning. Questions about thoughts on curriculum design aimed to uncover how participants observed and modelled their perceptions of the curriculum, considering the influence of the educational environment.

9. Observational Learning and Modelling (SCT): Directly aligned with SCT, these questions explored how participants observed, learned from others, and modelled behaviors in the postgraduate educational context, acknowledging the role of observational learning in shaping individual learning experiences.

10. Impact of Social and Cultural Factors: SCT highlights the influence of social and cultural factors on learning. Questions about the impact of social and cultural factors aimed to understand how these external factors were observed, learned from, and modeled in the participants' educational strategies.

4.3 Toots and Techniques Used

Qualitative data analysis software NVivo was employed to learn the concerns and focus of HEI's students in India. According to Reeves, Kuper, and Hodges (2008) and Holloway & Galvin (2016) the qualitative method provides in-depth, socio-contextual, and elaborate descriptions along with insightful interpretations. The present study follows the inductive approach which allows the development of categories and identifying from other theories before coding processes begin (Perry and Jensen,2001). The data obtained through detailed questionnaire collected from 10 students in higher educational institutes in India were stored as recordings. For the qualitative data analysis, these recordings were then converted to transcripts in word format. The NVivo software package was used to analyse the information gathered from all the participants. All responses were transcribed in word format (NVivo allows data entry from formats such as Word, PDF, Excel, or Picture) and collected into a file (called node) to theme the answers related to each question from each individual participant. Each question was coded, and all answers related to each question can be viewed separately. Open ended questions vary in responses, therefore, word frequency and word trees helped in identifying patterns in participants' responses, which helped the researchers to formulate and extract pertinent information from their responses. For better visualization of the results, Word cloud and Tree Map was generated, based on frequency and percentage of words. Figure ..... shows Word clouds where the keywords are represented according to their frequency in the dataset (Sinclair & Cardew-Hall, 2008) for themes generated by the software.

5. ANALYSIS OF RESULTS

In analyzing the participants' responses regarding hands-on learning experiences during their postgraduate studies, several key themes emerged, shedding light on the observational and modeling aspects within the SCT framework. Table 1 depicts the themes derived from participants' responses regarding hands-on learning experiences during postgraduate studies.

Table 1. Themes – Responses regarding hands-on learning experiences

Themes	Statement
Summer Internship and Corporate Exposure	- Participants highlighted the significance of summer internships in gaining practical exposure to corporate environments. - They learned about ongoing projects, departmental operations, and client engagements directly from professionals in the field.
Experiential Learning and Team Collaboration:	Experiential learning opportunities allowed participants to develop leadership skills and collaborate effectively within teams. Activities integrated collaboration, teamwork, and empathy, contributing to holistic skill development.
Application of Analytical Tools and Statistical Modeling	Participants utilized various analytical tools such as WEKA and R programming for data analysis and statistical modeling. Hands-on experience with these tools enhanced their understanding of analytical methods and techniques.
Real-World Applications of Theoretical Concepts	Guest lectures and theoretical subjects were complemented by real-world applications, providing insights into market scenarios and regulatory frameworks. Participants gained practical knowledge about financial markets, regulations, derivatives, and investment strategies.
Skill-Linked Immersion Program (SLIP) and Project-based Learning:	SLIP presentations and skill-linked immersion programs offered additional hands-on experiences beyond traditional coursework. Various projects within the curriculum facilitated practical learning and skill development

The participants' responses illustrate how observational learning plays a crucial role in their postgraduate education. Participants' narratives highlight the significance of modeling in their learning experiences. Table 2 depicts the themes derived from participants' responses regarding observational learning and modeling during postgraduate studies.

Table 2. Themes – Responses regarding observational learning

Themes	Statement
Cross-Disciplinary Collaboration and Peer Learning	Participants highlighted the value of collaborating with peers from different specializations, such as HR, marketing, and operations. Working on common projects with students from diverse backgrounds provided opportunities for interdisciplinary learning and knowledge exchange.
Foundational Learning and Knowledge Transfer:	Participants with backgrounds in different fields, such as science, emphasized the importance of foundational learning in transitioning to a new academic discipline. Learning from classmates, faculty members, and experienced peers facilitated the transfer of knowledge and skill acquisition
Diverse Problem-Solving Approaches:	Interactions with visiting faculty members exposed participants to diverse problem-solving approaches and perspectives. Participants learned the importance of considering various solutions and approaches to tackle complex problems effectively.
Efficient Work Management and Reduced Exam Anxiety	Observing peers' work management strategies helped participants improve their own time management and workload distribution. Learning from peers' experiences also contributed to reduced exam anxiety and improved confidence in academic performance.
Learning from Experienced Peers and Work Experience	Participants valued learning from peers with prior work experience, acknowledging their insights and perspectives. Observing and modelling behaviours of experienced peers enriched participants' learning experiences and broadened their understanding of real-world contexts.

Participants described effective teaching methods such as practical learning experiences, interactive sessions, case studies, and peer-led discussions as shown in Table 3. They recalled instances where these methods facilitated their learning by providing opportunities for observation and modeling of behaviors, strategies, and problem-solving approaches.

The participants' responses shed light on the integration of technology into their postgraduate education and how it positively impacted their learning experiences, particularly in terms of observational learning and modeling aspects within SCT. This occurred through observational learning through technology integration, modeling through software and tools, application of Software for learning, access to information and research resources. Table 4 depicts the themes derived from participants' responses regarding technology-enhanced education and self-efficacy.

As seen from Table 5, group projects during postgraduate studies influenced participants' social and cultural learning experiences within the SCT framework. By fostering collaboration, knowledge sharing, cultural sensitivity, and interpersonal skills, group projects contributed to individuals' overall development and preparedness for diverse professional environments. These findings underscore the significance of promoting inclusive and culturally responsive educational practices that nurture collaborative learning and social integration among students from diverse cultural backgrounds.

Table 6 highlights the need for changes in the postgraduate curriculum within the SCT framework. By prioritizing practical application, collaborative learning, flexibility, technological integration, and continuous improvement, educational institutions can create engaging and culturally responsive learning environments that empower students to succeed in diverse professional contexts.

Table 3. Themes – Responses regarding effective teaching methods

Themes	Statement
Practical Learning Experiences	Participants highlighted the effectiveness of practical learning experiences, such as corporate interaction sessions and hands-on activities. - Through these experiences, participants observed professionals and peers, learning from their expertise and real-world applications. - Observing professionals during corporate interaction sessions allowed participants to model effective strategies and gain insights into industry practices.
Interactive Sessions and Case Studies	Participants valued interactive teaching methods, including group discussions, question-and-answer sessions, and case studies. - These methods encouraged active participation and engagement, enabling participants to observe and learn from peers and instructors. - Case studies provided opportunities for participants to analyze complex scenarios, propose solutions, and observe different problem-solving approaches, fostering observational learning and modeling of effective strategies.
Peer-Led Learning	Participants recalled instances where peer-led discussions and presentations were particularly effective in their learning process. Peer-led sessions allowed participants to observe and learn from their peers, modeling effective communication, presentation skills, and content expertise. Through collaborative learning experiences, participants observed diverse perspectives and problem-solving techniques, enhancing their own understanding and skills through modeling.
Hands-On Learning and Problem-Solving Practice	Participants highlighted the effectiveness of hands-on learning experiences, such as solving practice problems and applying theoretical concepts to real-world scenarios. Engaging in practical exercises and solving a variety of problems enabled participants to develop problem-solving skills and gain a deeper understanding of course content

Table 4. Themes – Responses regarding integration of technology into higher education

Themes	Statement
Integrated Digital Platforms and Communication Tools	- Participants highlighted the role of digital platforms such as Outlook and management systems in facilitating communication and information dissemination. - Access to centralized email IDs and management systems streamlined administrative processes and provided a centralized hub for course-related communications and placement activities.
Data Analysis and Visualization Tools	- Technology-enabled learning encompassed subjects focusing on data analysis and visualization tools such as Power BI. - Participants benefited from workshops and courses that equipped them with practical skills in data analysis, enhancing their proficiency and employability in data-driven industries.
Specialized Software for Academic and Professional Development	- Participants utilized specialized software like ProVisIQ for accessing financial and non-financial information related to companies, enhancing their research capabilities and decision-making processes. - Engagement with software platforms such as Six Sigma certification tools empowered participants to apply theoretical frameworks and models in real-world contexts, fostering self-efficacy and practical knowledge application.
Excel Proficiency and Financial Modeling	- The incorporation of Excel proficiency and financial modeling subjects equipped participants with essential skills for financial analysis and project evaluation. - Learning how to create flow models and assess project profitability enhanced participants' understanding of financial concepts and their ability to evaluate business scenarios effectively.
Access to Research and Information Retrieval Tools	- Participants leveraged technology to access research papers and annual reports through platforms like Google Scholar. - Tools like TADGPT facilitated nuanced understanding and interpretation of complex research findings, enhancing participants' research capabilities and self-efficacy in navigating scholarly literature.

Table 5. Themes – Impact of group projects on social and cultural learning experiences

Themes	Statement
Diverse Group Dynamics and Knowledge Sharing:	- Participants highlighted the diversity of group dynamics, with members coming from various backgrounds and domains. - Collaborating with individuals from different disciplines facilitated knowledge sharing and exposure to alternative perspectives, enriching the learning experience.
Enhanced Learning through Teamwork	- Working in groups provided opportunities for participants to learn from each other's unique approaches and methodologies. - Engaging in brainstorming sessions and sharing conceptual insights contributed to a deeper understanding of course material and project objectives.
Development of Teamwork and Leadership Skills	- Group projects enabled participants to develop essential teamwork and leadership skills, including effective communication, task delegation, and time management. - Serving as team leaders allowed participants to hone their organizational abilities and learn how to navigate group dynamics to achieve project goals.
Efficient Work Allocation and Time Management	- Participants emphasized the importance of efficient work allocation and time management within group projects. - Learning how to delegate tasks, manage workloads, and coordinate efforts among team members contributed to improved productivity and project outcomes.
Smooth Collaboration and Compatibility	- Collaboration in group projects necessitated smooth coordination and compatibility among team members. - Understanding each other's work styles and strengths facilitated seamless workflow and minimized conflicts, ensuring successful project completion.

Table 6. Themes – Responses regarding need for changes in the postgraduate curriculum

Themes	Statement
Duration and Structure of Internships	- Participants expressed the need for longer durations for summer internships to gain a comprehensive understanding of corporate environments. - Suggestions were made to extend internships from two months to four months to allow for more immersive experiences and learning opportunities
Experiential Learning and Project-Based Curriculum	- Participants advocated for a shift towards experiential learning and project-based approaches in curriculum design. - Emphasizing hands-on projects and group activities was seen as a more effective way to enhance learning outcomes and develop practical skills.
Redundancy and Integration of Subjects	- Concerns were raised regarding the repetition of certain subjects throughout the trimesters, leading to redundancy in the curriculum. - Suggestions were made to integrate similar subjects into a single course to streamline learning and avoid duplication of content.
Balance Between Theory and Practice	- Participants highlighted the importance of striking a balance between theoretical knowledge and practical application in the curriculum. - While acknowledging the value of theory, participants suggested incorporating more practical aspects into subjects like financial regulation to enhance relevance and engagement.
Integration of Data Analytics and Emerging Trends	- The importance of integrating emerging topics like data analytics into the curriculum was emphasized by participants. - Updating the curriculum to reflect current trends and technologies, such as programming languages for data analysis, was seen as essential for staying relevant in the dynamic business landscape.

Table 7 presents the thematic analysis of participants' responses regarding the influence of social and cultural factors on their learning experiences, within the SCT framework. The analysis underscores the intricate interplay between social and cultural factors in shaping individuals' learning experiences, offering valuable insights for educators and researchers. Recognizing the influence of cultural diversity, social dynamics, institutional contexts, and individual identities can inform the development of inclusive and culturally responsive educational practices, aligned with the principles of SCT.

In the thematic analysis of participants' responses regarding opportunities to enhance postgraduate education experiences and improve educational strategies, several pertinent themes emerged, illuminating key aspects within the framework of SCT. Table 8 reveals the multifaceted nature of enhancing postgraduate education experiences within the context of SCT. By incorporating individualized learning approaches, fostering industry interaction, promoting peer collaboration, adapting educational programs, and providing practical experiences, institutions can create enriching learning environments that empower students to thrive in diverse socio-cultural contexts.

Table 7. Themes – Responses regarding influence of social and cultural factors on the student's learning experiences.

Themes	Statement
Cultural Diversity and Exposure	- Participants highlighted the enriching experience of studying in an institution with a different cultural background. - Exposure to diverse cultural norms and values broadened participants' perspectives and contributed positively to their learning experiences.
Interactions with International Clients and Cultures	- Participants shared experiences of interacting with clients from diverse cultural backgrounds during internships. - They observed differences in communication styles, emphasis on punctuality, and approaches to presenting
Influence of Peer Groups and Social Circles	- Peer groups and social circles were identified as significant influencers of learning experiences. - Participants emphasized the role of peer support and collaboration in enhancing understanding and knowledge acquisition.
Impact of Institutional Culture on Study Habits	- Participants reflected on the impact of institutional culture on their study habits and academic focus. - The emphasis on academic excellence and goal-oriented culture within the institution motivated participants to prioritize their studies and concentrate on their goals.
Practical Experiences and Business Backgrounds	- Participants noted the influence of classmates' practical experiences and business backgrounds on their learning. - Exposure to diverse professional backgrounds enriched classroom discussions and provided real-world insights into various subjects.

Table 8. Themes – Responses regarding opportunities to enhance postgraduate education experiences and improve educational strategies

Themes	Statement
Customization of Education	- Participants emphasized the need for personalized education tailored to individual skill sets and interests. - They suggested revising educational strategies to focus more on developing specific skills relevant to different career paths.
Industry Interaction and Corporate Sessions	- Participants highlighted the importance of interactions with corporates and industry professionals to complement regular classes. - They suggested integrating more Corporate Interaction Sessions (CIS) and similar initiatives to provide practical insights and real-world experiences.
Bridge between Academic and Practical Knowledge	- Postgraduate education was viewed as an opportunity to bridge the gap between theoretical knowledge and practical application, particularly for participants from diverse academic backgrounds. - Suggestions included increasing internship durations and incorporating live projects with organizations to enhance practical learning experiences.
Collaborative Learning and Knowledge Exchange	- Participants expressed interest in opportunities for collaborative learning and knowledge exchange with students from other institutions, especially prestigious ones like IITs and IIMs. - They proposed initiatives such as case study competitions and offline interactions to facilitate learning from peers and exposure to different learning methodologies.
Expanded Internship Opportunities	- Participants advocated for expanding internship opportunities by introducing winter internships in addition to summer internships. - They believed that multiple internship experiences would provide a more comprehensive understanding of corporate dynamics and enhance preparedness for professional roles.

Participants exemplified the practical application of theoretical knowledge by demonstrating how they utilized skills acquired in academic settings during real-world experiences as demonstrated in Table 9. This aligns with SCT's emphasis on observational learning, where individuals acquire new skills and behaviors by observing and imitating others. Thematic analysis underscores the behavioral aspects of SCT by demonstrating how individuals apply theoretical knowledge to real-world situations, engage in goal-setting and self-regulation, and develop self-efficacy to navigate professional challenges effectively.

Table 9. Themes – Responses regarding practical application of theoretical knowledge

Themes	Statement
Integration of Classroom Learning and Practical Experience	- Participants highlighted instances where they applied theoretical knowledge gained in the classroom to real-world situations during internships or projects. - They emphasized the importance of integrating theoretical concepts with practical applications to enhance understanding and proficiency.
Enhanced Understanding Through Application	- The application of theoretical knowledge to real-world scenarios facilitated a deeper understanding of concepts. - Participants noted how their ability to apply theoretical frameworks and analytical tools in practical contexts improved their comprehension and problem-solving skills.
Relevance of Curriculum to Professional Settings	- Participants appreciated how their academic curriculum equipped them with relevant skills and knowledge applicable in professional settings. - They cited examples such as financial analysis, data analytics, and marketing strategies where theoretical concepts directly contributed to their performance and effectiveness in real-world tasks.
Recognition of Transferable Skills	- Participants recognized the transferability of skills acquired through theoretical learning to diverse professional environments. - They emphasized the value of skills such as data analysis, financial modeling, and strategic planning in various industries and roles, underscoring the practical relevance of their academic training.
Feedback and Validation from Industry Mentors	- Participants received positive feedback and validation from industry mentors or supervisors regarding their application of theoretical knowledge in real-world projects or internships. - This feedback reinforced the significance of theoretical understanding in practical contexts and motivated participants to further integrate classroom learning with professional experiences.

Suggested Changes to Improve the Postgraduate Curriculum

Integrate more experiential learning opportunities within the curriculum to enhance practical application. Incorporate collaborative and project-based learning approaches to promote active engagement. Enhance curriculum flexibility and adaptability to accommodate diverse learning needs. Integrate emerging technologies and industry interactions for real-world experiences. Expand internship opportunities and duration to bridge the gap between theory and practice.

1. Customized Internship Programs:

Introduce personalized internship programs tailored to individual student interests and career goals. This will provide a more immersive and relevant experience for each participant.

2. Virtual Collaborative Learning Platforms:

Develop online platforms for students to engage in collaborative learning and knowledge exchange with peers from different institutions. This will facilitate continuous learning opportunities beyond physical boundaries.

3. Industry-Integrated Projects:

Collaborate with industry partners to create live projects embedded within the curriculum. This will offer students hands-on experience and exposure to real-world challenges.

4. Cross-Institutional Case Study Competitions:

Organize intercollegiate case study competitions to promote cross-institutional learning and foster healthy competition among students. This will encourage the exchange of diverse perspectives and innovative solutions.

5. Mentorship Programs with Industry Professionals:

Establish mentorship programs where students can be paired with industry professionals for guidance and practical insights. This will provide valuable networking opportunities and mentorship support for students' professional development.

6. CONCLUSIONS AND SCOPE FOR FUTURE WORK

Observational learning and modeling principles play a crucial role in shaping postgraduate students' educational experiences. By observing and imitating others, participants acquire new skills, knowledge, and problem-solving strategies, contributing to their overall learning and development within the academic context. These findings underscore the importance of considering observational learning and modeling behaviors in designing effective educational strategies and environments for postgraduate students. Hence there is a need to modify the core of the educational process: the teaching and learning process (Bridgstock,2016; Jollands, 2015; Mitchell, & Rost-Banik, 2020).

We also conclude that cultural diversity, peer influence, and institutional contexts further shape individuals' learning experiences, highlighting the intricate interplay between social and cultural factors within the SCT framework. Further, the integration of technology into learning experiences also aligns with SCT, providing students with tools and resources that support skill development and knowledge acquisition. In line with Huang & Jiang (2020) and Kalyuga et al. (2010), this study also concludes that through hands-on learning experiences, such as internships and projects, participants can apply theoretical knowledge to real-world scenarios, enhancing their understanding and proficiency. These findings are in line with Earnest et al. (2016), Romero (2010), Friedman, & Goldbaum (2016) and Lantu et al. (2022) which find that application of theoretical knowledge in practice enables students to face real world problems and also meet industry needs more effectively.

Accordingly, the study's outcomes may not only contribute to the professional development of educators but also help formulate educational policies at institutional and governmental levels, facilitating decisions regarding curriculum design, teaching practices, and student support services.

Data analysis can also be done by employing quantitative methods such as surveys or questionnaires to gather data on a larger scale. Additionally, qualitative methods such as interviews or focus groups can provide deeper insights into the experiences and perceptions of students from different regions and backgrounds. By including students from HEIs across the country, future researchers can examine variations in learning experiences, teaching methods, and cultural influences, contributing to a more comprehensive understanding of postgraduate education in India.

REFERENCES

Abdullah, N. A., Ahmad, M. S., & Aziz, A. A. (2017). A new pedagogical framework for enhancing self-regulation and social interactions in learning. *Journal of Educational Technology & Society*, *20*(1), 13–24. https://www.jstor.org/stable/26322208

Almaiah, M. A., Al-Khasawneh, A., & Althunibat, A. (2021). The impact of mobile learning on students' learning behaviours and performance: Integrating the technology acceptance model with social cognitive theory. *Interactive Learning Environments*, *29*(1), 1–16. doi:10.1080/10494820.2019.1692486

Bandura, A. (1986). *Social foundations of thought and action: A social cognitive theory*. Prentice-Hall.

Bowden, J. L.-H., Tickle, L., & Naumann, K. (2021). The four pillars of tertiary student engagement and success: A holistic measurement approach. *Studies in Higher Education*, *46*(6), 1207–1224. doi:10.1080/03075079.2019.1672647

Grusec, J. E. (1992). Social learning theory and developmental psychology: The legacies of Robert Sears and Albert Bandura. *Developmental Psychology*, *28*(5), 776–786. doi:10.1037/0012-1649.28.5.776

Hardin, M., & Greer, J. D. (2009). The influence of gender-role socialization, media use and sports participation on perceptions of gender-appropriate sports. *Journal of Sport Behavior*, *32*(2), 207–226.

Sohail, R. (2020). *Utilizing social cognitive theory to explore knowledge gaps in school health education: A phenomenological study*. California State University. https://scholarworks.calstate.edu/downloads/9019s503g

Chapter 4
Exploring Teacher Use of Augmented Reality (AR) and Virtual Reality (VR) in South Africa and Turkey

Huseyin Kocasarac
https://orcid.org/0000-0002-5846-9958
Ministry of Education, Ankara, Turkey

Handson Fingi Mlotshwa
https://orcid.org/0000-0002-2594-8426
Matthew Goniwe School of Leadership and Governance, South Africa

ABSTRACT

The purpose of this study was to explore the extent to which teachers in South Africa and Turkey are adopting and utilizing augmented reality (AR) and virtual reality (VR) in teaching and learning. A case study design`approach was utilized, and data was collected using a questionnaire using Google Forms. This study involved 29 teachers from both countries: 16 teachers from South Africa and 13 teachers from Turkey participated in a randomized sample. The results of the study reveal that 56% of South African teachers and 38% of Turkish teachers have explored the use of AR and VR in teaching and learning. Mathematics and science-oriented subjects were the most dominant in terms of the integration of AR and VR. The teachers who could not integrate were limited by the availability of digital resources in both countries.

DOI: 10.4018/979-8-3693-3015-9.ch004

Copyright © 2024, IGI Global. Copying or distributing in print or electronic forms without written permission of IGI Global is prohibited.

BACKGROUND

Virtual and augmented reality use for teaching and learning has become prominent due to technological advancement and access to digital resources that promote their use and adoption. There is very little research (Akgun, Instanbullu, and Avci,2012, Craig, Sherman, and Will, 2019, Lund and Wang, 2019, Mhlanga and Moloi) that has been done to investigate the effect of virtual and augmented reality in teaching and learning in South Africa and Turkey. There is a burgeoning literature (Penn and Umesh, 2019, Sarigoz, 2019, Alnaldi, 2018, Alquinas,2020) on the two concepts, however, the area appears to lack empirical studies on how these concepts are applied and understood within the basic education sector.

INTRODUCTION

Changes in teacher technological practices have been influenced by the proliferation of digital technologies, that have been perceived to create new forms of pedagogies. South Africa and Turkey have aggressively invested in digital technologies and are part of a small section of countries that invest heavily in the professional development of teachers. Understanding (AR) and (VR) use in teaching and learning will assist in policy formulation as well as resource prioritization by the departments of education in both countries. With the multimedia materials developed for (AR) and (VR) technologies, the student actively participates in the learning process, and permanent learning is achieved in the student. The basis of these concepts is that today, in addition to smartphones and tablets, other devices can show virtual reality, hear virtual sounds, and move virtual objects. There is a new generation of virtual reality glasses that can provide.

THE PURPOSE OF THE STUDY

The purpose of this book chapter is to explore the extent of use and adoption of augmented reality and virtual reality technologies amongst South African and Turkish teachers. Thus, this research will provide a comprehensive report underpinning the following research questions.

i. To what extent have teachers adopted and used augmented reality and virtual reality in South Africa and Turkey?
ii. Which grade or level of teaching are these technologies most used?

iii. Which augmented reality and virtual reality tools are used by the teachers for mediating learning?
iv. What are the benefits of using augmented and virtual reality in teaching and learning?

WHAT IS VIRTUAL REALITY?

The concept of virtual reality (VR) is defined as computer-aided three-dimensional environments in which the senses of one or more users can be stimulated, guided, and interacted in real-time (Gutiérrez A. et al., 2008; Guttentag, 2010). When virtual reality is considered as the state of being in a simulation-based environment outside of the physical space occupied by the individual in reality - based on experiencing a place and event different from what is happening around him - it means that a fictional content based on interactive, advanced computer screens is obtained from graphics and display technologies. It refers to an environment enriched with data (Craig, Sherman and Will, 2009). According to another definition, VR is defined as a technology that uses computers, software and peripheral hardware to create a simulated environment for the user (Sacks, Perlman and Barak, 2013). As can be understood from the definitions, virtual reality is a computer-generated simulation of a 3D environment that users can interact with using various electronic hardware. The development of technology, the importance of using technology in education has increased and it has been determined that education has become more effective with the support of technology (Drucker, 2000).

Virtual reality applications, which have spread over a wide area of use, have begun to significantly change education and lifestyle. In every field where computer-aided design is used, such as mechanical engineering, civil engineering, ergonomic design, aircraft and car design, architecture, interior design, clothing design; It is used in medical diagnosis and treatment, scientific experiments, flight simulators for the training of pilots and astronauts, defense, communication, marketing, tourism, entertainment, and all other sectors (Eryalçın, 1994; Emerson, 1994). Here are some of the opportunities provided by VR technology:

- Ability to carry out potentially dangerous experiments in the virtual world,
- Ability to carry out field work from the office,
- Ability to perform applications and experiments without using laboratory animals,
- Ability to examine and examine a virtual cadaver, any internal organ or an unborn fetus, as if you were holding it with your hand,

- Being able to watch an operation, experiment, film, theatre, fashion show or lecture as if you were in that environment,
- Being able to visit a city, museum or any building as if walking inside it,
- Ability to travel to Mars,
- Being able to walk on the moon,
- Ability to conduct military exercises almost anywhere in the world,
- Learning to ski, drive or dance,
- Providing training to astronauts for military training, flight training, and space studies,
- Being able to prepare for the real presentation by making a presentation in a virtually created environment,
- Ability to perform surgical intervention remotely with the help of a robot via teleoperation.

WHAT IS AUGMENTED REALITY?

Augmented reality (AR) is generally defined as reflecting a physically existing place onto electronic media using computer-aided images (Jung et al., 2015). Höllerer and Feiner (2004) define augmented reality; While defining it as a system that combines real and computer-generated information in a real environment, interactively and in real time, and aligns virtual objects with physical objects; Ludwig and Reimann (2005: 4) conceptualize augmented reality as human-computer interaction that adds virtual objects to real sensations provided by a video camera in real time. On the other hand, Trunfio et al. (2021) defines augmented reality as a technology in which physical reality is integrated with virtual elements and the physical world is expanded through information, images or videos.

AR technologies provide a more efficient learning environment because they can provide concrete examples in the learning process. For this reason, AR applications have an important place in terms of enriching education. In order for AR technologies to be used successfully in schools, content that meets the curriculum requirements must be provided and this technology must be introduced to teachers. Therefore, the purpose of this research is to evaluate teachers' opinions about the use of VR and AR applications in education.

The value and importance of using augmented and virtual reality applications in education and training processes is increasing day by day. Thanks to these developing technological tools and equipment, it is thought that Augmented and virtual reality applications will increasingly take place in education and training processes. Augmented reality and virtual reality technologies provide a more efficient learning environment because they can provide concrete examples in the learning process. For this reason, augmented reality and virtual reality applications have an important place in enriching education. For augmented reality technologies to be used successfully in schools, it is important to provide content that meets the curriculum requirements and to actively use this technology by teachers.

The use of augmented and virtual reality applications in the field of education plays a very important role in both attracting students to the lesson and bringing objects that are difficult to transport into the classroom environment as three-dimensional objects. In this context, this study is considered important in terms of adapting augmented and virtual reality technology to education. We think that this research will fill an important gap in the literature.

HOW DOES IT ENHANCE TEACHING AND LEARNING?

Use of Augmented Reality in Education

Augmented Reality technology is preferred and used in many different fields (education, health, military, museum, travel, etc.) (Alkhamisi and Monowar, 2013; Azuma, 1997; Damala, Marchal and Houlier, 2007). One of these areas is the field of education (Billinghurst, Kato and Poupyrev, 2001; Karakaş and Özerbaş, 2020). The use of augmented reality applications in education has many advantages. These include facilitating the use of educational materials that will make learning permanent, enabling learning by doing, experiencing, creating interactive and creative environments, making the content to be learned attractive, developing research skills, instilling the desire to discover, increasing attention and motivation, concretizing abstract and difficult-to-learn concepts and presenting them in a way that the student can understand, interpreting, It can be listed as increasing problem-solving and creative thinking skills (Ivanova and Ivanov, 2011). When the literature is examined, in the field of education; foreign language (Küçük, Yılmaz and Göktaş, 2014) mathematics (Akkuş and Özhan, 2017), physics (Abdüsselam, 2014; Kırıkkaya and Şentürk, 2018), medicine.

Using textbooks as virtual learning materials along with AR technologies (İbili & Şahin, 2015; Billinghurst, Kato, & Poupyrev, 2001) can be very useful in concretizing some abstract concepts. As a matter of fact, as the similarity and relationship of the content to real life increases, the effectiveness and efficiency of the education increases. AR technology; It gives independence from space, freedom and a feeling of personal privacy; increases the quality of learning (Etlican, 2012); It makes learning more fun and permanent by enriching educational environments (Wu et al., 2013) and It encourages the emergence of new opportunities in education.

Use of Virtual Learning in Education

It is known that virtual reality technology, which creates new teaching environments today, is very useful, especially in distance education, if the necessary infrastructure is provided. This technology can be used for educational purposes in areas that are very difficult to physically reach and experience (Can and Şimşek, 2016). For example, in virtual drill practices in military training, especially nuclear It is used practically on virtually created cadavers in engineering training where training will be carried out, in pilot and astronaut training by creating virtual cockpits, and in medical training (Kayabaşı, 2005). Students can have the chance to interact and communicate in the virtual environment with students in distant places where they do not have the opportunity to come together in a physical environment (Çoruh, 2011: 74). Thus, this technology can be used effectively in foreign language education, as it provides the opportunity to bring together students from different countries. In addition, students can learn abstract concepts in mathematics from virtual reality applications; They can also benefit from understanding historical events and earth formations in the fields of history and geography (Tepe et al., 2016).

WHAT ARE SOME OF THE TOOLS AND FEATURES USED FOR TEACHING AND LEARNING USING (AR) AND (VR)?

It is known that virtual reality technology, which creates new teaching environments today, is very useful, especially in distance education, if the necessary infrastructure is provided. This technology can be used for educational purposes in areas that are very difficult to physically reach and experience (Can and Şimşek, 2016). For example, it is used in virtual drill applications in military training, in engineering training, especially where nuclear studies will be carried out, in pilot and astronaut training by creating virtual cockpits, and in medical training on virtually created cadavers (Kayabaşı, 2005). Students can have the chance to interact and communicate in the virtual environment with students in distant places where they do not have the opportunity to come together in a physical environment (Çoruh, 2011). Thus, this technology can be used effectively in foreign language education, as it provides the opportunity to bring together students from different countries. In addition, students can learn abstract concepts in mathematics from virtual reality applications; They can also benefit from understanding historical events and earth formations in the fields of history and geography (Tepe et al., 2016).

The use of new approaches in the teaching-learning process is realized with virtual reality technology. Using innovative tools for education provides motivation to the student in the learning process. The use of virtual reality helps students understand concepts, especially abstract concepts. In the environment presented with virtual reality, the student feels himself in a more interesting and entertaining environment, improves his attention and learns with the motivation to explore. Since the objects in the environment in which the student is immersed create a sense of reality, it is ensured that the student learns the facts he is researching more permanently (Piovesan et al., 2012).

Virtual reality technologies provide opportunities to streamline teaching and learning and optimize learning. It guides the student with applications created with technology. It provides the basis for permanent learning, especially with the ability to practice the theoretical subjects. This shows that it supports the utilitarian understanding of education. Virtual reality technology is also making progress in development studies on psychological and pedagogical principles in promoting learning (Aiello, 2012).

McLellan (1996), in his work titled Virtual Realities, points out the existence of eleven types of virtual reality: 1. Immersive First-Person, 2. Augmented Reality, 3. Through the Window – Desktop VR, 4. Mirror World, 5. Waldo World - Virtual Characters, 6. Chamber world, 7. Cab simulator environment, 8. Cyberspace, 9. Telepresence/Teleoperation, 10. The VisionDome (Multi-User, Single Projection) 11. The Experience Learning System.

The student, who receives an education in an immersive and interactive environment based on 3D graphic images created in real-time by the computer, finds himself in discovery and learning by doing. To the student, the virtual world is presented through a window created by a monitor screen or projection screen, or by a head-mounted camera or multiple projection rooms (caves) and interactive devices. In this way, it becomes more possible to obtain information about places that are difficult to discover and situations that are difficult to understand. Virtual reality is used to make learning more interesting for students and to make learning simpler. It makes learning interactive and feedback is effective in evaluating the student (Piovesan et al., 2012).

Çavaş et al. (2004) suggest that there are many studies on the use of virtual reality in education. In a study in England, children with communication and especially mobility difficulties are trained to experience experiences that they cannot do due to their disabilities, using virtual reality technology. Showing past events and people in classrooms through virtual reality environments helps students understand the subjects better. Virtual reality environments provided in the history room are used for students to witness historical events, and in the room, students can interact with people from the past. Among science education, the importance of virtual reality is seen most in chemistry lessons. Complex molecules become meaningful with the help of 3D computer models. Thanks to the virtual reality environment, students can see and feel the connections and gravitational forces between molecules by interacting. Virtual reality, which is also used in mathematics education, makes it easier to understand graphs and equations that are difficult to understand visually. In solving equations with two unknowns, students try to keep the blocks representing the equation values in balance to solve the problem.

Method and Data Analysis

This is a case study that involves teachers in South Africa and Turkey. The data was obtained through a questionnaire that was randomly shared with teachers who have previously participated in professional development programs in South Africa and Turkey that involved information communications technology (ICT). A total of 29 teachers responded to the questionnaire in both countries, 16 teachers responded from South Africa, and 13 teachers responded from Turkey. Content analysis was used to analyze the data based on emergent themes.

Figure 1 below shows gender participation in both countries, 8 females and 8 males responded to the questionnaire in South Africa, while 8 females and 5 males responded to the questionnaire in Turkey.

Figure 1. Gender participation

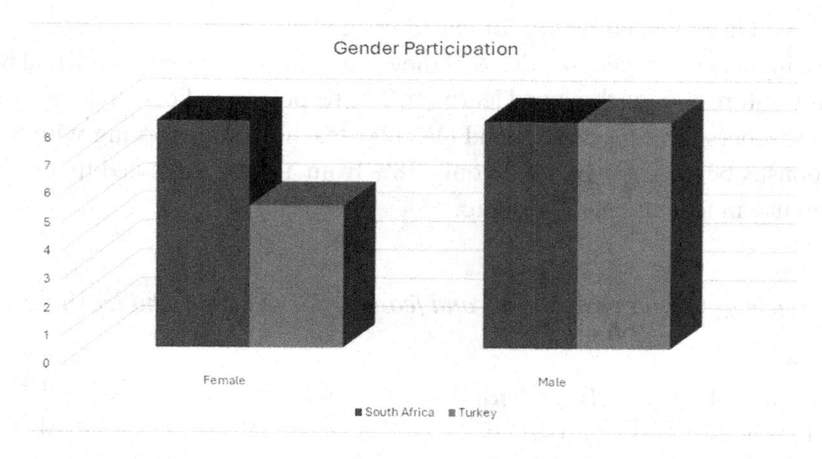

It is interesting to note that in both countries teachers who appear to be adopting and utilizing (AR) and (VR) are between the age category of 36 to 40 years as shown in Figure 2 below. The least adopters in both countries are in the age category of 51 years and above. The questionnaire included the age category 26-29 years, only South African teachers in this category responded to the questionnaire, while Turkey had no participants responding in this age category. Teachers within the age category

36 to 40 years responded the most in both countries with 31% in South Africa and 30% amongst Turkish teachers. Figure 2 shows that 13% of the responding teachers from South Africa are above 51 years old, while only 8% of Turkish teachers were in the same category.

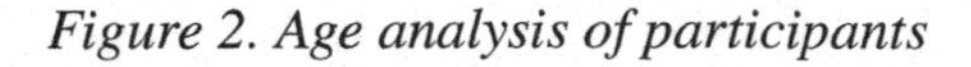

Figure 2. Age analysis of participants

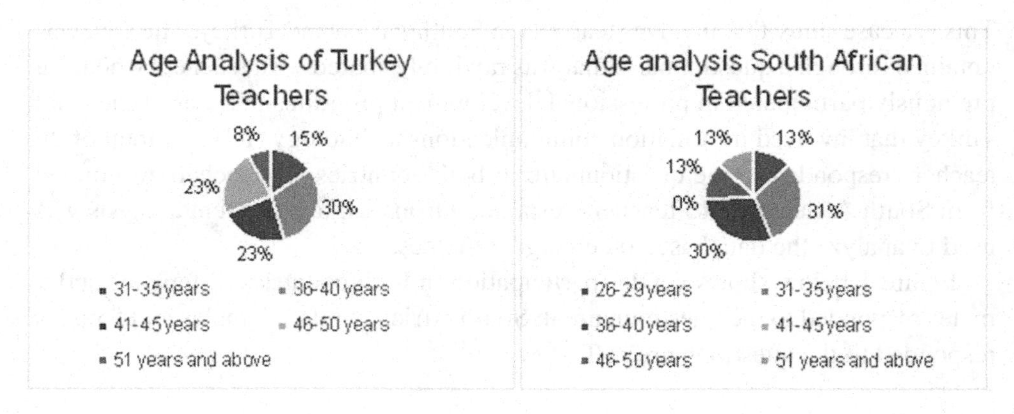

Have you used virtual reality for teaching and learning?

Participants were asked to indicate if they had used augmented and virtual reality tools and features for teaching and learning. The responses indicate that more South African teachers have used (AR) and (VR) for teaching and learning with 56% of the responses being positive, while only 38% from Turkey indicated that they had explored use in teaching and learning.

Figure 3. use of virtual reality tools and features for teaching and learning

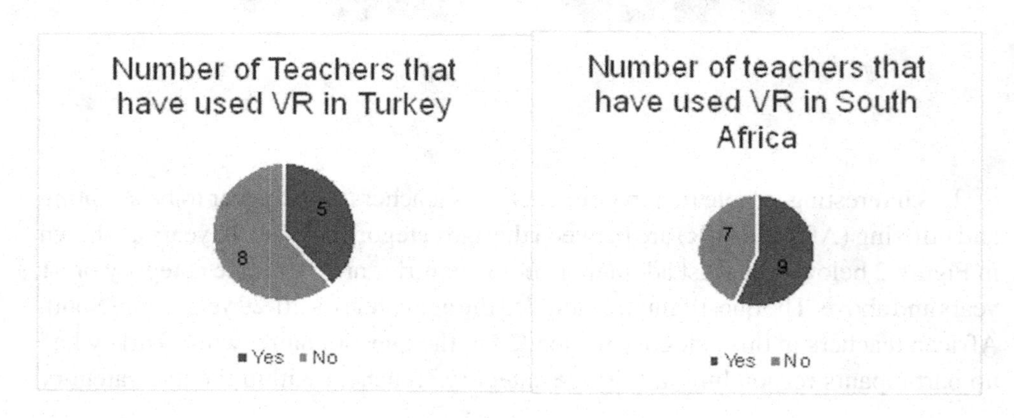

Most of the teachers who responded with a "No" indicated that the main limitation to their inability to explore the use of (AR) and (VR) in teaching and learning was a result of a lack of resources as well as professional development. The responses from both countries were similar.

Table 1. List of subjects where (AR and (VR) have been integrated.

South Africa	
List of subjects that adopted (AR) and (VR)	
1.	Social sciences
2.	English
3.	Mathematics Grade 12
4.	Coding and Robotics
5.	Business studies

The subjects in which these tools and resources were used are depicted in Tables 1 and 2 which show how subjects were distributed in both countries based on subjects or learning area. South Africa had 5 responses and it appears (AR) and (VR) are adopted in mathematics and science-oriented subjects.

Table 2. List of subjects where (AR and (VR) have been integrated.

Turkey	
List of subjects that adopted (AR) and (VR)	
1.	Science Grade 4
2.	Life sciences
3.	Mathematics
4.	Drama
5.	Music

The answers from Turkish teachers were varied with sciences still dominating in the forms of mathematics, Life science, and Grade 4 science. What stood out was the inclusion of music and drama. The limitation to non-exploration was like that given by South African teachers, which was lack of resources and professional development.

Figure 4. Teaching and grade level

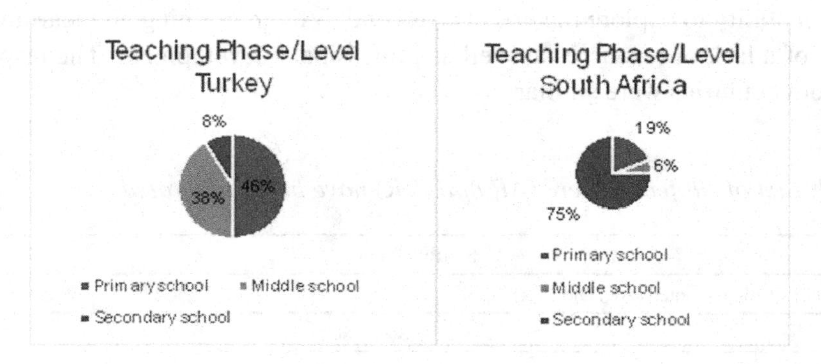

Figure 4 indicates a contrast in teacher participation, 75% of South African teachers who responded to the questionnaire are teaching in secondary schools, while 46% of responses received in Turkey were from primary school teachers. The South African responses are attributed to the device deployment of ICT resources that mainly targeted secondary school teachers. This also reveals an unequal distribution of resources amongst phase teachers. Turkey began its rollout of ICTs before South Africa and appears to have a balance of participation between primary school and middle school teachers as shown below.

Which Augmented Reality (AR) and Virtual Reality (VR) Tools Are Used by Teachers?

Table 3 reports on the identified tools and features that are common in the integration of (AR) and (VR) in teaching and learning. Virtual reality glasses were common amongst the two countries. A simulated lesson was used for cooking in South Africa, while a virtual tour was used in a Grade 4 science class in Turkey. Interactive books were mentioned in South Africa and the use of PowerPoint was visible amongst Turkish teachers.

Table 3: (AR) and (VR) tools and features used by teachers

No.	South Africa	Turkey
1.	VR Glasses	VR Glasses
2.	Simulated lesson (cooking)	PowerPoint cards
3.	Interactive e-books	Virtual tour

What Are the Benefits of Using Augmented Reality (AR) and Virtual Reality (VR) for Teaching and Learning?

Teacher responses about the benefits of (AR) and (VR) were positive in the two countries, teachers indicated that both (AR) and (VR) have the potential to improve learner engagement as noted below.

"Learning becomes more engaging, and learners pay attention to details."

Karakaş and Özerbaş, (2020) concur regarding the affordances of (AR) and (VR) affordances in improving teacher-learner engagement.

Teachers in South Africa were of the view that integrating (AR) and (VR) allows learners to learn new skills on how to use and manipulate (AR) and (VR) tools.

"Augmented reality exposes learners to technology and its use"

Emphasis was placed on the exposure and creation of learning opportunities where learners can extend their learning beyond the disciplinary knowledge mediated to them.

The Turkish teachers were of the view that (AR) and (VR) create an enabling environment for safer science experiments.

"VR allows safer experiments to be carried out at lower cost in experimental courses that require a laboratory environment, such as science."

The use of (AR) and (VR) is perceived to be a substitute for experiment laboratories and creates a simulated environment for learners to experience knowledge.

Teachers in Turkey are of the view that (AR) and (VR) can create knowledge retention as captured by the response below. (AR) and (VR) enables learners to deal with abstract concepts through the development of an artificial environment to learn a concept.

"Increasing motivation and permanence in learning through artificial experiences".

CONCLUSION AND DISCUSSION

This study sought to determine the extent to which teachers in South Africa and Turkey have adopted and used augmented reality (AR) and virtual reality (VR) tools for teaching and learning. The study was guided by four research questions which are, (i) to what extent have teachers used and adopted augmented reality (AR) and virtual reality (VR) in teaching and learning, (ii) which grade or level of teaching are these technologies used?, (iii) which augmented and virtual reality tools are used by teachers, and finally, what are the benefits of using augmented and virtual reality for teaching and learning. This study utilized a case study approach and administered a questionnaire that had closed questions as well as long-elaborated responses. Content analysis was used to analyse the collected data from 29 teachers in both countries, 16 teachers from South Africa and 13 teachers from Turkey.

Most of the teachers who responded to the question that sought to test their understanding of augmented reality (AR) and virtual reality (VR) showed that they are aware of the benefits of both technologies. The teachers indicated that the technologies could create opportunities for learners to broaden their knowledge and experiences. The results show that teacher educators who were able to use augmented reality (AR) and virtual reality (VR) were influenced by the availability of digital technologies as well as access to the tools and features. A case in point is the response participation of South African secondary teachers who were prioritized in the digital resource deployment program. When the results of both countries are compared against each other the factors that promote adoption as well as the factors that result in limitations for use were similar. Several teachers from both countries indicated that access to digital tools was an essential variable in determining the adoption and use of augmented reality (AR) and virtual reality (VR) technologies for teaching and learning.

LIMITATIONS OF THE STUDY

The sample size of this study was limited to 29 teachers who had participated in professional development programs involving information communications technologies at a foundation level. The sample type was randomly selected amongst teachers who taught different phases. This makes it difficult to generalize based on the results presented.

RECOMMENDATIONS

There is a need to increase the number of participating teachers in the study and to target specific phases of levels of teaching for better comparison concerning the knowledge and practices of the teachers. The data instruments need to be varied so that different dynamics and complexities are exposed, there is a limitation on the use of questionnaires since the interpretation of questions is left to the respondent. Interviews enrich the quality of responses and clarification of questions.

REFERENCES

Abdüsselam, S. M. (2014). Teachers' and students' views on using augmented reality environments in physics education: 11th Grade magnetism topic example. *Egitim ve Ögretim, 4*(1), 59–74. doi:10.14527/pegegog.2014.004

Aiello, P., D'Elia, F., Di Tore, S., & Sibilio, M. (2012). A constructivist approach to virtual reality for experiential learning. *E-Learning and Digital Media, 9*(3), 317–324. doi:10.2304/elea.2012.9.3.317

Akgun, E., Instanbullu, A., & Avci, S. (2017). Augmented reality in Turkey with researchers' comments for educational use: Problems, solutions, and suggestions. *Journal of Education and Training Studies, 5*(11), 201–218. doi:10.11114/jets.v5i11.2690

Akkuş, İ. & Özhan, U. (2017). Matematik ve geometri eğitiminde artırılmış gerçeklik uygulamaları. *İnönü Üniversitesi Eğitim Bilimleri Enstitüsü Dergisi, 4*(8), 19-33.

Alkhamisi, A. O., Arabia, S. & Monowar, M. M. (2013). Rise of augmented reality: Current and future application areas. *International Journal of Internet and Distributed Systems, 1*(4), 25.

Alqirnas, H. R. (2020). Students' perception of virtual classrooms as an alternative to real classes. *International Journal of Education and Information Technologies, 14*, 153–161. doi:10.46300/9109.2020.14.18

Azuma, R. T. (1997). A survey of augmented reality. *Presence (Cambridge, Mass.), 6*(4), 355–385. doi:10.1162/pres.1997.6.4.355

Billinghurst, M., & Kato, H. & Poupyrev, I. (2001). The magicbook-moving seamlessly between reality and virtuality. *IEEE Computer Graphics and Applications, 21*(3), 6–8.

Can, T. & Şimşek, İ. (2016). Eğitimde yeni teknolojiler: Sanal gerçeklik. Eğitim Teknolojileri Okumaları, 2016. The Turkish Online Journal of Educational Technology (TOJET), 21. *Bölüm, 351*, 363.

Cavas, B, Capar, S., Cavas, L, & Yahsi, Ö. (2021). Turkish STEM Teachers' Opinions About Scientist-Teacher-Student Partnership. *Journal of Turkish Science Education, 18*(4).

Çoruh, L. (2011). *Sanat tarihi dersinde bir öğrenme modeli olarak sanal gerçeklik uygulamasının etkililiğinin değerlendirilmesi: Erciyes Üniversitesi Mimarlık ve Güzel Sanatlar Fakülteleri örneği uygulaması (Yayımlanmamış Doktora Tezi)*. Gazi Üniversitesi Eğitim Bilimleri Enstitüsü.

Craig, A. B., Sherman, W. R., & Will, J. D. (2009). *Developing Virtual Reality Applications: Foundations of Effective Design*. Elsevier.

Damala, A., Marchal, I., & Houlier, P. (2007, October). Merging augmented reality-based features in mobile multimedia museum guides. In *Anticipating the Future of the Cultural Past, CIPA Conference 2007, 1-6 October 2007,* (pp. 259-264). Academic Press.

Drucker, P. (2000). *Yeni Gerçekler, Çev. Birtane Karanakçı*. Türkiye İş Bankası Kültür Yayınları.

Emerson, T. (1993). Mastering The Art Of VR: On Becoming The HIT Lab Cybrarian. *The Electronic Library, 11*(6), 385–391. doi:10.1108/eb045261

Eryalçın, B. (1994). Hayalle Gerçeğin Dansı Sanal Gerçeklik. *Bilim ve Teknik, 27*(323), 20–27.

Etlican, G. (2012). X ve Y Kuşaklarının Online Eğitim Teknolojilerine Karşı Tutumlarının Karşılaştırılması [Tezi. Bahçeşehir Üniversitesi Sosyal Bilimler Ens. İstanbul].

İbili, E. ve Şahin, S. (2015). Investigation Of The Effects On Computer Attitudes And Computer Self-Efficacy To Use Of Augmented Reality In Geometry Teaching, Necatibey Faculty of Education Electronic Journal of Science &. *The Mathematics Educator, 9*(1), 332–350.

Ivanova, M. ve Ivanov, G. (2011). Enhancement of learning and teaching in computer graphics through marker augmented reality technology. *International Journal on New Computer Architectures and Their Applications, 1*(1), 176–184.

Jung, T., Chung, N., & Leue, M. C. (2015). The determinants of recommendations to use augmented reality technologies: The case of a Korean theme park. *Tourism Management, 49*, 75–86. doi:10.1016/j.tourman.2015.02.013

Karakaş, M., & Özerbaş, M. (2020). Fizik dersinde artırılmış gerçeklik uygulamalarının öğrencilerin akademik başarılarına etkisi. *Eğitim Teknolojisi Kuram ve Uygulama, 10*(2), 452–468. doi:10.17943/etku.691179

Kayabaşı, Y. (2005). Sanal gerçeklik ve eğitim amaçlı kullanılması. *The Turkish Online Journal of Educational Technology, 4*(3), 151–166.

Kırıkkaya, E. B. (2018). Güneş sistemi ve ötesi ünitesinde artırılmış gerçeklik teknolojisi kullanılmasının öğrenci akademik başarısına etkisi. *Kastamonu Eğitim Dergisi, 26*(1), 181–189. doi:10.24106/kefdergi.375861

Küçük, S., Kapakin, S., & Goktas, Y. (2015). Medical faculty students' views on anatomy learning via mobile augmented reality technology. *Journal of Higher Education and Science*, *5*(3), 316–323. doi:10.5961/jhes.2015.133

Lund, B., & Wang, T. (2019). Effect of virtual reality on learning motivation and academic performance: What value may virtual reality have on library instruction? *Kansas Library Association College and University Libraries Section Proceedings*, *9*(1), 4. doi:10.4148/2160-942X.1073

McLellan, H. (1996). Virtual realities. In Handbook of research for educational communications and technology. Macmillan Library Reference.

Mhlanga, D., & Moloi, T. (2020). COVID-19 and the digital transformation of education: What are we learning on 4IR in South Africa? *Education Sciences*, *10*(7), 180. doi:10.3390/educsci10070180

Penn, M., & Umesh, R. (2019). The use of virtual learning environments and achievement in physics content tests. *Proceedings of the International Conference on Education and New Developments* (Vol. 1). https://eric.ed.gov/?id=EJ1236608

Piovesan, S. D., Passerino, L. M., & Pereira, A. S. (2012). Virtual reality as a tool in the education. *IADIS International conference on cognition and exploratory learning in digital age*, 295-298.

Sarigoz, O. (2019). Augmented reality, virtual reality and digital games: A research on teacher candidates. *Educational Policy Analysis and Strategic Research*, *14*(3), 41–63. doi:10.29329/epasr.2019.208.3

Tepe, T., & Kaleci, D. & Tüzün, H. (2016). Eğitim teknolojilerinde yeni eğilimler: Sanal gerçeklik uygulamaları. *10th International Computer and Instructional Technologies Symposium (ICITS)*, 547-555.

Wu, H. K., Lee, S. W. Y., Chang, H. Y., & Liang, J.-C. (2013). Current Status, Opportunities And Challenges Of Augmented Reality In Education. *Computers & Education*, *62*, 41–49. doi:10.1016/j.compedu.2012.10.024

Chapter 5
Fostering Academic Honesty for E-Content

Shefali Saluja
https://orcid.org/0000-0002-8560-5150
Chitkara Business School, Chitkara University, India

Amandeep Singh
https://orcid.org/0000-0002-0970-5467
Chitkara Business School, Chitkara University, India

Sandhir Sharma
https://orcid.org/0000-0002-3940-8236
Chitkara Business School, Chitkara University, India

ABSTRACT

Ensuring academic honesty is challenging in regular classrooms, but it is even more complex in online courses since the use of technology is fundamental to teaching and learning. The way content is presented to students in education has altered due to the internet. Due to the flexibility and convenience of receiving course materials via the internet, an increasing number of students are choosing to enroll in online courses nowadays. The behaviour of students, faculty, and staff is governed by the moral code or ethical policy of academia, which is known as academic honesty. This chapter identifies the thefts in e-learning and the ways to ensure ethics and governance in the development of online courses.

DOI: 10.4018/979-8-3693-3015-9.ch005

Copyright © 2024, IGI Global. Copying or distributing in print or electronic forms without written permission of IGI Global is prohibited.

1. INTRODUCTION

Since the Covid19 outbreak, there has been a substantial change in the education, which has been characterised by the advent of e-learning and the remote delivery of instruction via digital platforms. Academic integrity is the observance of the fundamental values of morality, faith, justice, esteem, accountability, and courageousness (Fishman et al., 2013). These principles form the basis for the meaning of ethical academic behaviour and also, establishing a community which is based on the exchange of data. Education institutions must immediately adapt to the new reality because technology is now the only way to keep education alive, regardless of their competence or drive. Making the transition from in-person instruction to online instruction has been extremely challenging for the higher education sector. Regardless of the e-course medium, discussions about learning and teaching always include academic integrity and responsible behaviour (online, hybrid, or face-to-face setting). An effective way to handle academic integrity is to "emphasise prevention and education above policing and punishment" (Sopcak, 2020). Academic integrity promotion strategies that are reasonable and successful have long been discussed in postsecondary education. However, it is widely believed that moral failings are increasing. New chances for "e-cheating" have emerged as a result of the integration of technology in the schoolroom and the acceptance of various online courses (Harmon & Lambrinos, 2008). Numerous novel methods of cheating have emerged, some of which are exclusive to online learning environments and others which are widely used in traditional classroom settings. These include, but are not limited to, copying essays from the internet and passing them off as one's own work, utilising prohibited materials on an online test, contacting other students online for help, and having someone else finish an online test or assignment in the student's place (Holden et al., 2021). One of the objectives of education is to promote ethics, but because of the open exchange of information and the disclosure of unethical behaviour in e-learning, it is vital to define ethical ideals. As a result, the goal of this study was examining the ways to ensure ethics in the development of online courses.

2. LITERATURE REVIEW

The 2019 coronavirus (COVID-19) pandemic has had widespread effects on the world's educational systems, both public and private. Because of the epidemic, many schools and institutions have been forced to close or function with severely reduced resources in order to protect their students and staff from contracting the disease. The hybrid or blended learning approach combines traditional classroom instruction with digital resources to give students the best of both worlds. Most lessons in older, more conventional schools only existed in face-to-face form before the pandemic. There are several advantages to learning in a face-to-face setting, including the opportunity for spontaneous, creative exchanges between teachers and students. In the classroom, students can get help with anything they don't understand or have a question about. Authors, scholars, thinkers, and educators from a wide range of backgrounds have offered their own unique definitions of online learning. There has been a shift in recent years towards evaluating schools not only on their ability to impart knowledge but also on their ability to foster the individual, social, and economic growth of its students. Tuition, fees, and the overall cost of attendance are only a few examples of the many possible sources of stress related to money. Because of this, conceptions of education and what it means to be a professor or a pupil have shifted. Many teaching models characterize the teaching and learning processes and also affect the interaction between the teacher and the learner. Nonetheless, the question of which teaching approach is more effective may arise. There seems to be a growing tendency in the educational literature of comparing the efficacy of alternative models or methods of instruction to more conventional approaches to education. E-learning, along with virtual, cyber, hybrid, and online modes of education, have been contrasted with more conventional classroom settings in numerous studies.E-learning theory demonstrates how the usage and design of educational technology can increase effective learning using cognitive science principles. The theory is based on the "Cognitive Load Theory" (Sweller et al., 2019). An educational approach known as the cognitive load hypothesis is based on how people think. Since the hypothesis was initially put forth in the 1980s, it has been used to achieve experimental and pedagogical results. Some studies explored the modality principle, which suggests that the use of visuals coupled by audio narration instead of on-screen text is more helpful for learning (Denecke, 2015). As an illustration, the research of Moreno in 2006 carried out a meta-analysis on modality effects. The results showed that the modality principle across various media had a considerable positive impact on learning. Now, that we're discussing regarding privacy issues, governments from across the world have passed privacy laws and regulations in an effort to stop the misuse of personal data. Individual control is necessary for the use of personal information, including the gathering, use, disclosure, preservation, and deletion of personal data by organisations that may handle such information, in nations with privacy legislation in effect. The verified E-Learning materials, such as textbooks, diplomas, test materials, lecture notes, and grade sheets, which are distributed by managers to students and authors to teachers, among others, may be altered or destroyed (Salimovna & Salimovna, 2019). The authors have made an effort to look at how to uphold ethics in online courses and content.

3. RESEARCH METHODOLOGY

The paper examines the elements that are essential for Academic Honesty for the academicians while posting their content online or on any other digital platform, several data bases using Scopus, Emerald, Web of Science were used to search the literature and understand about the factors that can be essential to protect data breach. The articles were used for the analysis primarily for the empirical research on the Academic Honesty, E-learning, Digital platforms across different counties.

4. E-LEARNING THREATS

The global market for eLearning is expanding and lucrative. A wide range of technology resources are available in this ecosystem, from comprehensive standalone educational platforms to specialised online tools and digital tools. The sector as a whole is predicted to be valued $331 billion by 2025.

Figure 1. Kinds of e-learning threats
Author's Compilation from various sources

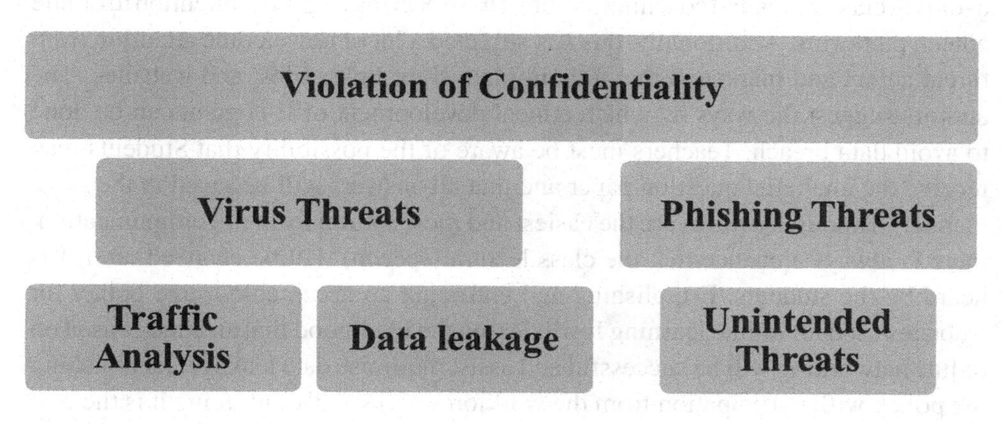

There are various kinds of threats that can hamper the security of the E-learning content posted on different websites/ sources. Online fraud is a fraud which results in personal or company damage (Saluja et al., 2021). To begin with, a third-party obtaining access to the E-Learning system's resources without authorization is the violation of confidentiality. Perhaps the most frequent kind of cybersecurity danger is a computer virus. It might start by changing a computer's software and progress to posing a hardware hazard. Like other cybersecurity concerns, computer viruses are spread through phishing, adware, and clicking on unidentified links. Phishing is the act of attackers sending malicious emails intended to trick recipients into falling for a scam. Typically, the goal is to get people to divulge confidential information, including system logins or financial information. Simply by listening to network data, the attacker can analyse it to find out where important nodes are, how routes are set up, and even how applications behave and that is traffic analysis. Sensitive data leakage occurs when it is mistakenly made available to the public while being used, stored, or in transit. Here are some typical instances: Data revealed while in transit Information sent through emails, API calls, chat rooms, and other channels of communication. Unintentional risks are non-malicious exposures of a company's IT systems, data, and infrastructure that have unanticipatedly detrimental repercussions on the company. The majority of these exposures are unintended or incidental. The above-mentioned threats impact the overall development of the E- learning platforms and contents.

5. THEORETICAL MODEL FOR SECURING E-LEARNING

Since the pandemic began, students seeking to supplement their education while avoiding classrooms and coaching facilities have been paying close attention to online edtech platforms. Additionally, this has attracted a lot of unwelcome attention from threat actors and marketers that hide in plain sight links, files, and websites. The authors suggest the ways by which ethical development of E-content can be done to avoid data breach. Teachers must be aware of the possibility that Students may receive the unaltered question paper and that all answers will be saved in the same manner. Although lectures are the easiest and most natural form of communication, there is always a chance that the class lecture (speech) will be changed after it is heard by the students. Establishing and enforcing an acceptable usage policy for websites used for online learning It will lessen the likelihood that an attack based on online networking will be successful and assist minimise data leakage. Establishing the policy with participation from the workforce and strictly enforcing it is the best way to guarantee its efficacy. Employees are less likely to transgress limitations if they are aware of its justification and were part in the policy's establishment. A few well-known methods are also used to defend the system against dangers. Teachers who design e-learning courses must take into account a variety of risks, as was previously discussed. To lessen the risks, it might be necessary to apply the ensuing technologies or methods. The authors have tried to conceptualize the methods through which Academic Integrity can be achieved. (Figure-1 below)

Figure 2. Securing e-learning (designed by the authors)

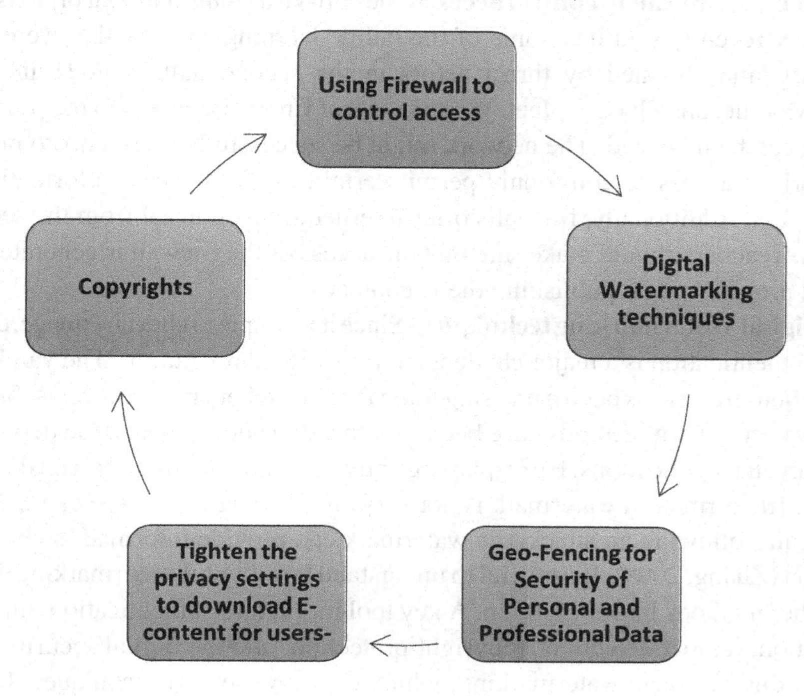

Figure 3. A secure firewall based e-learning system – Retrieved from Barik and Karforma (2012)

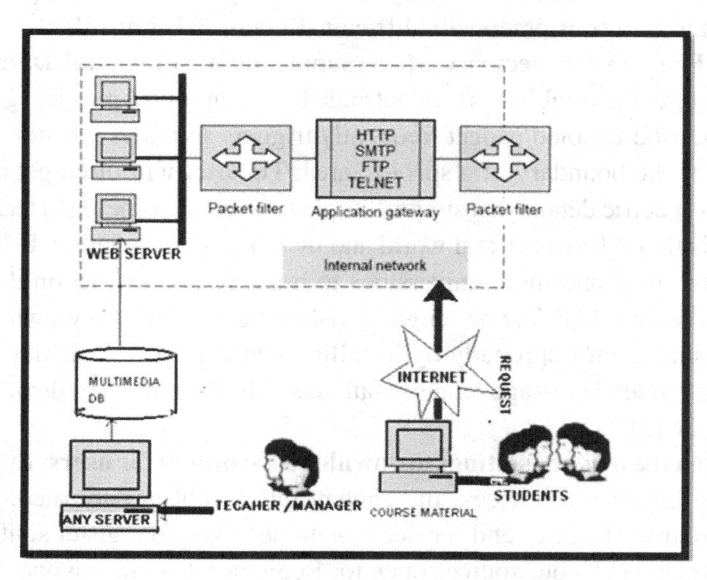

A) Using a firewall to control access- The anti-virus multinational organisation Kaspersky recently said that some of the online learning systems that were most frequently impersonated by threat actors in the second half of 2021 included Zoom, Moodle, and Google Meet. With the use of firewalls, access to the protected network can be managed. The network might be successfully closed off to prevent unauthorised access or could only permit certain users to access information or mail servers. Additionally, firewalls offer Internet access control from the secured network. Teachers should make sure that the access of the firewall is generated and checked properly while publishing the E-content.

B) Digital Watermarking techniques - Since it is simple to alter any image, digital image authentication is a major challenge for the digital revolution. The validity of digital photographs has been a pressing topic for researchers in recent years. Several viable watermarking methods have been developed to address this issue depending on the targeted applications. By displaying or transferring the watermarked data into different file formats, a watermark is not very simple to remove (Tao et al., 2014). As a result, following an attack, the watermark can provide information about the transition (Zhang, 2009). It's crucial to understand how digital watermarking differs from other methods like encryption. A key tool for picture authentication, integrity verification, tamper detection, copyright protection, and the digital security of an image is digital image watermarking, which uses a variety of techniques. Due to its multi-resolution capabilities, DWT is a high-quality and reliable technology for image watermarking. The key elements for building a successful watermarking system are robustness, imperceptibility, and capacity. However, completing all of these demands at once is practically difficult (Begum & Uddin, 2020).

C) Geo-Fencing for Security of Personal and Professional Data- A geo-fence is a feature that establishes an electronic border around a physical geographic region. A location-enabled gadget frequently triggers activities whenever the user enters or exits the boundary of a specific area. The user will often get a message that includes specific details that support its position in real time. This technology's key benefit is that it fuses the real world and the virtual one together. E-learning is being used by more and more universities to improve the instruction that college students receive. Students are no longer at risk of taking university-owned devices home and using them improperly by installing geofences on those devices. Geo-fences enforce intended usage while simultaneously guaranteeing device security (Yamanaka, 2019).

D) Tighten the privacy settings to download E-content for users- Every visitor to eLearning Industry can access the content that has been published. But some eLearning Industry features and services might need you to register so it is always recommended to keep your sources open for Registration while anyone downloads the content or try to use it (copy). To ensure that only users with permission can access more sensitive or important data, create restricted areas on the eLearning platform or inside the eLearning course itself. For instance, if a section of the online course is only open to registered users, then an individual can ask them to create their own passwords so that the conversations they have and the assignments they finish, stays private. Additionally, this will lessen the likelihood that your private information will be stolen and shared without your consent. Since only individuals with access rights will be able to see the data, there is little chance that a random person will steal it and post it online.

E) Copyrights- The Copyright Act 1957 governs copyright laws in India. At least five revisions to the Act have occurred: in 1983, 1984, 1992, 1994, 1999, and 2012. Securing the online content via copyright is a safe method. Once the work is copyright, others do not have permission to copy your data and they can eventually fall into a legal action. Additionally, once the work is copyrighted, you can also earn from the revenue generated out of the copyrighted material. However, in the cases of online data where teachers upload any content, it is in the open space for anyone to copy, which is why copyright plays a very important role. It is always recommended to get the data copyright (Czetwertyński, 2017).

5. CONCLUSION

It's difficult to go a few days after scanning the news without learning about a significant data breach that could have given hackers access to millions of customers' personal information (Syed-Abdul et al., 2019). The measures have to take to protect the content online via strong passwords, proper encryption and watch out for suspicious links and websites. The Virtual Private Network is also an essential element to save the data from hacking. As discussed by the authors above, there are certain measures which can prevent the E Content published. In the digital age, data and content protection is a pressing concern. Businesses that prioritise the security of their content and sensitive data are successful in building robust and trustworthy brands. Fortunately, there are numerous techniques to safeguard commercial information and data, such as encryption, DRM use, tokenization, watermarking, and geofencing (Sangeeta & Tandon, 2021). All of these techniques make sure that only permitted users can access digital information, prohibiting its unauthorised Internet distribution (Saluja, 2022). The further scope of the research will be to introspect the audience who is exposed to the thefts made on E-learning services and the aftermaths of the event.

REFERENCES

Barik, N., & Karforma, S. (2012). *Risks and remedies in e-learning system.* arXiv preprint arXiv:1205.2711

Begum, M., & Uddin, M. S. (2020). Digital Image Watermarking Techniques: A Review. *Information (Basel), 11*(2), 110. doi:10.3390/info11020110

Czetwertyński, S. (2017). Importance of copyrights in online society. *Managerial Economics., 18*(2), 147. doi:10.7494/manage.2017.18.2.147

Denecke, K. (2015). Ethical issues of social media usage in healthcare. *Yearbook of Medical Informatics, 24*(01), 137–147. doi:10.15265/IY-2015-001 PMID:26293861

Fishman, B. J., Konstantopoulos, S., Kubitskey, B. W., Vath, R., Park, G., Johnson, H., & Edelson, D. C. (2013). Comparing the impact of online and face-to-face professional development in the context of curriculum implementation. *Journal of Teacher Education, 64*(5), 426–438. Advance online publication. doi:10.1177/0022487113494413

Harmon, O. R., & Lambrinos, J. (2008). Are online exams an invitation to cheat? *The Journal of Economic Education, 39*(2), 116–125. doi:10.3200/JECE.39.2.116-125

Holden, O. L., Norris, M. E., & Kuhlmeier, V. A. (2021). "Academic integrity in online assessment: A research review." *Frontiers in Education. Frontiers.*

Salimovna, F. D., & Salimovna, Y. N. (2019). Security issues in E-Learning system. *2019 International Conference on Information Science and Communications Technologies (ICISCT).* IEEE.

Saluja, S. (2022). Identity theft fraud-major loophole for FinTech industry in India. *Journal of Financial Crime.*

Saluja, S., Aggarwal, A., & Mittal, A. (2021). Understanding the fraud theories and advancing with integrity model. *Journal of Financial Crime.*

Sangeeta, T., & Tandon, U. (2021). Factors influencing adoption of online teaching by school teachers: A study during COVID-19 pandemic. *Journal of Public Affairs, 21*(4), e2503. doi:10.1002/pa.2503 PMID:33173442

Sopcak, P. (2020). Academic integrity and the pandemic. *Canadian Perspectives on Academic Integrity, 3*(2), 41–42.

Sweller, J., van Merriënboer, J. J. G., & Paas, F. (2019). Cognitive architecture and instructional design: 20 years later. *Educational Psychology Review, 31*(2), 261–292. doi:10.1007/s10648-019-09465-5

Syed-Abdul, S., Malwade, S., Nursetyo, A. A., Sood, M., Bhatia, M., Barsasella, D., Liu, M. F., Chang, C.-C., Srinivasan, K., M, R., & Li, Y. C. J. (2019). Virtual reality among the elderly: A usefulness and acceptance study from Taiwan. *BMC Geriatrics, 19*(1), 1–10. doi:10.1186/s12877-019-1218-8 PMID:31426766

Tao, H., Chongmin, L., Zain, J. M., & Abdalla, A. N. (2014). Robust Image Watermarking Theories and Techniques: A Review. *Journal of Applied Research and Technology, 12*(1), 122–138. doi:10.1016/S1665-6423(14)71612-8

Yamanaka, G. (2019). *Geo-Fencing in Wireless LANs with Camera for Location-Based Access Control. 2019 16th IEEE Annual Consumer Communications & Networking Conference*. CCNC. doi:10.1109/CCNC.2019.8651877

Zhang, Y. (2009). Digital Watermarking Technology: A Review. *Proceedings of the ETP International Conference on Future Computer and Communication*, 250–252.

Chapter 6 Immersive Innovations: Exploring the Use of Virtual and Augmented Reality in Educational Institutions

Sabyasachi Pramanik
https://orcid.org/0000-0002-9431-8751
Haldia Institute of Technology, India

ABSTRACT

This chapter examines the transformative influence of immersive technology, namely virtual reality (VR) and augmented reality (AR), on higher education. The chapter illustrates the significant impact of VR and AR on education by tracing their evolutionary trajectory from their conceptual roots in the mid-20th century to their current implementations. Conventional lectures and textbooks are being replaced with immersive learning environments, leading to a transformation of traditional classroom paradigms. VR and AR enable students to immerse themselves in virtual environments, where they may engage with three-dimensional models, historical reenactments, and complex simulations. The chapter also explores the challenges and consequences associated with the integration of new technology, such as the need for specialized instruction and ensuring accessibility for all students.

INTRODUCTION

The educational domain is now experiencing a substantial and unprecedented transformation amidst relentless and swift technological progress. The conventional constraints that previously confined the classroom encounter are now liberating

DOI: 10.4018/979-8-3693-3015-9.ch006

Copyright © 2024, IGI Global. Copying or distributing in print or electronic forms without written permission of IGI Global is prohibited.

themselves from the confines of physical boundaries and temporal restrictions at an astonishing speed. Within the ever-changing educational landscape, we come across the influential and transformative capabilities of immersive technologies, specifically Virtual Reality (VR) and Augmented Reality (AR). These immersive technologies are not just mere instruments; they serve as the driving force behind a pedagogical revolution that has the potential to fundamentally change the way education is delivered. The newly generated opportunities they provide are very thrilling, and they have a really transformative impact on higher education. As we embark on this intellectual journey, we find ourselves in a cutting-edge environment where groundbreaking technologies, artificial intelligence, and teaching methods come together to provide us with a glimpse of an education future that surpasses our highest hopes. We aim to delve into the realms of immersive technologies in esteemed higher education institutions, going beyond traditional thoughts and engaging in a thorough exploration. Establishing a strong and comprehensive groundwork is the first stage of our investigation as it allows us to completely grasp the profound importance that virtual reality (VR) and augmented reality (AR) have in the realm of education. In the midst of limitless possibilities, we must also address the obstacles and moral deliberations that come with incorporating immersive technology into education. We will examine the complexities of privacy and ethics in immersive education and investigate the crucial role of responsible AI in guaranteeing the ethical use of these technologies in educational environments.

1. THE PROGRESSION OF IMMERSIVE TECHNOLOGIES IN EDUCATION

In order to fully comprehend the substantial influence of immersive technologies on education, it is necessary to delve into their evolutionary trajectory, retracing the origins of virtual reality (VR) and augmented reality (AR) to its nascent stages in the mid-20th century. The rudimentary research and first trials conducted during this era laid the groundwork for what has now evolved into an essential component of the educational environment. The progression from the first conceptualizations to the current advanced immersive experiences demonstrates a notable technical breakthrough. The origins of virtual reality (VR) and augmented reality (AR) may be traced back to the mid-20th century, when early innovators began investigating the possibilities of constructing artificial worlds. The notion of virtual reality, albeit in its early stages, was first developed via experiments such as Morton Heilig's Sensorama in the 1950s. These studies aimed to immerse individuals in a simulated world by stimulating several senses. The development of immersive technology reached a significant milestone with the creation of the first head-mounted display (HMD) by

Ivan Sutherland in the 1960s. These first endeavors established the basis for a trip that would ultimately revolutionize the field of education. The evolutionary path persisted over the years, observing incremental advancements in the capabilities of both hardware and software. The first flight simulators, created for military instruction during the 1960s, showcased the potential of virtual reality in producing authentic and engrossing encounters. However, it was not until the late 20th century, when more powerful processing technology became available, that VR and AR transitioned from experimental prototypes to practical applications. The advent of affordable and accessible technology during this time set the foundation for a more extensive incorporation of immersive technologies in various fields, such as education. The proliferation of VR and AR extended beyond research laboratories and began to permeate corporate and educational institutions. This transformation marked the beginning of a new era in which the transformative capabilities of immersive technologies became more and more apparent. In the realm of higher education, the adoption and incorporation of VR and AR have seen a recent surge (Hodgson, P., 2021). The formerly limited scope of specialized applications and experimental endeavors has now evolved into a transformative influence across several academic disciplines. Universities and educational institutions are increasingly embracing new technology as powerful tools to actively involve students in ways that conventional methods could not achieve.

The present educational environment is seeing a revival as immersive technology reevaluates instructional methodologies. VR and AR have evolved beyond being just supplementary tools and have now become catalysts for distinctive learning experiences. Educators in several domains, ranging from the sciences to humanities, are harnessing the potential of immersive technology to create interactive and captivating teaching material. New technologies are significantly impacting higher education by allowing for the replication of intricate scientific experiments, transporting students to historical locations, and facilitating practical training in healthcare. Specifically, in scientific fields, virtual laboratories equipped with simulations provide students with the opportunity to conduct experiments in a safe and regulated setting. These virtual activities enhance comprehension and foster the development of critical thinking and problem-solving abilities. VR and AR are revolutionizing medical training by facilitating lifelike surgical simulations and anatomy exploration, providing aspiring healthcare professionals with immersive experiences that were previously unattainable. In addition to the sciences, immersive technologies are reshaping the landscape of disciplines like history, literature, and the arts. Students have the ability to immerse themselves in historical locations, digitally explore ancient civilizations, or encounter the surroundings that influenced literary masterpieces. This hands-on learning goes beyond the limitations of traditional textbooks, allowing for a more profound and sophisticated understanding of historical events, literary narratives, and creative works. The use of virtual reality (VR) and augmented reality (AR) in education is leading to improved student involvement and participation. According to Adnan (2020), educational games and interactive simulations transform the process of learning into an exciting and unforgettable experience. The shift from passive consumption to active engagement is revolutionizing students' perception and interaction with educational content, fostering a sense of inquisitiveness and exploration. The progress of immersive technologies in education has also been driven by the continuous improvement of hardware. Contemporary virtual reality (VR) headsets include high-quality screens, precise motion tracking, and lifelike haptic feedback, resulting in immersive experiences that closely mimic the real world. AR programs for smartphones and tablets have evolved to seamlessly integrate digital information into the real world. As these technologies become more widely available, educators are faced with unprecedented opportunities to create inclusive learning environments. Students with different cognitive preferences and abilities might get advantages from immersive experiences that accommodate a wide range of requirements. Visual learners excel in interactive 3D environments, whereas kinesthetic learners flourish in simulations that require physical engagement. The advancement of immersive technology in education is not a linear progression, but rather a continuous process of investigation and improvement. The interaction between technological advancements and educational creativity consistently advances the boundaries of what may be achieved. In the future, there will be even more captivating breakthroughs, such as extended reality (XR), which encompasses virtual reality (VR), augmented reality (AR), and mixed reality (MR). These technologies will continue to diminish the boundaries between the physical and digital realms. The integration of immersive technology in education is a testament to the transformative power of innovation. From the first experiments conducted in the mid-20th century to the present age of advanced virtual reality (VR) and augmented reality (AR) applications, these technologies have made significant progress. The surge in adoption and integration inside higher education signifies a paradigm shift in instructors' pedagogical approaches and students' engagement with the learning process. As the process of development progresses, the capacity of immersive technology to transform education remains extensive and captivating, providing new opportunities to foster inquisitiveness, ingenuity, and a more profound comprehension of the universe.

2. REVOLUTIONIZING TEACHING METHODS: ENGAGING AND INTERACTIVE EDUCATIONAL ENCOUNTERS

The introduction of Virtual Reality (VR) and Augmented Reality (AR) has brought about a transformative period in higher education, challenging conventional classroom practices and transforming teaching methods. Traditional teaching methods, such as lectures and textbooks, are being replaced with immersive learning environments, in which students are not only passive recipients of information but actively interact with the subject matter. The profound influence of virtual reality (VR) and augmented reality (AR) on pedagogy lies in their capacity to transport students to virtual realms, providing exceptional opportunities for interactive learning through three-dimensional models, historical reenactments, and intricate simulations (Cicek, I., 2021). These immersive learning experiences bring about a fundamental change in the way knowledge is imparted and absorbed. Conventional approaches have faced difficulties in capturing students' interest and generating profound comprehension. VR and AR technologies overcome this challenge by creating immersive experiences that blend the boundaries between the physical and digital realms, providing an engaging and interactive educational journey (López Belmonte, 2019). The potential of immersive learning is particularly evident in its ability to transport students to virtual environments that would otherwise be inaccessible. Imagine a biology session where students had the opportunity to explore the intricate components of a human cell in three dimensions, as if they were on a trip within it. By using virtual reality (VR), students may explore the intricacies of cellular biology, gaining a deeper understanding that surpasses the limitations of conventional diagrams and textbooks. Engaging in this practical investigation not only enhances the process of acquiring knowledge but also fosters a sense of curiosity and inquiry.

AR has the potential to animate historical events, transcending temporal and spatial limitations in the realm of history. Students get the opportunity to see historical reenactments, fully engage in the cultural ambiance of past periods, and develop a direct understanding and admiration for pivotal times in history. Instead of simply reading about the construction of the pyramids in Egypt, students can use augmented reality (AR) applications to visually witness the ancient monuments, which provides a sense of scale and historical context that surpasses traditional methods (Choi, D. H., 2020). Immersive learning experiences offer more than just engagement; they greatly enhance retention and understanding. Research repeatedly demonstrates that active engagement and hands-on learning enhance knowledge retention. VR and AR technologies allow students to engage with educational information in a meaningful manner, resulting in memorable and captivating learning experiences (Jantjies, M., 2018). Illustrative instances from many academic fields further highlight the profound impact of immersive learning. VR simulations are revolutionizing medical education in the field of medicine. Students have the opportunity to enhance their surgical skills in a lifelike virtual setting, allowing them to practice surgical procedures without any potential risks, prior to performing them in an actual operating room. This not only enhances their technical expertise but also cultivates a crucial feeling of self-assurance in high-stress medical environments.

Similarly, in the field of architecture and design, virtual reality (VR) enables students to explore virtual structures and settings that they have constructed. They can analyze the intricacies of their designs, scrutinize spatial connections, and make immediate modifications. By adopting a comprehensive approach to education, students are able to improve their design abilities and gain valuable practical knowledge that goes beyond conventional drafting techniques. In the field of sciences, particularly physics and chemistry, virtual reality simulations allow students to conduct experiments that may pose risks or be impractical in a traditional laboratory environment. Students have the ability to alter virtual components, observe responses, and evaluate outcomes inside a regulated and immersive environment. This not only guarantees the security but also expands the possibilities for experimentation, enabling students to explore challenges that beyond the limitations of physical labs. The adaptability of virtual reality (VR) and augmented reality (AR) in accommodating diverse learning methods enhances their use in several educational settings. Visual learners may get advantages from the use of three-dimensional models and interactive visualizations, kinesthetic learners can actively participate in hands-on simulations, and auditory learners can engage in immersive experiences that include spatial sounds. The adaptability of these technologies allows instructors to meet the distinct needs and preferences of a varied student population.

As we examine these case studies, it becomes more and more clear that VR and AR are not just tools; they are agents for a transformative educational revolution. The transition from passively consuming information to actively engaging in experiential learning is reshaping the educational environment. Students are now liberated from the limitation of passively acquiring information. They actively engage in the learning process by exploring, experimenting, and internalizing knowledge in ways that were previously unimaginable. The effects of immersive learning experiences extend beyond the immediate academic setting and contribute to the development of essential skills necessary for success in today's society. Students that actively participate in virtual reality (VR) and augmented reality (AR) experiences improve their problem-solving capabilities, critical thinking aptitude, and adaptability. Engaging in virtual environments, making informed choices in simulated situations, and collaborating with peers in immersive spaces provide students with the necessary skills to tackle the demands of the digital era (Steele, P., 2020). While we acknowledge the profound impact that immersive learning experiences may have, it is important to recognize the constraints that arise when incorporating them. The allocation of resources towards technology and software, the need for instructors to undergo specialized training, and the imperative to address accessibility difficulties are substantial factors that require meticulous consideration. Ensuring equitable access to the advantages of immersive learning is crucial, regardless of students' socio-economic background or geographical location.

3. ENABLING EDUCATORS: CUTTING-EDGE TEACHING RESOURCES

Immersive technologies are at the forefront of a revolutionary approach to teaching, not only reshaping the educational environment for students but also fundamentally changing the role of teachers. Virtual Reality (VR) and Augmented Reality (AR) play important roles in the transformation of education, offering several aspects for the growth and empowerment of educators (Jamali, S., 2014). The mutualistic association between educators and immersive technology is expanding, resulting in the establishment of an educational environment that flourishes via novelty, involvement, and inclusiveness.

Teachers, acknowledging the capabilities of virtual reality (VR) and augmented reality (AR), are using these technologies to create educational experiences that go beyond conventional limitations. The key lies in their capacity to customize classes to accommodate various learning styles, addressing the distinct requirements of every learner. Through the use of virtual worlds and the integration of digital information into the actual world, educators create an interactive and captivating learning environment. The transition from traditional approaches to immersive experiences represents a significant advancement in the field of education, where learning is no longer restricted to textbooks and conventional teaching tools. As educators explore the realm of immersive technologies, the resources available to them become progressively more advanced (Muzyleva, I., 2021). These technologies go beyond being simple aids for visualization; they act as dynamic instruments that empower instructors to organize presentations that engage and clarify. Real-time feedback methods increase the learning process by enabling educators to promptly adjust their teaching tactics in response to students' comments (DePape, A., 2015). The incorporation of virtual reality (VR) and augmented reality (AR) into the educational toolset enables educators to surpass the limitations of traditional teaching methods, creating an atmosphere where learning becomes a customized and participatory experience.

In order for educators to fully harness the capabilities of immersive technologies, it is crucial to strategically include them into the curriculum. Implementing virtual reality (VR) and augmented reality (AR) into lesson plans necessitates a fundamental change in instructional design, with instructors actively integrating these technologies. The aim is not just to enhance conventional education, but to completely transform it, offering students experiences that go beyond the limitations of traditional classrooms. Lesson plans that include virtual situations and augmented aspects enhance comprehension and memory of intricate topics (Delello, J. A., 2015). In the field of assessment, educators are transforming conventional approaches by embracing the interactive features of virtual reality (VR) and augmented reality (AR). The era of static paper-and-pencil examinations has passed, giving way to dynamic and participative assessment experiences. Students engage in immersive simulated settings that require them to use their knowledge and problem-solving abilities in real-time. Assessing students' understanding and fostering their analytical and decision-making skills are the main benefits of using immersive technologies in the classroom. These technologies create a realistic environment that simulates real-world complexities. Furthermore, the transformative impact of immersive technologies is not confined to students; it also applies to the professional growth of educators. Educational institutions are adopting professional development programs that focus on immersive technology, acknowledging the need for a fundamental change in teaching approaches. The purpose of these programs is to provide educators with the essential skills and information required to effortlessly incorporate virtual reality (VR) and augmented reality (AR) into their teaching methods. Workshops, training sessions, and collaborative forums provide educators practical experience, promoting a community of professionals where they may exchange knowledge, effective methods, and creative strategies for immersive education.

The close connection between educators and immersive technologies is strengthening, leading to the emergence of a new kind of educators who are highly skilled in digital literacy and technology. This transformation extends beyond the development of technical skills; it incorporates a change in perspective, as educators transition from being providers of knowledge to being facilitators of experiential learning. Educators' job transitions from conventional teachers to facilitators of immersive experiences, leading students through virtual environments and augmented realities that enhance their educational journey (Nesenbergs, K., 2020). The influence of immersive technology on special education is remarkable. These technologies provide a wide range of options for meeting the different learning requirements of students, offering tailored and adaptable learning experiences for students with differing abilities. Virtual environments provide inclusive places that enable students, irrespective of their learning methods or physical limitations, to actively participate and interact with educational information. The accessibility and flexibility of immersive technologies enhance inclusivity and equity in the educational domain. The incorporation of Virtual Reality (VR) and Augmented Reality (AR) into education signals a significant shift in teaching methods, going beyond mere technology progress to bring about a transformative change in pedagogy. The immersive technologies have the ability to greatly impact educators by allowing them to go beyond conventional limits, offering a platform for customized and interactive learning experiences. To fully use immersive technologies, it is necessary to integrate them strategically into the curriculum, prepare creative lessons, and provide ongoing professional development for instructors. As education progresses, instructors play a crucial role in leading immersive learning experiences, which are altering the future of education in ways that were previously considered inconceivable.

4. ADDRESSING DISPARITIES: PROMOTING EQUAL OPPORTUNITY AND ACCESSIBILITY IN EDUCATION

Immersive technologies are seen as powerful tools in the ongoing effort to make education more accessible to everyone. These technologies provide innovative ways to overcome obstacles and provide equal opportunities for a wide range of learners. The advanced technologies of Virtual Reality (VR) and Augmented Reality (AR) have the potential to greatly transform the field of education. They can cater to the specific needs of individuals with disabilities and overcome the geographical obstacles that have historically limited access to high-quality education.

Immersive technology has great potential to meet the requirements of those with impairments. Conventional educational institutions may have difficulties in accommodating the distinct learning needs of persons with physical, sensory, or cognitive impairments. Nevertheless, the immersive nature of virtual reality (VR) and augmented reality (AR) presents novel opportunities for fostering inclusive education. These tools enable individuals with disabilities to engage in educational experiences that go beyond the limitations of traditional learning environments. For example, a visually impaired student can explore ancient civilizations through a virtual reality tour (Nabokova, L. S., 2019). This immersive experience enables students to explore historical landscapes via detailed descriptions and spatial audio cues, fostering autonomous engagement and understanding of the topic. In the same vein, individuals with auditory impairments might get advantages from augmented reality overlays that provide instantaneous textual subtitles during educational lectures or presentations. Immersive technologies have the ability to break down barriers and create an inclusive educational environment that can accommodate a wide range of abilities (Gudoniene, D., 2016). In addition to addressing physical impairments, these technologies are also important in meeting different learning styles and preferences. The process of education is highly individualized, and learners differ in their methods of absorbing knowledge. Virtual Reality (VR) and Augmented Reality (AR) provide a versatile platform for educators to develop educational programs that cater to various learning preferences, thereby guaranteeing that each student has the chance to excel. For example, a kinesthetic learner might actively participate in a biology class by digitally dissecting a frog, while a visual learner may examine three-dimensional representations of complicated chemical compounds. The creation of inclusive immersive content is at the forefront of this transformation. Innovators and educators are investing time and money in creating material that goes beyond standard pedagogical limits. This extends beyond the simple incorporation of accessibility features; it requires a thorough approach to creating material that takes into account the diverse needs and preferences of learners. Creating inclusive material requires meticulous attention to detail, including compatibility with assistive devices and providing several avenues for acquiring information (Liarokapis, F., 2010).

Content development that is inclusive is not only a technological endeavor; rather, it represents a fundamental change in educational philosophy. The statement advocates for a departure from a standardized approach to education and advocates for a strategy that embraces diversity. Collaboration between educators, content producers, and technologists is used to create an educational experience that is immersive and acknowledges and adapts to the unique qualities of each learner. The result is a learning environment that ensures no student is excluded and provides equal opportunities for development, regardless of their abilities or preferred learning methods. The influence of immersive technology on inclusivity goes beyond the individual learner and encompasses whole communities. Historically, geographical limitations have posed significant obstacles to education, especially in distant or economically disadvantaged areas. Virtual Reality (VR) and Augmented Reality (AR) are emerging as powerful tools to democratize education by providing a virtual platform that overcomes the barriers caused by distance and limited resources. Rural students, who were previously isolated from modern educational resources, now have the ability to access the same high-quality content as their urban peers. The democratization of education through immersive technology is not just about granting access to educational material; it is about fostering a feeling of empowerment and ambition. Formerly limited by their physical surroundings, students now have the capacity to explore virtual realms, conduct simulated experiments, and interact with educational material that surpasses the constraints of their real-world environment. Engaging in this activity not only expands their intellectual perspectives but also fosters a feeling of potential and ambition that surpasses the limitations of their immediate surroundings. The progress towards complete integration via immersive technology is not without its obstacles. As the popularity of these technologies increases in educational contexts, it is essential to tackle accessibility challenges at different levels. Addressing hardware costs, technical expertise, and infrastructural constraints is crucial to enable universal accessibility to immersive technology. The promotion of inclusion necessitates a synchronized effort by legislators, educators, and technology developers to create a setting where the advantages of immersive education are accessible to all students, irrespective of their socio-economic level or geographical location.

5. UTILIZING DATA TO INFORM DECISION-MAKING IN ORDER TO IMPROVE EDUCATIONAL OUTCOMES

Artificial intelligence (AI)-powered analytics have become a revolutionary force in the field of education, reshaping both the teaching methods used by educators and the decision-making processes of institutions to enhance educational results. In the midst of this technological revolution, immersive technologies like as Virtual Reality (VR) and Augmented Reality (AR) are not only tools for education, but also platforms that generate data. These technologies have the ability to uncover important information about student performance and engagement.

The integration of AI-powered analytics into education signifies a departure from conventional decision-making methods. Educators and institutions now have the opportunity to make informed choices by using data, rather than only relying on anecdotal observations and standardized assessments. The potential for transformation lies not only in the capacity to monitor student progress, but also in the ability to pinpoint specific areas that require additional support and to adjust teaching strategies accordingly. This transformation is driven by the recognition that each student is distinct, with individualized learning needs, abilities, and obstacles. AI-driven analytics empower instructors to go beyond a generic approach, providing personalized interventions based on specific student data. Through the use of data generated by immersive technologies such as virtual reality (VR) and augmented reality (AR), educators may get a detailed understanding of how students engage with instructional material. This surpasses conventional evaluation criteria by providing insights into nuanced aspects of learning, such as attention span, engagement levels, and problem-solving approaches. For instance, imagine a virtual reality (VR) history lesson where students immerse themselves in the experience of ancient civilizations. AI algorithms have the ability to observe and analyze the students' activities and behaviors in the virtual environment. This includes not just identifying right answers, but also understanding the cognitive processes that led to those answers. This level of detail enables educators to not only assess the knowledge of students but also understand the reasoning behind their decisions. Equipped with this knowledge, educators may personalize their interventions, providing supplementary materials or individualized assistance where it is most needed.

Data-driven decision-making in education has the potential to go beyond only helping individual students and may also lead to changes at the institutional level. Academic establishments are intricate ecosystems with several components that impact results. AI-driven analytics provide a comprehensive view of these dynamics, enabling institutions to identify patterns and trends that impact overall performance. By analyzing data on student engagement in several classes, a school may identify successful teaching methods and areas that may need improvements in the curriculum. Utilizing data to make decisions is a powerful force that drives ongoing advancement. It fosters a culture that promotes adaptability and responsiveness, allowing institutions to continuously refine teaching techniques, curriculum design, and support services using up-to-date information. The traditional method of evaluating performance through end-of-semester tests has been replaced by a flexible process that allows for adjustments to be made in real-time. This ensures that educational strategies can adapt to the constantly evolving needs of students. Numerous real-life examples exist of institutions harnessing the capabilities of AI-powered analytics to improve educational results. An exemplification of this is the use of virtual reality simulations in medical education. Medical education institutions that use virtual reality (VR) technology gather substantial amounts of data on student performance during simulated operations or diagnostic situations. AI systems may analyze this data to identify patterns in decision-making, accuracy in procedural tasks, and areas of difficulty for pupils.

By using these observations, teachers may modify training modules, provide targeted feedback, and guarantee that upcoming medical professionals not only acquire theoretical information but also improve their practical skills. Utilizing data-driven methods enhances the quality of medical education and contributes to advancements in medical training techniques, resulting in positive effects on the broader healthcare industry. With this information, instructors can optimize lesson plans, customize learning experiences, and allocate resources strategically for maximum effectiveness. The result is a classroom environment in which teaching is not a fixed or unchanging activity, but rather a flexible and adaptable practice that takes into account the evolving needs of each student, based on data and information. The use of AI-driven analytics in education is not devoid of challenges. The issues of privacy, ethical implications, and the need for transparent algorithms are crucial factors that need meticulous scrutiny. Given the substantial amount of student data that schools collect and analyze, it is crucial to manage this information responsibly, prioritizing the enhancement of educational outcomes rather than infringing upon individual privacy. Educators must engage in ongoing professional development to effectively navigate the complexities of data-driven decision-making. Proficiently comprehending and effectively using data necessitates a skill set that surpasses conventional educational methods. Institutions should allocate resources towards training programs that enable teachers to proficiently use AI-powered analytics for the advancement of their pupils.

6. OBSTACLES AND MORAL DELIBERATIONS

Within the ever-evolving field of education, where advanced technologies such as Virtual Reality (VR) and Augmented Reality (AR) are rapidly advancing, their ability to bring about substantial changes is accompanied with a complex set of problems and ethical issues. As educators and institutions use these technologies to enhance learning experiences, they must confront significant concerns, especially with privacy, responsible artificial intelligence, and the ethical consequences of using immersive technology in educational environments.

The integration of VR and AR in education is a significant barrier due to emerging privacy concerns. These immersive technologies, which are intended to provide customized and interactive learning experiences, often require the gathering of sensitive data on users. The use of virtual environments and augmented reality activities allows for extensive data collection on students' interactions and responses. This immersive nature goes beyond what traditional educational tools offer. However, educators and institutions face the challenge of navigating a complex landscape of data privacy regulations, each jurisdiction having its own distinct rules and requirements. The task at hand is not just to adhere to these standards, but also to build strong measures that beyond the bare minimum of what is legally required. Ensuring the protection of student information is of utmost importance, and institutions must take proactive steps to develop strict safeguards in order to safeguard the privacy of individuals interacting with immersive educational material (Radosavljevic, S., 2020). With the increasing convergence of physical and digital domains, the potential for data breaches and illegal access poses a significant and urgent threat. Institutions must allocate resources towards implementing cutting-edge security measures to protect the huge volumes of sensitive data produced by virtual reality (VR) and augmented reality (AR) apps. This encompasses encryption protocols, robust authentication procedures, and periodic security audits to detect and rectify vulnerabilities. Responsible AI, an integral aspect of the ethical considerations in immersive education, assumes a crucial function in guaranteeing equitable, transparent, and responsible algorithms. The use of artificial intelligence (AI) in educational environments gives rise to apprehensions about biases, discrimination, and the possibility of exacerbating pre-existing disparities. For example, if AI systems are taught using datasets that accurately represent social prejudices; they may unintentionally reinforce similar biases in educational decision-making processes.

In order to deal with these problems, educators and technologists need to take a proactive approach in using AI responsibly. This entails thorough examination of the algorithms used in immersive technologies, openness in the decision-making procedures of AI systems, and ways for holding algorithms accountable in case of mistakes or biases. Furthermore, it is crucial to continuously monitor and evaluate AI systems in order to detect and correct any biases that may arise over time. A fundamental element of responsible AI is ensuring that the algorithms used in immersive educational technologies can be explained and understood. The openness not only cultivates confidence among users but also enables instructors to comprehend the process of AI-driven decision-making. Educators who possess a comprehensive understanding of the reasoning behind AI-generated insights are more capable of responsibly utilizing this information. By having a clear comprehension of the underlying algorithms, they can customize interventions accordingly. The ethical dilemmas presented by immersive technologies in education extend beyond concerns of privacy and responsible AI. The inherent characteristics of modern technologies, characterized by their capacity to generate profoundly captivating and interactive encounters, give rise to inquiries on the likelihood of addiction and excessive dependence. As children increasingly engage in virtual worlds or augmented realities, there is a concern that new technologies may disrupt the equilibrium between screen time and other crucial components of a comprehensive education, such as physical exercise and in-person social connection.

Educators must confront the issue of achieving this equilibrium and advocating for responsible technology use. This entails establishing criteria for the proper use of immersive technology, as well as cultivating digital literacy among students. Developing digital literacy enables students to actively analyze and evaluate technology, comprehend its influence, and make well-informed choices about its use. It is important for educators to be aware of the possible socioeconomic inequalities in the availability of immersive technology. Although new technologies have the potential to transform education, there is a concern that students from economically disadvantaged families may face unequal access to VR headsets, AR gadgets, or high-end computer equipment. The presence of this digital gap might worsen pre-existing disparities in education, impeding the objective of establishing equal opportunities for all students. Tackling these difficulties requires a comprehensive and diverse strategy. Educational institutions should investigate novel finance mechanisms to provide equitable access to immersive technology for all students, irrespective of their financial status. Collaborations with technology firms, government programs, and community partnerships may have a crucial impact in closing the gap between those who have access to digital resources and those who do not, and in ensuring that immersive education is accessible to everyone.

Amidst these problems, it is crucial to highlight the significance of proactive ethical deliberations in the creation and use of immersive technologies in education. Creating ethical protocols and criteria that give priority to safeguarding student privacy, promoting responsible artificial intelligence, and fostering digital literacy will provide the groundwork for the conscientious use of these technologies. Effective implementation of this endeavor requires the cooperation of educators, legislators, technologists, and stakeholders in order to provide a comprehensive structure that promotes creativity and progress, while simultaneously ensuring the protection of students' welfare and rights. The use of immersive technology in education poses several problems and ethical issues that need meticulous attention. Educators and institutions must negotiate a difficult terrain that involves securing privacy, assuring responsible AI, addressing concerns of addiction, and fostering accessibility. To safely harness the transformational potential of immersive education, it is necessary to proactively address obstacles, encourage ethical standards, and prioritize inclusion. This will ensure that technology improves the educational experience for everyone, without compromising it.

7. PROSPECTS FOR THE FUTURE: INNOVATIVE OPPORTUNITIES

As we approach a future shaped by technology advancements, the combination of immersive technologies and generative Artificial Intelligence (AI) presents exciting opportunities for education. In this concluding segment, we go into unexplored domains of the future, investigating the potential impact of combining immersive technology and generative AI on learning experiences. This fusion has the potential to transform education into a dynamic, customized, and universally empowering pursuit.

Generative AI, a branch of artificial intelligence focused on machines autonomously producing material, has the potential to significantly transform the educational field. Envision an educational setting where AI algorithms not just aid but actively engage in the development of dynamic and tailored learning experiences (Martín-Gutiérrez, 2015). This signifies a shift from conventional methods, where educational content remains fixed and consistent, to a time where educational materials continuously change, adjusting to the distinct requirements and preferences of individual learners. One of the most revolutionary uses of generative AI in education is the development of customized learning paths. Artificial intelligence systems, powered by extensive datasets and sophisticated machine learning methods, have the capability to examine the learning patterns, strengths, and areas for growth of individual students. By possessing this detailed insight, the AI system is capable of producing information that closely corresponds to the specific requirements of the student, offering a customized educational experience that optimizes both involvement and understanding.

This customized approach goes beyond traditional fields to provide a comprehensive perspective on education. Generative AI has the capability to provide transdisciplinary learning experiences, enabling students to identify connections between many courses in a seamless and integrated way. An example of this is when a history lecture seamlessly incorporates elements of literature, art, and science, resulting in a comprehensive comprehension of historical events and their wider implications. The future of education is not limited to the traditional classroom setting; it encompasses lifelong learning in the larger world. Generative AI has the capacity to transform the manner in which people interact with the process of learning, by creating customized pathways for professional growth, acquisition of skills, and intellectual exploration. Envision experts using immersive technology to explore virtual environments that accurately reflect real-world problems, led by AI-generated information tailored to their specific professional objectives and learning preferences. The combination of generative artificial intelligence and immersive technology has the potential to fundamentally rethink the notion of evaluations. Conventional examinations and standardized tests might be replaced with dynamic assessments powered by artificial intelligence. These assessments would not only measure information retention but also evaluate problem-solving ability, critical thinking skills, and creativity. Utilizing generative AI, immersive simulations have the potential to expose students to authentic situations, assess their reactions, and provide immediate feedback to facilitate their educational progress.

The notion of the virtual classroom assumes a novel perspective in this utopian future. Immersive technologies, powered by generative AI, have the potential to enable worldwide collaborations and cultural exchanges, beyond geographical limitations. Students from various global locations may convene in virtual environments, participating in cooperative initiatives, cultural interactions, and collective educational encounters. The realization of establishing a worldwide community of students, united by their common quest for knowledge, is made possible. Creativity, often regarded as the fundamental element of innovation, has a prominent role in this futuristic vision. Generative artificial intelligence, with the ability to comprehend and produce imaginative material, assumes the role of a partner in the educational journey. Students have the opportunity to participate in immersive experiences where they collaborate with AI algorithms to generate material, allowing them to explore new areas of creative expression, scientific investigation, and problem-solving.

Within this future context, the function of educators experiences a profound metamorphosis. Teachers assume the role of facilitators and mentors, providing guidance to students as they navigate the ever-changing realm of AI-enhanced, immersive learning experiences. The emphasis transitions from imparting fixed knowledge to fostering students' abilities in critical thinking, creativity, and flexibility. Teachers engage with AI systems that generate material, construct learning experiences, and provide personalized assistance to individual students. As we enthusiastically explore these innovative possibilities, ethical questions become of utmost importance. Transparency, accountability, and a dedication to fairness are essential for the proper use of generative AI in the field of education. It is essential for educators and technologists to guarantee that the algorithms powering individualized learning experiences are equitable, impartial, and devoid of discriminating inclinations. Ensuring a harmonious equilibrium between the advantages of AI-powered customization and the possible hazards of perpetuating preexisting disparities emerges as a critical factor in creating this next era. The issue of privacy, which has always been a difficult problem in the field of technology, requires further focus. Given that AI algorithms are collecting and examining extensive quantities of data to customize educational experiences, it is imperative to ensure the protection of learners' privacy. In order to establish and maintain trust in this advanced educational environment, it is crucial to implement strong data security measures, clearly communicate data use regulations, and continuously monitor AI systems. The future of education, influenced by the combination of immersive technology and generative AI, has great potential. It imagines a future in which learning is not a fixed procedure, but a flexible, customized experience that adjusts to individual need. The capacity to cultivate creativity, analytical thinking, and continuous learning is limitless. As we go towards the future, it is crucial that ethical concerns play a central role in the development and deployment of new technologies. Collaboratively, educators, technologists, politicians, and learners may influence a future in which education is not limited, and where there are endless possibilities for development and exploration.

CONCLUSION

Our analysis of immersive technologies, namely Virtual Reality and Augmented Reality, in the context of higher education uncovers a world of remarkable change and unprecedented possibilities. As we progress through the chapters of this book, it is clear that immersive technologies have the potential to significantly change the way we learn, in ways that were not previously considered. The combination of artificial intelligence, disruptive technologies, and advanced educational methods is creating a dynamic learning environment. For effective use of these tools, collaboration between educators and technologists is essential. There are a wide range of possibilities, including revamping the educational environment, empowering educators, and promoting inclusiveness. As we embark on this groundbreaking endeavor, we must also be aware of the challenges and ethical quandaries that arise from incorporating immersive technology into the educational setting. In order to guarantee an ethical and equal future for education, it is imperative that we prioritize responsible AI and data protection. Ultimately, the purpose of this chapter is to encourage and stimulate both educators and technologists to collaborate closely, with the aim of establishing a future in which education is really empowering and available to everyone. The revolution has started, and as we explore the uncharted territories of immersive education, we invite you to accompany us on this groundbreaking journey. Collectively, we have the power to transform education and introduce a period of unimaginable opportunities.

REFERENCES

Adnan, A. H. M. (2020, September). From interactive teaching to immersive learning: Higher Education 4.0 via 360-degree videos and virtual reality in Malaysia. *IOP Conference Series. Materials Science and Engineering*, *917*(1), 012023. doi:10.1088/1757-899X/917/1/012023

Choi, D. H., Dailey-Hebert, A., & Estes, J. S. (Eds.). (2020). *Current and prospective applications of virtual reality in higher education*. IGI Global. doi:10.4018/978-1-7998-4960-5

Cicek, I., Bernik, A., & Tomicic, I. (2021). Student thoughts on virtual reality in higher education—A survey questionnaire. *Information (Basel)*, *12*(4), 151. doi:10.3390/info12040151

Delello, J. A., McWhorter, R. R., & Camp, K. M. (2015). Integrating augmented reality in higher education: A multidisciplinary study of student perceptions. *Journal of Educational Multimedia and Hypermedia*, *24*(3), 209–233.

DePape, A. M., Barnes, M., & Petryschuk, J. (2019). Students' experiences in higher education with virtual and augmented reality: A qualitative systematic review. *Innovative Practice in Higher Education*, *3*(3).

Gudoniene, D., & Rutkauskiene, D. (2019). Virtual and augmented reality in education. *Baltic Journal of Modern Computing*, *7*(2), 293–300. doi:10.22364/bjmc.2019.7.2.07

Gurevych, R., Silveistr, A., Mokliuk, M., Shaposhnikova, I., Gordiichuk, G., & Saiapina, S. (2021). Using augmented reality technology in higher education institutions. *Postmodern Openings*, *12*(2), 109–132. doi:10.18662/po/12.2/299

Hodgson, P., Lee, V. W., Chan, J. C., Fong, A., Tang, C. S., Chan, L., & Wong, C. (2019). Immersive virtual reality (IVR) in higher education: Development and implementation. *Augmented reality and virtual reality: The power of AR and VR for business*, 161-173.

Jamali, S., Shiratuddin, M. F., & Wong, K. (2014). An overview of mobile-augmented reality in higher education. *International Journal on Recent Trends In Engineering & Technology*, *11*(1), 229–238.

Jantjies, M., Moodley, T., & Maart, R. (2018, December). Experiential learning through virtual and augmented reality in higher education. In *Proceedings of the 2018 international conference on education technology management* (pp. 42-45). 10.1145/3300942.3300956

Liarokapis, F., & Anderson, E. F. (2010). *Using augmented reality as a medium to assist teaching in higher education*. Academic Press.

López Belmonte, J., Moreno-Guerrero, A. J., López Núñez, J. A., & Pozo Sánchez, S. (2019). Analysis of the productive, structural, and dynamic development of augmented reality in higher education research on the web of science. *Applied Sciences (Basel, Switzerland)*, *9*(24), 5306. doi:10.3390/app9245306

Martín-Gutiérrez, J., Fabiani, P., Benesova, W., Meneses, M. D., & Mora, C. E. (2015). Augmented reality to promote collaborative and autonomous learning in higher education. *Computers in Human Behavior*, *51*, 752–761. doi:10.1016/j.chb.2014.11.093

Muzyleva, I., Yazykova, L., Gorlach, A., & Gorlach, Y. (2021, June). Augmented and Virtual Reality Technologies in Education. In *2021 1st International Conference on Technology Enhanced Learning in Higher Education (TELE)* (pp. 99-103). IEEE. 10.1109/TELE52840.2021.9482568

Nabokova, L. S., &Zagidullina, F. R. (2019). Outlooks of applying augmented and virtual reality technologies in higher education. *Professional education in the modern world*, *9*(2), 2710-2719.

Nesenbergs, K., Abolins, V., Ormanis, J., & Mednis, A. (2020). Use of augmented and virtual reality in remote higher education: A systematic umbrella review. *Education Sciences*, *11*(1), 8. doi:10.3390/educsci11010008

Radosavljevic, S., Radosavljevic, V., & Grgurovic, B. (2020). The potential of implementing augmented reality into vocational higher education through mobile learning. *Interactive Learning Environments*, *28*(4), 404–418. doi:10.1080/10494820.2018.1528286

Steele, P., Burleigh, C., Bailey, L., & Kroposki, M. (2020). Studio thinking framework in higher education: Exploring options for shaping immersive experiences across virtual reality/augmented reality curricula. *Journal of Educational Technology Systems*, *48*(3), 416–439. doi:10.1177/0047239519884897

Videnov, K., Stoykova, V., & Kazlacheva, Z. (2018). Application of augmented reality in higher education. ARTTE Applied Researches in Technics. *Technologies and Education*, *6*(1), 1–9.

Chapter 7
Immersive Learning:
Navigating the Future With Virtual and Augmented Reality in Education

Garima Arora
https://orcid.org/0000-0001-8348-0721
Maharishi Markandeshwar University (deemed), India

Vinod Kumar
https://orcid.org/0000-0002-3578-8155
Maharishi Markandeshwar University (deemed), India

Ankur Mangla
https://orcid.org/0000-0003-1152-6289
Maharishi Markandeshwar University (deemed), India

Rajit Verma
https://orcid.org/0000-0003-0643-4718
Maharishi Markandeshwar University (deemed), India

ABSTRACT

Immersive learning and technology are instructional strategies that use cutting-edge technologies to create dynamic and captivating learning environments. With this combination, the learning environment should be more immersive and productive, increasing the impact and engagement of education. Virtual reality (VR) and augmented reality (AR) are such innovative technologies that increase opportunities in education. This chapter examined how AR and VR are used in education, particularly during the knowledge dissemination. These technologies offer both teachers and students novel platforms for teaching by providing interactive environments, immersives

DOI: 10.4018/979-8-3693-3015-9.ch007

Copyright © 2024, IGI Global. Copying or distributing in print or electronic forms without written permission of IGI Global is prohibited.

and simulations that have revolutionised the field of learning tactics. However, to meet the huge demand in education, these technologies are still at their growing stage and require more resources. The chapter also focuses on the differences, and educational benefits of AR and VR, as well as the possibilities for mobile learning environments and future applications of these technologies in education.

BACKGROUND

Modern technology has contributed to major shifts in society and the economy by integrating and applying cutting-edge instruments and techniques. These include improvements in the field of telecommunications (da Cruz *et al.*, 2018), an emphasis on sustainability, and a rise in technological advancement (Muniz *et al.*, 2020). These changes, which are spreading quickly and widely, led several technical studies to propose the beginning of the fourth industrial revolution, known as "Industry 4.0" (Gilchrist, 2016). Applications of artificial intelligence techniques are increasingly being used including time series forecasting (Stefenon *et al.*, 2021) and classification (Stefenon *et al.*, 2022). These applications are also found in fields like energy (Stefenon *et al.*, 2020), security (Stefenon *et al.*, 2022d), and education (Zhai *et al.*, 2021).

With Industry 4.0 driving constant digitization and the never-ending problem of handling the deluge of information, education struggles to hold students' attention in the midst of a plethora of interactive materials. The teaching profession is undergoing a significant transition to better fit the current global environment in reaction to the complexity of 21st-century education. This change entails the use of fresh teaching strategies that acknowledge and address how people fit into the dynamics of modern society (Cilliers, 2017).

The expanding integration of technology into educational practices is being driven by the rising use of artificial intelligence (AI) and the introduction of new technologies (Vieira *et al.*, 2022; Stefenon *et al.*, 2022b; Stefenon *et al.*, 2022c). Mendes *et al.* (2021) have shown that this tendency is promising for the application of these principles in the classroom. In response to the need for a more modern educational system, interactive technologies such as virtual reality (VR) and augmented reality (AR) are finding their way into instructional applications (Silva *et al.*, 2022).

INTRODUCTION

Some of the most cutting-edge technical advancements of the modern era, virtual reality (VR) and augmented reality (AR), have the power to drastically alter the educational landscape. The use of virtual reality (VR) and augmented reality (AR) in education has increased noticeably in recent years, offering several chances to use technology for better educational results. With the help of these technologies, learning experiences can be greatly enhanced and students can be engaged in novel ways (Tan *et al.*, 2022). Phakamach *et al.* (2022) stated that combination of augmented reality (AR) and virtual reality (VR) exposes pupils to immersive digital experiences that surpass the limitations of conventional teaching approaches. This technology transcends the boundaries of traditional lectures and textbooks and enables students to interact more effectively with difficult content (Sun *et al.*, 2022). Additionally, as discussed by Childs *et al.* (2021), VR and AR enable teachers to customise information based on each student's unique learning preferences, enabling a customised and flexible approach to teaching. Seidametova *et al.* (2021), explained that these technologies not only improve immersion but also give educators the chance to use simulations and enable virtual field excursions, removing the limitations connected with actual travel. Moreover, the incorporation of cutting-edge technologies such as Virtual Reality (VR) and Augmented Reality (AR) offers concrete benefits for professional development by reducing the disparity between traditional classroom training and actual-life situations. This method is in line with the changing needs of education, where technology is essential to educating students about real-world problems in their disciplines.

Augmented Reality (AR) is the use of technology to allow people to extend or improve their range of view by superimposing digital objects onto real-world situations in real time. This calls for merging computer vision and computer graphics techniques. The interaction between the user and virtual elements happens safely and smoothly when digital content blends in with the user's real-world surroundings. This procedure can be carried out using the mobile device's camera without the need for additional equipment (Duan *et al.*, 2018).

Hantono *et al.*, (2018) define augmented reality (AR) as a technology that modifies the physical world by superimposing digital content on top of it. Antonioli *et al.* (2014) have emphasised the numerous professional applications of this adaptable technology across a range of industries, such as education, manufacturing, healthcare, and retail. Because AR may improve experiences in the actual world, it's a useful tool with a wide range of significant applications in various fields and industries (Kumar *et al.*, 2023). Employers are using Augmented Reality (AR) more frequently to improve worker safety by simulating virtual training sessions and allowing employees to see how equipment will operate before it is ever manufactured. In many different industries, this use of AR leads to more efficient training and risk prevention strategies (Velev & Zlateva, 2017) and virtual reality (VR), on the other hand, stands out as a cutting-edge technical advancement that has revolutionised how we perceive and interact with digital worlds. Virtual reality (VR) produces lifelike digital experiences that mimic real-world situations and have a wide range of uses in industries like gaming, training, and education.

Furthermore, the integration of AR and VR technologies into online, mobile, and mixed learning settings yields numerous benefits, such as the creation of more captivating learning environments and immersive learning experiences. These technologies make it possible to build simulations and virtual worlds, which let students interact with real life settings without having to step outside of the classroom. By providing dynamic and interactive content, this use of VR and AR improves learning experiences and encourages learners to become more engaged and have a deeper knowledge of the material (Young *et al.*, 2020).

LITERATURE REVIEW

Augmented Reality (AR) and Virtual reality (VR) are recent developments and dissimilarities were also seen between the two. The characteristics of virtual reality include interaction, sensory feedback, an imaginary realm, and immersion in virtual worlds (Javornik, 2016; Krüger *et al.*, 2019; Kim *et al.*, 2018). Conversely, AR (Augmented Reality) is distinguished by its contextual quality, which includes the blend of virtual and physical components at the very same time, simultaneous interaction, and spatiality in the three-dimensional space. These characteristics have made it easier to incorporate virtual and augmented reality into the classroom and have led to the development of creative teaching strategies, especially during the Covid-19 pandemic. The increasing acceptance of Virtual Reality (VR) and Augmented Reality (AR) technologies can be attributed due to their rapid development (Beck, 2019; Chen *et al.*, 2017; Rutkauskiene & Gudoniene, 2019). Nonetheless, current studies done within the field of education related to Augmented Reality and Virtual Reality involving investigating quality shifts in the learning setting during the Coronavirus period (Lakshmi Priya & Raja, 2022); social learning spaces (Scavarelli *et al.*, 2021); use by elementary school instructors (Alalwan *et al.*, 2020); issues with current and upcoming teaching approaches Al-Azawi (2018) and meta-analysis (Hantono *et al.*, 2018).

According to Garzón *et al.* (2019), learning efficacy is positively impacted by both virtual reality (VR) and augmented reality (AR). The aforementioned technologies are among the most cutting-edge instruments available, and they have the power to significantly enhance the quality of education. Kumar *et al.* (2022), found that augmented and virtual reality allow instructors can take students on online field trips, offering dynamic and interesting teachings that can be accessed from any location. Furthermore, by utilising Augmented Reality (AR) and Virtual Reality (VR), students can participate in tasks in a virtual environment and receive constructive feedback on their performance, thereby promoting engaging learning experiences. Furthermore, incorporating virtual and augmented reality into the classroom has the potential to lower expenses associated with travel and course materials, improving accessibility and affordability for a larger population. Teachers can get the finest performance from their students by using VR and AR technology and can deliver courses in a way that is much more interesting and successful.

Using AR and VR technology, educators can develop lively, engaging classes which are cater to the specific requirements of each student, making for a more individualised educational experience. According to Oberdörfer *et al.* (2021), virtual reality (VR) and augmented reality (AR) give students the chance to investigate simulated environments and mimic situations from life, which improves their comprehension of a wide range of disciplines. Furthermore, AR and VR can improve student-teacher communication. Learners can collaborate on group projects and participate in educational activities by immersing themselves in virtual environments, which promotes interaction and engagement. Teachers can use augmented reality (AR) and virtual reality (VR) to incorporate gaming into their lessons. By adding game components, student engagement and learning more fun. Technology such as augmented reality and virtual reality can be very helpful in the evaluation process by providing students with interactive tests and challenges that are tailored to their specific learning levels. This method helps professors analyse students' grasp of a subject more precisely and give quick feedback, which improves the efficacy of the evaluation system.

In the sphere of education, augmented reality (AR) and virtual reality (VR) are increasingly prominent because they may offer a distinctive and engaging learning experience. Nevertheless, several problems need to be fixed until these technologies are used effectively. Nguyen *et al.* (2019) have highlighted cost as a major impediment among these problems. Financial obstacles prevent the widespread use of VR and AR in education since the required hardware and software are expensive. Budgeting for these technologies may be difficult for schools. In addition, the need for frequent updates for the software that creates immersive experiences adds to the costs. Biswas *et al.* (2021) have highlighted accessibility as a noteworthy difficulty. Since not every student has access to the required gear and software, schools need to figure out how to make these resources available to every kid. Furthermore, some students may find the use of augmented reality and virtual reality in the classroom to be overwhelming, based on their age as well as their level of technological expertise. Furthermore, scaling is also a problem (Scavarelli *et al.*, 2019). As AR and VR become more commonly used, educational institutions will need to find out how to stay up to speed with the latest technology developments to improve their curriculum and produce deeper experiences.

CHALLENGES IN CONVENTIONAL EDUCATION

Students with varying learning styles and schedules may not be capable to have their requirements met by the uniform method utilised in traditional schooling. Contrarily, personalised learning takes into account these variations and enables students' study at their own speed using methods that best meet their individual needs (Tomlinson, 2001). The curriculum in conventional educational institutions might not always keep up with the rapid changes in society and technology. Due to this delay, students may be taught material that is out-of-date or does not fairly reflect the state of research in various subjects today. To effectively prepare students for the difficulties of the modern world, the curriculum must be updated continuously to incorporate the most recent knowledge and abilities (Cuban, 1986). Students may become disinterested and less motivated to learn if traditional education fails to successfully engage them. Routine memorization and lectures are two examples of traditional teaching methods that might cause students to become disengaged. Increasing students' interest and participation in the learning process can be accomplished by using interactive and participatory teaching strategies (Fredricks *et al.,* 2004).

A "teaching to the test" mentality may be developed by placing an excessive emphasis on standardised testing as a measure of academic success. This narrow emphasis could limit the scope of education by excluding important components like creativity, critical thinking, and problem-solving abilities. To obtain a thorough grasp of students' abilities, it is essential to take a more well-rounded approach to assessment that incorporates a variety of evaluation methods (Koretz, 2008). It's possible that traditional education does not always place a strong emphasis on developing critical thinking abilities, which are crucial for making decisions and addressing problems effectively. Proficiency in critical thinking, which includes information processing, reasoning, and problem solving, is essential for success in a variety of life domains. Including critical thinking in the curriculum helps students acquire the abilities needed to deal with the difficulties of today's world (Ennis, 1987).

A teacher-centered approach is commonly used in traditional education, providing few opportunities for student-driven and collaborative learning. This approach places a lot of emphasis on the teacher as the information provider, with the expectation that pupils will just take it in and repeat it. Students may not be encouraged to think independently or to work together under such a technique. Making the shift to a student-centered approach, in which students participate actively in their education and work together with classmates, creates a more vibrant and engaging learning environment (Kagan & Kagan, 1994). It could be difficult for many traditional classrooms to smoothly integrate modern technology into the teaching and learning process. To provide students with the skills they need to live in a technologically advanced environment, interactive and digital learning experiences can be hindered by a lack of technology integration. According to Becker (1994), integrating technology into the classroom can boost student participation and provide them with practical digital literacy abilities. Through traditional education, students might not always gain the information and practical skills necessary for success in real-world situations. Theoretical knowledge may occasionally precede the practical abilities needed for real-world applications in conventional schooling. Students can be better prepared for the obstacles they may face in their future jobs by including problem-solving activities, real-world scenarios, and hands-on experiences in the curriculum (Trilling *et al.*, 2012). Students from poor families may face barriers including limited money, restricted access to instructional technologies, and fewer extracurricular activity options, socioeconomic inequities lead to unequal access to high-quality education. Policies and procedures that ensure all students have equitable access to educational opportunities and resources must be put in place to address these disparities (Sirin, 2005).

EDUCATIONAL BENEFITS OF AUGMENTED REALITY AND VIRTUAL REALITY

Two modern developments that have broad applications are virtual reality (VR) and augmented reality (AR). These days, the teaching and learning process commonly makes use of digital technologies. The power of AR and VR is pushing education into the realm of experience these days. Students have access to a multitude of knowledge and learning materials, and teachers are increasingly serving as learning facilitators. The curriculum is adapted to the needs of the students. In order to close certain learning gaps and improve comprehension of particular subjects that call for more in-depth learning interventions, educators develop online courses. In addition, the use of enhanced audio-visual effects, 3D visuals, and simulations to maximise learning results has led to the introduction of VR and AR technology.

AR-based media has a lot of potential to improve biology lessons, especially when it comes to studying the anatomy of creatures. A single cell can only be seen from one perspective under the constrained standard microscope vision. On the other hand, three-dimensional visualisation is made possible by augmented reality (AR), which lets learners examine the form of the cell from various perspectives. Beyond the capabilities of the conventional instructional medium, this immersive experience not only offers a thorough grasp of the structure of the cell but also adds pertinent theories and extra information to it. This technology is very useful for Earth and space-related instructional products. Many academic institutions have adopted augmented reality (AR) to improve geography education by tackling the frequently difficult ideas related to these courses. Moving beyond conventional resources like atlases and globes, educators are now excited to lead their students through interactive studies of Earth's features and space. These traditional props are thought to be less relevant in the dynamic educational environment of today since they might be inflexible and unengaging. The introduction of augmented reality (AR) represents a positive development in education by providing a fresh path for quick and effective growth (Fitria, 2023).

Based on the research findings, it appears that one of the areas where augmented reality has been used the most is education. Given that augmented reality is a technology that must be taught before being applied, it was intriguing to discover that education and training are latent in all professions. Furthermore, there were some coincidental advantages of applying AR in education, the majority of which led to a significant increase in learning motivation. With the use of an AR education (AREd) software, students of various academic levels were given 3D resources to use in their coursework. When the knowledge acquired was assessed, it was discovered that AREd increased learning comprehension and speed. However, some of the students found it difficult to adjust to AREd (Pan *et al.,* 2021). Furthermore, a biological microscope for a learning system in medicine was created using AR and VR technologies. VR was utilised to create a comprehensive three-dimensional model, and AR served as the microscope's guiding system, enabling users to transition between VR and AR subsystems. For AREd in open settings, this technique is viewed as a significant accomplishment (Zhou *et al.*, 2020). Additionally, AREd, a smartphone application for UG courses based on ARTutor, was introduced by the 'Institute of Technology of Eastern Macedonia and Thrace'. By including digital content, it made it possible for high school students to read books more enjoyable, as evidenced by the 84% of users who reported satisfied outcomes.

Because the human digestive system is inside, it is challenging to study and difficult to observe directly. The effectiveness of traditional visual aids to illustrate dynamic processes like as heart rate, blood flow, and interactions with other organs in the body is restricted. The application of virtual reality (VR) in the study of biology presents a strong way around these challenges. Students are given an interesting platform for learning about the complexities of the digestive system through the use of virtual reality (VR). This immersive approach not only piques their curiosity but also makes it possible to comprehend the intricate processes involved in digestion in great detail. In the past, schools have aided in the study of the galaxy by arranging field trips to planetariums and observatories, which include models of planets and other celestial bodies in addition to night sky simulations. But this strategy is less effective, particularly during pandemics. Using VR technology in the classroom offers a game-changing alternative that lets learners explore the galaxy from the comfort of their homes. Compared to traditional visual aids found in books or videos, the immersive VR experience that showcases three-dimensional concepts offers a clearer and more interesting comprehension of planets and other celestial objects. Virtual flight simulators are useful for both beginner and seasoned pilots as they let them practise flying without requiring a real aircraft. This not only works well for improving skills, but it also drastically lowers the possibility of accidents. Virtual reality (VR) in particular allows trainees to practise realistic scenarios, including simulated shooting exercises, without using live ammunition, especially for fighter pilot training. VR simulations' immersive quality imitates real-world settings, offering a risk-free and effective training platform for skill development without the expenses and dangers associated with more conventional training approaches (Fitria, 2023).

MOBILE LEARNING ENVIRONMENT

According to Pol´akov´a & Klímov´a (2019) and Criollo-C *et al.* (2022), mobile applications have grown widespread in the field of education for the last few years. According to Huang *et al.* (2019), the proliferation of smartphones and tablets has made it easier for developers to create a wide range of educational applications, from interactive educational games to language learning programs. This pattern emphasises how mobile technology is being used more and more to improve learning across a wide range of subject areas. Numerous advantages come with mobile apps for education: they let students' study at their own pace, boost motivation and engagement levels, and give them anytime, anywhere access to learning resources (Criollo-C *et al.,* 2021). In the opinion of Bernacki *et al.* (2020), the emergence of mobile learning, or m-learning, has drastically changed how education is delivered. M-learning enables students to access learning resources and online courses while on the go, giving them the freedom to acquire knowledge at their own speed and from anywhere (Klimova & Polakova, 2020). This revolutionary method to education breaks down the traditional boundaries of time and place by utilising the widespread use of mobile devices to facilitate learners' seamless engagement with instructional content. Mobile learning has become even more powerful with the advent of VR and AR technology in recent years.

In their work on a theory of learning for the mobile age, Sharples *et al.* (2007) talk about the flexibility and accessibility provided by mobile learning. With the flexibility that mobile learning offers, students can access instructional materials whenever it's convenient for them. It improves accessibility, particularly for people who might have time or location restrictions. M-learning encourages ubiquitous learning, which allows for learning to take place outside of the traditional classroom in a variety of formal and informal environments (Traxler, 2007). MLEs offer individualised learning experiences by adjusting to the interests and requirements of each individual learner. By tailoring the content, mobile learning may adjust to the requirements, interests, and development of every single student. Learning experiences become more effective because of this personalisation. The theories and practices of mobile learning, as well as adaptive learning in the setting of small screens, are covered by Sharples *et al.* (2009). Within MLEs, mobile applications and platforms are essential for delivering interactive features, collaboration tools, and instructional content. With their many features, mobile applications meet a variety of learning demands. A historical review of mobile learning is given by Crompton (2013), who also discusses the contribution of mobile apps to the development of this kind of instruction.

AR APPLICATIONS USED IN EDUCATION

Here are just a few examples of the various augmented reality apps used in education.

1. Google Expeditions: One widely used AR tool that helps with virtual field trips in educational settings is Google Expeditions. It provides students with immersive learning chances to explore a variety of areas, such as science, geography, and history. Research suggests that virtual reality (VR), which is comparable to augmented reality (AR), can improve educational outcomes (Akcayir and Akcayir, 2017).

2. Anatomy 4D: Anatomy 4D is an augmented reality application that lets users explore three-dimensional models of the human anatomy. It helps to visualise anatomical structures and is often used in anatomy instruction. Research has demonstrated that augmented reality (AR) can improve learning results in anatomy instruction. In a study comparing the effectiveness of AR-enhanced learning with standard teaching techniques in anatomy education, for example, Kugelman *et al.* (2018) found that the AR approach raised student engagement and retention to higher levels.

3. ZooBurst: Using an augmented reality (AR) storytelling platform, ZooBurst enables students to create customised pop-up books enhanced with three-dimensional (3D) components. This creative application allows students to create and share interactive stories with digital characters and objects, which develops literacy skills and creativity. Studies highlight the benefits of using digital storytelling in teaching methods. For instance, Robin (2008) found significant improvements in both learning outcomes and student engagement while studying the impact of digital storytelling.

VR APPLICATIONS USED IN EDUCATION

Here are just a few examples of the various virtual reality apps used in education.

1. **Tilt Brush:** One virtual reality (VR) tool that lets users create three-dimensional art in a simulated setting is called Tilt Brush. It provides an extensive selection of brushes, colors, and effects, encouraging experimentation and artistic expression. Research has clarified the benefits of using VR technology to support creativity and artistic expression (Fetzner *et al.,* 2021).
2. **MEL Chemistry VR:** Students can use the MEL Chemistry VR platform to participate in safe and realistic virtual chemistry experiments and simulations. It enhances the learning process by providing practical learning opportunities without the need for actual laboratory equipment. Studies investigating the application of virtual reality chemical simulations suggest that these tools can enhance student learning outcomes and foster curiosity about the subject. For example, a study by Eitel *et al.* (2017) investigated the effects of VR chemical simulations on student understanding and engagement, finding positive effects on both fronts.
3. **VRMath2:** A virtual reality (VR) setup called VRMath2 is designed to help learners learn mathematics in a simulated environment. It helps with mathematical concept exploration and comprehension by offering interactive exercises, simulations, and virtual manipulatives. Research efforts are still underway to determine how well VRMath2 and similar VR-based teaching resources might improve maths learning for students. Positive study results point to positive results in terms of improving students' comprehension and engagement with mathematical subjects in virtual reality settings (Hinojosa & Barreto, 2017).

FUTURE OF VIRTUAL AND AUGMENTED REALITY FOR MOBILE LEARNING

It is expected that VR and AR would be more smoothly integrated into mobile devices. Users will be enabled to access immersive experiences directly through their mobile devices, offering a more accessible and user-friendly interface, thanks to the development of lightweight and powerful VR headsets and AR glasses. The flexibility and accessibility of VR and AR applications can be improved by this integration. As VR and AR applications develop, collaborative learning environments with virtual areas for student interaction may result. Fostering cooperation and communication skills could become commonplace through shared experiences, group projects, and cooperative problem-solving scenarios (Bower *et al.,* 2017).

Enhancing the personalisation of VR and AR learning experiences may be the main emphasis of future improvements. In order to customise information delivery to each learner's needs and learning style, adaptive algorithms and machine learning may be combined to analyse learner behaviours and preferences (Klopfer & Squire, 2008). The continuous advancements in mobile hardware, which are marked by faster processors, better graphics capabilities, and better sensors, are expected to be crucial in raising the level of sophistication and realism of Augmented Reality (AR) and Virtual Reality (VR) experiences on mobile devices. Higher resolutions, quicker refresh rates, and enhanced tracking technologies are among the anticipated advancements that will help to improve the overall quality of immersive entertainment. With their increasingly potent processors and sophisticated sensors, mobile hardware is evolving, which could result in the creation of sophisticated VR and AR apps for mobile devices. The observations made by Mc Graw & Westerman (2017) highlighted the possibility of revolutionary developments as mobile hardware develops further, bringing in a new era of immersive experiences.

Learning experiences that are more intelligent and responsive could arise from the combination of AI technology with VR and AR. Artificial intelligence systems possess the ability to evaluate user interactions, offer instantaneous feedback, and dynamically modify the content according to each learner's progress and output (Gupta *et al.*, 2024). The intelligence and responsiveness of VR and AR applications in mobile learning may be improved through integration with AI. AI algorithms are able to assess user interactions, offer adaptive feedback, and tailor information according to the progress of learners (Johnson *et al.*, 2018). Robust evaluation tools and analytics are integrated with Virtual Reality (VR) and Augmented Reality (AR) applications in mobile learning, going beyond simple content distribution. These technologies allow teachers to keep an eye on students' development and gain insightful knowledge about how they are performing. This data-driven method helps to assess the efficacy of immersive learning experiences in addition to providing guidance for instructional design. In VR and AR applications for mobile learning, Johnson *et al.* (2015) emphasise the need of integrating assessment tools and analytics, stressing their role in improving the whole educational experience by providing a thorough understanding of learner engagement and achievement.

Technology advancements and economies of scale are expected to drive down the overall price of AR and VR equipment. These technologies may become more affordable for educational institutions, even those with tight budgets, as a result of this decline in cost. As a result, the possibility of democratising access to immersive learning opportunities exists. Bacca *et al.* (2014) draw attention to how technical advancements may affect how affordable VR and AR solutions become, opening the door to more widespread accessibility and use in educational contexts.

The growing usage of VR and AR in sector of education is probably going to lead to a greater emphasis on the creation of ethical standards and norms. In order to guarantee inclusive and equitable learning experiences, this imperative entails addressing a number of issues, such as privacy concerns, encouraging the responsible use of immersive technology, and developing best practices. The necessity for ethical frameworks grows as these technologies become more integrated into educational contexts. These entails managing concerns like safety, privacy, and responsible use, highlighting the significance of developing an ethical basis for the incorporation of VR and AR in education.

FUTURISTIC ROLE OF VR AND AR TECHNOLOGIES IN EDUCATION

With the help of immersive simulations as well as opportunities offered by virtual reality AR VR, students can explore historical moments, visit remote regions, or conduct scientific investigations in a virtual environment. Because VR and AR reflect real-world situations, they can produce immersive learning environments (Deterding *et al.*, 2011). Virtual reality (VR) technology also makes virtual laboratories possible, enabling students to perform experiments in subjects such as biology and chemistry without having to search for real materials. This creates a controlled and secure learning environment (Papastergiou, 2009). Augmented reality (AR) can improve traditional textbooks and provide a more dynamic and engaging learning environment by adding 3D models or other information. This visual enhancement makes complex ideas easier for pupils to understand, which increases learning interaction (Akçayır & Akçayır, 2017). Furthermore, technologies such as AR and VR can adjust to various learning styles and advancements, providing a personalised learning environment. This adaptability ensures that the curriculum is tailored to the individual requirements and tastes of the students (Johnson *et al.*, 2015). With virtual reality (VR), students may take virtual field trips and fully immerse themselves in different cultures, historical sites, or natural environments without ever having to leave the classroom. By raising engagement, this immersive experience improves learning. Additionally, VR is especially useful for training and skill development, especially in the healthcare industry. Before working with actual patients, medical students can improve their practical abilities by polishing their surgical methods in a virtual environment (Rosen, J. *et al.,* 2019). Gamification components can be incorporated into the learning process using VR and AR. Education becomes more engaging when game-like elements are added, which motivates students to actively participate in their education (Deterding *et al.*, 2011). VR can be utilized as a platform to simulate physical activities and sports training, providing students with a safe and controlled environment to hone their physical talents (Pombo *et al.,* 2019). Virtual reality (VR) can be customised for special education, offering students with disabilities individualised experiences. It can more successfully meet each person's demands and provide opportunities for multisensory learning (Kizilcec *et al.*, 2017).

REFERENCES

Akçayır, M., & Akçayır, G. (2017). Advantages and challenges associated with augmented reality for education: A systematic review of the literature. *Educational Research Review*, *20*, 1–11. doi:10.1016/j.edurev.2016.11.002

Al-Azawi, R. (2018, April). Embedding augmented and virtual reality in educational learning method: present and future. In *2018 9th International Conference on Information and Communication Systems (ICICS)* (pp. 218-222). IEEE. 10.1109/IACS.2018.8355470

Alalwan, N., Cheng, L., Al-Samarraie, H., Yousef, R., Alzahrani, A. I., & Sarsam, S. M. (2020). Challenges and prospects of virtual reality and augmented reality utilization among primary school teachers: A developing country perspective. *Studies in Educational Evaluation*, *66*, 100876. doi:10.1016/j.stueduc.2020.100876

Bacca Acosta, J. L., Baldiris Navarro, S. M., Fabregat Gesa, R., & Graf, S. (2014). Augmented reality trends in education: A systematic review of research and applications. *Journal of Educational Technology & Society*, *17*(4), 133–149.

Beck, D. (2019). Augmented and virtual reality in education: Immersive learning research. *Journal of Educational Computing Research*, *57*(7), 1619–1625. doi:10.1177/0735633119854035

Becker, H. J. (1994). How exemplary computer-using teachers differ from other teachers: Implications for realizing the potential of computers in schools. *Journal of Research on Computing in Education*, *26*(3), 291–321. doi:10.1080/08886504.1994.10782093

Bernacki, M. L., Greene, J. A., & Crompton, H. (2020). Mobile technology, learning, and achievement: Advances in understanding and measuring the role of mobile technology in education. *Contemporary Educational Psychology*, *60*, 101827. doi:10.1016/j.cedpsych.2019.101827

Biswas, P., Orero, P., Swaminathan, M., Krishnaswamy, K., & Robinson, P. (2021, May). Adaptive accessible AR/VR systems. In *Extended Abstracts of the 2021 CHI Conference on Human Factors in Computing Systems* (pp. 1-7). Academic Press.

Bower, M., Howe, C., McCredie, N., Robinson, A., & Grover, D. (2014). Augmented Reality in education–cases, places and potentials. *Educational Media International*, *51*(1), 1–15. doi:10.1080/09523987.2014.889400

Chen, P., Liu, X., Cheng, W., & Huang, R. (2017). A review of using Augmented Reality in Education from 2011 to 2016. *Innovations in smart learning*, 13-18.

Childs, E., Mohammad, F., Stevens, L., Burbelo, H., Awoke, A., Rewkowski, N., & Manocha, D. (2021). An overview of enhancing distance learning through augmented and virtual reality technologies. arXiv preprint arXiv:2101.11000.

Cilliers, E. J. (2017). The challenge of teaching generation Z. PEOPLE. *The International Journal of Social Sciences (Islamabad)*.

Criollo-C, S., Altamirano-Suarez, E., Jaramillo-Villacís, L., Vidal-Pacheco, K., Guerrero-Arias, A., & Luján-Mora, S. (2022). Sustainable teaching and learning through a mobile application: A case study. *Sustainability (Basel)*, *14*(11), 6663. doi:10.3390/su14116663

Criollo-C, S., Guerrero-Arias, A., Jaramillo-Alc'azar, ´. A., & Luj'an-Mora, S. (2021). Mobile learning technologies for education: Benefits and pending issues. *Applied Sciences (Basel, Switzerland)*, *11*(9), 4111. doi:10.3390/app11094111

Crompton, H. (2013). A historical overview of m-learning: Toward learner-centered education. In *Handbook of mobile learning* (pp. 3–14). Routledge.

Cuban, L. (1986). *Teachers and machines: The classroom use of technology since 1920*. Teachers college press.

da Cruz, F. C., Stefenon, S. F., Furtado, R. G., Dela Rocca, G. A., & Silva Ferreira, F. C. (2018). Financial feasibility study for radio installation link on the mobile telephone network. *Revista Geintec-Gestao Inovacao E Tecnologias*, *8*(3), 4447-4460.

da Silva, L. M., Dias, L. P., Barbosa, J. L., Rigo, S. J., dos Anjos, J., Geyer, C. F., & Leithardt, V. R. (2022). Learning analytics and collaborative groups of learners in distance education: A systematic mapping study. *Informatics in Education*, *21*(1), 113–146.

Duan, G., Han, M., Zhao, W., Dong, T., & Xu, T. (2018). Augmented reality technology and its game application research. *2018 3rd Int. Conf. Autom. Mech. Control Comput. Eng.*, 701–705.

Eitel, A., Krey, O., Sodian, B., & Dörfler, T. (2017). Learning from virtual agents: Empowering students for science learning by coupling them with virtual characters. *Computers & Education*, *106*, 46–58.

Ennis, R. H. (1987). *A taxonomy of critical thinking dispositions and abilities*. Academic Press.

Fetzner, M., Hirt, E. R., & Bläsi, B. (2021). Learning to create in immersive virtual reality: Effectiveness of a VR drawing intervention in supporting creativity and spatial skills. *Educational Technology Research and Development*, *69*(1), 75–96.

Fitria, T. N. (2023). Augmented Reality (AR) and Virtual Reality (VR) Technology in Education: Media of Teaching and Learning: A Review. *International Journal of Computer and Information System*, *4*(1), 14–25.

Fredricks, J. A., Blumenfeld, P. C., & Paris, A. H. (2004). School engagement: Potential of the concept, state of the evidence. *Review of Educational Research*, *74*(1), 59–109. doi:10.3102/00346543074001059

Frizzo Stefenon, S., Kasburg, C., Nied, A., Rodrigues Klaar, A. C., Silva Ferreira, F. C., & Waldrigues Branco, N. (2020). Hybrid deep learning for power generation forecasting in active solar trackers. *IET Generation, Transmission & Distribution*, *14*(23), 5667–5674. doi:10.1049/iet-gtd.2020.0814

Gilchrist, A. (2016). *Industry 4.0: the industrial internet of things*. Apress. doi:10.1007/978-1-4842-2047-4

Gudoniene, D., & Rutkauskiene, D. (2019). Virtual and augmented reality in education. *Baltic Journal of Modern Computing*, *7*(2), 293–300. doi:10.22364/bjmc.2019.7.2.07

Gupta, S., Sharma, P., Chaudhary, S., Kumar, V., Singh, S. P., Lourens, M., & Beri, N. (2024). Study on the Beneficial Impacts and Ethical Dimensions of Generative AI in Software Product Management. *International Journal of Intelligent Systems and Applications in Engineering*, *12*(8s), 251–264.

Hantono, B. S., Nugroho, L. E., & Santosa, P. I. (2018, July). Meta-review of augmented reality in education. In *2018 10th international conference on information technology and electrical engineering (ICITEE)* (pp. 312-315). IEEE. 10.1109/ICITEED.2018.8534888

Hinojosa, J., & Barreto, E. (2017). Virtual reality in mathematics education: A study on the effects of immersive VR on students' mathematical achievement and spatial ability. In *Proceedings of the 49th Annual Southeast Regional Conference* (pp. 273-278). ACM. https://doi.org/10.1145/3077286.3077330

Huang, K. T., Ball, C., Francis, J., Ratan, R., Boumis, J., & Fordham, J. (2019). Augmented versus virtual reality in education: An exploratory study examining science knowledge retention when using augmented reality/virtual reality mobile applications. *Cyberpsychology, Behavior, and Social Networking*, *22*(2), 105–110. doi:10.1089/cyber.2018.0150 PMID:30657334

Javornik, A. (2016). Augmented reality: Research agenda for studying the impact of its media characteristics on consumer behaviour. *Journal of Retailing and Consumer Services*, *30*, 252–261. doi:10.1016/j.jretconser.2016.02.004

Johnson, L., Adams Becker, S., Cummins, M., Estrada, V., Freeman, A., & Ludgate, H. (2018). *NMC/CoSN Horizon Report: 2018 Higher Education Edition*. The New Media Consortium.

Johnson, L., Adams Becker, S., Estrada, V., & Freeman, A. (2015). *NMC/CoSN Horizon Report: 2015 K-* (12th ed.). The New Media Consortium.

Kagan, S., & Kagan, M. (1994). Cooperative Learning. Academic Press.

Kim, C., Yoon, H. C., Kim, D. H., & Do, Y. R. (2018). Spectroscopic influence of virtual reality and augmented reality display devices on the human nonvisual characteristics and melatonin suppression response. *IEEE Photonics Journal*, *10*(4), 1–11. doi:10.1109/JPHOT.2021.3107852

Klimova, B., & Polakova, P. (2020). Students' perceptions of an EFL vocabulary learning mobile application. *Education Sciences*, *10*(2), 37. doi:10.3390/educsci10020037

Klopfer, E., & Squire, K. (2008). Environmental Detectives—The development of an augmented reality platform for environmental simulations. *Educational Technology Research and Development*, *56*(2), 203–228. doi:10.1007/s11423-007-9037-6

Koretz, D. M. (2008). *Measuring up*. Harvard University Press. doi:10.4159/9780674039728

Krüger, J. M., Buchholz, A., & Bodemer, D. (2019, December). Augmented reality in education: three unique characteristics from a user's perspective. In Proc. 27th Int. Conf. on Comput. in Educ (pp. 412-422). Academic Press.

Kugelman, A., Shaoul, J., Ben-Ami, R., Shoenfeld, Y., & Wientroub, S. (2018). Use of augmented reality technology in orthopedic surgery. *Acta Orthopaedica*, *89*(5), 503–507. PMID:29790397

Kumar, P. P., Thallapalli, R., Akshay, R., Sai, K. S., Sai, K. S., & Srujan, G. S. (2022, May). State-of-the-Art: Implementation of Augmented Reality and Virtual Reality with the Integration of 5G in the Classroom. In AIP Conference Proceedings (Vol. 2418, No. 1). AIP Publishing.

Kumar, V., Sharma, D., & Chauhan, S. (2023). Role of Customer Experience-Driven Business Innovation Framework for the Modern Enterprises. In Innovation, Strategy, and Transformation Frameworks for the Modern Enterprise (pp. 310-326). IGI Global. doi:10.4018/979-8-3693-0458-7.ch013

McGraw, K. L., & Westerman, D. L. (2017). Innovations in Augmented Reality: Pedagogical Shifts for Mobile Learning. *TechTrends*, *61*(1), 5–12.

Mendes, A. S., Silva, L. A., Blas, H. S. S., de La Iglesia, D. H., Encinas, F. G., Leithardt, V. R. Q., & González, G. V. (2021). Physical movement helps learning: teaching using tracking objects with depth camera. In Trends and Applications in Information Systems and Technologies: Volume 4 9 (pp. 183-193). Springer International Publishing. doi:10.1007/978-3-030-72654-6_18

Nguyen, V. T., Jung, K., & Dang, T. (2019, December). Creating virtual reality and augmented reality development in classroom: Is it a hype? In *2019 IEEE International Conference on Artificial Intelligence and Virtual Reality (AIVR)* (pp. 212-2125). IEEE. 10.1109/AIVR46125.2019.00045

Ninno Muniz, R., Frizzo Stefenon, S., Gouvêa Buratto, W., Nied, A., Meyer, L. H., Finardi, E. C., & Ramati Pereira da Rocha, B. (2020). Tools for measuring energy sustainability: A comparative review. *Energies, 13*(9), 2366. doi:10.3390/en13092366

Oberdörfer, S., Birnstiel, S., Latoschik, M. E., & Grafe, S. (2021, June). Mutual benefits: Interdisciplinary education of pre-service teachers and hci students in vr/ar learning environment design. *Frontiers in Education, 6*, 693012. doi:10.3389/feduc.2021.693012

Pan, X., Zheng, M., Xu, X., & Campbell, A. G. (2021). Knowing your student: Targeted teaching decision support through asymmetric mixed reality collaborative learning. *IEEE Access : Practical Innovations, Open Solutions, 9*, 164742–164751. doi:10.1109/ACCESS.2021.3134589

Phakamach, P., Senarith, P., & Wachirawongpaisarn, S. (2022). The metaverse in education: The future of immersive teaching & learning. *RICE Journal of Creative Entrepreneurship and Management, 3*(2), 75–88.

Poláková, P., & Klímová, B. (2019). Mobile technology and Generation Z in the English language classroom—A preliminary study. *Education Sciences, 9*(3), 203. doi:10.3390/educsci9030203

Raja, M., & Lakshmi Priya, G. G. (2022). Using virtual reality and augmented reality with ICT tools for enhancing quality in the changing academic environment in COVID-19 pandemic: An empirical study. In *InTechnologies, artificial Intelligence and the Future of learning post-COVID-19* (pp. 467–482). Springer. doi:10.1007/978-3-030-93921-2_26

Robin, B. R. (2008). Digital storytelling: A powerful technology tool for the 21st century classroom. *Theory into Practice, 47*(3), 220–228. doi:10.1080/00405840802153916

Scavarelli, A., Arya, A., & Teather, R. J. (2019). Circles: exploring multi-platform accessible, socially scalable VR in the classroom. In 2019 IEEE Games, Entertainment, Media Conference (GEM) (pp. 1-4). IEEE. 10.1109/GEM.2019.8897532

Scavarelli, A., Arya, A., & Teather, R. J. (2021). Virtual reality and augmented reality in social learning spaces: A literature review. *Virtual Reality (Waltham Cross)*, *25*(1), 257–277. doi:10.1007/s10055-020-00444-8

Seidametova, Z. S., Abduramanov, Z. S., & Seydametov, G. S. (2021, July). Using augmented reality for architecture artifacts visualizations. *CEUR Workshop Proceedings*.

Sharples, M., Arnedillo-Sánchez, I., Milrad, M., & Vavoula, G. (2009). Mobile learning. Small Screens, Big Ideas: Theories and Applications of Mobile Learning. Academic Press.

Sharples, M., Taylor, J., & Vavoula, G. (2007). A theory of learning for the mobile age. In The Sage Handbook of E-learning Research (pp. 221-247). Sage Publications.

Sirin, S. R. (2005). Socioeconomic status and academic achievement: A meta-analytic review of research. *Review of Educational Research*, *75*(3), 417–453. doi:10.3102/00346543075003417

Stefenon, S. F., Bruns, R., Sartori, A., Meyer, L. H., Ovejero, R. G., & Leithardt, V. R. Q. (2022b). Analysis of the ultrasonic signal in polymeric contaminated insulators through ensemble learning methods. *IEEE Access : Practical Innovations, Open Solutions*, *10*, 33980–33991. doi:10.1109/ACCESS.2022.3161506

Stefenon, S. F., Ribeiro, M. H. D. M., Nied, A., Mariani, V. C., Coelho, L. D. S., Leithardt, V. R. Q., & Seman, L. O. (2021). Hybrid wavelet stacking ensemble model for insulators contamination forecasting. *IEEE Access : Practical Innovations, Open Solutions*, *9*, 66387–66397. doi:10.1109/ACCESS.2021.3076410

Stefenon, S. F., Ribeiro, M. H. D. M., Nied, A., Yow, K. C., Mariani, V. C., dos Santos Coelho, L., & Seman, L. O. (2022d). Time series forecasting using ensemble learning methods for emergency prevention in hydroelectric power plants with dam. *Electric Power Systems Research*, *202*, 107584. doi:10.1016/j.epsr.2021.107584

Stefenon, S. F., Seman, L. O., Neto, N. F. S., Meyer, L. H., Nied, A., & Yow, K. C. (2022). Echo state network applied for classification of medium voltage insulators. *International Journal of Electrical Power & Energy Systems*, *134*, 107336. doi:10.1016/j.ijepes.2021.107336

Stefenon, S. F., Singh, G., Yow, K. C., & Cimatti, A. (2022c). Semi-ProtoPNet deep neural network for the classification of defective power grid distribution structures. *Sensors (Basel)*, *22*(13), 4859. doi:10.3390/s22134859 PMID:35808353

Sun, J. C. Y., Ye, S. L., Yu, S. J., & Chiu, T. K. (2023). Effects of Wearable Hybrid AR/VR Learning Material on High School Students' Situational Interest, Engagement, and Learning Performance: The Case of a Physics Laboratory Learning Environment. *Journal of Science Education and Technology*, *32*(1), 1–12. doi:10.1007/s10956-022-10001-4

Tan, Y., Xu, W., Li, S., & Chen, K. (2022). Augmented and Virtual Reality (AR/VR) for Education and Training in the AEC Industry: A Systematic Review of Research and Applications. *Buildings*, *12*(10), 1529. doi:10.3390/buildings12101529

Tomlinson, C. A. (2001). *How to differentiate instruction in mixed-ability classrooms*. Ascd.

Traxler, J. (2007). Defining, discussing, and evaluating mobile learning: The moving finger writes and having writ..... *International Review of Research in Open and Distance Learning*, *8*(2), 1–12. doi:10.19173/irrodl.v8i2.346

Trilling, B., & Fadel, C. (2012). *21st century skills: Learning for life in our times*. John Wiley & Sons.

Vieira, J. C., Sartori, A., Stefenon, S. F., Perez, F. L., De Jesus, G. S., & Leithardt, V. R. Q. (2022). Low-cost CNN for automatic violence recognition on embedded system. *IEEE Access : Practical Innovations, Open Solutions*, *10*, 25190–25202. doi:10.1109/ACCESS.2022.3155123

Young, G. W., Stehle, S., Walsh, B. Y., & Tiri, E. (2020). Exploring virtual reality in the higher education classroom: Using VR to build knowledge and understanding. *Journal of Universal Computer Science*, *26*(8), 904–928. doi:10.3897/jucs.2020.049

Zhai, X., Chu, X., Chai, C. S., Jong, M. S. Y., Istenic, A., Spector, M., & Li, Y. (2021). A Review of Artificial Intelligence (AI) in Education from 2010 to 2020. *Complexity*, *2021*, 1–18. doi:10.1155/2021/8812542

Zhou, X., Tang, L., Lin, D., & Han, W. (2020). Virtual & augmented reality for biological microscope in experiment education. *Virtual Reality & Intelligent Hardware*, *2*(4), 316–329. doi:10.1016/j.vrih.2020.07.004

ADDITIONAL READING

Dunleavy, M., Dede, C., & Mitchell, R. (2009). Affordances and limitations of immersive participatory augmented reality simulations for teaching and learning. *Journal of Science Education and Technology*, *18*(1), 7–22. doi:10.1007/s10956-008-9119-1

Lytridis, C., & Tsinakos, A. (2018). Evaluation of the ARTutor augmented reality educational platform in tertiary education. *Smart Learning Environments*, *5*(1), 1–15. doi:10.1186/s40561-018-0058-x

Milgram, P., & Kishino, F. (1994). A taxonomy of mixed reality visual displays. *IEICE Transactions on Information and Systems*, *77*(12), 1321–1329.

Mystakidis, S., Fragkaki, M., & Filippousis, G. (2021). Ready teacher one: Virtual and augmented reality online professional development for K-12 school teachers. *Computers*, *10*(10), 134. doi:10.3390/computers10100134

Velev, D., & Zlateva, P. (2017). Virtual reality challenges in education and training. *International Journal of Learning and Teaching*, *3*(1), 33–37. doi:10.18178/ijlt.3.1.33-37

KEY TERMS AND DEFINITIONS

Artificial Intelligence (AI): AI is the branch of technology that develops intelligent machines for carrying out tasks that traditionally require human intelligence.

Augmented Reality: It refers to a technology that projects digital data like pictures, movies, or three-dimensional models in form of real environment. It is usually seen with a smartphone, tablet, or AR headset.

Education: The process of gaining knowledge, skills, values, beliefs, and habits through organized instruction, hands-on activities, and interactions is referred to as education.

Immersive Learning: It is a teaching strategy that involves completely engrossing students in a virtual or interactive setting, frequently with the aid of technology.

Mobile Environment: The digital ecology and infrastructure that surround mobile devices, such as smartphones, tablets, and wearable technology, is referred to as the mobile environment.

Technology: It refers to the practical application of scientific knowledge, instruments, and methods, especially in business, industry, education, and other domains.

Virtual Reality: It is a technology in which users may interact with and experience three-dimensional (3D) digital environments as though they were actually there. VR immerses users in a simulated, computer-generated environment.

Chapter 8
Influence of Virtual Reality as a Tool to Revolutionize Industry Education

Tanushree Thakur
Chitkara University, India

Shraddha Bhatia
Chitkara University, India

Gurpreet Kaur
Manav Rachna University, India

ABSTRACT

Virtual reality (VR) improves learning and ensures the engagement of students in grabbing effective and efficient knowledge and skills. A real and imaginary world is created, which helps a student to understand what is being taught by interacting with a virtual world. VR helps students to experience destinations from across the world without having to leave the classroom. Even though virtual reality has provided new teaching and learning models to meet the requirements of the learners in 21st century, it's not fully implemented. Therefore, the present study aims to review the literature pertaining to the application of virtual reality in the educational industry. Further, the study recommends ways to bring about revolution in the education industry by re-establishing new advanced education techniques which will help the students in gaining better understanding of concepts.

DOI: 10.4018/979-8-3693-3015-9.ch008

Copyright © 2024, IGI Global. Copying or distributing in print or electronic forms without written permission of IGI Global is prohibited.

INTRODUCTION

Virtual Reality (VR) is a computer-generated environment with scenes and objects that appear to be real, making the user feel they are submerged in their surroundings. Virtual Reality (VR) has emerged as a transformative technology that has the potential to revolutionize many industries, including education. The use of VR in industry education can enhance learning experiences by providing learners with immersive and realistic simulations that allow them to experience real-world scenarios in a safe environment. Augmented reality (AR) is a technology that overlays digital information on the real-world environment. This technology has recently gained attention in the education industry, as it provides students with a unique and engaging way to interact with the learning material. AR has become an increasingly popular tool in the industry education, as it enhances the learning experience by providing a more interactive and practical approach.

While both virtual reality and augmented reality are planned to bring a imitate environment to the user and each of its concept is unique and involves different using mechanism.

In this paper, we will explore the influence of VR and AR as a tool to revolutionize industry education. We will examine how VR and AR technology can be used to enhance traditional teaching methods, improve retention rates, and provide students with practical skills that are essential in the industry. In this paper will explore the influence of virtual reality and augmented reality as a tool to revolutionize industry education. We will discuss the benefits of using VR and AR in education, its impact on learner engagement, and the potential applications of VR and AR in various industries.

OBJECTIVE

The objective of this article is to explore the potential of virtual reality (VR) as a tool to revolutionize industry education. The study aims to review how VR is proving itself as a new stepping stone in education, also it describes how VR and AR technologies is used to strengthen teaching and learning. The study aims to understand how virtual reality can improve education by providing students with impressive and mesmerizing experiences that would otherwise not be possible and it enables users to explore and interact with a virtual surrounding in a way that approximates reality, as it is perceived through the users' senses. It helps to explore how virtual reality improves teamwork and social skills through creating exciting, collaborative learning environments. Ultimately, this article aims to showcase the transformative power of VR in the field of industry education and its potential to shape the future of work.

METHOD

Paszkiewicz et al (2021), researched on expansion and application of adequate courses with the help of comprehensive methodology, including the design, creation, implementation and evaluation of individual courses in the VR environment which might help to lower the costs and increase the safety and efficiency of employees' performed activities and with this they tried to create customized and specialized virtual environments which might focus on the specific needs of individual industries.

Khan, Rabbani (2021), in India, were engrossed in learning from pandemic situation and develop a learning and teaching model for the future generation by focusing on artificial intelligence and cloud-based computing services is the future and as quickly as it is accepted in the education sector, it will be more beneficial for the next generation.

Raja, Priya (2021), in India, with the help of PowerPoint presentations, videos and animations, the research highlighted the core concepts, the creation of the technology, its impact, associated problems, and future directions of VR concerning education and the methods considered by infamous researchers which helped to overcome the identified gaps.

Hamzah, Ambiyar, et al, (2021), in Indonesia, studied how to build AR-based applications in learning computer network devices in order to increase understanding, generate motivation and student interest; also, how the application of augmented reality recognizes computer network devices that are capable of realizing the virtual world to the real world.

Kaplan et al (2020), in Florida, USA, tried to give a systematic review and explore the presently available findings on transfer of training from virtual (VR), augmented (AR), and mixed reality (MR) and determine whether will it make such a great reality (XR)-based on training is as effective as traditional training methods.

Moreno et al (2020), in Spain studied about the utility of technologies highlighted by the existence of specific apps for physical activity which can be used inside and outside the classroom to know the physical condition, as well as through the potential that virtual and augmented reality can have in such assessment.

Vasilevski, Birt (2020), the study focused on expanding existing course, learning outcomes for professional skill development in real-world environments, by engaging in strategic and analytic thinking capabilities using situated authentic learning, self-analysis and reflective learning skills combined with emerging professional practices

VR and AR; also it explained the combination of mapping of the environment and display of 3D virtual content tie up in space and time.

Scavarelli, Arya et all (2020), in London, the study laid a foundation to explore properties and interactions, with the help of constructivism, social cognitive theory, connectivism, and activity theory relevant to educational use in social learning spaces; further to study how virtual reality/augmented reality which helped in building a theoretical foundation for future educational frameworks.

Philippe, Souchet, et al, (2020), in United Kingdom, highlighted the application of multimodal VR-based teaching and training as a pedagogically rich strategy that may be designed, mapped and visualized through distinct VR-design elements and features by explaining the design and usage of VR for multimodal teaching, learning and training.

Iatsyshyn, Lyubchak et al (2020), in Ukraine, the objectivity of the research was to know the application of augmented reality in educational projects which would help to increase students' interest for educational material by overcoming difficulties with AR technologies application in educational institutions.

Souchet et al. (2020), in Paris, the research focused in finding how digital learning is outlined, mainly when it is in work with highly interactive and immersive learning environments such as Virtual Reality (VR) by explaining the connection between VR learning and multimodality and the instruction concepts related to it.

Kovach, Romanenko, et al, (in 2020), in Ukraine, researched a study to understand main benefits that educational institutions would receive from introduction of augmented reality technology are highlighted, the study focused on application of augmented reality technologies in education would contribute to these technologies development and therefore need increase for specialists in the augmented reality; growth of students' professional level due to application of augmented reality technologies is proved.

Elmqaddem (2019), observed the work which consists of the reasons behind the successful rise of AR and VR and how its adoption in education will be a reality in a near future.

Uppot, Laguna et al., (2019) in California researched about clinical utility of both AR and VR in patient education and perioperative planning is becoming more promising day by day.

Demitriadou, Stavroulia et al., (2019), the research focused the implementation of new technologies in education of virtual and augmented reality which helps to improve interactivity and student interest in mathematics education, contributing to more efficient learning and understanding of mathematical concepts when compared to traditional teaching methods. The research explained the usage of AR and VR applications which provides higher impact on student's learning and understanding of mathematical concepts compared to traditional teaching approaches.

Buchholza, Bodemer et al., (2019), focused on experience provided by AR/VR in the real world. Secondly, it includes the possibilities to interact with AR through the influencing both real objects and virtual properties. At the end, the research concludes how VR/AR is efficiently useful for providing several opportunities by increasing: - student engagement, providing constructivist, genuine experiences to impact student identity, etc.

Huang, Francis et al (2019), studied about the gap in the literature by comparing AR and VR technologies regarding their impact on learning outcomes, such as retention of science information. The study determined how AR and VR have their own set of strengths and weaknesses which can be considered while combining these technologies into learning environments.

Haus, Ludovico, et al (2019), in Italy, studied how to deal with the adoption of 5G technologies in educational field, is focusing on activities based on Augmented Reality (AR) and Virtual Reality (VR), which helped in opening new perspectives in the deployment of innovative educational scenarios.

Sallah, et al., (2019), in Saudi Arabia, the study concentrated on various steps which can be useful for students to anticipate the RMS design, interact with it, understand its operation, and evaluate its performance by focusing on effectiveness of the VR-based teaching methodology.

Liagkoua, & Sallmasa et al (2019), in Greece, researched about the aspects of VR technology and limitations for supporting the VR developers for creating VR industrial environment that produce reliable/feasible simulations of the machines. The research proved that Virtual Reality helps to decrease design and production costs, maintain product quality and overcome several technical tradeoffs like reducing rendering, complexity or increasing resolution while providing a stable VR experience.

Kiryakova et al., (2018), in Bulgaria, found out how the smart technologies has made learning interactive; also, how knowledge and skills are more effective and learning experience is improving when learners are vigorously engaged in the learning process.

Drigas et al (2018), studied the challenges in front of the adoption of virtual reality on educational practices, VR/AR applications do comes up with an effective tool to enhance learning and memory of students.

Alltinpulluk (2018), in Turkey, focused on present examples about how the utility of virtual reality lead to new chances that support effective and efficient learning through data collection tools, tables and graphics and in the end concluded how AR/VR is closely related to disciplines such as human-computer interaction, robotics and remote laboratory systems etc.

Kiryakova, et al., (2018), the focus of the research was to create an environment where the training is consistent with the needs and characteristics of digital learners and present-day society, by determining that the technology offers an innovative way of learning which helps transform education into smart education.

Elliot Hu-Au and Joey J. Lee (2017), examined how VR is useful in providing several chances by increasing: - student engagement, providing constructivist, genuine experiences to impact student identity.

Elliot Hu-Au and Joey J. Lee (2017), the study mainly focused on present examples of how the supply of virtual reality lead to new opportunities that support learners, by concluding that concludes that VR is especially useful for providing several opportunities: increase in student engagement; providing humanistic, authentic experiences to impact student identity; allowing for new outlook taking and empathy; and supporting creativity and the ability to visualize difficult models.

Kesim, Ozarslan (2016), in Turkey, the research concentrated in providing an introduction about technology of augmented reality (AR) and its possibilities in education sector which aimed to achieve realistic solutions we need to design and coordinate multi-disciplinary research project to enhance content and environment.

Pantelidis (2010), research focused on the pros and cons of using virtual reality are presented, as well as suggestions on when to use and when not to use virtual reality. This study played a part in the continuing search for ways to use virtual reality in education and training courses.

Wentz et al (2009), focused that how virtual reality and augmented reality technologies can be used to strengthen teaching; also, how a student and teacher can join hands together to open doors to new chances and opportunities in the digital age.

Billinghurst (2002), the research focused enveloping Virtual Reality, AR interfaces, which allow users to see the real world at the same time as virtual representation attached to real locations and objects; it determines different other computing technologies about how AR interfaces offer absolute interaction between the real and virtual worlds, a tangible interface metaphor and a means for transitioning between real and virtual worlds.

Allessandro (2001), in Italy, researched about the pros and cons of using the technology of VR in the classrooms and in the end, he concluded that the student's engagement and focus have now started increasing with the use of virtual reality technology.

RESEARCH GAP

In VR-based courses, it is just learners and software, and this can deteriorate the relationship between students and instructors. The lack of flexibility in VR-based classrooms can be a disadvantage for students, as education is not a fixed activity, and each student learns at a different pace. Some of the key issues in implementing clinical VR research include theoretical immaturity, a lack of technical standards, the problems of separating effects of media versus medium, practical in vivo issues, and costs. This may especially affect low-income sections of the population and vulnerable groups who prefer virtual experiences to those of the real world. One of the main disadvantages is the health risks associated with using VR headsets. These headsets can cause eye problems, such as eyestrain, headaches, and nausea. They can also cause motion sickness because they can make users feel like they are moving when they are not.

Figure 1. Top 5 cited papers

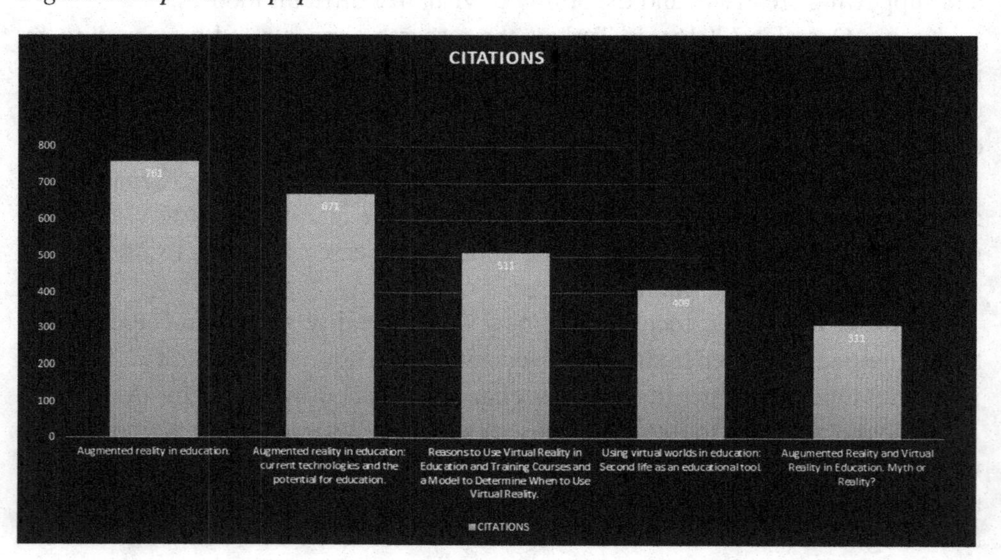

Table 1.

TITLE	CITATIONS
Augmented Reality in Education	761
Augmented reality in education: current technologies and the potential for education.	671
Reasons to Use Virtual Reality in Education and Training Courses and a Model to Determine When to Use Virtual Reality.	511
Using virtual worlds in education: Second Life as an educational tool.	409
Augmented reality and Virtual reality in Education. Myth or Reality?	311

Table 2.

YEAR OF PUBLICATION	AUTHOR NAMES	TITLE OF PAPER	JOURNAL NAME
2021	Andrzej Paszkiewicz, Mateusz Salach, Pawe Dymora, Marek Bolanowski, Grzegorz Budzikand Przemysław KubiaK	Methodology of Implementing Virtual Reality in Education for Industry.	Sustainability
2021	Shahnawaz Khan, Mustafa Raza Rabbani	Corona virus pandemic paving ways to next generation of learning and teaching: futuristic cloud based educational model.	
2021	M. Raja, G.G. Lakshmi Priya	Conceptual Origins, Technological Advancements, and Impacts of Using Virtual Reality Technology in Education.	Webology
2021	Muhammad Luthfi Hamzah, Ambiyar, Fahmi Rizal, Wakhinuddin Simatupang, Dedy Irfan, Refdinal	Development of Augmented Reality Application for Learning Computer Network Device.	Development of Augmented Reality Application for Learning Computer Network Device.
2020	Alexandra D. Kaplan, Jessica Cruit, P. A. Hancock	The Effects of Virtual Reality, Augmented Reality, and Mixed Reality as Training Enhancement Methods: A Meta-Analysis.	Human Factors
2020	Ferran Calabuig-Moreno, María Huertas González-Serrano, Javier Fombona and Marta García-Tascón	The emergence of technology in physical education: A general bibliometric analysis with a focus on virtual and augmented reality.	Sustainability
2020	N Vasilevski, J Birt	Analysing construction student experiences of mobile mixed reality enhanced learning in virtual and augmented reality environments	Research in Learning Technology
2020	Anthony Scavarelli, Ali Arya & Robert J. Teather	Virtual reality and augmented reality in social learning spaces: a literature review	Immersive Learning Environments
2020	Anna V. Iatsyshyn,Volodymyr O. Lyubchak,Yurii O. Zuban	Application of augmented reality technologies for education projects preparation.	Digital transformation of learning

Table 2 continued

YEAR OF PUBLICATION	AUTHOR NAMES	TITLE OF PAPER	JOURNAL NAME
2020	Stéphanie PHILIPPE1*, Alexis D. SOUCHET1,2, Petros LAMERAS3, Panagiotis PETRIDIS4, Julien CAPORAL1, Gildas COLDEBOEUF5, Hadrien DUZAN	Multimodal teaching, learning and training in virtual reality: a review and case study	Virtual Reality & Intelligent Hardware
2020	Anna V. Iatsyshyn, Valeriia O. Kovach, Yevhen O. Romanenko, Iryna I. Deinega, Yulii G. Kutsan, Svitlana H. Lytvynova	Application of augmented reality technologies for preparation of specialists of new technological era	Creative Commons License Attribution 4.0 Internationational
2019	Noureddine Elmqaddem	Argumented reality and Virtual reality in Education. Myth or Reality?	International Journal of Emerging Technologies in Learning
2019	Raul N. Uppot, Benjamin Laguna, Colin J. McCarthy, Gianluca De Novi, Andrew Phelps, Eliot Siegel, Jesse Courtier	Implementing Virtual and Augmented Reality Tools for Radiology Education and Training, Communication, and Clinical Care.	Radiology
2019	Jule M. KRÜGERa, Alexander BUCHHOLZa and Daniel BODEMER	Augmented Reality in Education: Three Unique Characteristics from a User's Perspective	A Media-based Knowledge Construction
2019	Kuo-Ting Huang, Christopher Ball, Jessica Francis, Rabindra Ratan, Josephine Boumis, and Joseph Fordham	Augmented Versus Virtual Reality in Education: An Exploratory Study Examining Science Knowledge Retention When Using Augmented Reality/Virtual Reality Mobile Applications.	CYBERPSYCHOLOGY, BEHAVIOR, AND SOCIAL NETWORKING
2019	Eleni Demitriadou, Kalliopi-Evangelia Stavroulia & Andreas Lanitis	Comparative evaluation of virtual and augmented reality for teaching mathematics in primary education.	Education and Information Technologies
2019	Adriano Baratè, Goffredo Haus, Luca A. Ludovico, Elena Pagani, & Nello Scarabottolo	5G TECHNOLOGY FOR AUGMENTED AND VIRTUAL REALITY IN EDUCATION	Education and New Developments
2019	B Salah, MH Abidi, SH Mian, M Krid	A Modern Approach towards an Industry 4.0 Model: From Driving Technologies to Management.	The Role of Engineering Education in Industry 4.0 Era

Table 2 continued

YEAR OF PUBLICATION	AUTHOR NAMES	TITLE OF PAPER	JOURNAL NAME
2019	Vasiliki Liagkoua, Dimitrios Salmasa, Chrysostomos Styliosa	Realizing Virtual Reality Learning Environment for Industry 4.0	Procedia CIRP
2019	Gabriela Kiryakova, Nadezhda Angelova, Lina Yordanova	The Potential of Augmented Reality to Transform Education into Smart Education.	TEM Journal.
2019	George Papanastasiou,thanasios Drigas, Charalabos Skianis, Miltiadis Lytras & Effrosyni Papanastasiou	Virtual and augmented reality effects on K-12, higher and tertiary education students' twenty-first century skills.	Virtual Reality
2018	Hakan Altinpulluk	Determining the trends of using augmented reality in education between 2006-2016	Education and Information Technologies
2018	Gabriela Kiryakova, Nadezhda Angelova, Lina Yordanova	The Potential of Augmented Reality to Transform Education into Smart Education	TEM Journal
2017	Elliot Hu-Au and Joey J. Lee	Virtual Reality in education: a tool for learning in the experience age.	Int. J. Innovation in Education
2016	Mehmet Kesim, Yasin Ozarslan	Augmented reality in education: current technologies and the potential for education	Procedia - Social and Behavioral Sciences
2010	Veronica S. Pantelidis	Reasons to Use Virtual Reality in Education and Training Courses and a Model to Determine When to Use Virtual Reality.	THEMES IN SCIENCE AND TECHNOLOGY EDUCATION
2009	Baker, Suzanne C., Ryan K. Wentz, and Madison M. Woods.	Using virtual worlds in education: Second Life as an educational tool.	Teaching of Psychology
2002	Mark Billinghurst	Augmented Reality in Education.	New horizons for learning
2001	Antonietti Alessandro	Virtual reality and hypermedia in learning to use a turning lathe.	Journal of Computer Assisted Learning

DISCUSSION

Virtual Reality (VR) technology has the potential to revolutionize industry education by providing immersive and interactive learning experiences. With VR, students can engage in simulations that replicate real-life scenarios and gain practical knowledge and skills that are difficult to acquire through traditional classroom teaching methods. For instance, medical students can practice surgical procedures on virtual patients, engineers can explore complex systems and structures, and pilots can operate flight simulators that simulate different weather conditions and emergency situations. This not only improves retention and recall but also reduces the chances of accidents or mistakes in the workplace. VR also allows for collaborative learning, where students from different parts of the world can learn and work together on projects. In summary, VR is an innovative tool that can transform industry education by providing an engaging and effective way to learn, train, and prepare for the workforce.

CONCLUSION

The world is changing fast, and the demand for skilled professionals is growing rapidly. This has led to industry leaders investing in VR as a tool to revolutionize education. VR allows students to explore real-life scenarios and gain practical experience, that too in a safe and controlled environment. This technology is especially beneficial in hazardous fields like engineering, medicine, and construction, where mistakes can be costly, and safety is of paramount importance. VR technology has also helped to enhance team collaboration and communication, enabling new levels of efficiency and productivity.

When we talk about virtual reality, it is worth mentioning the platforms on which virtual reality is made for education. Virtual Reality has the potential to increase capability and confidence of students providing approachable and repeatable learning opportunities in a fail-safe environment. The main goal of the technology is to become accessible to a broader audience through a web browser. VR provides the optimal compromise between students and educators. So, in the future, when VR in education is used on a full scale by schools, we will see amazing results.

In conclusion, the influence of virtual reality as a tool to revolutionize industry education has massive potential. With the growth of VR technology, the future of education looks exciting, interactive, and innovative. The integration of VR with traditional teaching methods is the key to enhancing knowledge and practical skills, preparing students for the industries of the future.

REFERENCES

Altinpulluk, H. (2019). Determining the trends of using augmented reality in education between 2006-2016. *Education and Information Technologies*, *24*(2), 1089–1114. doi:10.1007/s10639-018-9806-3

Antonietti, A., Imperio, E., Rasi, C., & Sacco, M. (2001). Virtual reality and hypermedia in learning to use a turning lathe. *Journal of Computer Assisted Learning*, *17*(2), 142–155. doi:10.1046/j.0266-4909.2001.00167.x

Baker, Wentz, R. K., & Woods, M. M. (2009). Using virtual worlds in education: Second Life® as an educational tool. *Teaching of Psychology*, *36*(1), 59–64. doi:10.1080/00986280802529079

Baratè. (2019, June). 5G technology for augmented and virtual reality in education. In *Proceedings of the International Conference on Education and New Developments* (Vol. 2019, pp. 512-516). 10.36315/2019v1end116

Billinghurst, M. (2002). Augmented reality in education. *New horizoKuo-Ting Huangns for learning, 12*(5), 1-5.

Calabuig-Moreno, González-Serrano, M. H., Fombona, J., & García-Tascón, M. (2020). The emergence of technology in physical education: A general bibliometric analysis with a focus on virtual and augmented reality. *Sustainability (Basel)*, *12*(7), 2728. doi:10.3390/su12072728

Demitriadou, Stavroulia, K.-E., & Lanitis, A. (2020). Comparative evaluation of virtual and augmented reality for teaching mathematics in primary education. *Education and Information Technologies*, *25*(1), 381–401. doi:10.1007/s10639-019-09973-5

Demitriadou, Stavroulia, K.-E., & Lanitis, A. (2020). Comparative evaluation of virtual and augmented reality for teaching mathematics in primary education. *Education and Information Technologies*, *25*(1), 381–401. doi:10.1007/s10639-019-09973-5

Elmqaddem, & .... (2019). Augmented reality and virtual reality in education. Myth or reality? *International Journal of Emerging Technologies in Learning*, *14*(3), 234. doi:10.3991/ijet.v14i03.9289

Hamzah, Ambiyar, A., Rizal, F., Simatupang, W., Irfan, D., & Refdinal, R. (2021). Development of Augmented Reality Application for Learning Computer Network Device. *International Journal of Interactive Mobile Technologies*, *15*(12), 47. doi:10.3991/ijim.v15i12.21993

Hu-Au. (2017). Virtual reality in education: A tool for learning in the experience age. *International Journal of Innovation in Education, 4*(4), 215–226. doi:10.1504/IJIIE.2017.091481

Huang, Ball, C., Francis, J., Ratan, R., Boumis, J., & Fordham, J. (2019). Augmented versus virtual reality in education: An exploratory study examining science knowledge retention when using augmented reality/virtual reality mobile applications. *Cyberpsychology, Behavior, and Social Networking, 22*(2), 105–110. doi:10.1089/cyber.2018.0150 PMID:30657334

Iatsyshyn. (2020a). *Application of augmented reality technologies for preparation of specialists of new technological era*. Academic Press.

Iatsyshyn. (2020b). *Application of augmented reality technologies for education projects preparation*. Academic Press.

Kaplan, Cruit, J., Endsley, M., Beers, S. M., Sawyer, B. D., & Hancock, P. A. (2021). The effects of virtual reality, augmented reality, and mixed reality as training enhancement methods: A meta-analysis. *Human Factors, 63*(4), 706–726. doi:10.1177/0018720820904229 PMID:32091937

Kesim. (2012). Augmented reality in education: current technologies and the potential for education. *Procedia-social and behavioural sciences, 47*, 297-302.

Khan. (2020). Corona virus pandemic paving ways to next generation of learning and teaching: futuristic cloud based educational model. Available at SSRN 3669832. doi:10.2139/ssrn.3669832

Kiryakova. (2018). The potential of augmented reality to transform education into smart education. *TEM Journal, 7*(3), 556.

Krüger. (2019, December). Augmented reality in education: three unique characteristics from a user's perspective. In *Proc. 27th Int. Conf. on Comput. In Educ* (pp. 412-422). Academic Press.

Liagkou, Salmas, D., & Stylios, C. (2019). Realizing virtual reality learning environment for industry 4.0. *Procedia CIRP, 79*, 712–717. doi:10.1016/j.procir.2019.02.025

Pantelidis, V. S. (2010). Reasons to use virtual reality in education and training courses and a model to determine when to use virtual reality. *Themes in Science and Technology Education, 2*(1-2), 59–70.

Papanastasiou, Drigas, A., Skianis, C., Lytras, M., & Papanastasiou, E. (2019). Virtual and augmented reality effects on K-12, higher and tertiary education students' twenty-first century skills. *Virtual Reality (Waltham Cross)*, *23*(4), 425–436. doi:10.1007/s10055-018-0363-2

Paszkiewicz, Salach, M., Dymora, P., Bolanowski, M., Budzik, G., & Kubiak, P. (2021). Methodology of implementing virtual reality in education for industry 4.0. *Sustainability (Basel)*, *13*(9), 5049. doi:10.3390/su13095049

Philippe, Souchet, A. D., Lameras, P., Petridis, P., Caporal, J., Coldeboeuf, G., & Duzan, H. (2020). Multimodal teaching, learning and training in virtual reality: A review and case study. *Virtual Reality & Intelligent Hardware*, *2*(5), 421–442. doi:10.1016/j.vrih.2020.07.008

Raja. (2021). Conceptual Origins, Technological Advancements, and Impacts of Using Virtual Reality Technology in Education. *Webology, 18*(2).

Salah, Abidi, M., Mian, S., Krid, M., Alkhalefah, H., & Abdo, A. (2019). Virtual reality-based engineering education to enhance manufacturing sustainability in industry 4.0. *Sustainability (Basel)*, *11*(5), 1477. doi:10.3390/su11051477

Uppot, Laguna, B., McCarthy, C. J., De Novi, G., Phelps, A., Siegel, E., & Courtier, J. (2019). Implementing virtual and augmented reality tools for radiology education and training, communication, and clinical care. *Radiology*, *291*(3), 570–580. doi:10.1148/radiol.2019182210 PMID:30990383

Vasilevsk. (2020). Analysing construction student experiences of mobile mixed reality enhanced learning in virtual and augmented reality environments. *Research in Learning Technology*, *28*(0), 28. doi:10.25304/rlt.v28.2329

Vasilevski, & Birt, J. (2020). Analysing construction student experiences of mobile mixed reality enhanced learning in virtual and augmented reality environments. *Research in Learning Technology*, *28*(0), 28. doi:10.25304/rlt.v28.2329

Chapter 9
Leveraging Minecraft for Enhanced Spatial Perception and Academic Achievement

Şevket Huntürk Acar
Sinop University, Turkey

Hülya Karaçalı Taze
Sinop University, Turkey

Tugra Karademir Coşkun
Sinop University, Turkey

ABSTRACT

This study aims to reveal the impact of using the digital game Minecraft: Education Edition in teaching geographical features in social studies on the achievement and spatial perception skills of 5th grade students. The research adopts a sequential explanatory mixed-method design. Quantitative data was collected using self-assessment and teacher assessment forms on spatial perception skills, and an achievement test developed by the researchers. Qualitative data was gathered through interviews. The study found that using Minecraft led to an increase in students' achievement and their skills in examining space. This study provides valuable insights for educators and curriculum developers, offering a potential pathway to enhance students' understanding of geographical concepts and spatial perception skills through interactive digital tools such as Minecraft: Education Edition in the future.

DOI: 10.4018/979-8-3693-3015-9.ch009

Copyright © 2024, IGI Global. Copying or distributing in print or electronic forms without written permission of IGI Global is prohibited.

INTRODUCTION

Technological advancements at the dawn of the 21st century have fundamentally transformed educational approaches and teaching methods, with one of the key components of this shift being the utilization of digital and interactive games in educational processes. As of today, the global user count in the video game segment has reached 401.8 million, with the number of players in the United States alone accounting for 18.7 million within the video game segment (Statista, 2023). In 2022, the digital game industry was observed to possess a substantial profit share with revenues amounting to 197 billion dollars worldwide. At this juncture, it is appropriate to question what makes digital games so prevalent. The ubiquity of digital games is due to a series of factors. Technological advancements, widespread availability of the internet, and penetration of mobile devices have enabled games to reach a broader audience. In particular, the increased use of smartphones and tablets has enhanced the accessibility and portability of games (Newzoo, 2020). Furthermore, a wide range of games and various game genres cater to the interests of diverse demographic groups. Games offer users a host of experiences, such as social interaction, competitive challenges, and even storytelling (Bányai et al., 2019). A broad spectrum of cognitive abilities can be stimulated by video games, which may contribute to their popularity. Lastly, the gaming industry itself constantly introduces innovations and advancements to attract more users and retain the interest of existing ones. This not only sustains demand for games but also generally boosts their popularity (Kaplan & Haenlein, 2020).

On the other hand, when examining the literature pertaining to the use of digital games in education, which is the focus of this study, it is seen that digital games contribute to improvements in many areas such as attention, visual-spatial abilities, and psychomotor skills (Green & Bavelier, 2012). In addition, strategic games can enhance problem-solving and flexible thinking, while puzzle games generally target logic and abstract thinking skills (Sala & Gobet, 2019). Research has proven that digital games enhance problem-solving and strategic thinking skills (Granic, Lobel, & Engels, 2014), and multiplayer games improve social and communication skills (Adachi & Willoughby, 2013). Academically, digital games have the potential to improve abilities to understand and recall information (Clark et al., 2016). In particular, educational games offer students the opportunity to understand and apply complex concepts (Sung & Hwang, 2013), have positive cognitive, behavioral, and affective effects (Connolly et al., 2012) and increase students' procedural knowledge (Perini et al., 2018). Studies reveal that students who play games perform better on tests compared to students who use other traditional teaching methods (Flores, Paiva, & Cruz, 2020). Games make learning more engaging by providing fun and interactive learning experiences, as digital games offer students real-world experiences (Squire, 2008).

Today, digital games are used for educational purposes in many fields. Among these fields, the use of digital games in Social Studies education is also valuable. The subject of social studies has an interdisciplinary structure that organizes learning, where related knowledge, skills, and values can be viewed as a whole (MEB, 2018). This situation leads to the intensity of information load and the diversity of comprehensive topics, which makes teaching social studies difficult. The first of these difficulties is that students have difficulty relating the subjects to their personal lives (Schug, Todd & Beery, 2013). On the other hand, the need to teach abstract concepts in social studies lessons can make understanding these topics more complicated. Another significant difficulty is that teachers often struggle to effectively teach social studies topics and present these topics to students in an engaging and meaningful way (Fitchett & Heafner, 2010). The need to present topics within a broad and complex framework puts pressure on both teachers and students (Bolick, Adams & Willox, 2019). At this point, digital games appear as an alternative in overcoming some of the difficulties in social studies education as characterized above. In some studies in the field literature, it is seen that thanks to digital educational games used in different acquisitions of the social studies course, students' academic achievements (Koka, 2018; Öztürk & Yeşiltaş 2015; Doğan 2017), permanence of information (Koka, 2018; Çalışkan & Biter 2019), interest in the course (Koka, 2018; Çalışkan & Biter 2019; Erkan, 2019; Sousa & Rocha, 2019) and attention increased (Koka, 2018) and it prepared an environment for concrete learning experiences (Koka, 2018). Digital games in social studies education can provide students with information about social and cultural diversity (McGonigal, 2011), social skills (Blumberg & Altschuler, 2011), thinking and problem-solving abilities about complex social and political concepts (Squire, 2008; Gee, 2007), and the opportunity to understand social and cultural diversity (McGonigal, 2011). Particularly, digital and interactive games can assist students in experiencing social studies topics such as history, geography, economics, and politics, and in developing a more comprehensive understanding of these subjects (Squire, 2008).

Digital games can be incorporated into social studies education through various methods such as teachers developing games, using commercial games, and students learning by designing games. Particularly with the development of technology, designing and developing real-life environments in games seem to have significantly eased for teachers (Udeozor et al., 2022). However, this requires teachers to have a certain level of technological literacy, knowledge of gamification (Sanchez-Mena & Marti-Parreño, 2017), and sufficient time (Gros, 2017). This is because gamification, in its most explicit form, requires a level of expertise as it involves engaging students with the performance of predetermined and routinized activities where learning becomes a secondary issue (Smeyer, 2018). An alternative to teachers developing their games is to incorporate commercial games into the class. However, challenges such as the non-scientific design of commercial games, their inconsistency with the learning outcomes, unsatisfactory, and student-incompatible game results can arise (Bi & Song, 2011). Additionally, the selection of ready-made games can pose a challenge for teachers in terms of determining the appropriateness of the content within the game (Gros, 2017).

Finally, students learning by designing games is actually an example of learning by doing. Constructivism explains its main aim as providing more opportunities for students to create their own games instead of directly embedding "lessons" into games and assisting them in establishing new relationships with knowledge during this process (Kafai, 2006). From this perspective, learning by designing games emerges as a constructivist practice where the student constructs the knowledge himself. However, the game software to be used in the game design learning process is critical.

One of this software, Minecraft, provides students with the experience of 3D design and various geography areas. Especially considering some of the outcomes taught in the social studies class, it can be an effective tool by making knowledge construction possible by supporting constructivist learning and by evoking positive emotions such as fun and motivation brought about by playing games. Minecraft offers a series of tools that allow students to construct the earth primarily through geometric shapes (Kapp, 2012). Minecraft, consisting of square blocks, is an open-world game played by millions of users worldwide and one of the largest learning communities (Reich, 2020). It motivates students to creativity, discovery, and teaching by doing (Elliott, 2014). Although studies conducted in different fields show that Minecraft game is a significant tool in understanding 3D geometric shapes (Carrera et al.,, 2021), developing spatial visualization and mental rotation skills (Sms, 2021); teaching cooperation and design skills (Mørch, Eie & Mifsud, 2018), construction of critical thinking (Hill, 2015; Gauquier & Schneider, 2013), encouraging communication and group collaboration (Egbert & Borysenko, 2019), increasing social interaction (Choo, Karamnejad, & May, 2013; Mavoa, Carter & Gibbs, 2018), developing problem-solving skills (Marcon & Faulkener, 2016), it is seen that the number of researches aiming to demonstrate its effectiveness in social studies class is limited.

In social studies education, the focus isn't solely on teaching the learning outcomes. There are also certain skills intended to be imparted to students. One of these skills, spatial perception, is defined as recognizing and perceiving elements in space, interpreting these elements with their physical and human effects, and explaining these effects along with their causes and consequences (MEB, 2004). Spatial perception is highly important in education as part of a broader set of knowledge and skills. It is not only significant for the associated field of social studies but is also proven to be essential for developing skills in various other disciplines such as mathematics (Mix et al., 2016), STEM (Wai, Lubinski & Benbow, 2009), and geography (Kastens & Ishikawa 2006). For instance, Sorby (2009) found that spatial perception education could help women achieve greater success in the field of engineering. This skill is crucial in many aspects of daily life and is related to navigation, memory, and attention (Wolbers & Hegarty, 2010). People possessing spatial perception skill are expected to perform several sub-dimensions such as visualizing an object or a shape on paper, seeing a shape in three dimensions, and being able to visualize a space, sketch, street, or building (MEB, 2004). Although there's no specific tool or method for teaching these skills, they are expected to be imparted during the teaching of the outcomes. To develop spatial perception skills, students should be taught to construct mental images of spaces and organize these images into meaningful wholes (Mathewson, 1999). At this point, digital games can play an important role in enhancing students' spatial perception skills. For example, games like Minecraft are powerful teaching tools that help improve navigational abilities (Peppler et al., 2010), spatial visualization and mental rotation (Sms, 2021), as well as building 3D models and visual spatial reasoning (Junco, 2014). Additionally, Minecraft can be an effective design and mapping tool in sketching and interpreting, which are among the sub-dimensions of spatial perception skills (Bashandy, 2021), and it can be said to present a spatial representation of real life (Wood, 2010). Because games like Minecraft allow players to transition between 2D and 3D (Carrera et al., 2021), utilize cartography effectively (Sena & Jordãob, 2021), and design environments aimed at developing creativity (Blanco-Herrera, Gentile, & Rokkum 2019; Checa-Romero & Pascual Gomez, 2018).

Considering these features, the question arises, 'Could the game Minecraft be an effective teaching tool in enhancing students' spatial perception skills and academic performance?' However, when literature is surveyed in this regard, studies typically focus on reviews or seeking opinions (Erol & Akpinar, 2021). Indeed, there are limited studies on the use of digital games in social studies education (Yeşiltaş & Cantürk, 2022; Güneş et al., 2021; Karamustafaoğlu & Kılıç, 2020). Given the effectiveness of digital games in social studies education and their relationship with the sub-dimensions of spatial perception skills, it becomes apparent that more studies are needed in this area.

In this context, the motivation for this research is to test the effectiveness of Minecraft in teaching both landforms and spatial perception skills through a game-based design. Accordingly, the aim of this study is to reveal the effect of digital game-supported teaching of landforms concepts in social studies on the performance and spatial perception skills of fifth-grade students. Under this general aim, specific objectives sought to be answered are as follows:

1. Is there a significant difference between the pre- and post-test achievement scores of students as a result of teaching landforms concepts with Minecraft: Education Edition?
2. How is the distribution of students' spatial perception skills according to their self-assessment in teaching landforms concepts with game-based learning?
3. Is the effect of game-based learning in teaching landforms concepts on the categories of students' spatial perception skills significant according to teacher evaluation?
4. What are the opinions of fifth-grade students on the impact of Minecraft: Education Edition, which they used in teaching landforms concepts in social studies, on their spatial perception skills?

METHOD

Research Design

In this study, a sequential explanatory mixed methods design, one of the mixed design typologies proposed by Creswell (2021), has been utilized as it was considered appropriate for the research problem and questions. The choice of the mixed method has two reasons. Firstly, this study aims to reveal the effects of learning landforms through a digital game on students' achievement and spatial perception skills. During this process, it was thought that a single measurement tool and method would not be sufficient to measure achievement and track the development of competence. Because this study aims to produce integrated results that are more valid, complete, deep, thought-provoking, or broad-based according to the results obtained (Morin, Olsson, & Atikcan, 2021). Another reason is to eliminate possible measurement errors due to the low number of participants and to utilize multiple different measurement tools and methods for this. In line with this, the steps of the sequential explanatory mixed methods design applied in this study are given in Figure 1.

Figure 1 shows that the research started with the application of the pre-test. After the test applications, teaching of the Social Studies course achievements determined with Minecraft has been passed on, and post-tests were applied after the teaching was completed. After the analysis of quantitative data, meetings were held with students to detail the determined points and reveal latent variables, and the analysis of the products they produced was performed. The data obtained as a result of the analyzes were interpreted as a whole.

Figure 1. Research Process

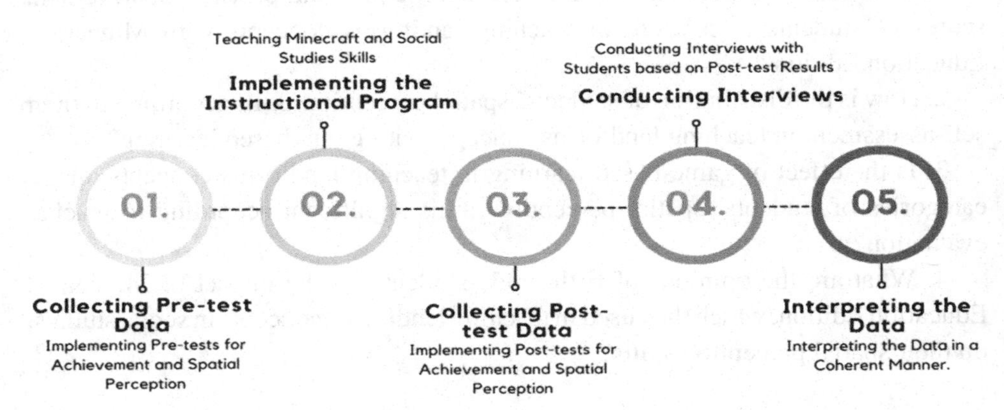

Research Group

The study group of this research consists of seven 5th grade students who were studying in a village middle school in the 2021-2022 academic year. Due to the COVID-19 pandemic that occurred during the implementation phase of the research, the appropriate sampling method was used in the selection of the study group. Suitable sampling is used when data cannot be collected from different groups due to obstacles such as research permission, cost, or time (Kılıç, 2013; Baştürk & Taştepe, 2013). Some validity and reliability methods have been applied to eliminate the generalization problems that may arise due to the sample size, and the details are included under the "Method" heading. The research included seven students, 42.85% of whom were male and 57.15% were female. The students had not previously taken a lesson on the achievement of "SB.5.3.1. Describes the landforms of his/her place and its surroundings on maps in general (MEB, 2018)." Before the research, the students were provided with the skills of using the general tools, menus, and scene of the Minecraft EDU application and designing in general terms as part of the Information Technologies course. In the research process, to minimize the problems that may arise from the hardware, a smooth gameplay experience at a stable 60 FPS was provided to the students on all platforms. It can be said that equal opportunities were provided to the students in terms of game experience.

Data Collection Tools

In the context of this research, "Spatial Perception Skills Form - Teacher Evaluation Version", "Game-Supported Learning Student Self-Evaluation Form", and "Achievement Test", developed by the researchers, were used to collect quantitative data, and a semi-structured interview form was used to collect qualitative data. Additionally, the games developed by the students were subjected to document analysis. The steps proposed by Yurdugül (2005) for theoretical scale development were followed for the validity and reliability studies of the measurement tools. Initially, the features to be measured were determined, literature reviews were conducted, and interviews were held with field/subject experts, and based on the obtained information, scale items were prepared. After the development of the prospective measurement tool, studies were conducted for face validity and then for content validity. Assistance was taken from both experts and the age group in the study sample for face validity, and for content validity, Content Validity Ratios (CVR) for the items were calculated using the Lawshe (1975) technique. According to the Lawshe (1975) technique, CVR ratios are calculated by dividing the number of experts who say "appropriate" for the item by half of the total number of experts, then taking one less. According to the calculations, the minimum content validity ratio for five experts should be over 0.99 at the .05 significance level (Veneziano & Hooper, 1997). In this research, since feedback was received from five experts, items below 0.99 were removed from the scale considering their representation powers. Detailed information about the scales is provided below.

Spatial Perception Skills Form - Teacher Evaluation Version. The Spatial Perception Skills Form was developed to measure the changes in students' spatial perception skills during the 3D game design process by the teacher. Initially, during the development stage, searches were conducted in both native and foreign field literature on "Spatial perception skills", "3D game design", "Minecraft", "social sciences education achievements" themes and the concepts in the combined common themes were concretely defined. The defined concepts were converted into items that could be used for observation by the teacher, and a pool of 15 items was created and compiled in a draft form. The draft form was first sent to experts for compliance validity, and necessary changes were made in sentence structures based on their recommendations. The obtained form was sent to five experts, four in the field of Social Studies and one in the field of instructional technologies with associate professor degree, for the calculation of CVR ratios. Scope CVR ratios for the items were calculated using the Lawshe (1975) technique based on the feedback received from the experts. According to the content validity ratios obtained, it was determined that the items took values between 1 and 0.6. It was determined that items 3 and 5 had a CVR ratio below 0.99 at the .005 significance level. Before removing the items from the measuring tool, a literature review was conducted again to look at the necessity power for the measurement tool. It was determined that there was no inconvenience in removing them from the form as a result of the research, and items 3 and 5 were removed from the scale. The Spatial Perception Skills Form -

Teacher Evaluation Version was structured as a three-point Likert scale, consisting of "Agree", "Disagree", "Undecided", in a total of 13 items.

Game-Supported Learning Student Self-Evaluation Form. The Game-Supported Learning Student Self-Evaluation Form was used to determine whether the spatial perception skill originated from game-supported learning from the student's perspective. In the writing phase of the items related to this form, a literature review was first conducted on 'game-supported learning dimensions' and 'game-based learning in social studies'. Using the sign table prepared for the achievement test, 38 items were written. The draft form containing the items was first sent to experts for fit validity, and the related items were reorganized considering the suggestions of the evaluators. The obtained form was sent to five experts again for the calculation of CVR ratios, and the CVR ratios were calculated using the Lawshe (1975) technique with the data obtained. It was determined that items 5-6-13-14-26 and 38 had a CVR ratio below 0.99 at the .005 significance level. Before removing the items from the measurement tool, a literature review was conducted again to examine the necessity power for the measurement tool. As a result of the research, it was decided that some of the items were important for the form, four items were removed, and others were used with corrections in line with the suggestions from the experts. The Game-Supported Learning Student Self-Evaluation Form was structured as a three-point Likert scale, consisting of "Agree", "Disagree", "Undecided", with a total of 34 items.

Achievement Test. In the preparation stage of the Achievement Test, a sign table was first established for the related achievements, and following expert opinions, 48 multiple-choice exam questions were prepared for the 24 achievements in the sign table. The items were read to three fifth-grade students for language comprehensibility, and necessary corrections were made in the item stems after receiving feedback. The draft test was applied to a group of 90 individuals who had previously received education on topics about landforms to test the significance of the difference between item scores. The top and bottom 27% groups were calculated from the collected data and the significance of the difference between the group's item scores was examined. In the third step, the item discrimination indexes of the test questions were calculated. It is accepted that items with a value between 0.00 and 0.20 are not good at discrimination and should not be included in the test, items with a value between 0.20 and 0.30 are moderately discriminating and should be included in the test after corrections, and items with an item discrimination index above 0.30 are good at discrimination and should be included directly in the test (Erkuş, 2003). Therefore, to construct a robust achievement test, questions with an item discrimination index below 0.30 have been removed from the test. In the next step, difficulty indexes were calculated for the items, and the necessary adjustments were made so that the difficulty of the test would be close to .50. In each step, when removing items, the power to represent the achievements in the sign table was considered. Finally, the KR-20 value was calculated to test the internal consistency of the test, and it was concluded that the reliability coefficient was at the desired level with .82. As a result of the analyses, the final form was given to the achievement test consisting of 22 items.

Structuring the Semi-Structured Interview Form. A semi-structured interview form was prepared to validate the qualitative data obtained during the research process and to identify latent variables. The interview form is quite important for this study as it will be used to reduce potential measurement bias due to sample size, which is among the limitations of the study, and to increase its generalizability. The semi-structured interview form used for semi-structured interviews is considered a hybrid form according to its degree of structuring and even though the questions are predefined, the interviewer can easily change the order or exact formulation of the questions (Kallio et al., 2016). The semi-structured interview form was used to determine the relationship between the students' spatial perception skills and the changes in their achievements with the MinecraftEDU application, measure the learning situations of the achievements, and reveal other implicit variables within the scope of the research. In addition, other conditions, such as the age status of the students and their socio-economic levels, which are thought to affect the structure of the interview items, were considered as prerequisites. In this phase, it was first started with the preparation of interview questions (Whiting, 2008) related to the relevant purpose and literature, and 40 open-ended questions were prepared for the preliminary interview guide. Among these questions, 20 are main questions and 20 are follow-up questions. The purpose of the follow-up questions is to facilitate the participant's understanding of the main themes (Turner, 2010) and to guide the conversation towards the subject of the study (Baumbusch, 2010). Care was taken to ensure that the questions were prepared to be flexible and free from guidance (Dearnley, 2005), allowing dialogue during the interview process (Whiting, 2008), enabling easy transition between questions, participant-focused (Astedt-Kurki & Heikkinen, 1994), and unidirectional (Baumbusch, 2010). The prepared interview questions were examined by two different groups to eliminate ambiguities and inappropriate guiding questions (Barriball & While, 1994). The second examination was carried out by field experts to evaluate the appropriateness and comprehensiveness of the questions in relation to the research objectives and subjects. At this stage, opinions were received from two computer and instructional technology experts and two social studies experts. Finally, the obtained form was read to a group close to potential study participants to test the comprehensibility (Chenail, 2011), order, and timing of the questions (Cridland et al., 2015). Finally, a guide was prepared that included the purpose (Barriball & While, 1994) of the semi-structured interview form and usage instructions (Krauss et al., 2009) that guide other researchers in using the form, and the final form was given to the form.

Research Process

The research, including data collection and implementation, was completed in a total of nine weeks. Table 1, demonstrating the application steps of the research, is given below.

Table 1. Research Application Steps

Research Flow	Duration	Course Name
Minecraft Instruction	4 hours	Information Technologies
Pre-Test Application	1 hour	Information Technologies
Teaching of Achievements with Minecraft: EDU		
Stream 1: Knows that streams are water flowing within a certain bed. Stream 2: Distinguishes the stream from other landforms. Stream 3: Can associate the stream with the regions they live in. Stream 4: Establishes a connection between the concept of stream and human elements	3 hours	Social Studies
Plateau 1: Knows that plateaus are high compared to their surroundings. Plateau 2: Knows that plateaus are flat compared to their surroundings. Plateau 3: Realizes that plateaus are formed as a result of rivers deeply cutting into their beds. Plateau 4: Can distinguish the plateau from other landforms.	3 hours	Social Studies
Lake 1: Knows that lakes are waters accumulated in hollows. Lake 2: Knows that lakes are stagnant waters. Lake 3: Can associate the lakes with the regions they live in. Lake 4: Establishes a connection between the concept of lake and human elements. Lake 5: Distinguishes the lakes from other landforms.	3 hours	Social Studies
Plain 1: Expresses that plains are flat compared to their surroundings. Plain 2: Knows that plains are lower than their surroundings. Plain 3: Knows that plains are agriculturally productive. Plain 4: Can provide examples of the reasons for high population in plains. Plain 5: Distinguishes the plain from other geographical shapes. Plain 6: Can associate the plains with the regions they live in. Plain 7: Establishes a connection between the concept of plain and human elements.	3 hours	Social Studies
Mountain 1: Knows that mountains are the highest landform. Mountain 2: Distinguishes the mountains from other landforms. Mountain 3: Can associate the mountains with the regions they live in. Mountain 4: Establishes a connection between the concept of mountain and human elements.	3 hours	Social Studies
Post-test Application	2 hours	Social Studies
Analysis of Quantitative Data		
Conducting the Interview		
Analysis of Interview Data		
Data Reporting		

The research initially began with the instruction of the MinecraftEDU application within the scope of the Information Technology course. Over the course of four hours in total, the students were taught the game menus and mechanics related to MinecraftEDU, and they were generally taught the skill of design. Exercises were conducted for the taught tools. At the end of the training, a pre-test application for the research was conducted. Following the preliminary preparations and trainings, instruction for research acquisitions was initiated in the Social Studies course. Three hours were allocated for each topic area in the Social Studies course. Deductive learning, as suggested by De Cecco (1968), Klausmeier (1992), and Taba (1967) for acquisition instruction, was used in the instruction of the acquisitions. The steps of the deductive learning method used for the instruction of the concepts were structured on the example of the first concept, the River, as follows:

1. At the beginning of the lesson, the concept of the river was verbally expressed to the students.
2. In the second stage, a Minecraft game containing river drawings was examined by the students. Classification of the river's features was requested and the classifications were written on the board.
3. In the third stage, a Minecraft game featuring other landforms was examined by the students. Classification of the features of some other landforms was requested and written on the board. An example Minecraft drawing and an example video including these two stages are given below.

Figure 2. Minecraft Sample Lesson Drawings

4. The features of the river were compared with the features of other landforms, and their similarities and differences were revealed.
5. From all the features, they were asked to define the concept of a river.

6. Finally, based on this definition, the students were asked to draw an example of a river on the Minecraft application. Examples of the students' drawings are given in Figure 3.

Figure 3. Sample River Drawings by Students

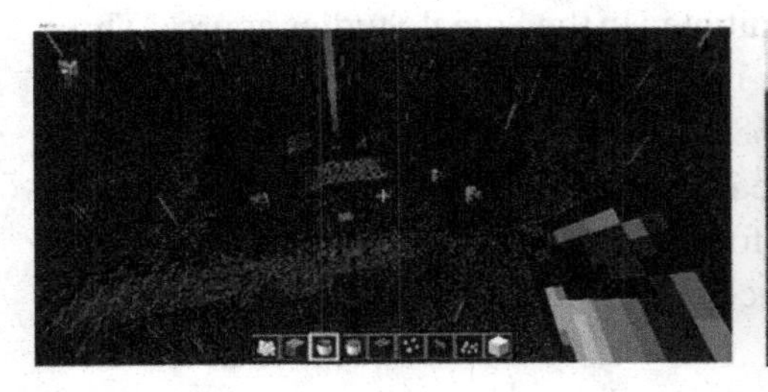

The instruction of the acquisitions was completed in 15 hours over 5 weeks. The drawings made by the students as a result of the training were recorded for analysis, and the final tests were applied. Quantitative data was analyzed and interviews were held with the students to support the results. Each student was interviewed for an average of 14 minutes using a semi-structured interview form physically in the school library. Explicit consent was obtained from the students in order to record the interviews, and all interviews were recorded with the help of a digital device. The total 99 minutes of recorded sound was transcribed and prepared for data analysis. A total of 51 pages of interview data was obtained.

Data Analysis

For sub-objective 1, when the pre-test and post-test achievement scores of the students were examined, it was found that the obtained data did not provide normal distribution (skewness and kurtosis coefficient> +-2) and the difference scores had a symmetric population distribution. The measurement values include the prior (pre-test) and posterior (post-test) measurement values of the same sample. Measurements are quantitative and continuous variables. Considering all these features, it was decided that the most suitable test is the Wilcoxon signed ranks test. At this stage, the games prepared by the students were also subjected to document review. Document review, when combined with other qualitative data collection methods, especially interviews and observations, provides researchers with the opportunity to understand and interpret the subject more holistically (Merriam, 2009). That is, document review is an important research tool that has the potential to provide researchers with a more comprehensive perspective on a subject. The students' drawings were subjected to document analysis based on critical criteria related to landform concepts, and evidence was provided for sub-objective 1.

It's important to note that the use of games such as Minecraft in educational settings provides a unique opportunity to assess student understanding of complex topics. This study leverages this potential in order to provide a novel perspective on the application of game-based learning methodologies in the classroom. Through the analysis of the students' game creations and in-depth interviews, valuable insights into the learning process can be gleaned. Such findings can prove instrumental in the further development and application of technology-enhanced learning strategies. For the second sub-objective, self-evaluation results were subjected to frequency analysis. Data collected in three categorical groups, 'agree', 'disagree' and 'undecided', were divided into frequencies and comparisons were made between categories. With the data obtained, the impact of game-based learning on attainments was evaluated from the student's perspective. In sub-objective 3, the teacher's evaluation scores of spatial perception skills for each student were compared to verify the self-evaluation results regarding students' spatial perception skills. Because the data perform ordinal measurements, they have two independent groups, namely teacher and student evaluations, no correlation between the observations in each group, and the data does not show normal distribution, it was decided that the Man Whitney-U Test was the most suitable test.

Transcripts obtained from student interviews were analyzed using content analysis. Before the analysis, the literature and quantitative interviews were examined, and preliminary categories related to spatial perception skills that would be considered significant in the interviews were determined and the results are given in Table 2.

The preliminary categories identified in Table 2 have been determined to be appropriate to the aim of the study and the definitions of the relevant concepts. For example, after the interviews, the definitions in the field literature of the spatial perception skill variable that was measured were extracted, and the common features in the definitions were placed in the table as categories. When the literature was examined, it was determined that the common themes of the definitions regarding spatial perception skills were 'visualization in the mind', 'seeing in three dimensions', 'drawing and interpreting sketch maps', and 'comparison with reality'. The data obtained from the interviews were coded in a single cycle according to these categories. For coding, the hypothesis coding from the explanatory methods categorized by Saldana (2009) was used. First cycle coding, hypothesis coding, is the application of a predetermined code list created by the researcher, especially to evaluate a hypothesis created by the researcher, to qualitative data (Saldana, 2009). In this study, the interview data obtained from the students were subjected to hypothesis analysis based on the preliminary categories obtained from the literature review in Table 2. In order to verify the findings obtained as a result of the analysis, the Miles-Huberman model was taken as the basis and expert approval (Merriam, 1998) was applied. In this context, the findings were sent to three researchers (one computer and instructional technologies expert, two social studies experts) and the agreement between the coders was examined using the Miles and Huberman formula ($\Delta = \text{C} \div (\text{C} + \partial) \times 100$) according to the feedback received (Δ: Reliability coefficient, C: The number of agreed topics/terms, ∂: The number of disagreed topics/terms). The coding check that gives internal consistency is expected to be at least 80% agreement between coders (Miles & Huberman, 1994; Patton, 2002). In this context, findings with agreement below 80% were removed from the study.

Table 2. Preliminary categories for spatial perception skills

Themes	Definition
Visualization	In the mind, visualizing the form of an object in space or a shape on paper (MEB, 2004).
Perceiving in Three Dimensions	Seeing a shape in three dimensions (MEB, 2004).
Sketching and Interpreting Map	Map, plan, sketch, graph, diagram drawing and interpretation (MEB, 2004).
Comparing with Reality	Can compare a place with its representation drawn on paper (MEB, 2004).
Knows Basic Information Related to Space Draws Basic Information About Space on Minecraft Giving Examples	Space perception includes processes such as people perceiving, knowing and interpreting their environment (Öcal, 2007). They are learning its relationship with physical and human processes (Demircioğlu and Akengin, 2012).
Spatial Differences Relationship of Spatial Differences with Human Activities	Recognizes that separate places have similar and different characteristics, how this situation affects human activities, the interdependence of distant spaces (Demircioğlu and Akengin, 2012).
Draws Basic Information About Space on Minecraft Visualization	Individual's perception of the space they live in, obtaining information about the space, designing the space in their mind, and putting forth actions related to spatial cognition can be expressed (Köşker, 2012). The ability to perceive space is particularly important in expressing space in different ways, in other words, simply drawing it (Sönmez, 2010).
Relationship of Spatial Differences with Human Activities Draws Basic Information About Space on Minecraft Giving Examples	Children's perception of space develops by recognizing, understanding, and interpreting the effects of the physical and human processes of the space they are in on human life (Akengin, 2011).

Validity: Reliability Studies

In the study, some validity and reliability studies have been carried out to eliminate the limitations of the study. In this context, long-term interaction and expert reviews, as also suggested by Holloway and Wheeler (1996), have been applied to ensure the credibility of the study. In the long-term interaction, the researcher spent time with the students before the implementation, gaining a deep understanding of their culture, language, and views. Both in structuring the measurement tools and confirming the findings obtained from the qualitative data, expert opinions were frequently obtained and two experts (Computer and instructional technologies expert, social studies instruction expert) provided expertise to the researcher throughout the application.

Triangulation has been used to increase the internal validity of the study. Researcher-source triangulation and method triangulation, types of triangulations proposed by Denzin (1978), were used. In researcher-source triangulation, two field experts have assisted the researcher in developing data collection tools, data collection, analysis, and interpretation throughout the study. Triangulation, another method applied to increase internal validity, was used to eliminate the limitation of working with a small group and to increase the generalizability of quantitative data by resorting to different data collection methods. In the study planned as a mixed design, data were collected both quantitatively and qualitatively with observations and interviews. Especially, the process of collecting qualitative data was planned in a way that would allow in-depth information related to the purpose of the study. Because; the more usable data collected from each person, the less participant is needed (Beins, 2017).

Various methods have also been applied to ensure the confirmability of the research. For instance; detailed descriptions and explanations were given for the method and application procedures in the text, the study process was occasionally supported with visuals, the analysis of the findings was explained in detail, how and with which tools the measurements were made, and the validity and reliability studies of the performed tools (Holloway & Wheeler, 1996) were described in detail. In addition, to ensure both confirmability and transferability, direct quotations have been made regarding the interviews under the findings heading (Holloway & Wheeler, 1996; Guba & Lincoln, 1982), presenting the raw data to the readers. In addition to these, the researcher has preferred the mixed design, a known method in the literature, and used the application steps suggested for the mixed design in the study. The findings obtained were shared with users supported by literature.

FINDINGS

Is There a Significant Difference Between Students' Pre- and Post-Test Achievement Scores After Teaching Geographic Formations Concepts With Minecraft: Education Edition?

To determine whether there is a significant difference between the pre- and post-test rank averages of 5th grade middle school students taught the concepts of rivers, lakes, plains, plateaus, and mountains using Minecraft: Education Edition, the Wilcoxon Signed-Ranks Test was conducted based on both total scores and individual concepts. The table below contains the results of the test conducted on total scores.

Table 3. Wilcoxon signed-rank test results

Pre-Post Test	N	Rank Mean	Rank Sum	z	p
Negative Rank	0	-	-		
Positive Rank	7	4.00	28,00	-2.317	,018
Equal	0	-	-		

Upon examining Table 3, a significant difference was found between students' pre- and post-test achievement rank averages (Z=-2.371, p=.018). Reviewing the results, an increase in achievement scores was seen in all seven students who participated in the study. The collected interview statements and drawings confirm these data. For instance, while drawing a mountain, Student K4 noted paying attention to it being "high and having a pointed peak", similarly, Student K2 indicated paying attention to it being "protruding and upward". Student K3's definition of a plateau was seen in their statements: "Teacher, [I paid attention] to it being high, flat", and "Teacher, for the river... I was leveling its sides, so it became flat as I level the rocks". Also, after Student K1 responded "I paid attention to it being higher than its surroundings and to its top being flat", they further explained this by saying "weather events like rain, smooths its surroundings".

In the drawing of the plain concept, Student K6 said, "I paid attention to it being low, then to it being flat and the surface being smooth", Student K4 said, "I paid attention to its surroundings being high but itself being low", and Student K1 stated, "I made the surroundings of the plains a bit higher because the surroundings of the plains are high. I made it flat because it is flat and it is easier for people to live". These statements show that they learned the characteristics related to the concept of a plain. Student K1 expressed the contribution of the drawing process with Minecraft to learning the concept of a river as, "For example, while rivers flow straight, I considered them passing through a certain path by carving the soil from somewhere". K2 explained this as, "It being thin, flat, and also flowing...".

Additionally, upon examining the students' drawings, it is seen that they reflect the key points of the relevant geographical formations. For example, in the literature, it is known that the concept of a plain includes features such as being lower than its surroundings (1) and having flat or near-flat (2) large flatlands (Doğanay, 2017; Sanır, 2000; MEB, 2021). When students' plain drawings are examined, it is observed that these details are included in the drawings.

Figure 4. Students' River Drawings

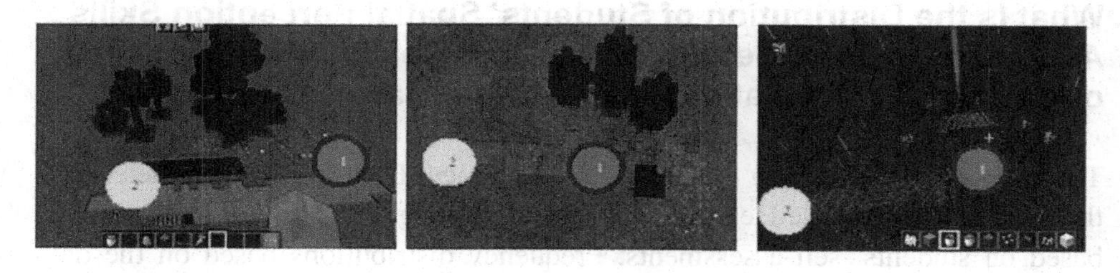

When assessing the above criteria and the student drawings in Figure 4, it's evident that the characteristics related to the concept of a plain are present in the students' drawings. Beyond the physical characteristics of the concept, students have also included human characteristics related to the concept, such as livestock farming, agriculture, and population density, in their drawings. From this perspective, it can be said that the concept of a plain is learned cohesively, encompassing both physical and human factors.

Figure 5. Students' Plateau Drawings

To give another example, in the literature, it is known that the concept of a plateau includes features such as being deeply dissected by rivers (1) and flat or near-flat (2) landforms (Doğanay, 2017; Sanır, 2000; MEB, 2021). Upon examining the students' plateau drawings, it can be observed that these details are also present in their illustrations.

When assessing the above criteria and the student drawings in Figure 5, it can be seen that the physical characteristics related to the concept of a plateau are present in the students' drawings. Further drawings and criteria within the scope of the research are included in the appendices. From these findings, it can be inferred that Minecraft is successful in teaching geographical formations.

What Is the Distribution of Students' Spatial Perception Skills According to Their Self-Assessment in Teaching the Concepts of Geographic Formations Using Game-Based Learning?

The Game-Based Learning Student Self-Assessment Form was used to determine the impact of game-based learning in concept teaching on spatial perception skills, based on students' self-assessments. Frequency distributions based on the data obtained and the learning outcomes are given in Table 4.

Table 4. Frequency and percentage results of the students' self-evaluation form related to their spatial perception ability

Learning Outcome	Category	Frequency	Percentage
River	Neutral	2	28,6
	Agree	5	71,4
Mountain	Disagree	1	14,3
	Agree	6	85,7
Plain	Agree	2	28,6
	Agree	5	71,4
Plateau	Disagree	1	14,3
	Agree	6	85,7
Lake	Disagree	1	14,3
	Neutral	1	14,3
	Agree	5	71,4
Total	Neutral	1	14,3
	Agree	6	85,7

Upon examining Table 4, regarding whether or not the process of teaching concepts through MinecraftEDU had any effect on spatial perception skills, for the concept of a river, 71.4% of students selected the option "I agree," whereas 28.6% opted for "I am undecided." For the concept of a mountain, 85.7% agreed, and 14.3% disagreed. For the concept of a plain, 71.4% agreed, and 28.6% remained undecided. For the concept of a plateau, 85.7% of students agreed, while 14.3% disagreed. A similar distribution was observed for the concept of a lake, with 71.4% agreeing, 14.3% disagreeing, and the remaining 14.3% being undecided. However, when looking at all categories, it is observed that more students selected the "I agree" option. Based on this, it could be stated that according to student self-assessments, game-based learning is effective in enhancing students' spatial perception skills. To verify this data, interviews with students were also conducted.

Table 5. Quotes obtained after the interview

Sub Themes	Direct Quotes
Knows basic information about space	K3: It being sloped, causing a flow and also, how can I put it, being near to agricultural activities (River). K1: For instance, I paid attention to its roundness because the lake is round. I took the examples of touring with ships, I made agricultural lands around. They irrigate with the water of the lake (Lake). K4: I paid attention to the fact that its surroundings are high, but it itself is low. And I built houses to show that there are many people (Plain). K2: I paid attention to being high relative to its surroundings and being flat (Plateau). K1: The highness of the mountain. I realized that mountains are the exact opposite of plateaus, they are sloping, like a triangle (Mountain).
Visualizes in mind	K1: When I was drawing with Minecraft, I really saw the river in the real world before my eyes. K4: I imagined a picture I saw somewhere. K1: Let me explain. After doing the thing, I also made decorations inside, for instance, I went inside and looked at my houses. I looked from above to see how it looks. I took our village as an example, since our village is a plain, I understood that it was a plain when I looked. K1: I wanted to visualize a real plateau, but I've never seen one. For instance, I visualized the plateau as a flat mountain, it was better when I looked at what was in my mind.
Sees in three dimensions	K6: Ma'am, I looked, for instance, I looked from above, it was curved, I saw and made it again. K1: Yes. I looked from top to bottom, from the left, and tried to make it round. It resembled the real shape like that. K6: If I had made the sides protruding, that plateau would not stand there, it would collapse. K3: Ma'am, I climbed to the top and looked (Mountain). K7: From the side and bird's eye view (Mountain).
Draws and interprets sketches	K4: I paid attention to it being long and having water inside. And I added fields to the edges, put fish inside. K3: I used water. To erode around it. I used a pickaxe and also put a block for flatness. (Plateau). K2: I used soil, stone and minerals. (Mountain)
Compares with reality	K1: I understood that life is difficult in the mountains. I understood that there are fewer people because it is sloping.
Gives examples	K4: For instance, I didn't know that this village was a plain, I learned.

What Are the Fifth-Grade Students' Opinions on the Effect of the Game Minecraft: Education Edition, Which They Use in Teaching the Concepts of Geographical Formations in Social Studies Lessons, on Their Spatial Perception Skills?

Based on the interview results, the quotes obtained in accordance with the table of spatial perception skills determined prior to the research, which is supported by literature, are given in

Upon examination of Table 5, it can be seen that there are direct quotes indicating that students have improved their spatial perception skills in teaching the concepts of plateau, lake, mountain, plain, and river. To summarize some points; when examining the first concept, the river, it is observed that K1's statement "While drawing with Minecraft, I really visualized the river in the real world," directly expresses one of the sub-themes of spatial perception skills, mental imagery. K6's statement, "I looked from above, it was crooked, so I redid it," encompasses the sub-theme of seeing in three dimensions, and also shows that they used this feature to correct faults in their concept drawings. K4's statement, "I paid attention to it being long and having water in it. I added fields to the sides and put fish in it," meets the sub-theme of sketching and interpreting. Moreover, it is crucial as it not only defines the physical features of the concept but also shows that human influences such as agriculture and aquaculture were learned. This is in line with the integrated nature of social studies.

On the other hand, the sub-theme of the spatial perception skill related to the concept of a lake, the mental visualization theme, is depicted in K4's statement, "I envisioned a picture I saw somewhere." Students' expressions indicate that they mentally visualized real forms. This situation could be attributed to the presence of different types of lakes in their environment. K1's statement, "Yes. I looked from above, below, from the left and tried to form it into a circle. It looked similar to its real shape," relates to the sub-theme of three-dimensional visualization. This statement not only shows that this sub-theme was utilized but also indicates that students' visual drawings were organized in this manner.

Examining the concept of a plain, K1's sentences, "For instance, let me explain. After completing that task, I also decorated the inside; for instance, I examined my houses. I observed from above how it appears. I took our village as an example, as there's a plain in our village, and when I looked at it, I recognized it as a plain," encompasses both three-dimensional and mental visualization sub-themes. From K4's statement, "For example, I wasn't aware that this village was a plain until I learned," it can be inferred that students were able to establish connections with the real world and create examples after their drawings related to the concept of a plain.

Regarding the concept of a plateau, K6's expression, "If I had made its sides protrude, that plateau wouldn't have stood there; it would have collapsed," directly articulates the three-dimensional viewing theme, one of the spatial perception skills' sub-themes. It's also intriguing that three-dimensional visualization is considered in terms of gravity. Similarly, K1 conveyed the mental visualization theme, another spatial perception skill sub-theme, saying, "I aimed to visualize a real plateau, but I had never seen one." He explained his drawing process of an unfamiliar landform with the phrase, "For instance, I visualized a plateau as a flat mountain. I looked at it in my mind's eye; it was more beautiful that way." K3's statement, "I used water. To erode its surroundings. I used a pickaxe, and I also placed a block for its flatness..." in the sketching and interpreting sub-theme subtly alludes to water's role in plateau formation. It could be inferred that he attempted to draw the eroded parts of plateaus from a bird's eye view.

Examining the final theme, the concept of a mountain, K1's statement, "I realized that life is challenging in the mountains. I understood that there are fewer people because it is sloping," directly relates to the sub-theme of comparing reality within spatial perception skills. Also, K1's statement allows for a comparison between the structure of mountains in reality and his three-dimensional drawing. This statement also exemplifies why population density is low. To achieve three-dimensional visualization, students examined their drawings from various angles; K3 articulated this as "Teacher, I climbed to the top and looked," and K7 expressed it as "From the side and bird's-eye view." Unlike other students, K2 attempted to sketch not only the external appearance but also the cross-section of the mountain, saying, "I used soil, rocks, and minerals."

In general, when evaluating the interviews with the students, it is apparent that during the process of illustrating the taught landform concepts through Minecraft, the students were able to execute all the themes encompassed within their spatial perception skills: "Understanding basic information related to space," "Mental visualization," "Three-dimensional viewing," "Sketching and interpreting," "Comparing with reality," and "Providing examples." Hence, it could be argued that the illustration of landforms with Minecraft positively enhances students' spatial perception skills.

CONCLUSION AND DISCUSSION

In the boundless universes of digital games, learning social studies subjects such as geography, history, and culture within the limits set by our imagination turns into an adventure. The interactive, experiential, and visual-based features of digital games can assist students in understanding these complex concepts more profoundly (Sung

& Hwang, 2013). Therefore, the integration of digital games into social studies education emerges as a significant strategy for improving quality in education. In this context, this study examined the impact of digital game-assisted teaching (Minecraft: Education Edition) of landform concepts included in the Social Studies course on the success and spatial perception skills of 5th-grade students.

As a result of the research, firstly, it was found that teaching the concepts of landforms with Minecraft led to an increase in students' success scores, in other words, improved their performance. Similarly, González et al. (2021) found that Minecraft allows the concept of geographical space, its components, and features to be deepened. In another study, it was demonstrated that Minecraft produced positive results in remote education processes for learning the basic concepts of cartography (Sena & Jordãob, 2021) and increased students' interest and awareness in landforms and geology (Iwahashi et al., 2020). The effectiveness of Minecraft in teaching basic geological concepts has also been highlighted (Rader et al., 2021; Short, 2012). Although these findings directly relate this increase in success to the Minecraft game and prevent us from inferring that digital games are effective in social studies teaching, it is understood that different types of digital games also have positive effects such as geography, perspective-taking, cultural spread (Maguth, List, & Wunderle, 2015); map and, relatedly, scale building (Zheng & Spires, 2014; Nietfeld, 2019), promoting geographical creativity (Kim & Shin, 2016). These studies enable the generalizability of our study findings and indicate that when combined with other research, we can infer that digital games positively affect students' success in social studies teaching. In fact, these findings eliminate the problem of the small group among the limitations of the study while adding Minecraft to the games that could be effective in social studies teaching. Especially when considering the potential of digital games in teaching abstract concepts in social studies education (Maguth, List, & Wunderle, 2015; Khurshid & Bibi, 2020), Minecraft can be used to ensure academic success (Koka, 2018; Öztürk & Yeşiltaş, 2015; Doğan 2017) and the permanence of their knowledge (Koka, 2018; Çalışkan & Biter 2019). The reason for this could be the concretization of these concepts (Maguth, List, & Wunderle, 2015; Khurshid & Bibi, 2020) as a result of teaching abstract concepts in 3D with digital games (Carbonell et al. 2017; Carbonell et al., 2021), and the living ecosystem of MinecraftEDU (Short, 2012), even if virtual, being experienced from a first-person perspective (Carbonell et al., 2020), which can be associated with the feeling of enjoyment experienced in line with the nature of game-based teaching (Spires & Lester, 2016).

Another finding revealed by the research is that MinecraftEDU enhances students' spatial perception skills. Both student views and teacher observations indicate that students' spatial perception skills have improved during educational activities conducted with Minecraft. Although not directly related to social studies teaching, similar findings can be encountered in studies conducted with different digital games and gains. For example, in a study conducted by Aydoğan and Karabağ (2020) using a game called Atayolu, it was determined that the game used improved students' spatial perception skillsA study conducted by Feng, Feng, Spence, and Pratt (2007) revealed that action video games could improve spatial skills such as spatial perception, mental rotation, and the ability to switch between multiple tasks. Boot et al. (2008) have shown that strategy-based video games can enhance cognitive skills such as spatial perception and memory. Green and Bavelie (2006) claim that action video games can enhance visual-spatial attention and rapid decision-making ability. Again, in another study, Green and Bavelie (2003) have shown that people who play action video games have significantly better spatial perception skills than those who do not. Of course, at this point, it would be appropriate to discuss some of the reasons as well. The Minecraft game facilitates the transition between 2D and 3D (Carbonell et al., 2021), making mental rotation and spatial visualization easier (Sms, 2021). Mental rotation refers to the ability to rotate 2D and 3D objects in the mind (Shepard, 1971). This situation seems to correspond exactly to the "ability to see a shape in three dimensions", which is attributed as important for spatial perception skill. The Committee on Support for Thinking Spatially (2006) sees spatial thinking as a high-value geographic skill that helps us understand, reason, and represent spatial methods, the properties of represented spaces, and the relationships that arise between them (Carbonell et al., 2020). The features of spatial thinking skills reflected in the field literature also focus on the representation of space and the depiction of objects. Minecraft's open world and user-centric design (Kafai & Burke, 2015), unique storytelling (Dezuanni, O'Mara, & Beavis, 2015), and the possibility of building with simple blocks might have played a role in enhancing students' spatial perception skills.

The results of this study reveal the values that digital games, especially Minecraft: Education Edition, add to social studies teaching. There is a fact supported by both the current findings in the literature and the results of this study, that digital games are an effective tool in social studies teaching, especially in teaching subjects such as geography, history, and culture. This study has shown that Minecraft can be a learning tool that helps students understand complex concepts, beyond just being an entertaining game.

SUGGESTIONS

In future studies, along with the impact of Minecraft on improving students' achievements, its effects on other spatial and social skills can be examined in more detail. In particular, the investigation of other digital games that can enhance students' spatial perception skills can make significant contributions to the accumulation of knowledge in this field. Furthermore, it is recommended that games like Minecraft: Education Edition be used more extensively in schools. Providing teachers with training to integrate these types of games into their classes will ensure that students benefit from these games in the best possible way. These games can increase the quality of education and make students' learning process more fun and effective.

Lastly, educators and researchers are encouraged to delve deeper into the potential of digital games in teaching social studies. The topic of how Minecraft and similar games can be used to particularly enhance students' academic achievements and knowledge retention could be the focus of future research.

LIMITATIONS

This study has a number of limitations. First, due to the restrictions of the COVID-19 pandemic, the study could only be conducted on a limited group of students. This could limit the generalizability of the sample and necessitates caution when extrapolating the results to the entire student population. Second, this study focused on specific social studies concepts. This situation limits the breadth and depth of the results. Focusing solely on specific concepts may lead to a lack of complete understanding of the effects on the teaching of the entire social studies curriculum. These limitations indicate that future research needs to expand this study using larger and more comprehensive sample groups and wider sets of concepts.

ACKNOWLEDGMENT

Ethical Approval: No ethical approval was required for this study as it did not involve any experiments on animals or humans.

Competing Interests: The authors declare that they have no financial or personal conflicts of interest in relation to this study.

Authors' Contributions: All authors have equally contributed to the design of the research, data collection, and the writing of the paper.

Funding: This study has not been funded by any institution or organization.

Availability of Data and Materials: The datasets and materials used in this study will be made publicly available in an appropriate data repository.

REFERENCES

Adachi, P. J., & Willoughby, T. (2013). Do video games promote positive youth development? *Journal of Adolescent Research, 28*(2), 155–165. doi:10.1177/0743558412464522

Åstedt-Kurki, P., & Heikkinen, R. L. (1994). Two approaches to the study of experiences of health and old age: The thematic interview and the narrative method. *Journal of Advanced Nursing, 20*(3), 418–421. doi:10.1111/j.1365-2648.1994.tb02375.x PMID:7963044

Aydoğan, O., & Karabağ, G. (2020). The effect of history teaching supported by educational computer games on students' chronological thinking and space perception skills. *Uluslararası Sosyal Bilgilerde Yeni Yaklaşımlar Dergisi, 4*(1), 106–130.

Bányai, F., Griffiths, M. D., Király, O., & Demetrovics, Z. (2019). The psychology of esports: A systematic literature review. *Journal of Gambling Studies, 35*(2), 351–365. doi:10.1007/s10899-018-9763-1 PMID:29508260

Barriball, L. K., & While, A. (1994) Collecting Data Using a Semi-Structured Interview: A Discussion Paper. *Journal of Advanced Nursing, 19*, 328-335.

Bashandy, H. (2021). Playing, mapping, and power a critical analysis of using minecraft in spatial design. *American Journal of Play, 12*(3), 363–369.

Baştürk, S., & Taştepe, M. (2013). *Bilimsel araştırma yöntemleri* [Scientific research methods]. Vize Yayıncılık.

Baumbusch, J. (2010). Semi-structured interviewing in practice-close research. *Journal for Specialists in Pediatric Nursing, 15*(3), 255–258. doi:10.1111/j.1744-6155.2010.00243.x PMID:20618640

Beins, B. C. (2017). *Research method: a tool for life*. Cambridge University Press.

Bi, T., & Song, S. (2011). *Problems and solutions of educational game development* [Conference presentation]. 2011 International Conference on Consumer Electronics, Xianning, China.

Blanco-Herrera, J. A., Gentile, D. A., & Rokkum, J. N. (2019). Video games can increase creativity, but with caveats. *Creativity Research Journal, 31*(2), 119–131. doi:10.1080/10400419.2019.1594524

Blumberg, F. C., & Altschuler, E. (2011). From the playroom to the classroom: Children's views of video game play and academic learning. *Child Development Perspectives, 5*(2), 99–103. doi:10.1111/j.1750-8606.2011.00163.x

Bolick, C., Adams, R., & Willox, L. (2019). The marginalization of elementary social studies in teacher education. *Social Studies Research & Practice*, *14*(3), 31–44.

Boot, W. R., Kramer, A. F., Simons, D. J., Fabiani, M., & Gratton, G. (2008). The effects of video game playing on attention, memory, and executive control. *Acta Psychologica*, *129*(3), 387–398. doi:10.1016/j.actpsy.2008.09.005 PMID:18929349

Çalışkan, H., & Biter, M. (2019). Values education with educational in social studies courses: An action research. *Journal of Interdisciplinary Education: Theory and Practice*, *1*(1), 1–28.

Carbonell, C., Avarvarei, B. V., Chelariu, E. L., Draghia, L., & Avarvarei, S. C. (2017). Mapreading skill development with 3d technologies. *The Journal of Geography*, *116*(5), 197–205. doi:10.1080/00221341.2016.1248857

Carbonell, C., Gunalp, P., Saorin, J. L., & Hess-Medler, S. (2020). Think spatially with game engine. *ISPRS International Journal of Geo-Information*, *9*(03), 159. doi:10.3390/ijgi9030159

Carbonell-Carrera, C., Jaeger, A. J., Saorín, J. L., Melián, D., & de la Torre-Cantero, J. (2021). Minecraft as a block building approach for developing spatial skills. *Entertainment Computing*, *38*, 1–7. doi:10.1016/j.entcom.2021.100427

Checa-Romero, M., & Pascual Gómez, I. (2018). Minecraft and machinima in action: Development of creativity in the classroom. *Technology, Pedagogy and Education*, *27*(5), 625–637. doi:10.1080/1475939X.2018.1537933

Chenail, R. J. (2011). Ten Steps for Conceptualizing and Conducting Qualitative Research Studies in a Pragmatically Curious Manner. *The Qualitative Report*, *16*(6), 1715–1732.

Choo, A., Karamnejad, M., & May, A. (2013). *Maintaining long distance togetherness Synchronous communication with Minecraft and Skype* [Conference presentation]. 2013 IEEE International Games Innovation Conference, Vancouver, Canada.

Clark, D. B., Virk, S. S., Barnes, J., & Adams, D. M. (2016). Self-explanation and digital games: Adaptively increasing abstraction. *Computers & Education*, *103*, 28–43. doi:10.1016/j.compedu.2016.09.010

Committee on Support for Thinking Spatially. (2006). *Learning to think spatially*. National Academies Press.

Connolly, T. M., Boyle, E. A., MacArthur, E., Hainey, T., & Boyle, J. M. (2012). A systematic literature review of empirical evidence on computer games and serious games. *Computers & Education*, *59*(2), 661–686. doi:10.1016/j.compedu.2012.03.004

Creswell, J. W. (2021). *Araştırma deseni nitel, nicel ve karma yöntem yaklaşımları*. Nobel Akademik.

Cridland, E. K., Jones, S. C., Caputi, P., & Magee, C. A. (2015). Qualitative research with families living with autism spectrum disorder: Recommendations for conducting semistructured interviews. *Journal of Intellectual & Developmental Disability, 40*(1), 78–91. doi:10.3109/13668250.2014.964191

De Cecco, J. P. (1968). *The psychology of learning and instruction: educational psychology*. Prentice-Hall.

Dearnley, C. (2005). A reflection on the use of semi-structured interviews. *Nurse Researcher, 13*(1), 19–28. doi:10.7748/nr2005.07.13.1.19.c5997 PMID:16220838

Denzin, N. K. (1978). Triangulation: A case for methodological evaluation and combination. *Sociological Methods*, 339-357.

Dezuanni, M., O'Mara, J., & Beavis, C. (2015). 'Redstone is like electricity': Children's performative representations in and around Minecraft. *E-Learning and Digital Media, 12*(2), 147–163. doi:10.1177/2042753014568176

Doğan, E. & Koç, H. (2017). The impact of instruction through digital games on students' academic achievement in teaching earthquakes in a social science class. *Uluslararası Türk Eğitim Bilimleri Dergisi, 5*(8).

Doğanay, H. (2017). *Coğrafya bilim alanları sözlüğü* [Dictionary of geography science fields]. PEGEM Akademi.

Egbert, J., & Borysenko, N. (2019). Standards, engagement, and Minecraft: Optimizing experiences in language teacher education. *Teaching and Teacher Education, 85*, 115–124. doi:10.1016/j.tate.2019.06.015

Erkuş, A. (2003). *Psikometri üzerine yazılar* [Articles on psychometrics]. Türk Psikologlar Derneği Yayınları.

Erol, F. Z., & Akpınar, E. (2021). A review on experimental studies on the ability to perceive space carried out in the field of social studies education. *International Journal of Social Science Research, 10*(1), 1–16.

Feng, J., Spence, I., & Pratt, J. (2007). Playing an action video game reduces gender differences in spatial cognition. *Psychological Science, 18*(10), 850–855. doi:10.1111/j.1467-9280.2007.01990.x PMID:17894600

Fitchett, P. G., & Heafner, T. L. (2010). A national perspective on the effects of high-stakes testing and standardization on elementary social studies marginalization. *Theory and Research in Social Education, 38*(1), 114–130. doi:10.1080/00933104.2010.10473418

Flores, N., Paiva, A. C., & Cruz, N. (2020). Teaching software engineering topics through pedagogical game design patterns: An empirical study. *Information (Basel), 11*(3), 153. doi:10.3390/info11030153

Gauquier, E., & Schneider, J. (2013). Minecraft programs in the library. *Young Adult Library Services, 11*(2), 17–19.

Gee, J. P. (2007). *Good video games good learning: Collected essays on video games, learning, and literacy*. Peter Lang. doi:10.3726/978-1-4539-1162-4

González, C., Barreda, G., Ortega, M., Ampuero, C., & Norambuena, M. (2021). Geografía y Minecraft: Potencialidades de una herramienta para la enseñanza a partir de un videojuego de mundo abierto. *Informes Científicos Técnicos, 13*(1), 30–53. doi:10.22305/ict-unpa.v13.n1.788

Granic, I., Lobel, A., & Engels, R. C. (2014). The benefits of playing video games. *The American Psychologist, 69*(1), 66–78. doi:10.1037/a0034857 PMID:24295515

Green, C. S., & Bavelier, D. (2006). Effect of action video games on the spatial distribution of visuospatial attention. *Journal of Experimental Psychology. Human Perception and Performance, 32*(6), 1465–1478. doi:10.1037/0096-1523.32.6.1465 PMID:17154785

Green, C. S., & Bavelier, D. (2012). Learning, attentional control, and action video games. *Current Biology, 22*(6), R197–R206. doi:10.1016/j.cub.2012.02.012 PMID:22440805

Gros, B. (2017). Game dimensions and pedagogical dimension in serious games. In Handbook of Research on Serious Games for Educational Applications (pp. 402-417). IGI Global. doi:10.4018/978-1-5225-0513-6.ch019

Guba, E. G., & Lincoln, Y. S. (1982). Epistemological and methodological bases of naturalistic inquiry. *Educational Communication and Technology, 30*(4), 233–252. doi:10.1007/BF02765185

Güneş, G., Ayantaş, T., Güneş, C., Güleryüz, O., & Arıkan, A. (2021). Review of theses on the use of technology in social studies education. *Türkiye Sosyal Araştırmalar dergisi, 25*(3), 859-890.

Hill, V. (2015). Digital citizenship through game design in Minecraft. *New Library World, 116*(7-8), 369–382. doi:10.1108/NLW-09-2014-0112

Holloway, I., & Wheeler, S. (1996). *Qualitative research for nurses*. Blackwell Science.

Junco, R. (2014). Beyond screen time: What minecraft teaches kids. *Atlantic (Boston, Mass.)*.

Kafai, Y. B. (2006). Playing and making games for learning. *Games and Culture, 1*(1), 36–40. doi:10.1177/1555412005281767

Kafai, Y. B., & Burke, Q. (2015). Constructionist gaming: Understanding the benefits of making games for learning. *Educational Psychologist, 50*(4), 313–334. doi:10.1080/00461520.2015.1124022 PMID:27019536

Kallio, H., Pietilä, A. M., Johnson, M., & Kangasniemi, M. (2016). Systematic methodological review: Developing a framework for a qualitative semi-structured interview guide. *Journal of Advanced Nursing, 72*(12), 2954–2965. doi:10.1111/jan.13031 PMID:27221824

Kaplan, A., & Haenlein, M. (2020). Rulers of the world, unite! The challenges and opportunities of artificial intelligence. *Business Horizons, 63*(1), 37–50. doi:10.1016/j.bushor.2019.09.003

Kapp, K. M. (2012). *The gamification of learning and ınstruction: game-based methods and strategies for training and education*. John Wiley & Sons.

Karamustafaoğlu, O., & Kılıç, M. F. (2020). Investıgatıon of natıonal scıentıfıc studıes about educatıonal games. *Atatürk Üniversitesi Kazım Karabekir Eğitim Fakültesi Dergisi*, (40), 1–25.

Kastens, K. A., & Ishikawa, T. (2006). Spatial thinking in the geosciences and cognitive sciences: A cross-disciplinary look at the intersection of the two fields. *Special Papers-Geological Society of America, 413*, 53. doi:10.1130/2006.2413(05)

Khurshid, F., Bibi, M., & Bibi, M. (2020). Effectiveness of educational videos and games for the concepts clarity and understanding of social studies subject: An intervention study. *Pakistan Journal of Education, 37*(2), 61–78. doi:10.30971/pje.v37i2.1310

Kılıç, S. (2013). Sampling methods. *Journal of Mood Disorders, 3*(1), 44–46. doi:10.5455/jmood.20130325011730

Kim, M., & Shin, J. (2016). The pedagogical benefits of SimCity in urban geography education. *The Journal of Geography, 115*(2), 39–50. doi:10.1080/00221341.2015.1061585

Klausmeier, H. J. (1992). Concept learning and concept teaching. *Educational Psychologist, 27*(3), 267–286. doi:10.1207/s15326985ep2703_1

Koka, V. (2018). *Sosyal bilgiler dersinde kullanılan bilgisayar destekli eğitsel oyunların öğrencilerin ders başarısına olan etkisi* [The effect of computer aıded educatıonal games used ın socıal scıences course] (Unpublished master thesis), İnönü Üniversitesi Eğitim Bilimleri Enstitüsü, Malatya.

Köstlbauer, J. (2018). The strange attraction of simulation realism, authenticity, virtuality. In Playing with the Past: Digital Games and the Simulation of History (pp. 169-183). Bloomsbury Academic.

Krauss, S. E., Hamzah, A., Omar, Z., Suandi, T., Ismail, I. A., Zahari, M. Z., & Nor, Z. M. (2009). Preliminary investigation and interview guide development for studying how Malaysian farmers' form their mental models of farming. *The Qualitative Report, 14*(2), 245.

Lawshe, C. H. (1975). A quantitative approach to content validity. *Personnel Psychology, 28*(4), 563–575. doi:10.1111/j.1744-6570.1975.tb01393.x

Maguth, B. M., List, J. S., & Wunderle, M. (2015). Teaching social studies with video games. *Social Studies, 106*(1), 32–36. doi:10.1080/00377996.2014.961996

Marcon, N., & Faulkner, J. (2016). Exploring minecraft as a pedagogy to motivate girls' literacy practices in the secondary English classroom. *Engineers Australia, 51*(1), 63–69.

Mathewson, J. H. (1999). Visual-spatial thinking: An aspect of science overlooked by educators. *Science Education, 83*(1), 33–54. doi:10.1002/(SICI)1098-237X(199901)83:1<33::AID-SCE2>3.0.CO;2-Z

Mavoa, J., Carter, M., & Gibbs, M. (2018). Children and minecraft: A survey of children's digital play. *New Media & Society, 20*(9), 3283–3303. doi:10.1177/1461444817745320

McGonigal, J. (2011). *Reality is broken: Why games make us better and how they can change the world*. Penguin.

MEB. (2004). İlköğretim sosyal bilgiler dersi 4-5. sınıflar öğretim program [Elementary social studies curriculum for 4th and 5th grades]. Talim ve Terbiye Başkanlığı, Ankara: MEB.

MEB. (2018). Sosyal bilgiler dersi (4, 5, 6 ve 7. sınıflar) öğretim program [Social studies curriculum for 4th, 5th, 6th and 7th grades]. Ankara.

MEB. (2021). *5. Sınıf sosyal bilgiler ders kitabı* [5th grade social studies textbook]. Millî Eğitim Bakanlığı.

Merriam, S. B. (1998). *Qualitative research and case study applications in education*. Jossey-Bass Publishers.

Miles, M. B., & Huberman, A. M. (1994). Qualitative data analysis: An expanded sourcebook. Thousand Oaks.

Mix, K. S., Levine, S. C., Cheng, Y.-L., Young, C. J., Hambrick, D. Z., & Konstantopoulos, S. (2017). The latent structure of spatial skills and mathematics: Further evidence from wave 2. *Journal of Cognition and Development*, *4*, 465–492. doi:10.1080/15248372.2017.1346658

Mørch, A. I., Eie, S., & Mifsud, L. (2018). Tradeoffs in combining domain-specific and generic skills' practice in minecraft in social studies in teacher education. *Cultures of Participation in the Digital Age*, *2101*(6), 44–52.

Morin, J. É., Olsson, C., & Atikcan, E. Ö. (2021). *Research methods in the social sciences: An az of key concepts*. Oxford University Press. doi:10.1093/hepl/9780198850298.001.0001

Newzoo. (2020). *The Impact of Coronavirus on Games and Esports: Our First Thoughts*. Retreived 13 June 2023 from https://newzoo.com/news/impact-of-coronavirus-on-games-and-esports-our-first-thoughts/

Nietfeld, J. L. (2019). Predicting transfer from a game-based learning environment. *Computers & Education*, 146.

Öztürk, T., & Yeşiltaş, E. (2015). The effect of computer supported instruction on students achievements in civics topics of social studies lesson. *E-International Journal of Educational Research*, *6*(2), 86–101.

Patton, M. Q. (2002). *Qualitative research and evaluation methods*. Sage Publications.

Peppler, K., Danish, J., Zaitlen, B., Glosson, D., Jacobs, A., & Phelps, D. (2010). BeeSim: Leveraging wearable computers in participatory simulations with young children. *Proceedings of the Ninth International Conference on Interaction Design and Children (IDC 2010)*, (pp. 246–249). ACM. 10.1145/1810543.1810582

Perini, S., Oliveira, M., Margoudi, M., & Taisch, M. (2018). The use of digital game based learning in manufacturing education–a case study. *Learning and Collaboration Technologies. Learning and Teaching: 5th International Conference, LCT 2018, Held as Part of HCI International 2018, Las Vegas, NV, USA, July 15-20, 2018 Proceedings*, *5*(Part II), 185–199.

Rader, E., Love, R., Reano, D., Dousay, T. A., & Wingerter, N. (2021). Pandemic minecrafting: An analysis of the perceptions of and lessons learned from a gamified virtual geology field camp. *Geoscience Communication*, *4*(4), 475–492. doi:10.5194/gc-4-475-2021

Reich, J. (2020). *Failure to disrupt: why technology alone can't transform education*. Harvard University Press.

Sala, G., & Gobet, F. (2019). Cognitive training does not enhance general cognition. *Trends in Cognitive Sciences*, *23*(1), 9–20. doi:10.1016/j.tics.2018.10.004 PMID:30471868

Saldana, J. (2009). *The Coding Manual for Qualitative Researchers*. Sage Publications.

Sanchez-Mena, A., & Marti-Parreño, J. (2017). Drivers and barriers to adopting gamification: Teachers' perspectives. *Electronic Journal of e-Learning*, *5*(15), 434–443.

Sanır, F. (2000). *Coğrafya terimleri sözlüğü* [Dictionary of geography terms]. Gazi Kitapevi.

Schug, M. C., Todd, R. J., & Beery, R. (1982). *Why kids don't like social studies*. National Council for the Social Studies.

Sena, C. C. R. G., & Jordãob, B. G. F. (2021). Challenges in the teaching of cartography during the COVID-19 pandemic: use of minecraft in the remote classroom setting. *Proceedings of the ICA*, (4). 10.5194/ica-proc-4-99-2021

Shepard, R. N., & Metzler, J. (1971). Mental rotation of three-dimensional objects. *Science*, *171*(3972), 701–703. doi:10.1126/science.171.3972.701 PMID:5540314

Short, D. (2012). Teaching scientific concepts using a virtual world: Minecraft. *Teaching Science*, *58*(3), 55-58.

Smeyers, P. (2018). *International handbook of philosophy of education*. Springer. doi:10.1007/978-3-319-72761-5

Sms, S. (2021). Recognizing mental rotation and spatial visualization skills in Minecraft in-game practices. *Proceedings of the International Conference on Future of Education, 4*(1), 47-57.

Sorby, S. A. (2009). Educational research in developing 3-D spatial skills for engineering students. *International Journal of Science Education, 31*(3), 459–480. doi:10.1080/09500690802595839

Sousa, M. J., & Rocha, Á. (2019). Leadership styles and skills developed through game-based learning. *Journal of Business Research, 94*, 360–366. doi:10.1016/j.jbusres.2018.01.057

Spires, H. A., & Lester, J. C. (2016). Game-based learning: Creating a multidisciplinary community of inquiry. *On the Horizon, 24*(1), 88–93. doi:10.1108/OTH-08-2015-0052

Squire, K. D. (2008). Video game–based learning: An emerging paradigm for instruction. *Performance Improvement Quarterly, 21*(2), 7–36. doi:10.1002/piq.20020

Statica. (2023). *Video gaming worldwide*. Statista. Retreived june 2023 from https://www.statista.com/topics/1680/gaming/#topicOverview

Sung, H. Y., & Hwang, G. J. (2013). A collaborative game-based learning approach to improving students' learning performance in science courses. *Computers & Education, 63*, 43–51. doi:10.1016/j.compedu.2012.11.019

Taba, H. (1967). *Teachers' handbook for elementary social studies*. Addison-Wesley.

Turner, D. W. (2010). Qualitative interview design: A practical guide for novice investigators. *The qualitative report, 15*(3), 754.

Udeozor, C., Toyoda, R., Russo Abegão, F., & Glassey, J. (2022). Digital games in engineering education: Systematic review and future trends. *European Journal of Engineering Education, 48*(2), 321–339. doi:10.1080/03043797.2022.2093168

Veneziano, L., & Hooper, J. (1997). A method for quantifying content validity of health-related questionnaires. *American Journal of Health Behavior, 21*(1), 67–70.

Wai, J., Lubinski, D., & Benbow, C. P. (2009). Spatial ability for STEM domains: Aligning over 50 years of cumulative psychological knowledge solidifies its importance. *Journal of Educational Psychology, 101*(4), 817–835. doi:10.1037/a0016127

Whiting, L. S. (2008). Semi-structured interviews: Guidance for novice researchers. *Nursing Standard, 22*(23), 35–40. doi:10.7748/ns2008.02.22.23.35.c6420 PMID:18323051

Wolbers, T., & Hegarty, M. (2010). What determines our navigational abilities? *Trends in Cognitive Sciences*, *14*(3), 138–146. doi:10.1016/j.tics.2010.01.001 PMID:20138795

Wood, D. (2010). *Rethinking the power of maps*. Guilford Press.

Yeşiltaş, E., & Cantürk, A. (2022). Trends of researches on the use of games in social studies education: 1971 – 2021. *Journal of History School*, *15*(61), 4434–4466.

Yurdugül, H. (2005). Ölçek geliştirme çalışmalarında kapsam geçerliği için kapsam geçerlik indekslerinin kullanılması [Using content validity indices for content validity in scale development studies]. XIV. Ulusal Eğitim Bilimleri Kongresi. Pamukkale Üniversitesi.

Zheng, M., & Spires, H. A. (2014). Fifth graders' flow experience in a digital game-based science learning environment. *International Journal of Virtual and Personal Learning Environments*, *5*(2), 69–86. doi:10.4018/ijvple.2014040106

Chapter 10
Navigating the Complexities of Academic Integrity in E-Learning:
Challenges and Strategies

Rajni Bala
https://orcid.org/0000-0002-1225-939X
Chitkara Business School, Chitkara University, Punjab, India

Prachi Gupta
https://orcid.org/0009-0007-2757-7212
Chitkara Business School, Chitkara University, Punjab, India

ABSTRACT

Learning has been transformed by e-learning, which makes it simpler to learn from any location. It can be challenging, tough, to make sure people are being truthful when they learn online. As it is very easy to get material online, people can engage in practices like copying from the internet and cheating in online tests. We need to come up with innovative strategies to fight cheating and maintain equitable education for all as technology advances. To guarantee that everyone adheres to the same standards of honesty, educational institutions require support and well-defined policies. The study investigates the driving force behind student involvement in academic dishonesty. The solutions and difficulties of upholding the academic integrity in online learning contexts are also covered in the study. This chapter discusses the factors responsible for students' involvement in academic dishonesty. The chapter also discusses strategies that educational institutions can adopt to maintain academic integrity.

DOI: 10.4018/979-8-3693-3015-9.ch010

Copyright © 2024, IGI Global. Copying or distributing in print or electronic forms without written permission of IGI Global is prohibited.

INTRODUCTION

E-learning offers a dynamic platform to individuals where they can acquire knowledge and skill. But these days due to virtual landscape of education, it is not easy to maintain academic honesty. Academic integrity is the ethical cornerstone where students can learn with transparency, honesty and committed to ethical behavior. In the e-learning environment, where students may physically be miles apart but share the same virtual classroom, preserving of academic integrity takes on a unique challenges and opportunities (E. Orok et al., 2023). Examinations, an assessment method in higher education, aim to evaluate students' proficiency in meeting course objectives (Ahmad & Hamed, 2014). However, this method is also facing challenges due to increasing academic dishonesty and misconduct. A culture of cheating among students undermines the intended purpose of assessing knowledge through examination (Diego 2017; Forkuor et al. 2019). With technological advancement, new e-tools are coming to reduce academic dishonesty. But yes educational institutions need to explore strategies that can promote academic honesty among students. So the objectives of the study are:

A. Explore the potential strategies to maintain academic integrity in e-learning.
B. Examine the existing tools to promote academic integrity in e-learning.
C. Identify the challenges to academic integrity in e-learning environments.

ACADEMIC INTEGRITY

Academic integrity means five core principles as respect, trust, fairness, honesty & responsibility (TEQSA, 2021). It requires that all researchers, teachers, academicians, students show above five principles in their actions. It means to conduct any research, study with ethical behavior. Actually, it describes the behavior of an individual with faced with multiple choices. Violations of ethical behavior are termed as Academic Dishonesty. Academic Dishonesty not only applicable for students but to each and everyone who is involved in academic environment. (Cizek, 2003; Whitley, Jr. & Keith-Spiegel, 2002). Academic Dishonesty is a big crime, whether it is done deliberately or not (NIU, 2023).

ACADEMIC DISHONESTY

Academic dishonesty encompasses engaging in or facilitating dishonest behaviours within teaching, learning, research, and associated academic endeavors, applying to all academic community members (Whitley, Jr. & Keith-Spiegel, 2002). It is considered a grave transgression irrespective of intent (NIU, 2023). The issues extend globally, impacting developed and developing nations (Ubaka et.al 2013). Notably, there appears to be a growing incidence of academic dishonesty in developing countries, potentially attributed to cultural and socioeconomic disparities countries (Al-Qahtani & Guraya 2019), along with variations in the perception of academic misconduct (McGurgan et al. 2020).

TYPES OF ACADEMIC DISHONESTY

Figure 1. Types of Academic Dishonesty

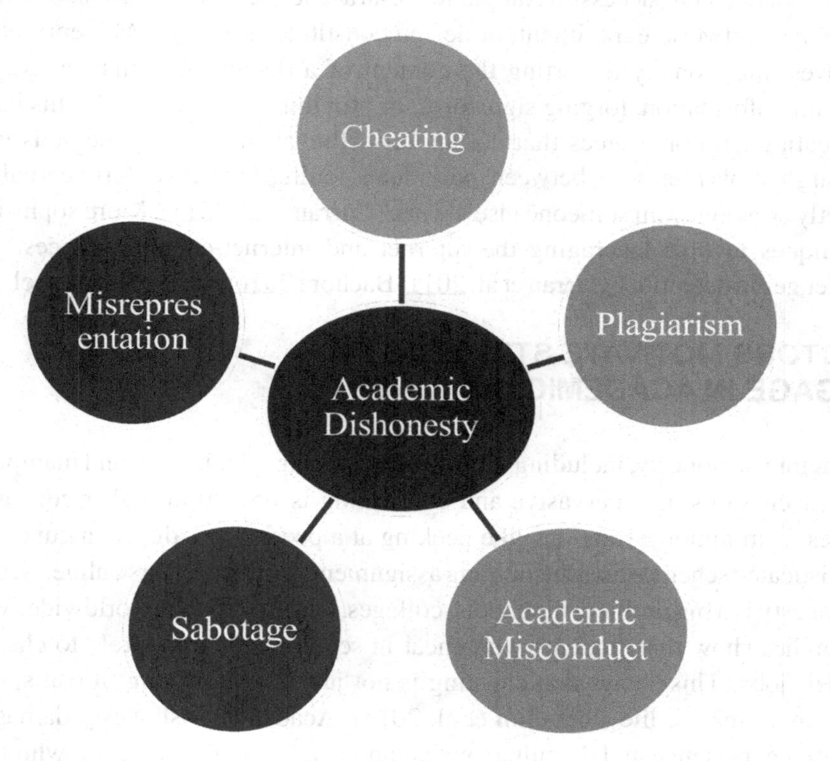

Academic dishonesty manifests in various forms, broadly categorized as cheating, plagiarism, academic misconduct, sabotage, and misrepresentation (Whitley, Jr. & Keith-Spigel, 2002; Pavela, 1978). Cheating entails the unauthorized utilization of information, materials, devices, sources, or practices to complete academic tasks. For example, They are copying from another student's test or homework, employing materials like textbooks or notes during a test without instructor approval, or enlisting someone else to compose or design a paper. Plagiarism involves intentionally or unintentionally, presenting another individual's words or ideas as one's own without proper attribution. Instances include copying and pasting content from websites, books, journals, or magazines into one's document without citation or failing to acknowledge materials created by others. Additionally, submitting identical work for multiple courses without instructor consent constitutes plagiarism.

Academic misconduct entails violating regulations by manipulating grades or accessing and disseminating any portion of a test or assignment. Examples include acquiring a test copy before its administration, distributing tests before they are officially given, altering grades in grade books or digital systems, and continuing to work on a test after time has expired. Sabotage involves destroying another person's work to hinder their successful completion of an academic task. For instance, damaging someone's artwork, experiment, or design constitutes sabotage. Misrepresentation involves intentionally distorting the content of a document, either by adding or omitting information, forging signatures, or providing false material. This includes fabricating data or sources that do not exist. Prevalent cheating methods include passing handwritten notes between individuals, jotting down notes on one's palm, and directly copying from someone else's work (Curran et al. 2011). More sophisticated techniques involve leveraging the internet and internet-enabled devices, posing challenges in detection (Curran et al. 2011; Bachore 2016; Kayişolu & Temel, 2017).

FACTORS MOTIVATE STUDENTS TO ENGAGE IN ACADEMIC DISHONESTY

Academic dishonesty, including actions like cheating, plagiarism, and manipulating data or citations, is a pervasive and concerning issue within higher education. It ranges from minor infractions like peeking at a peer's work during a quiz to more sophisticated schemes like outsourcing assignments to ghostwriters online. Academic dishonesty is a big problem in schools, colleges, and universities worldwide. Various researches show that students who cheat in schools are more likely to cheat later in their jobs. This shows that cheating is not just a school thing; it can spill over into other areas of life (Iberahim et al. 2013). Academic Dishonesty damages the learning experience and defaulters get an undue advantage over those who follows the rule. Previous studies show that those who are involved in cheating at school and college level, they also do cheating at work place also. This shows that dishonest behavior is not situation based.

Research shows that most students consider academic dishonesty ethically wrong. Academic dishonesty can sometimes arise from a need for more understanding about academic integrity principles rather than a deliberate intent to violate them (Baird 1980; Haines et al. 1986; Hughes and Mccabe 2006). Sometimes, while doing cheating people are not aware about the rules. Due to ignorance of rules, they are involved in academic dishonesty. There can be multiple reasons to involve in academic dishonesty like some time students have a high pressure from parents' sides to get good academic record so that they can increase their chances of placement, or promotion at workplace. Sometimes students do not get enough time to prepare for their exam this also motivates students for cheating. Idleness, huge competition, failure fear, difficult exams and pressure from peers can also be motivational factors for cheating (Bachore, 2016; Kayişolu & Temel, 2017).

Previous studies shows that gender is also an factor that motivate students for cheating like males are more involved in cheating as compared to females. They have very moderate views regarding the cheating behavior (Arnett et al. 2002; Hensley et al. 2013; Jereb et al. 2018). In school, colleges or universities, where there is more competition among students about academic performance, they have a higher rate of cheating. But in colleges where more focus on learning values, students are less involved in cheating (Miller et al. 2007). Cheating badly affect the reputation of educational institutions. When students of these institutions, where students are more involved in cheating, go for job, they are unable to perform and fail to justify their certificates. This poorly impacts the reputation of institution and affect the image of students who may attend these institutions in future (Dusu et al. 2016).

Figure 2. Causes of Academic Dishonesty

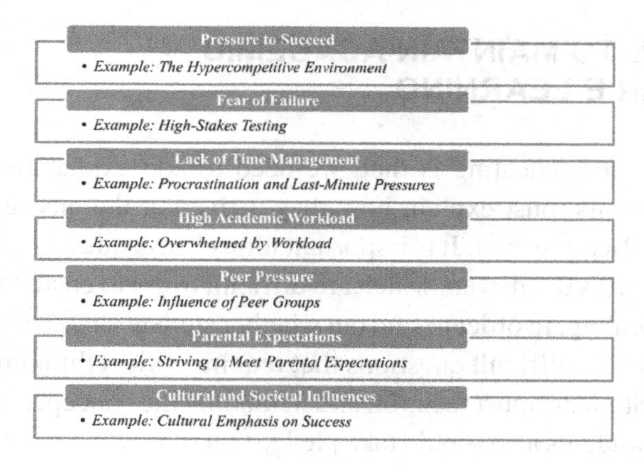

There is an intense pressure on students to be successful in high pressure academic environments (Sharma et al., 2023). Competitiveness means a greater chance of dishonest practices (McCabe & Treviño, 2001). The fear of being left behind by peers and the possible consequences may push students to cheat so as to maintain their competitive edge thus making it their major motivation for engaging in such behavior (Kayişolu & Temel, 2017). This heightened fear of failure, partly due to increased emphasis on standardized test results, makes cheating a viable option for many students who are afraid they might fail. It has been established that some students view cheating as an alternative way out when they feel that poor grades can have an outright impact on their future (Lang et al., 2013). They could be discouraged from taking up this act by the dread of being caught and punished if they are caught while in most cases, cheating is more serve than failing fairly. Poor time management skills contribute to academic dishonesty (Grijalva et al., 2006). These days parents expect that their child must maintain a specific GPA to get nay financial aid from the government or educational institutions, to take part in sports etc. It has been observed that students who are very good in studies, sometimes they also involve in cheating to maintain their GPA target.

Peer pressure, which has been impacted in promoting academic dishonesty, is also found to be one of these factors (Davis et al., 2009). Some students cheat because they are influenced by their friends' interest in the behavior (Davis et al., 2009). Culture also plays an important role in shaping the child behavior. Socities that give high importance to academic achievement, there students mostly involve in cheating to maintain a positive image in the society (Gomez, 2001). It is also seen that males do cheat more as compare to females during exams (Arnett et al. 2002; Hensley et al. 2013; Jereb et al. 2018). Some factors such as laziness, stress, difficult level of exam are also motivate students for cheating (Abiodun et al. 2011; Bachore 2016).

STRATEGIES TO MAINTAIN ACADEMIC INTEGRITY IN E-LEARNING

The best way to stop cheating is that, we need to add explanation part into the assessment. Students must explain how they arrived at the answer and also they need to give clarification on it. It is important for us to ask questions about what was discussed in the class or answers which are difficult to get to ensure that students do not involve in cheating. In order to find out whether students understand concepts; an instructor should ask difficult questions that require critical thinking, not the recall of information. Students must focus on understanding the concept deeply rather than memorizing it. Students also should take pledge that they will not involve in cheating before sitting for final exams. Previous researches show that if students take oath then they less involve in cheating. To achieve this, we should create online forums where students can discuss openly on issues like honesty, cheating and ethical behavior etc. We can utilize many platforms like Microsoft teams or slack, where students can ask questions, solve their assignments which reduce their urge to cheat. Much plagiarism detection software like Grammerly, Copyspace & Turnitin etc. are used to compare students data against data available in journals, magazines, publications & online content etc, (Kaur & Singh, 2023). Multiple softwares are used to ensure the reliability of online evaluation. These softwares use strategies like screen mirroring, webcam and voice detector to detect the cheating during exams. These tools limit the students' access of external website or any other browser during online exam.

Educational institutions use a lockdown browser that can stop the access of websites during online exam. It stops the access of any other website or browser by students during online exam. With the help of lockdown browser all shortcut keys are locked on keyboard and student can't make use of it. It can also block the use of shortcut keys that students may use during online exam. Educational institutions must design modules based on academic integrity, ethical values and how to proper cite content that can motivate students to complete their work with honesty. Student can make use of software like Mendely, endnote or Zotero that can help students in managing references easily. A varied approach is required to reduce academic dishonesty.

CHALLENGES IN MAINTAINING ACADEMIC INTEGRITY

These days to maintain academic integrity is not easy. It is easy for student to copy stuff as so much information is available online. Even it is not easy to recognize that who is giving online exam. Someone else might be doing them! Using special machines to check who is taking the test is sometimes perfect. They might make mistakes. Watching students at home during exams can be creepy and invade their privacy. Technical problems during online exams can be frustrating and unfair. Students might use special computer programs such as virtual machines or let others see their screens to cheat on exams. Phones and tablets can tempt students to peek at answers during exams. Some students might use texting apps or chartrooms to cheat on exams. Technology is not easily accessible to all. Some students might need better computers or the internet, making online learning harder. Not all students are equally familiar with online tools, making it confusing to know what's allowed and what's not in online education. Teachers also need training as they might need more preparation to handle online cheating and ensure everyone plays fair.

Recommendation for future Research

To find the impact of training programs designed for faculty on decreasing academic dishonesty

How different factors like regional, personal, cultural, geographical etc. affect the students' perceptions of academic dishonesty

To find the correlation between digital literacy of students and their perception regarding academic integrity.

CONCLUSION

As online education becomes more popular, it's more challenging to ensure everyone is doing their work and following the rules. It is complex to maintain fairness and honesty in online learning. Several strategies, such as incorporating explanation components into assessments, making questions un-Google-able, encouraging higher-order processing, implementing a code of conduct, and utilizing various e-tools like plagiarism detection software and online proctoring services, can be more effective in combating academic dishonesty. The multi-faceted approach, combining technological solutions with educational measures, is crucial in effectively addressing academic dishonesty. Not only that, but it is also must to teach students a culture of integrity and ethical behavior to reduce academic misconduct behavior. Teachers can play an essential role in fostering academic integrity among students.

REFERENCES

Abiodun, G., Gbadebo, O., & Tola, O. (2011). Forms of Academic Cheating During Examination among Students with Hearing Impairment in Nigeria: Implication for Counselling Practice. *Eur J Soc*, *26*(2), 276.

Ahmad RG, Hamed OA (2014). Impact of adopting a newly developed blueprinting method and relating it to item analysis on students' performance. *Med Teach, 36*(1), S55–S61. . doi:10.3109/0142159X.2014.886014

Al-Qahtani, M. F., & Guraya, S. Y. (2019). Comparison of the professionalism behaviours of medical students from four GCC universities with single-gender and Co-educational learning climates. *The Open Nursing Journal*, *13*(1), 193–200. doi:10.2174/1874434601913010193

Arnett, J. L., Arnett, J. J., Feldman, S. S., & Cauffman, E. (2002). It's wrong, but everybody does it: Academic dishonesty among high school and college students. *Contemporary Educational Psychology*, *27*(2), 209–228. doi:10.1006/ceps.2001.1088

Bachore, M. M. (2016). The nature, causes and practices of academic dishonesty/ cheating in higher education: The case of Hawassa University. *Journal of Education and Practice*, *7*(19), 222–1735.

Baird, J. S. Jr. (1980). Current Trends in College Cheating. *Psychology in the Schools, 17*(4), 515–522. doi:10.1002/1520-6807(198010)17:4<515::AID-PITS2310170417>3.0.CO;2-3

Cizek, G. J. (2003). *Detecting and preventing classroom cheating: Promoting integrity in assessment*. Corwin Press.

Curran, K., Middleton, G., & Doherty, C. (2011). Cheating in exams with technology. *International Journal of Cyber Ethics in Education, 1*(2), 54–62. doi:10.4018/ijcee.2011040105

Davis, F., Drinan, F., & Gallant, B. (2009). *Cheating in Schools: What We Know And What We Can Do*. Wiley. doi:10.1002/9781444310252

Diego, A. (2017). Friends with benefits: Causes and effects of learners 'cheating practices during examination. *IAFOR J Educ, 5*(2), 121–138. doi:10.22492/ije.5.2.06

Dusu, P. B., Gotan, A., Mohammed, J. D., & Gambo, B. (2016). Management of re-occurring cases of examination malpractice in plateau state college of health technology, Pankshin. *Nigeria J Educ Pract, 7*(6), 38–43.

Forkuor, J. B., Amarteifio, J., Attoh, D. O., & Buari, M. A. (2019). Students' perception of cheating and the best time to cheat during examinations. *The Urban Review, 51*(3), 424–443. doi:10.1007/s11256-018-0491-8

Gomez, D. (2001). Putting the shame back in student cheating. *Education Digest, 67*(4), 1–6.

Grijalva, T., Nowell, C., & Kerkvliet, J. (2006). Academic Honesty and Online Courses. *College Student Journal, 40*(1), 180–185.

Haines, V. J., Diekhoff, G. M., LaBeff, E. E., & Clark, R. E. (1986). College Cheating: Immaturity, Lack of Commitment, and the Neutralizing Attitude. *Research in Higher Education, 25*(4), 342–354. doi:10.1007/BF00992130

Hensley, L. C., Kirkpatrick, K. M., & Burgoon, J. M. (2013). Relation of gender, course enrollment, and grades to distinct forms of academic dishonesty. *Teaching in Higher Education, 18*(8), 895–907. doi:10.1080/13562517.2013.827641

Hughes, J. M., & McCabe, D. L. (2006). Understanding Academic Misconduct. *Canadian Journal of Higher Education, 36*(1), 49–63. doi:10.47678/cjhe.v36i1.183525

Iberahim, H., Hussein, N., Samat, N., Noordin, F., & Daud, N. (2013). Academic dishonesty: Why business students participate in these practices? *Procedia: Social and Behavioral Sciences*, *90*, 152–156. doi:10.1016/j.sbspro.2013.07.076

Jereb, E., Urh, M., Jerebic, J., & Šprajc, P. (2018). Gender differences and the awareness of plagiarism in higher education. *Social Psychology of Education*, *21*(2), 409–426. doi:10.1007/s11218-017-9421-y

Kaur, B., & Singh, J. P. (2023). *Empowering Research Communities: Implementing ETDs as Catalysts for Knowledge Sharing at Chitkara University Punjab*. Academic Press.

Kayisolu, N. B., & Temel, C. (2017). An Examination of Attitudes towards Cheating in Exams by Physical Education and Sports High School Students. *Universal Journal of Educational Research*, *5*(8), 1396–1402. doi:10.13189/ujer.2017.050813

Lang, J. M. (2013). *Cheating Lessons: Learning From Academic Dishonesty*. Harvard University Press. doi:10.4159/harvard.9780674726239

McCabe, D. L., Treviño, L. K., & Butterfield, K. D. (2001). Cheating in academic institutions: A decade of research. *Ethics & Behavior*, *11*(3), 219–232. doi:10.1207/S15327019EB1103_2

McGurgan, P., Calvert, K. L., Narula, K., Celenza, A., Nathan, E. A., & Jorm, C. (2020). Medical students' opinions on professional behaviours: The Professionalism of Medical Students' (PoMS) study. *Medical Teacher*, *42*(3), 340–350. doi:10.1080/0142159X.2019.1687862 PMID:31738619

Miller, Y., & Izsak, R. (2017). Students' involvement in academic dishonesty and their attitudes towards copying in exams and academic papers. *Sociology and Anthropology (Alhambra, Calif.)*, *5*(3), 225–232. doi:10.13189/sa.2017.050306

NIU. (2023). *Academic Dishonesty Definition and Types*. https://www.niu.edu/academic-integrity/faculty/types/index.shtml

Orok, E., Adeniyi, F., Williams, T., Dosunmu, O., Ikpe, F., Orakwe, C., & Kukoyi, O. (2023). Causes and mitigation of academic dishonesty among healthcare students in a Nigerian university. *International Journal for Educational Integrity*, *19*(1), 13. doi:10.1007/s40979-023-00135-2

Pavela, G. (1978). Judicial review of academic decision-making after, *Horowitz. School Law Journal*, *55*, 55–75.

Sharma, R., Mehta, K., & Vyas, V. (2023). Investigating academic dishonesty among business school students using fraud triangle theory and role of technology. *Journal of Education for Business*, *99*(2), 69–78. doi:10.1080/08832323.2023.2260925

TEQSA. (2021). *What is academic Integrity.* https://www.teqsa.gov.au/students/understanding-academic-integrity/what-academic-integrity

Ubaka, C., Gbenga, F., Sunday, N., & Ndidiamaka, E. (2013). Academic dishonesty among Nigeria pharmacy students: A comparison with United Kingdom. *African Journal of Pharmacy and Pharmacology*, *7*(27), 1934–1941. doi:10.5897/AJPP2013.3587

Whitley, B. E., & Keith-Spiegel, P. (2002). *Academic dishonesty. An educators guide*. Lawrence Erlbaum Associates Publishers.

Chapter 11
Pedagogical Transformation:
Integrating Innovative Approaches in Teaching

Yogita Rawat
ITM Business School, India

Prachi Yadav
ITM Business School, India

ABSTRACT

Over time, education has transformed, requiring innovative pedagogical techniques to stay relevant. This chapter offers an array of research-based teaching strategies, providing educators with an overview of transformational pedagogy. It consists of fundamental pedagogical concepts and explores evolving trends like gamification, blended learning, storytelling, project-based learning, and experiential learning. Each approach is examined comprehensively, including theoretical foundations, their ability to foster critical thinking, collaborative learning impact, and overall influence on student development. Given the distinct advantages and disadvantages of each technique, educators must discern the most suitable for their classrooms to enhance student engagement and ensure inclusive learning opportunities. Ultimately, it serves as a guide for teachers seeking to innovate learning methods and empower every student to actively participate, thus preparing them for success in our constantly evolving world.

DOI: 10.4018/979-8-3693-3015-9.ch011

Copyright © 2024, IGI Global. Copying or distributing in print or electronic forms without written permission of IGI Global is prohibited.

NEED OF THE STUDY

Pedagogical practices must be continuously reevaluated due to the ever-changing landscape of education. The chapter addresses this concern by providing a critical examination of emerging pedagogical approaches, giving teachers a wide range of innovative tools, backed by research, to plan and reinvent their teaching strategies.

This chapter seeks to cover the gap between old and new pedagogy techniques, by providing teachers with a comprehensive framework to understand and implement innovative approaches, including:

1. **Blended Learning**: The strategic and evidence-based blending of online and offline environments, providing flexibility and personalized learning experiences.
2. **Gamification**: Using the motivational power of game mechanics to promote student engagement, encourage problem-solving skills and student engagement.
3. **Project-based learning**: Using projects that are driven by students, help cultivate critical thinking, teamwork and practical problem solving in them.
4. **The art of storytelling**: Making use of the power of narration to take hold of imaginations, help build empathy, and improve understanding of complex concepts.
5. **Experiential Learning**: Creating indulging learning environments that actively involve students in real-world situations, helping them retain information through practice, and encouraging a lifetime love of learning are all components of experiential learning.

Considering the difficulties and complications that come with implementation, this chapter explores the theoretical foundations and possible advantages of each strategy. Teachers will be more equipped to integrate these approaches into their teaching when they have access to new perspectives. Eventually it is about creating conditions that support holistic growth of students.

PURPOSE OF THE STUDY

This chapter's sole purpose is to investigate the potential of pedagogical transformation to cater to the evolving needs of education in the 21st century. By critically examining diverse approaches like blended learning, gamification, project-based learning, storytelling, and experiential learning, the study here aims to:

1) Provide teachers with a comprehensive understanding of potential benefits, theoretical foundations, and challenges regarding implementation of these approaches.
2) Empowering teachers in making informed decisions regarding context-specific integration of innovative practices in their own teaching environments.
3) Contribute to the ongoing discourse on pedagogical transformation by highlighting the potential of emerging approaches to enhance student engagement, promote personalized learning experiences, and enable students with the critical skills essential for success in the 21st century.

INTRODUCTION

What Is Pedagogy?

Pedagogy is a technique of teaching where both theoretical and practical approaches are used by the educator. It is a combination of culture and learning techniques.

Pedagogy helps students to get a thorough understanding of the subject, which also helps them to apply their classroom learning in the practical world (Shirke, 2021).

PEDAGOGICAL TRANSFORMATION IN TEACHING

Given the world's social and economic developments and the need for new skills, education is ripe for change.

Education systems around the world are finding ways to capitalize on and contribute to a growing environment of innovation and creativity, keeping pace with societal change. A focus on promoting educational reforms, especially in countries with growing youth populations, will promote responsible citizens, enhance human capabilities, and support transitioning to a knowledge-driven economy.

A learning-centered approach has taken over the teacher-centered approach in education in recent years. Introduction of educational technologies like virtual reality, video games, and robotics will assist educators and learners in this shift and promote the development of 21st century skills like creativity, problem-solving, teamwork, and critical thinking.

A. Blended Learning

An innovative concept known as Blended Learning combines the advantages of both traditional classroom instructions and learning supported by Information and communication technology (ICT), covering both offline and online learning.

It offers areas for collaborative learning, constructive learning, and computer-assisted learning (CAL). Successfully implementing blended learning requires rigorous effort, the right attitude, a big budget, and highly motivated teachers and students. It is complex and a difficult task to organize as it contains various modes like:

1. Face to face teaching
2. Student interaction with course content
3. Peer group interaction
4. Group discussion and exchange of ideas.
5. Accessing e-library
6. Virtual classroom
7. Online assessment
8. Webinars
9. Online learning through videos and audios
10. Virtual laboratories

Components of Blended Learning

Blended learning consists of 5 components:

1. **Face-to-face instructor-led**: Students participate in an experiential class where the teacher presents learning content and there is little interaction, training, or practice.
2. **Face-to-face collaboration**: Promotes the participation of students in educational activities together at school.
3. **Online instructor-led**: The teacher assesses learning progress and interactions throughout the teaching process in an online manner.
4. **Online collaboration**: Provides students with an opportunity to take part in learning activities via the internet.
5. **Online self-paced:** Allows students to study at their own pace, with flexible time and space.

MODELS

Five models are classified, based on where content is shared and practical activities are carried out, such as flipped, combined, flexible, supplementary online practice models.

1. **Flipped Model**: Students are guided to access prepared materials before class begins. Preparation occurs outside of school hours in an online format and is used to maximize opportunities for teachers and students to interact, collaborate, troubleshoot, and manipulate during face-to-face instruction.
2. **Blended model**: Delivering learning content and exercises in presence and online.
3. **Flex model**: Learning content and practical tasks are conveyed through online education. However, students participate in face-to-face sessions to check their progress and receive feedback on their learning process. Teachers allow students to learn at their own pace, and students meet in person regularly for lessons.
4. **Supplemental model:** Acquisition of knowledge and practice is improved through face-to-face instruction. However, online activities have been added to improve student engagement.
5. **Online Exercise Model**: This model allows students to practice, solve problems, and receive instant feedback online through an online learning platform.

ADVANTAGES OF BLENDED LEARNING

Some of the learning with ICT takes place in online or offline modes, allowing teachers and students in the classroom to spend more time on creative and collaborative exercises.

Students can benefit from online learning and her CAI without losing the element of social interaction and the human touch of traditional education. This provides more space for communication. The communication cycle is completed with blended learning. This is not possible if only traditional approaches are followed. Students become more technologically savvy and improve their digital fluency. Students develop in themselves qualities such as responsibility, discipline, and initiative, so they have stronger professionalism, update course content, and breathe new life into established courses (Tong et al., 2022).

BEST PRACTICES FOR IMPLEMENTING BLENDED LEARNING

Blended learning is a flexible and innovative approach to teaching that offers significant benefits to both teachers and students. However, successful implementation requires careful planning and consideration. Below are some best practices for implementing blended learning (Lata Dangwal, 2017).

Set clear goals: It's important to start with a clear understanding of what one wants to achieve with blended learning. Do you want to increase student engagement, provide a more personalized learning experience, and improve learning outcomes? By setting clear goals, you can tailor your blended learning approach to your specific goals.

Incorporate lectures, discussions, hands-on activities, group work, and online resources to accommodate a variety of learning styles. By changing your teaching strategies, you can create a more engaging and effective learning experience.

Using technology to improve learning: Technology is a key element of blended learning. Use digital tools to enhance your learning experience. Integrate technology to achieve your goals and support your teaching strategy.

Promoting student autonomy and responsibility: Blended learning gives students more flexibility and control over their learning. Encourage students to take ownership of their education by setting goals, managing their time, and asking for help when needed. Foster a sense of ownership by setting clear expectations and providing regular feedback.

Continuous evaluation and improvement of blended learning approaches: Implementing blended learning is a continuous process. Continually evaluate the effectiveness of your approach by collecting feedback from students, analyzing performance data, and reflecting on your own experiences.

Blended learning has many benefits, but its successful implementation requires careful planning and consideration. By setting clear goals, incorporating a variety of instructional strategies, leveraging technology, encouraging student autonomy and responsibility, and continually evaluating and improving our approach, we provide an engaging and tailored approach to student needs. Create an effective blended learning environment. As the educational landscape continues to evolve, innovative approaches such as blended learning can help both teachers and students thrive in this ever-changing world (Dearmer, 2023).

B. Gamification in Education

The usage of game components in non-gaming environments is known as gamification. Applications for Information Systems (IS) gamification are expanding in various fields like business, healthcare, education and ideation for new projects. The notion that gamification is effective emerges from the connection with the gaming experience, considering its qualities of enjoyment and inherent motivation (Domínguez et al., 2013).

The goal of a gamified system is to foster user engagement and improve a target outcome, such as user participation, learning, purchase, social interaction, and ultimately productivity.

In the context of education, the use of playful elements has increased considerably in recent years, and pieces have attracted the attention of researchers. Informational activities alone have significant potential to improve student learning outcomes through gamified learning systems. The goal is to motivate students in new ways, reducing the feeling of fatigue in some activities, which would positively affect learning results.

Although elements of gamification such as marks, grades and leaderboards can be implemented in educational systems to motivate or engage students to increase participation and learning, the IS literature again lacks a clear distinction to characterize experiential and instrumental outcomes of gamified educational systems. Thus, although the different constructs are used interchangeably in the literature, additional research is needed to advance this topic (Best 8 Principles of Gamified Learning, 2023; Saunders & Katula Mwila, 2023).

BENEFITS OF GAMIFICATION

1. **Student engagement:** Gamification can be a powerful tool in increasing motivation and interest through rewards.
2. **Collaboration and Social Interaction**: Along with providing opportunities for teamwork, competition, and feedback from peers, gamification also fosters a sense of community and belonging.
3. **Promotes feedback and reflection**: Gamification offers immediate and frequent feedback, further encouraging self-assessment and goal setting.
4. **Support learning and retention**: Gamification reinforce and apply knowledge, skills and attitudes which further creates enjoyable and memorable experiences (Codish & Ravid, 2014).

PRINCIPLES OF GAMIFICATION

The concept of utilizing games as a teaching aid is not new, nor are the gamified learning ideas. However, gamification has now become one of the biggest education trends of the last decade due to the widespread adoption of gamified adaptive learning patterns, the rise in popularity of gamified strategies and the spread of mobile learning apps (Smiderle et al., 2020).

Following are the 8 principles of Gamified Learning-

1. Conceptual Challenges
2. Productive failure
3. Careful Calibration
4. Boost Persistence
5. Builds Confidence
6. Enhances Intrinsic Motivation
7. Accessibility
8. Deeper Learning

1. **Conceptual Challenges-** The best games mix rigorous education with engaging challenges to teach students more than just facts. The best games don't mix fun with education quizzes. Instead, the best games map to widely accepted standards. This makes it easier to incorporate them into your existing curriculum and tests, while ensuring that you are getting the material you need. Game designer Nigel Nisbet said that the new common core state standards for math are "exciting" because they "reinvigorate the spirit of curiosity and inquiry." It's hardwired in a document that is probably going to be the basis for teaching and learning math for years to come."
2. **Productive failure** - The best games give the players a chance to make mistakes, but they also receive constructive criticism. It takes a great deal of work and input from the author's audience to develop accurate mental models. The children learn by making forecasts and putting them to the test, then reflecting on their results.
3. **Careful Calibration**- The space between a student's current knowledge and his or her current skills is identified and maintained by effective educational frameworks. Good games strike a nice balance between being too easy and too hard, neither of which is desirable.
4. **Boosts persistence**- Author, researcher, and game advocate Dr. Jane McGonial argues that the gaming mindset- the willingness to fail and keep trying- boosts resilience, perseverance, and prepares pupils in the virtual world to cope better with obstacles in the real world. With an unusual blend of scoreboards, some instructors keep track of team work on large projects on an interactive whiteboard.
5. **Builds confidence**- One of the main benefits of gamification, as noted by Elizabeth Corcoran, founder of Lucere, an organization dedicated to assisting educators in identifying and implementing the most appropriate technology

for inspiring students, is that it helps students gain confidence as they learn how to have a winning learning experience, and makes them hungry for tools that put them in control. A sense of control and mastery is fostered by the best games and methods of play.

6. **Enhances Intrinsic Motivation**- Thanks to the constant feedback and prizes, students are highly engaged and motivated by gamification, which also aids in the development of problem-solving abilities and a feeling of success. Effective games and principles of Gamified learning do not replace the intrinsic drive of a student, which is stronger and more long term, with the extrinsic one, but give a mix of the two for a higher performance.
7. **Accessibility**- All players should have equal access to resources and knowledge and although the degree of advancement may vary from one level to another, there is still a chance that they will be able to master skills at all levels. Like effective game designers, instructors must build the learning environment and process to allow equitable access to the information and resources required by our students to succeed in learning.
8. **Deeper learning**- In game-based and adaptive learning tools students are exposed to new settings which require a combination of creativity and analytical thinking in order to attain difficult and important objectives. We must offer our teachers and students the opportunity to explore mathematics, so that it's no longer about remembering processes but rather creating strong mathematical concepts and understandings which will serve a student for life, not just an exam (Barata et al., 2014).

APPLICATION OF GAMIFICATION

1. **Increased Engagement and Motivation:** Game elements like points, badges, and leaderboards spark a sense of accomplishment and healthy competition, driving students to actively participate and persevere through challenges. Interactive and immersive learning journeys with storylines, avatars, and quests make information absorption more engaging and memorable. Personalized learning paths with adaptive challenges cater to individual strengths and weaknesses, keeping students motivated and on track.
2. **Enhanced Knowledge Acquisition and Retention:** Gamified activities like quizzes, simulations, and puzzles actively reinforce understanding and provide immediate feedback, leading to better knowledge retention. Interactive storytelling and branching narratives encourage critical thinking, problem-solving, and decision-making skills. Collaboration and teamwork through

in-game elements foster communication, peer support, and social learning, enhancing the learning experience.

3. **Development of 21st-century Skills:** Gamification promotes essential skills like creativity, communication, critical thinking, and problem-solving through engaging challenges and collaborative tasks. Adaptive learning platforms personalized to individual needs and pace build resilience and self-directed learning skills. Immersive simulations and virtual environments provide safe spaces to practice real-world skills and decision-making in a non-threatening setting.
4. **Beyond Engagement:** Blended gamification fosters a positive learning environment by reducing anxieties and making learning fun, leading to higher attendance and completion rates. Data-driven insights from game mechanics allow educators to track student progress, identify areas of difficulty, and tailor their teaching methods accordingly. Gamification can cater to diverse learning styles by offering various gamified activities and making learning more inclusive for all students (Iahad & Ahmad, 2015).

C. Project Based Learning:

A teaching method known as project-based learning (PBL) allows students to apply their theoretical knowledge in the context of a classroom. The manner that classrooms are set up allows students to work together on assignments or difficulties in the real world. Through practical learning activities, students gain and reinforce knowledge that is relevant to their everyday lives.

PBL is suitable for students from preschool to higher secondary and above. Various activities like classroom discussions, community service projects, field trips and language immersion programs are included. The length of PBL engagements may vary from less than 1 class period to more than one year for completion.

For an activity to be considered PBL, it must meet at least one of the following 7 criteria:

1. Questions, challenges, or problems that are open-ended
2. A process based on inquiry that builds curiosity and leads to questions
3. Acquiring new knowledge, skills that build on previous knowledge
4. Utilizing higher level skills like critical thinking, communication, creativity
5. Promoting student voice, choice
6. Providing opportunities for instructor, peer feedback and review
7. Public presentation of problem, research process, methods, results

PBL is commonly used in STEM (science, technology, engineering and medicine) or STEAM (science, engineering and math) instruction because so many of our daily lives are shaped by science, technology, engineering, art and math. For many students, learning by doing makes a potentially intimidating, challenging subject much easier and more "real".

CHALLENGES

1) Time constraints: Teachers struggle to fit project- based learning within curriculum demands.
2) Teacher capability: Lack of training and project mastery hinder effective facilitation.
3) Student Skills: Indiscipline and inadequate teamwork affect project execution.
4) Project type: Difficulty depends on teacher perception and resource availability.
5) Cost: Financial limitations restrict material acquisition and project scope (Cintang et al., 2018).

STRATEGIES

1) Teacher's belief and commitment: Strong belief in the benefits of project-based learning fuels commitment to overcome obstacles and carry out their duties.
2) Combining projects or learning: Integrate related learning or merge projects to save time and fit within curriculum demands.
3) Semester program planning: Calculate effective weeks and allocate appropriate time for project implementation.
4) Modifying project details: Adapt project tools, materials, and procedures to student environment and capabilities.
5) Choosing easy projects: Select suitable projects and allocate sufficient time to ensure successful completion.

D. Art of Storytelling

Storytelling plays an important role in childhood development and throughout one's life. Some stories are imagined while others are based on real experiences. Stories have the power to both celebrate life's experiences and teach valuable lessons across different aspects of life.

For generations, parents and teachers have effectively conveyed important values and guidance to children through the engaging format of storytelling. The practice of imparting knowledge through narrative has been recognized across civilizations as an impactful means of instruction.

There are several definitions of storytelling, but broadly speaking, storytelling can be defined as conveying stories and sharing information through various tools and resources. In the notable chapter Storytelling in the Classroom by Oller, the author describes storytelling as a creative process in which a traditional story is combined with personal experiences such as insights, inspiration, and relevant memories. (Duncan et al., 2019).

The influence and possibilities of storytelling are evident in our culture, as demonstrated by the Panchatantra, an ancient Indian collection of interrelated animal fables presented in verse and prose with a frame story structure. These stories are said to have transformed unfocused individuals into capable administrators considered geniuses by the society at that time.

Storytelling is an effective teaching tool that can nurture emotional intelligence and provide insight into human behavior. It also supports language learning by enriching vocabulary and exposing learners to new language structures and sentences. Some research even suggests storytelling may be more impactful for language acquisition than traditional textbooks.

Studies note storytelling's effectiveness stems from how engaging and enjoyable it is for learners, raising their interest in listening, speaking, writing, and reading related stories (Choudhury, 2022).

STORYTELLING AND INTERCULTURAL UNDERSTANDING

There are several ways in which storytelling can enhance intercultural understanding and communication-

1. Stories allow children to explore their own cultural roots and experience diverse cultures, enabling them to empathize with unfamiliar people, places, and situations.
2. Stories offer insights into different traditions and values, helping children understand how wisdom is common across all peoples and cultures.
3. Stories also provide insights into universal life experiences and allow children to consider new ideas while revealing differences and commonalities among cultures worldwide (Importance of Storytelling for Tech Jobs & Career Growth, 2022).

Other benefits of using Storytelling in the Classroom-

1. Stories promote a feeling of well-being and relaxation for children, increasing their willingness to communicate thoughts and feelings.

2. Storytelling also encourages active participation and increases verbal proficiency.
3. Stories further encourage the use of imagination and creativity while promoting cooperation among students.
4. Storytelling enhances listening skills (Manwani, 2022).

EXAMPLE OF STORYTELLING IN VARIOUS FIELDS

1. **Storytelling in science:** Mastering the art of storytelling in science will help one succeed. By crafting compelling narratives, researchers can help audiences understand innovations and believe in their effectiveness. Digital storytelling in science is an emerging method combining various digital modes, like video, audio, images, and text. Blending artistic media and interactive tools on social platforms shows promise engaging diverse audiences. It is no surprise storytelling in science through online channels has become vital for outreach by modern researchers.
2. **Storytelling in Business Communication:** In business communication, storytelling refers to telling a story rather than listing facts when communicating with customers. Stories provide an advantage over competitors. For example, Hutch (now Vodafone) used a pug named Cheeka in their ad "You & I". The ad showed the dog following a boy in unlikely places, with the tagline "Wherever you go, our network follows". It became hugely popular and led to increased pug sales in India despite high prices. Developing stories for connection and entertainment helps build an emotional relationship with the brand to foster trust, loyalty, and value.
3. **Storytelling in Healthcare**: In healthcare storytelling has been employed with success. One major area of impact is patient safety. Patients and families sharing stories of preventable harm has highlighted process issues that can cause injury. It likely adds humanity to case details, tapping empathy. It increases accountability and urgency for improvement. The result was a national effort to improve patient safety (Cox, 2019).

E. Experiential Learning as a Comprehensive Learning Tool

Experiential learning is a method of teaching that is very different from the theory driven method used in most of the classrooms. It is based on the simple idea that knowledge is created through transformation of experience. Instead of simply listening and observing, it encourages active engagement and reflection, to gain a deeper understanding.

Experiential learning combines action with reflection, theory with practice. It recognizes that learning is personal and interactive, and adapts to changing educational environments, making it an essential methodology in modern education.

PRINCIPLES OF EXPERIENTIAL LEARNING

Experiential learning is based on three fundamental principles that set it apart from traditional learning approaches:

Learning through experience, reflection, and application.

1. **Learning through experience:** Unlike passive learning practices that include sitting and reading textbook in a lecture, experiential learning focuses on active participation in the learning process through hands-on learning. Students can take part in field research, laboratory experiments, or other practical learning experiences. It is important to keep in mind that learners are being active participants in the process and not just observing it.
2. **Reflection**: A very important part of the experiential learning process is Reflection. Examine your experiences critically, methods you used and the lessons you learnt. The reflective process helps you connect theoretical knowledge with real-world applications. It supports self-evaluation and helps you internalize your learning, making sure that the experience is more than just an activity.
3. **Application**: This is the third principle. The application is where you put your newly learned knowledge or skills to the test. You can use it to solve real-world problems, create new projects, or apply concepts to other contexts. The application makes sure that your learning is not just theoretical but practical, useful, and relevant (Learning, n.d.).

BENEFITS OF EXPERIENTIAL LEARNING

1. **Make real-world relevance:** Students may skip a lecture if they believe the material is not relevant to the real world. Experiential learning takes data and concepts and applies them to real-life tasks, creating real-world results.
2. **Providing opportunities for creativity:** Through experiential learning students can use their creative parts of their brain and find their own solutions to problems or tasks. The creative problem solving, and diverse outcomes produced enriches the classroom.

3. **Provides opportunity for reflection:** Reflective observation is an integral part of experiential learning theory. Students analyze how their actions affect results and how their results may differ from those of other students. This analysis helps them better understand how to apply the concepts learned to other situations.
4. **Teaching the value of mistakes**: Experiential learning involves trial and error. As students engage in real-world tasks, they discover that some approaches are more effective than others. Students learn not to be afraid of making mistakes but learn to enjoy and remember them.
5. **Accelerate learning**: Hands-on activities require practice, problem solving and decision making. As student engagement increases through these processes, learning accelerates, and retention improves.
6. **Guiding students to the future:** Many experiential learning projects are career focused. Through these activities, students begin to explore and develop their skills, abilities and passions.
7. **Prepare students for adult life:** Through group projects, students learn how to work together more effectively, develop action plans and take advantage of each group member's unique strengths. Students learn how to lead, think critically, and adapt to changing circumstances (The Benefits of Experiential Learning for Students, n.d.).

CHALLENGES AND CONSIDERATIONS

1. **Adjusting Experiential and Conventional learning strategies**: One of the essential challenges is finding the proper adjustment between experiential and conventional learning. Whereas experiential learning is important, conventional strategies like lectures and reading material still play a significant part in giving foundational information.
2. **Addressing resource constraints and logistical issues**: Experiential learning often requires more resources than traditional classroom education. Additionally, logistical issues such as planning, coordinating with external partners, and managing team dynamics pose significant challenges.
3. **Ensuring safety and ethical considerations in Experiential Environments:** Safety is paramount in experiential learning environments, especially during physical tasks or fieldwork activities. Additionally, ethical considerations are essential, especially in service learning and community engagement.

4. **Adapting experiences to diverse learning styles and needs**: Finally, experiential learning must be inclusive and adapt to diverse learning styles and needs. Some may thrive in a hands-on setting, while others may find thoughtful observation more beneficial (Learning, n.d.).

While experiential learning is a powerful educational tool, it requires careful attention to balance, resources, safety, ethics, and inclusion. Addressing these challenges is essential to creating effective, rich, and safe learning experiences for all students.

CURRENT EDUCATION TRENDS

Advantages and Challenges

The word 'education', originally from Latin, means 'to learn, know, and lead'. Its meaning has changed significantly in modern times due to advances in technology. This section will talk about the benefits and drawbacks of modern pedagogical techniques with the aim of offering challenges and institutions useful information to enhance the learning outcomes (Pramoth, 2022).

Prospects for Current Educational Trends

The emphasis in modern education is on developing students' practical skills in addition to their academic knowledge. Global skills are critical for understanding the interconnected world of globalization and they can be developed by combining Science and technology, engineering, arts and mathematics (STEAM) education.

Advantages of Modern Education Trends

1. Practical skill development: Curriculum design prioritizes real-world problem-solving, nurturing critical thinking and analytical abilities from an early age.
2. Accessibility: Technological advancements facilitate universal access to learning resources, transcending geographical barriers
3. Global Skill Development: Emphasis on global competencies equips learners to thrive in diverse cultural and technological landscapes.
4. STEAM Education: Integrated learning approaches promote holistic understanding and application of STEAM subjects, enhancing students' problem-solving skills.

5. Innovative teaching methods: Student-centered methodologies, such as eLearning, hybrid learning, gamification, and mobile learning, enhance engagement and comprehension.
6. Experiential learning: Conceptual knowledge and retention are enhanced through practical experiences and project-based learning.
7. Teacher Transformation: Educators evolve into mentors, guiding personalized learning journeys and leveraging technology for customized instruction.
8. Technological integration: Artificial Intelligence, virtual reality, and Augmented Reality enrich learning experiences, fostering immersive and interactive engagement.

Challenges in Modern Education Trends

1. Cost implications: The adoption of digital learning tools may pose financial barriers, limiting access for certain demographics.
2. Linguistic impact: English dominance in educational discourse marginalizes regional languages, hindering linguistic diversity and proficiency.
3. Social interaction deficiency: Overreliance on technology diminishes interpersonal communication and peer collaboration, affecting motivation and social skills development.
4. Educational inequality: Disparities in resource allocation exacerbate educational inequalities, necessitating governmental intervention and equitable funding.
5. Diminished intellectual skills: Excessive dependence on technology risks undermining critical thinking and problem-solving skills, necessitating a balanced approach to technology integration.
6. Distraction and Detrimental effects: Prolonged exposure to digital devices may lead to distraction, disengagement, and adverse physical and mental health outcomes among students.
7. Computer literacy challenges: The demand for tech-savvy educators presents challenges in skill acquisition and technical proficiency, requiring ongoing professional development.

CONCLUSION

While modern education trends present challenges, their benefits outweigh drawbacks with strategic planning and moderation. By leveraging innovative pedagogical approaches, educators can cultivate dynamic learning environments conducive to holistic skill development and academic excellence.

REFERENCES

Agrawal, A. K., & Mittal, G. K. (2018). The role of ICT in higher education for the 21st century ICT as a change agent for education. Multidisciplinary Higher Education, Research, Dynamics & Concepts Opportunities & Challenges for Sustainable Development, 1(1), 76–83.

Albert, T.C., & Rennella M. (2021, November 11). *Readying students for their careers through project-based learning*. Harvard Business Publishing Education.

American Association of Colleges for Teacher Education. (2010, March). The clinical preparation of teachers. *Policy Brief.*

Ball, D. L., & Forzani, F. M. (2009). The work of teaching and the challenge for teacher education. *Journal of Teacher Education*, *60*(5), 497–511. doi:10.1177/0022487109348479

Barata, G., Gama, S., Jorge, J. A., & Gonçalves, D. J. (2014). Relating gaming habits with student performance in a gamified learning experience, *Proceedings of the first ACM SIGCHI annual symposium on Computer-humaninteractioninplay CHI PLAY'14*. 10.1145/2658537.2658692

Best 8 Principles of Gamified Learning. (2023, June 26). Future Education Magazine. https://futureeducationmagazine.com/8-principles-of-gamified-learning/

Brier, D. J., & Lebbin, V. K. (2004). Teaching information literacy using the short story. *RSR. Reference Services Review*, *32*(4), 383–387. doi:10.1108/00907320410569734

Choudhury, P. K. (2022, August 26). *The art of storytelling in science and research*. Researcher.Life. https://researcher.life/blog/article/storytelling-in-science-and-research

Cintang, N., Setyowati, D. L., & Handayani, S. S. D. (2018). The Obstacles and Strategy of Project Based Learning Implementation in Elementary School. *Journal of Education and Learning*, *12*(1), 7–15. doi:10.11591/edulearn.v12i1.7045

Codish, D., & Ravid, G. (2014). Personality based gamification-educational gamification for extroverts and introverts. *CHAIS Conference for the Study of Innovation and Learning Technologies, 1.* https://www.openu.ac.il/innovation/chais2014/download/E2-2.pdf

Cox, E. (2019). *Narrative Medicine: The Importance of Storytelling in Health Care*. US News & World Report. https://health.usnews.com/health-care/for-better/articles/narrative-medicine-the-importance-of-storytelling-in-health-care

Dearmer, A. (2023, August 16). *Unlocking Blended Learning: Strategies, Benefits & Tools*. Appsembler. https://appsembler.com/blog/unlocking-blended-learning-strategies-benefits-tools/#:~:text=Incorporating%20Varied%20Instructional%20 Strategies%3A%20In

Domínguez, A., Saenz-de-Navarrete, J., de-Marcos, L., Fernández-Sanz, L., Pagés, C., & Martínez-Herráiz, J.-J. (2013). Gamifying learning experiences: Practical implications and outcomes. *Computers & Education*, *63*(1), 380–392. doi:10.1016/j.compedu.2012.12.020

Duncan, M., Cunningham, A., & Eyre, E. (2019), A combined movement and storytelling intervention enhances motor competence and language ability in preschoolers to a greater extent than movement or storytelling alone. European Physical Education Review, 25(1), 221-235.

Iahad, N. A., & Ahmad, N. (2015). Gamification in online collaborative learning for programming courses: A literature review. *ARPN Journal of Engineering and Applied Sciences, 10*(23), 1–3.

Importance of Storytelling for Tech Jobs & Career Growth. (2022, April 21). Stoodnt.com. https://stoodnt.com/blog/storytelling-tech-jobs-career/

Lata Dangwal, K. (2017). Blended Learning: An Innovative Approach. *Universal Journal of Educational Research*, *5*(1), 129–136. doi:10.13189/ujer.2017.050116

Learning, E. (n.d.). Appsembler. https://appsembler.com/glossary/what-is-experiential-learning/

Learning, S. (2022, June 15). 12 Project Based Learning (PBL) Examples. Creative Learning Systems. https://www.smartlablearning.com/project-based-learning-examples/

Manwani, K. (2022, April). *An empirical study on using storytelling as a learning tool for online and offline education*. http://Journalppw.com

McDury, J., & Alterio, M. (2001). Achieving Reflective Learning using storytelling pathways. *Innovations in Education and Teaching International*, *38*(1), 63–73. doi:10.1080/147032901300002864

Pramoth, A. (2022, November 18). Modern trends in education pros and cons. *The Times of India*. https://timesofindia.indiatimes.com/readersblog/modern-trends-in-education-pros-and-cons/modern-trends-in-education-pros-and-cons-46765/

Raju, G. V. (2020). Art of Storytelling: A Critical Perspective on English Language Teaching. *Journal of Emerging Technologies and Innovative Research*.

Saunders, R., & Katula Mwila, N. (2023, September 16). *How can you use gamification to enhance student engagement in higher education?* [Review of How can you use gamification to enhance student engagement in higher education?]. Linkedin. www.linkedin.com

Shirke, A. (2021, October 7). *What is Pedagogy? Importance of pedagogy in teaching and learning process*. Www.iitms.co.in

Smiderle, R., Rigo, S. J., Marques, L., de Miranda Coelho, J. A. P., & Jaques, P. (2020). *The impact of gamification on students' learning, engagement and behavior based on their personality traits* [Review of The impact of gamification on students' learning, engagement and behavior based on their personality traits]. doi:10.1186/s40561-019-0098-x

Storytelling - benefits and tips. (n.d.). Teaching English. https://www.teachingenglish.org.uk/professional-development/teachers/managing-resources/articles/storytelling-benefits-and-tips

T.C. (2019, May 22). *Successful project-based learning*. Harvard Business Publishing Education.

The Benefits of Experiential Learning for Students. (n.d.). Retrieved February 27, 2024, from https://www.envisionexperience.com/blog/the-benefits-of-experiential-learning#

Tong, D. H., Uyen, B. P., & Ngan, L. K. (2022). The effectiveness of blended learning on students' academic achievement, self-study skills and learning attitudes: A quasi-experiment study in teaching the conventions for coordinates in the plane. *Heliyon*, *8*(12), e12657. doi:10.1016/j.heliyon.2022.e12657 PMID:36643330

Tvarozek, J., & Brza, T. (2014). Engaging students in online courses through interactive badges. *2014 International Conference on-Learning*. https://pdfs.semanticscholar.org/fe68/ 5176c8d4bf7f6507f3870815f56a65097c89.pdf

Chapter 12
Powerful AI in Social Science Research

Satinder Singh
Chitkara University, India

Rashmi Aggarwal
https://orcid.org/0000-0002-5010-5068
Chitkara University, India

ABSTRACT

The never-ending improvements in artificial intelligence models have been astonishing in each sphere of life, especially the business segments and academic research. Even though the involvement of AI in social and business environments has already raised many key concerns, academia and business world experts recommend safely deploying this next digital revolution. Several key aspects of AI can bring forth marvelous results. In this chapter, the authors advocate a safety model of AI which can not only speed up the research tools and technique but also open the broader window to achieve the research objectives with more depth and explanatory answers. This chapter's major contribution is exploring viable and secure solutions to use powerful AI models to improve and faster the social science research approaches.

INTRODUCTION

Social Science Research opens new horizons for policymakers, decision-makers, academicians, psychologists, professionals, and scholars. However, it is not easy to decode the philosophical as well as theoretical conditions that are the pillars of Social Science research (Moon & Blackman, 2014). Embarking upon social science

DOI: 10.4018/979-8-3693-3015-9.ch012

Copyright © 2024, IGI Global. Copying or distributing in print or electronic forms without written permission of IGI Global is prohibited.

research always brings forth a bumpy road for all researchers; some continuously strive to ensure the juxtapositions of all research ethos without compromising the nobility of research; and others struggle to explore the appropriate keywords on search engines and apply tools to fetch the desired previous quality of studies in one report. According to McGrath, (1995), Social science entails unique phases and human actions based on behaviors of different stakeholders in purchasing a car, casting a vote, disobeying the parking etiquettes, communicating with family etcetera. This takes a huge amount of time in screening, sorting, polishing, fetching the right information, and noting appropriate findings. As of now, social science has been upgraded with new innovative tools and techniques which made the tasks of researchers easier than ever before. For instance, Artificial Intelligence, Chat GPT, and Open AI software have proved themselves more than tech assistants for any researcher. However, every innovation brings positive as well as negative outcomes hence Artificial Intelligence, Chat GPT, and Open AI software have brought serious concerns related to their impact on research ethos. So, this research is an attempt to explore a safety model while using AI tools.

VARIANTS OF AI TOOLS

AI replicates human intelligence in every task (Dias & Torkamani, 2019). There is a growing number of AI tools used in social science research such as Chat GPT, QuillBolt, Semantic Scholar, Grammarly, AI chatbots, AI copywriting tools, Synthesia, Elicit, Scholarcy, Knewton, IBM Watson, Tableau, Consensus, and many more. These tools are empowered with super intelligence technology that makes every tool function like unimaginable power in every sphere of life. Moreover, different AI tools accede to each other in terms of their better and faster results which always catches the attention of different individuals. Notably, these tools run their algorithms on stored information which means they still cannot generate new information and this exhibits a major drawback of AI technology. Likewise, all AI-based research tools maximize the risk of copyright data and this usually spoils the quality of research. AI supports businesses to touch growth in the digital time and enables them to be innovative (Verganti et al., 2020). How these different AI tools can create a safe research model is yet to be explored.

NEW AVATAR CHATGPT IN RESEARCH

The new Avatar ChatGPT is a blend of numerous technologies, for example, deep learning, auto-pilot, instruction fine-tuning, multi-task learning, text-to-text,

text-to-image, image-to-text, image-to-image, image-to-video, text-to-video, and video-to-video result (Wu et al., 2023). Since its introduction in 2018, ChatGPT has gained momentum in every sphere of life and it has been successfully finding its real applications despite being sharply criticized by well-known philosophers throughout the world. Kocoń et al., (2023), strongly support ChatGPT as a Jack of All of the Trades; efficient in decoding mathematical equations (Frieder Simon et al., 2023); and ChatGPT 4.0 version capable of blurring the line between reality and artificial. In research, ChatGPT has become a crucial tool for all researchers that ask them to first adopt and then adapt to its fast-processing results-generating machine. Scholars must align their learning efforts as well as match the pace of fast-processed information concerning research purposes. Moreover, the new data-driven era backed by AI technology requires precise and appropriately sorted information on time thus the New Avatar of ChatGPT shows its readiness to deal with the fast to fastest commands in research. Unquestionably, the ChatGPT technique is the future of Social Science research.

USES OF SEARCH ENGINES IN SOCIAL SCIENCE RESEARCH

One of the complex tasks for today`s scholars is to navigate precisely between the information stored on the internet and the appropriate uses of search engines for the same. The life of a researcher has fully augmented ever since search engines like 'Google Scholar have become more ready to offer tens of hundreds of results on specific keywords. It does not end here because year after year new search engines are available with loaded information and some have premium subscriptions due to the higher quality of data available. According to (Waller, 2011) there is no significant deviation between any words typed or topics related to different types of stakeholders for netizens. However, the availability of data over search engines raises a question about its true representativeness towards the asked information (Scheitle, 2011). It is always one of the challenging tasks for the publisher to accept the manuscript in a straightway manner once they receive any publication request from the researcher for their research findings. Day by day, breach of copyright always catches the attention of the research community. It demoralizes the true contribution of the original researcher of their finding if anyone tries to give a name to such findings of someone`s work. Even though many research-related ethos and rules already have been put in place to prevent and detect plagiarism of research works, search engines supported by AI influence many minds to get the research paper ready in a short period merely commanding AI to do the task on your behalf. This phenomenon creates a new lacuna to be addressed by AI tools in the AI-driven era.

CHALLENGES IN THE DIGITAL ERA

There are key areas in Social Science research in the Digital era where lack of awareness towards breaching research ethics leads to severe consequences for the defaulter. For instance, the Digital world makes every task easy with just one click and generates plenty of organized results into a beautiful summary at the end nevertheless the authenticity of such outputs brings forth much-copied information which is being reused to reclaim the true credits of any findings. Research agencies or Institutions throughout the globe work together to combat this serious issue in a Social Science domain with a set of rules and guidelines framed to minimize the possibility of breaching copyright rights. The Digital world draws a very thin line between the data available in a stored format and information published multiple times on different platforms. Hence, the Social Science research community is required to enhance ethical literacy among different stakeholders who are using the published findings for their uses.

MAPPING RESEARCH ETHICS WITH AI FUNCTIONS

Research ethics are the combination of ethical approaches, regulating ethics, informed consent, confidentiality, avoiding harm and doing good, relationships, integrity, care, ethical conduct, and regulatory compliance (Israel & Hay, 2006). All these are instrumental for the qualitative outcome from every research attempt in social science domain. However, the ever-increasing the technological development in the social science research domain has brought up so many serious concern about the appropriate usage of the technology. For instance, the Artificial intelligence has made many researcher process task more easier than ever before and every bit of information can be fetched, organised, redesigned, refined, copied, and pasted. This type of growing phenomena everywhere has created a very thin line between human creativity and AI reproduction and it's really hard for human eyes and brain to detect the involvement of AI tools. (Hagendorff, 2020) advocated in this context that ethics of AI or general ethics both are extremely incapable in enforcing their own normative related to core principles.

HOW CAN RESEARCHERS AVOID PLAGIARISM AND ENSURE THE SAFETY OF RESEARCH?

In the present time of AI tools, the social science research attempts have become more challenging, day by day, and plagiarism is one among all those (Katju, 2011).

Plagiarism is a real threat to the academic integrity (Sudhakar, 2023) and impacts scientific publications (Dien, 2023). To address this serious issue, all the research institution across the globe are working to bring forth the concrete solution against the use of all AI tools. This paper is an attempt to highlight the key factors and their composition matching with the research ethics while using Artificial Intelligence in social science research. We have prepared a five key checks which not only detect the early stages of plagiarism but also assist in detecting the copyright material to avoid any breach of law. This five key checks focus from bottom to top and depicted in Figure 1.

Figure 1. Authors compilations

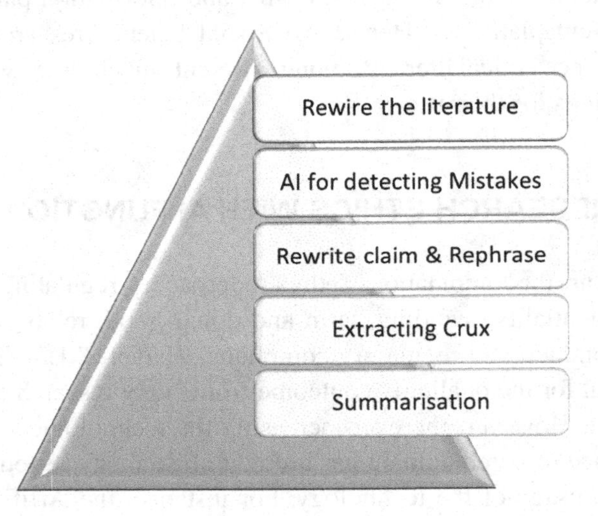

Summarisation: The first crucial step for a social science researchers is to hone the skill how to summarise the previous research findings along with redesigning the both left and right sides of one key aspects. Researchers, for instance, must quote or requote when requires the different school of thoughts addressing one specific area.

Extracting Crux: Once the summarisation phase is fully taken care of by any individual researcher thus they must highlight or pen down the crux of the overall research findings. This offers precise focus on the current identified problems not addressed by the previous researchers.

Rewrite Claim & Rephrase: It is the onus on the researcher to give the true credit to previous work done by anyone in their research background. Moreover, this must be rewrite the established opinion but this time with rephrasing technique.

AI for Detecting Mistakes: The AI research tools are ubiquitous and cannot be overlooked. However, AI could only be appropriate if it is used to detect any grammatical error or sentence formation mistakes. This further leads to minimise the percentage of plagiarism possibilities.

Rewire the Literature: One of the toughest task for a researcher is to synch their opinion based on the identified problem with covered area by the previous researchers. However, with the advent of AI tools this task has become much easier than ever and AI fetch every possible thread from the stored data on internet with artificially redesigned format. This format usually breaches the intellectual property rights. Thus, rewiring the literature review using AI to explore the much room of the internet data not only improves the quality of literature part but also amend many new ways to adequately design the past saga of specific problem.

CONCLUSION

The world is changing rapidly and exploring new ways of solving the complex problems of the society. Artificial Intelligence has been astonishing in each sphere of life, especially the business segments and academic research. The ever-increasing acceptance of AI in social science domain produces faster results however becomes responsible too for breaching the intellectual property rights clause. Thus, it requires a special attention from researchers to work on a safe model while embarking upon on a journey of new research problem. In fact, this study proposed five key essential checks such summarising, extracting the crux, rewrite claims & rephrase, uses of AI for detecting mistakes, and rewiring the literature review with the help AI can minimise the chances of plagiarism. This safety model of AI which can not only speed up the research tools and technique but also open the broader window to achieve the research objectives with more depth & explanatory answers.

REFERENCES

Dias, R., & Torkamani, A. (2019). Artificial intelligence in clinical and genomic diagnostics. *Genome Medicine*, *11*(1), 70. doi:10.1186/s13073-019-0689-8 PMID:31744524

Dien, J. (2023). Editorial: Generative artificial intelligence as a plagiarism problem. *Biological Psychology*, *181*, 108621. doi:10.1016/j.biopsycho.2023.108621 PMID:37356702

Hagendorff, T. (2020). The Ethics of AI Ethics: An Evaluation of Guidelines. *Minds and Machines*, *30*(1), 99–120. doi:10.1007/s11023-020-09517-8

Israel, M., & Hay, I. (2006). *Research Ethics for Social Scientists*. SAGE Publications, Ltd. doi:10.4135/9781849209779

Katju, M. (2011). Plagiarism and social sciences. *Economic and Political Weekly*, 45–48.

Kocoń, J., Cichecki, I., Kaszyca, O., Kochanek, M., Szydło, D., Baran, J., Bielaniewicz, J., Gruza, M., Janz, A., Kanclerz, K., Kocoń, A., Koptyra, B., Mieleszczenko-Kowszewicz, W., Miłkowski, P., Oleksy, M., Piasecki, M., Radliński, Ł., Wojtasik, K., Woźniak, S., & Kazienko, P. (2023). ChatGPT: Jack of all trades, master of none. *Information Fusion*, *99*, 101861. doi:10.1016/j.inffus.2023.101861

McGrath. J. E. (1995). Methodology matters: Doing research in the behavioral and social sciences. In Readings in Human–Computer Interaction (pp. 152–169). Elsevier. doi:10.1016/B978-0-08-051574-8.50019-4

Moon, K., & Blackman, D. (2014). A Guide to Understanding Social Science Research for Natural Scientists. *Conservation Biology, 28*(5), 1167–1177. doi:10.1111/cobi.12326

Scheitle, C. P. (2011). Google's Insights for Search: A Note Evaluating the Use of Search Engine Data in Social Research. *Social Science Quarterly*, *92*(1), 285–295. doi:10.1111/j.1540-6237.2011.00768.x

Simon, F., Luca, P., Alexis, C., Ryan-Rhys, G., Tommaso, S., Thomas, L., Philipp, P., & Julius, B. (2023). Mathematical Capabilities of ChatGPT. *37th Conference on Neural Information Processing Systems (NeurIPS 2023) Track on Datasets and Benchmarks*, 1–46. https://ghosts.friederrr.org

Sudhakar, M. (2023). *Enhancing Plagiarism Detection: The Role of Artificial Intelligence in Upholding Academic Integrity*. Library Philosophy & Practice.

Verganti, R., Vendraminelli, L., & Iansiti, M. (2020). Innovation and Design in the Age of Artificial Intelligence. *Journal of Product Innovation Management, 37*(3), 212–227. doi:10.1111/jpim.12523

Waller, V. (2011). Not just information: Who searches for what on the search engine Google? *Journal of the American Society for Information Science and Technology, 62*(4), 761–775. doi:10.1002/asi.21492

Wu, T., He, S., Liu, J., Sun, S., Liu, K., Han, Q.-L., & Tang, Y. (2023). A Brief Overview of ChatGPT: The History, Status Quo and Potential Future Development. *IEEE/CAA Journal of Automatica Sinica, 10*(5), 1122–1136. doi:10.1109/JAS.2023.123618

Chapter 13
Revolutionizing Education:
The Transformative Power of EdTech

Shivangi Shukla Bhavsar
Narayana Business School, India

Yogi Agravat
Narayana Business School, India

Imroz Mansuri
https://orcid.org/0000-0003-3757-940X
Narayana Business School, India

ABSTRACT

The incorporation of educational technology (EdTech) into modern educational practices has resulted in a paradigm change in teaching and learning approaches. This chapter explores the diverse landscape of EdTech tools and platforms, categorizing them into learning management systems (LMS), interactive learning tools (ILT), virtual and augmented reality (VR and AR) tools, massive open online courses (MOOCs), and other online learning platforms. It goes into EdTech's evolution, charting its historical development and emphasizing major milestones, as well as assessing its scope and significance in today's educational context. The chapter emphasizes how EdTech transforms education by increasing student engagement, interaction, and personalized learning experiences.

DOI: 10.4018/979-8-3693-3015-9.ch013

Copyright © 2024, IGI Global. Copying or distributing in print or electronic forms without written permission of IGI Global is prohibited.

INTRODUCTION

Educational Technology, commonly referred to as EdTech, represents a dynamic and innovative field that merges technology with educational practices to enhance teaching and learning experience. At its core, EdTech tools and platforms encompass a wide range of software, applications, and technology-based infrastructure designed to facilitate, enrich, and personalize the educational process. These tools are not confined to digital textbooks or e-learning modules; they span a vast array of digital resources, from comprehensive learning management systems and interactive learning applications to cutting-edge virtual reality environments and adaptive learning software.

EdTech is truly revolutionizing the way we approach education by integrating technology seamlessly into the teaching and learning journey. From interactive learning applications to virtual reality environments, these tools are reshaping traditional educational practices and making learning more engaging, personalized, and effective. By leveraging EdTech solutions, educators can create dynamic and immersive learning experiences that cater to diverse student needs and preferences. The possibilities are endless with EdTech, as it continues to push boundaries and unlock new opportunities for both teachers and learners alike.

(Cowling et al., 2022) gives a detailed historical review of educational technology, beginning in the late 1970s with the introduction of personal computers and culminating in the 1980s with a shift away from traditional teaching methods and towards more technology-driven approaches. Its basic premise is that technological interventions in education must be deliberate, with the goal of improving learning experiences across several educational modalities. It emphasizes the importance of theoretical frameworks and methodological rigor in EdTech practices, arguing for a human-centered approach that recognizes the behavioral dynamics inherent in educational technology research.

Mohit Sharma (2020) highlights the enormous impact of the COVID-19 pandemic on the online education sector and the birth of educational technology (EdTech) companies, demonstrating the abrupt shift to online learning caused by the worldwide health crisis. It emphasizes the need to investigate various types of e-learning, particularly during times of crisis, and looks into the capabilities, limitations, motivations, and obstacles of online education. Furthermore, it covers the boom in EdTech start-ups during the pandemic and environmental upheavals, providing educators with counsel on how to navigate the hurdles of online learning.

The analysis of the COVID-19 pandemic's impact on the educational landscape, particularly through the eyes of teachers in Delhi and the National Capital Region (NCR) of India, provides light on crucial challenges in the field (Jain et al., 2020). A survey done during the early phases of the epidemic highlighted significant issues compounded by the quick shift to online education. The findings highlighted the growing disparity between private and public schools, which disproportionately affects economically poor pupils who are already marginalized. Insufficient training in online pedagogies has emerged as a serious barrier for educators, limiting their ability to effectively adapt to virtual teaching environments. Despite the rise of educational technology (Ed-Tech) companies that provide answers, their interventions frequently fail to meet the needs of poor students and schools.

RESEARCH METHODOLOGY

This study is a qualitative approach, with a systematic literature review methodology used to achieve the objectives described below. Given the exploratory character of the study, a qualitative research design is used, with the goal of providing a full assessment and analysis of existing literature on Educational Technology (EdTech) and its impact on modern education. Scholarly articles, reports, case studies, and other EdTech-related publications were identified through comprehensive searches of academic databases, digital libraries, and relevant online repositories.

The objectives are as follows:

1. Define the scope and significance of EdTech in the contemporary educational context.
2. Examine the evolution of EdTech, tracing its historical development and highlighting key milestones.
3. Explore the diverse spectrum of EdTech tools and platforms, showcasing their applications and impact on teaching and learning.
4. Investigate the transformative potential of EdTech, focusing on its ability to foster personalized learning, improve accessibility, and drive educational inclusivity.
5. Address the ethical considerations and challenges posed by the integration of technology in education.

EDTECH TOOLS AND TRANSFORMATIVE POWER

Learning Management Systems (LMS) have evolved as the foundation of digital education, providing structured and integrated platforms to support teaching and learning processes. Aside from material distribution, these systems offer a wide range of features such as course administration, student progress monitoring, interactive participation, and evaluation tools. Among the prominent LMS platforms addressed is Moodle, which is noted for its open-source nature and customizable features that promote learner-centered methods. Moodle's support for various activities, including forums and quizzes, allows educators to design collaborative learning environments suited to their individual educational goals. Blackboard, another popular platform, provides a complete set of features that cater to both asynchronous and real-time learning methods. It prioritizes inclusivity by making educational materials available to all pupils, creating an environment in which every learner may interact with the subject and broaden their knowledge. Google Classroom has become popular among educators because of its seamless connection with Google's productivity tools, which streamlines communication and task management between teachers and students. Schoology distinguishes itself by emphasizing cooperation and mobile learning while also offering a comprehensive set of features to support community-building inside educational institutions.

Furthermore, innovative platforms like as BrightSpace and Docebo use predictive analytics and artificial intelligence to personalize learning experiences, reflecting a larger trend in modern education towards technology-driven, adaptive solutions. These LMS systems work together to modernize education by meeting a variety of needs in digital learning settings and pave the way for future improvements in the area. Interactive Learning Tools (ILT) have transformed passive learning into dynamic and engaging experiences, hence revolutionizing education. Platforms like Kahoot use gamification to make education more enjoyable and participatory, whilst Quizlet provides diverse study tools to reinforce learning across multiple areas. Edpuzzle allows teachers to augment video content with interactive aspects, promoting active learning and delivering vital feedback to students. TED-Ed uses chosen instructional videos to pique interest and stimulate debates, enhancing the learning experience with varied viewpoints. ClassDojo's broad communication tools are designed to foster classroom communities and encourage positive behavior. These ILT solutions improve education by catering to different learning styles while also encouraging creativity, cooperation, and communication in the classroom. Virtual and Augmented Reality (VR & AR) technologies are transforming education by enabling immersive and experience learning. Platforms such as Oculus Rift, Jigspace, and ClassVR provide virtual worlds in which students can investigate complicated concepts in fields ranging from science and history. Avanti's World provides students immersive learning experiences through a virtual theme park, whereas Kai's Clan uses coding, robotics, and augmented reality to teach problem-solving skills in an interesting way. These VR and AR solutions bridge the gap between academic knowledge and practical application, allowing students to gain a better comprehension of the curriculum and revolutionizing the learning experience. MOOCs and other online learning platforms have democratized education by providing high-quality courses and programmes from leading universities and institutions around the world.

Platforms such as Coursera, Udacity, Edx, Future Learn, Swayam, and Udemy cater to a wide range of learning demands, offering learners flexible and accessible opportunities to improve their skills and knowledge. These platforms represent a broader trend in online education, allowing students to easily pursue lifetime learning and professional development possibilities.

Table 1. Categorization of EdTech Tools and Platforms

Platform/Tool	Features	Benefits
Learning Management Systems (LMS)	- Organized and integrated platform for teaching and learning processes - Course administration - Student progress monitoring - Facilitating interaction and teamwork - Evaluation and feedback mechanisms	- Structured approach to digital education - Streamlined management of courses and student progress - Enhanced collaboration and engagement among students - Efficient assessment and feedback mechanisms for instructors and learners
Moodle	- Open-source and highly customizable - Support for various learner-focused tools - Diverse forms of engagement including discussions and assessments	- Customizable learning environments tailored to educational objectives - Rich collaborative features for vibrant learning spaces - Empowerment of instructors to facilitate diverse forms of engagement
Blackboard	- Comprehensive suite of capabilities supporting asynchronous and real-time learning - Cohesive experience integrating resources, assessments, and analytics	- Inclusive platform ensuring educational material accessibility for all students - Seamless integration of resources and assessments for an enhanced learning experience - Facilitation of analytics-driven insights for informed decision-making
Google Classroom	- Integration with Google's productivity tools - Streamlining communication between teachers and learners - User-friendly layout and free model	- Simplified distribution, collection, and grading of assignments - Enhanced communication and collaboration between teachers and learners - Accessibility and affordability for schools seeking to adopt digital learning
Schoology	- Emphasis on teamwork and mobile learning - Complete set of capabilities for managing courses and building community - Compatibility with third-party tools and materials	- Encouragement of collaborative learning and community-building within educational institutions - Adaptable platform for improving teaching and learning experiences - Compatibility with a wide range of tools for enhanced functionality
BrightSpace	- Adaptive platform utilizing predictive analytics for personalized learning experiences	- Personalized learning experiences tailored to individual student needs - Utilization of predictive analytics for informed decision-making and adaptive learning pathways

Table 1 continued

Platform/Tool	Features	Benefits
Docebo	- Focus on artificial intelligence to customize content and support social learning and mobile use - Personalized and dynamic features	- Customized learning content and experiences based on individual learner profiles - Support for social learning and mobile accessibility for enhanced engagement and flexibility
Interactive Learning Tools (ILT)	- Leverage technology to make learning more engaging, interactive, and accessible - Support a wide range of learning styles and preferences of students	- Dynamic and engaging learning experiences for students - Versatile study tools to reinforce learning across various subjects - Transformation of passive learning into active and enjoyable processes
Kahoot	- Games and quizzes to make education enjoyable - Custom surveys for real-time student response - Fosters learning through competitive yet educational environment	- Engagement through gamification and real-time interaction - Encouragement of learning through competitive spirit - Flexibility to customize surveys for diverse educational purposes
Quizlet	- Method for studying, practicing, and mastering subjects through flashcards - Various engaging ways of learning such as matching games and practice exams	- Ease of studying and reinforcing ideas and vocabulary - Versatility in learning methods to cater to diverse learning preferences - Enhancement of learning outcomes through interactive engagement
Edpuzzle	- Conversion of any video into interactive learning lessons - Addition of questions, voiceovers, and annotations to videos - Tracking student engagement and understanding through analytics	- Transformation of passive video watching into active learning experiences - Enhanced student engagement and understanding through interactive elements - Informed feedback on learning progress for both students and teachers
TED-Ed	- Educational videos on a wide range of topics - Customized lessons around TED-Ed original and YouTube videos - Sparking curiosity and fostering learning through curated content	- Access to diverse educational content from reputable sources - Enhancement of learning experiences through curated videos and discussions - Flexibility to customize lessons based on individual student interests and preferences
ClassDojo	- Building classroom communities through communication and involvement - Sharing of photos, videos, and updates - Encouragement of good behavior through point system	- Strengthening of classroom relationships and communication - Clarity and transparency in classroom activities for teachers, students, and parents - Promotion of positive behavior and recognition of student achievements
Virtual and Augmented Reality (VR & AR Tools)	- Immersive and lifelike scenarios for experiential learning - Engagement of students in interactive learning experiences - Visualization of complex concepts through 3D technologies	- Enhancement of learning experience through immersion and interactivity - Clearer understanding of complex concepts through visualization - Bridging the gap between theoretical knowledge and practical application through experiential learning

Table 1 continued

Platform/Tool	Features	Benefits
MOOC and Other Online Learning Platforms	- Democratization of access to high-quality education - Offering courses and programs from top universities and institutions - Social learning through discussion and interaction	- Access to diverse educational content from reputable institutions worldwide - Flexibility and convenience in learning opportunities - Encouragement of collaboration and interaction among learners through social learning
Oculus Rift	- Provides unlimited educational experiences in VR - Immersive virtual environment for students to engage in various activities - Realistic simulations enhancing understanding of complex concepts	- Enhanced learning experiences through immersion in virtual environments - Engagement with lifelike scenarios making learning enjoyable and memorable - Clearer understanding of complex concepts through realistic simulations
Jigspace	- Utilizes 3D technologies to visualize complex subjects - Allows interaction with various models in a virtual space - Clearer understanding of subjects ranging from human anatomy to mechanical engineering to circuit designing	- Simplified learning of complex subjects through visualization in 3D space - Enhanced engagement with interactive models - Improved comprehension of concepts through hands-on exploration
ClassVR	- Brings real-life environments into the classroom using VR technology - Offers a library of immersive educational experiences - Easy-to-use interface for teachers to guide students through lessons	- Deeper understanding of curriculum topics through immersion in real-life environments - Access to a wide range of educational experiences for enriched learning - Facilitation of seamless integration into classroom instruction by teachers
Avanti's World	- Offers immersive learning zones covering historical events, scientific concepts, and natural environments - Provides a completely virtual experience using VR and AR technologies	- Exploration of diverse educational topics through immersive virtual experiences - Engagement with historical events, scientific concepts, and natural environments in a virtual setting - Integration of VR and AR technologies for enhanced learning experiences
Kai's Clan	- Collaborative learning platform merging coding, robotics, and augmented reality - Enables students to create digital robots and navigate through challenges in a virtual world - Develops problem-solving, teamwork, and computational thinking skills in an engaging manner through Augmented Reality	- Encouragement of collaboration and teamwork among students through coding and robotics challenges - Development of problem-solving and computational thinking skills through interactive and engaging experiences - Integration of AR technology for futuristic learning opportunities

Source: Created by authors

A BRIEF OVERVIEW OF EDTECH TOOLS TRANSFORMING LEARNING

As depicted in Table. 1, which categorizes EdTech Tools and Platforms, the following details outline how these tools can be effectively utilized across various training sessions.

Learning Management Systems (LMS)

Learning Management Systems (LMS) have become the foundation of digital education, providing an organized and integrated platform for instructing, managing, and improving teaching and learning processes. These systems provide a wide variety of capabilities that go beyond simple content delivery, encompassing course administration, monitoring student advancement, facilitating interaction and teamwork, and offering mechanisms for evaluation and comments. Below, we investigate several major LMS platforms that have notably influenced education.

Moodle is an open-source learning management system that is highly customizable with a wide range of learner-focused tools. (Moodle.org, n.d. 2024) It supports various activities such as forums, databases, and quizzes, allowing educators to build rich and collaborative learning environments. Moodle facilitates diverse forms of engagement including discussions, data organization, and assessments, empowering instructors to generate vibrant, cooperative learning spaces. This adaptability is a key reason for its embrace across different educational organizations seeking to tailor the solution specifically for their unique educational objectives.

Blackboard possesses a comprehensive suite of capabilities supporting both asynchronous and real-time learning models. Blackboard facilitates a cohesive experience integrating resources, virtual classrooms, assessments, and analytics. (Blackboard, n.d. 2024) Ensuring educational material is available to all students irrespective of their capabilities is a core principle of Blackboard. It excels at providing an inclusive platform where every learner can engage with content and build upon their knowledge.

Google Classrooms has rapidly become a beloved choice among educators due to its integration with Google's collection of productivity instruments. It facilitates job distribution, collection, and grading, streamlining communication between teachers and learners. (Google Classroom. 2024) Its user-friendly layout and free model make it particularly attractive for schools seeking to apply or enhance their digital learning foundation.

Schoology differentiates itself by strongly emphasizing teamwork and learning using mobile devices. It provides a complete set of capabilities that back not just managing courses but also building a sense of community within educational institutions. (Schoology, n.d. 2024) Its user-friendly layout combined with compatibility with a wide range of third-party tools and materials make it an adaptable choice for improving teaching and learning experiences.

BrightSpace and **Docebo** demonstrate innovative approaches to meet changing educational needs. BrightSpace uses predictive analytics on its adaptive platform to personalize learning experiences. Docebo focuses on using artificial intelligence to customize content as well as social learning and mobile use. (Docebo, n.d. 2024) Both systems aim to support modern education through technology that analyzes users and adapts accordingly. They seek to enhance user experience and support through personalized, dynamic features.

The learning management platforms like Moodle, Blackboard, Google Classrooms, Schoology, BrightSpace, and Docebo play a vital role in modern education. By providing holistic solutions addressing the manifold needs of digital learning environments, these systems not only help teaching and learning but also clear a path for the future of education. Through their varied capabilities and dedication to bettering educational results, LMS platforms have become indispensable instruments in the EdTech world.

Interactive Learning Tools (ILT)

Interactive learning tools have revolutionized the way educators engage students, turning passive learning into an active and enjoyable process. These platforms leverage technology to make learning more engaging, interactive, and accessible, thereby supporting a wide range of learning styles and preferences of the students.

Kahoot is a learning platform that uses games and quizzes to make education more enjoyable. Educators can build custom surveys on any subject matter which students can then respond to in real time using their own devices. (Kahoot, n.d. 2024) This competitive yet educational environment fosters learning through playing games, making it a favorite tool of both – the educators and the students.

Quizlet provides an easy but effective method for studying, practicing, and mastering whatever students are learning. (Quizlet, n.d. 2024) Users can make study sets of flashcards that can then be utilized through various engaging ways of learning such as matching games, practice exams, and live quizzes. Quizlet's adaptability makes it an exceptionally helpful instrument for strengthening ideas and vocabulary across many topics.

Edpuzzle empowers teachers to convert any video into the learning lessons for the students. By enabling the addition of questions, voiceovers, and annotations to educational videos, it transforms passive video watching into an active learning experience. (Edpuzzle, n.d. 2024) It tracks student engagement and understanding through analytics and provides feedback on learning to the students as well as teachers.

TED-Ed is an extension of the popular TED platform, offering educational videos on a wide range of topics. These carefully curated videos, created by educators and animators, are designed to spark curiosity and foster learning. (TED-Ed, n.d. 2024) TED-Ed also allows teachers to create customized lessons around TED-Ed original, TED Talk or YouTube videos, enhancing the learning experience with discussions and activities.

ClassDojo is an ILT product aiming to build classroom communities by connecting teachers, students, and parents. It facilitates 360-degree communication and involvement. (ClassDojo, n.d. 2024) Teachers can share photos, videos, and updates on ClassDojo. This makes classroom activities clearer for everyone. In addition, ClassDojo encourages good behavior. Teachers can give points to students for participation and conduct. This recognizes students for positive choices they make. Together, these ILT products are reshaping education by making learning more dynamic, engaging, and tailored to individual learners' needs. They not only complement traditional teaching methods but also open new avenues for creativity, collaboration, and communication in the classroom.

Virtual and Augmented Reality Tools (VR and AR Tools)

Virtual and Augmented Reality (VR and AR) technologies are at the forefront of transforming educational experiences by immersing students in interactive and lifelike scenarios. These tools provide unique opportunities for experiential learning, making complex concepts easier to understand and engaging students in unprecedented ways.

Oculus Rift bring an unlimited felt of educational experiences in VR. The outcomes are just incredible due to the quality of virtual reality. (Oculus Rift,n.d. 2024) Students may take a trip to the virtual world, do virtual exercises, and involve themselves in many other activities just as if they are there.

Jigspace uses 3D technologies to make learning complex subjects much easier and realistic. (Jigspace, n.d. 2024) By visualizing concepts in 3-dimensions, students can interact with various models in a virtual space, providing a clearer understanding of subjects ranging from human anatomy to mechanical engineering to circuit designing.

ClassVR brings a real-life environment into the classroom using virtual reality technology. With a library of educational experiences and an easy-to-use interface, teachers can guide students through immersive lessons in science, history, and art, fostering a deeper understanding of the curriculum. (ClassVR, n.d. 2024)

Avanti's World is the first educational VR theme park. (Avanti's World, n.d. 2024) It hosts numerous immersive learning zones where students can explore historical events, scientific concepts, and natural environments through a completely virtual experience using VR and AR technologies.

Kai's Clan is a collaborative learning platform that merges coding, robotics, and augmented reality. (Kai's Clan, n.d. 2024) Students can write their own code to create digital robots that navigate through challenges in a virtual world seen through Augmented Reality. It develops problem-solving, teamwork, and computational thinking in the students in an engaging and futuristic manner. Integrating Virtual and Augmented Reality Technology into education not only enhances the learning experience for the students, in fact, it completely revolutionizes it. These technologies provide a bridge between theoretical knowledge and practical application, making education an immersive, and interactive experience for students.

MOOC and Other Online Learning Platforms

MOOC and Other Online Learning Platforms have democratized access to high-quality education, enabling learners worldwide to enhance their skills and knowledge with just a click of a button. Coursera partners with universities and organizations to offer courses, specializations, and degrees across a wide range of subjects, facilitating access to top-tier educational content. (Coursera, n.d. 2024) Udacity focuses on tech-related skills and subjects, offering "Nanodegree" programs in areas like programming, data science, and artificial intelligence, designed to equip the students with job-ready skills (Udacity, n.d. 2024). Edx, founded in collaboration by Harvard and MIT, provides a platform for higher education learning, offering courses from universities across the world in various disciplines (edX, n.d. 2024). FutureLearn offers a diverse selection of courses from leading universities and cultural institutions, emphasizing social learning through discussion and interaction (FutureLearn, n.d. 2024). Swayam, an initiative by the Government of India, aims to provide free online courses, ensuring that quality education is accessible to all (Swayam, n.d. 2024). Udemy offers a wide array of courses on various topics, allowing experts to create and share content, catering to the learning needs of professionals (Udemy, n.d. 2024).

IMPACT ON TEACHING AND LEARNING

Enhanced Engagement and Interaction

EdTech tools and platforms enhance student engagement significantly by making learning a highly interactive experience through dynamic content, and collaborative projects.

EdTech platforms like Kahoot and Quizlet employ gaming into their core pedagogy making learning more fun and challenging, which ultimately boosts student participation. Various learning Management Systems offer synchronous and asynchronous communications between the teachers and learners. This accomodates different learning styles of students at different knowledge levels. In addition, EdTech products let use multimedia and Virtual Reality which enables the transition from the lifeless classes to a more active learning environment with visual and auditory perception. This way, students will be able to improve their comprehension and will have more chances to understand and remember new learnings. Individual learning is provided through personalized learning paths, which specifically fragment the content according to the student's strengths and weaknesses thereby offering more personalized learning. Also, another mechanism in these platforms is the creation of forum or discussion.

Data Driven Insights

Data analytics capabilities of EdTech tools transform teaching and learning by offering deep insights into students' performance and their engagement with the content offered. Through the analysis of data collected from various EdTech platforms, educators can identify trends and patterns in the learning behavior of the students, they can pinpoint areas where students struggle and areas where they excel. This enables the creation of targeted interventions and personalized learning experiences by modifying the course content as per the level of the students. Real-time feedback mechanisms allow for immediate adjustments to teaching approaches, which ultimately enhances the learning process. In addition to this, predictive analytics can forecast student outcomes, enabling preemptive action to address potential challenges. Overall, the use of data-driven insights in education leads to improved educational outcomes, and a more enjoyable learning journey for students.

THE SCOPE AND SIGNIFICANCE OF EDTECH IN THE CONTEMPORARY EDUCATIONAL CONTEXT

(Selwyn et al., 2019) provides a detailed analysis of the critical terrain in educational technology scholarship, identifying six main problems that are expected to affect the discipline in the following decade. It advocates for ongoing collective debate and proactive engagement to effectively handle these problems. By recognizing and expanding on these problems, the paper gives vital guidance for future research endeavors while also emphasizing the importance of scholars remaining aware of the changing dynamics of educational technology. Furthermore, it emphasizes the practical implications of these issues, allowing educators and academics to foresee and plan for the complexities of critical educational technology scholarship in the coming years. Despite the lack of concrete empirical data, the paper acts as a catalyst for promoting a greater awareness of the complex challenges surrounding educational technology, paving the way for informed discourse and action in the field.

Ed tech the word has been derived from Education and Technology making it word Edtech. Since the days of usage of computers with regards to teaching, it can be said that technology was being deployed to impart education. The proper usage of computers in education can be traced back in 1965 when the act of Elementary and Secondary Education Act was passed in United States (US). (California State University., 2008) The major thrust of the act was to provide quality education to every child in US.

Educational Technology (EdTech) has a significant impact on today's educational scene, indicating a radical shift in teaching and learning paradigms. As technology permeates all aspects of society, its incorporation into education has become critical, providing unparalleled prospects for innovation and growth. EdTech comprises a wide range of tools and platforms, including Learning Management Systems (LMS) and Virtual and Augmented Reality (VR & AR) technologies, all meant to improve educational experiences and outcomes. EdTech not only improves information access in today's educational context, but it also promotes participation, collaboration, and personalised learning experiences. Its significance stems from its potential to meet varied learning needs, democratise access to education, and equip students for success in an increasingly digital environment. Furthermore, EdTech is critical in addressing the evolving difficulties in education, such as the requirement for flexible learning environments, personalised instruction, and the development of 21st-century skills. As a result, understanding the extent and impact of EdTech is critical for educators, policymakers, and stakeholders as they negotiate the complexity of modern education and aim to maximise the potential of technology to assist learning and growth.

The next wave had overhead projectors being used in the classrooms similarly around the same era. Overhead projectors required very little setting up and only a plug in to light the bulb on the instrument to reflect the light. It had very limited functionality where the class can only view the content on A4 paper on large screen. It was only possible to view a static image or document, there was no possibility of watching a video. Therefore, this technology also had its own limitations. Also, the institutions also may not have enough budget to scale up the technology because of which this has become quite prevalent in earlier times.

Simultaneously there was the use of radio and television to broadcast various courses. This medium was extensively used by government to promote basic courses to teach the masses. (Sriram ARULCHELVAN, & D. VISWANATHAN, 2008) Slowly during these times was the advent of computers in the education system. Therefore, 20th century had projectors, radio, television and computers in education. With the onset of 21st century, more technology embraced the education sector. Couple of technologies that came in are

- Laptops and Tablets
- E Books and E Readers
- Smartphones
- Massive Open Online Courses (MOOCs)
- Virtual and Augmented Reality
- Artificial Intelligence
- Video Conferencing

The crux of all the above technologies is that it made education a very involving and interactive activity.

The market size of Edtech Industry in India is $6 billion as per CNBC TV18 (Anand, 2023). This market is set to expand further going ahead with more and more gaps being explored by edtech companies in India. A total of 13,771 edtech startups are there in India (*Top 10 startups in EdTech in India - tracxn* 2023).

The scope of using technology is immense in the education system. The development of artificial intelligence and machine learning would create way for better learning experience for the students. Earlier also simulations were taught in physical classroom set up but now with the help of virtual reality its very much possible to create a very interactive environment for delivery of a concept. Newer concepts of augmented reality are giving user a very unique experience and the same can be replicated in education. In fact the Department of State Education Research and Training of Bengaluru have been using QR (Quick Response) code in textbooks for classes 6 to 10 since 2018. The student can connect digitally by using the QR code. (*School textbooks to turn smarter with QR codes from this year* 2018)

The current size of Indian Edtech industry is $ 6 billion as per CNBC TV18 (Anand, 2023). This market is expected to grow to $ 10 billion by 2025 (*Growth and expansion of India's Edtech Industry: IBEF* 2023). Things started to burst when schools and educational institutions reopened post the pandemic. Obviously, the reason for exponential growth has been solved because of which the industry couldn't see much beyond. Funding to edtech start-ups came down to $2.6 billion in the year 2022 and in the year 2023 it had fallen to $ 297.3 million. These things were not enough, and problems started to crop up in bellwether edtech firm Byju's. The valuation of Byju's crashed from $ 22 billion to $1 billion by Blackrock (R et al., 2024). The failure of Byju's came because of multiple reasons of mis management which included mis selling of staff, providing loans to parents who were not capable, failing to file the financials on time, unproportionate marketing expenditures and leverages taken for doing the businesses.

NAVIGATING ETHICAL FRONTIERS: CHALLENGES AND CONSIDERATIONS IN INTEGRATING TECHNOLOGY IN EDUCATION

It is crucial to thoroughly analyze the ethical implications and obstacles that come with the incorporation of technology in education, as it rapidly evolves. As educators, administrators, and stakeholders eagerly embrace the advantages of educational technology (EdTech), it is essential to negotiate the intricate terrain with a heightened consciousness of ethical ramifications. This section explores crucial factors that require meticulous attention to guarantee the responsible and fair utilization of educational technology.

Amidst the rapid development of educational technology, it is of utmost importance to prioritize the protection of student data. Geoffrey Alphonso, the Chief Executive Officer at Alef Education, emphasizes the increasing difficulties encountered by EdTech companies and calls for strong cybersecurity measures (Alphonso, 2023).

Educational Technology (EdTech) solutions frequently entail the gathering and examination of vast quantities of student data. It is of utmost importance to prioritize the implementation of strong privacy safeguards, consent processes, and secure data storage practices to protect the sensitive information of learners. Joseph Evanick, (Joseph Evanick, 2023) an expert in Cultural Transformation in Educational Technology, examines the crucial significance of implementing efficient measures to protect student data privacy. The author highlights the ethical obligations related to educational technology, emphasizing the importance of openness, data retention policies, and design principles that prioritize privacy. Evanick supports a well-rounded strategy that improves education while also safeguarding student privacy.

Although EdTech can make education more accessible to all, there are ethical concerns around discrepancies in access. The chapter explores the difficulties associated with disparities in device availability, access to high-speed internet, and digital resources. The rise of Massive Open Online Courses (MOOCs) is a promising opportunity to utilize technology for the achievement of long-awaited benefits in global higher education. As the MOOCs landscape develops with promising opportunities, it also presents a complex set of ethical problems inherent in different efforts. (Marshall, 2014) This address concerns things such as the possible commercialization of students and explores the ethical dilemmas presented by the analytical and research initiatives carried out by scholars and organizations.

Ensuring educators and students possess the essential abilities to appropriately navigate the digital realm is a crucial ethical concern. The field of EdTech frequently involves collaborations with external vendors, which can give rise to ethical concerns regarding the possible impact of commercial interests on educational practices. To ethically incorporate EdTech, instructors must be dedicated to continual professional development. There is a significance of training programs that prioritize not only technical proficiency but also ethical considerations, cultivating a culture of conscientious technology utilization inside educational institutions.

Addressing ethical considerations is crucial in order to establish a sustainable, inclusive, and responsible future for learning as education experiences a paradigm shift through the transformative impact of EdTech. Through proactive planning and careful attention to detail, educators can effectively utilize technology to optimize the educational experience while maintaining ethical norms and values.

FINDINGS AND FUTURE IMPLICATIONS

The integration of Educational Technology (EdTech) has resulted in a substantial alteration of teaching and learning procedures. Educators observed increased possibilities of student engagement, interaction, and personalised learning experiences by the varied range of EdTech tools and platforms accessible. EdTech applications like Moodle, Blackboard, Google Classroom, Kahoot, and Quizlet have been shown to greatly improve student engagement and participation. Gamification, multimedia content, and collaborative learning settings were particularly helpful in encouraging students to participate actively and communicate with one another.

The study recognised EdTech platforms' ability to create personalised learning experiences based on individual student needs and preferences. Adaptive learning algorithms, interactive simulations, and personalised feedback systems were identified as important aspects that contribute to the customisation of learning routes and delivery.

EdTech was discovered to accelerate the evolution of established educational procedures, allowing educators to implement novel pedagogical techniques and instructional strategies. The integration of virtual and augmented reality tools, interactive learning software, and Massive Open Online Courses (MOOCs) has broadened instructors' teaching techniques, encouraging creativity and experimentation in instructional design.

Despite EdTech's transformative potential, the study revealed ethical concerns and hurdles in its integration. Concerns about data privacy, inequality in access to technology, and the commercialization of education were identified as topics that require serious consideration and ethical thought.

Educators emphasised the need for ongoing professional development in order to fully realise the promise of EdTech in educational contexts. Training programmes that focus on technological competency, ethical considerations, and pedagogical best practices were highlighted as critical for preparing educators to traverse the digital domain responsibly and ethically.

The study's findings have important implications for future research and practice in educational technology. Further research should focus on developing comprehensive frameworks for evaluating the effectiveness of EdTech interventions, addressing equity and access issues, and investigating innovative uses of emerging technologies in education, such as artificial intelligence and immersive simulations.

CONCLUSION

This study sheds light on the transformative effect of Educational Technology (EdTech) in revolutionising teaching and learning techniques at Narayana Business School. The incorporation of EdTech tools and platforms has resulted in increased student involvement, interaction, and personalised learning experiences, as well as the progression of traditional educational approaches. The findings emphasise the significance of ongoing professional development for educators to fully leverage the potential of EdTech in educational contexts. Training programmes that emphasise technological competency, ethical considerations, and pedagogical best practices are critical for preparing educators to navigate the digital domain responsibly and ethically. Despite EdTech's transformative potential, the study revealed ethical concerns and hurdles in its integration. Concerns about data privacy, inequality in technological access, and educational commercialization highlight the importance of rigorous consideration and ethical discussion while implementing EdTech solutions.

Future research should focus on developing comprehensive frameworks for evaluating the effectiveness of EdTech interventions, addressing equity and access challenges, and investigating new uses of emerging technology in education. Using the findings of this study, educators, administrators, policymakers, and other stakeholders may collaborate to build inclusive, engaging, and successful learning environments that maximise the potential of educational technology.

REFERENCES

Alphonso, G. (2023, August 4). Council post: Empowering learners and protecting privacy: Advancing Data Security in EdTech. *Forbes*. https://www.forbes.com/sites/forbestechcouncil/2023/08/02/empowering-learners-and-protecting-privacy-advancing-data-security-in-edtech/?sh=378880db3053

Althunibat, A., Alzyadat, W., Almarashdeh, I., Alsmadi, M., Al Shawabkeh, A. O., Abuhamdah, A., & Alzaqebah, M. (2023). Learning experience of students using the Learning Management System: User's perspective on the use of Moodle in the University of Jordan. *Advances in Human-Computer Interaction, 2023*, 1–11. doi:10.1155/2023/6659245

Anand, A. (2023, April 12). *India's Edtech market expected to grow to $10 billion by 2025*. CNBCTV18. Retrieved March 1, 2024, from https://www.cnbctv18.com/education/india-edtech-market-expected-to-grow-to-10-billion-by-2025-startups-unicorns-16391151.htm

California State University. (2008). History, the History of Computers, and the History of Computers in Education. History of computers in Education. https://home.csulb.edu/~murdock/histofcs.html

Corporate Author. (2023b, June 16). Top 10 startups in EdTech in India - tracxn. Retrieved March 1, 2024, from https://tracxn.com/d/explore/edtech-startups-in-india/__fpQpYpejRQUpr2Den-JxfLl7qv4ORAU4R34IA5folf0/companies

Cowling, M. A., Crawford, J., Vallis, C., Middleton, R., & Sim, K. (2022). The EdTech difference: Digitalisation, digital pedagogy, and technology enhanced learning. *Journal of University Teaching & Learning Practice*, *19*(2), 1–13. doi:10.53761/1.19.2.1

Hurix, C. A. (2024, January 23). *Top eleven education solution providers in India - Hurix Digital*. Digital Engineering & Technology | Elearning Solutions | Digital Content Solutions. Retrieved March 1, 2024, from https://www.hurix.com/top-edtech-companies-in-india-edtech-excellence-2/

IBEF. (2023, February). *Growth and expansion of India's Edtech Industry: IBEF*. India Brand Equity Foundation. Retrieved March 1, 2024, from https://www.ibef.org/research/case-study/growth-and-expansion-of-india-s-edtech-industry

Jain, S., Lall, M., & Singh, A. (2020). Teachers' voices on the impact of covid-19 on school education: Are Ed-tech companies really the Panacea? *Contemporary Education Dialogue*, *18*(1), 58–89. doi:10.1177/0973184920976433

Joseph Evanick. (2023, November 21). Ethical dilemmas in student data privacy: Navigating edtech safeguards. eLearning Industry. https://elearningindustry.com/ethical-dilemmas-in-student-data-privacy-navigating-edtech-safeguards

K, P. (2018, November 4). *School textbooks to turn smarter with QR codes from this year*. The New Indian Express. Retrieved March 1, 2024, from https://www.newindianexpress.com/cities/bengaluru/2018/Oct/29/school-textbooks-to-turn-smarter-with-qr-codes-from-this-year-1891393.html

Marshall, S. (2014). Exploring the ethical implications of moocs. *Distance Education*, *35*(2), 250–262. doi:10.1080/01587919.2014.917706

Mohit Sharma. (2020). Impact of COVID-19 on online education sector and edtech companies. *PalArch's Journal of Archaeology of Egypt / Egyptology, 17*(12), 1278-1288. Retrieved from https://archives.palarch.nl/index.php/jae/article/view/6802

R, V., Dimri, A., Chhetri, V., Fyler, T., & Prabhu, A. (2024, February 5). *Byju's valuation down 99%: India's Edtech Decacorn seeking $200m at $225M valuation, what exactly happened? - TFN*. Tech Funding News. Retrieved March 1, 2024, from https://techfundingnews.com/byjus-valuation-down-99-indias-edtech-decacorn-seeking-200m-at-225m-valuation-what-exactly-happened/#:~:text=However%2C%20the%20same%20year%20witnessed,its%20peak%20of%20%2422%20billion

Sarma, A., & Jaybhave, S. (2024, January 24). *Edtech in India: Boom, Bust, or bubble?* Edtech in India: Boom, bust, or bubble? Retrieved March 1, 2024, from https://www.orfonline.org/expert-speak/edtech-in-india-boom-bust-or-bubble#:~:text=The%20country%20had%20emerged%20decisively,4.73%20billion%20in%202021%20alone

Selwyn, N., Hillman, T., Eynon, R., Ferreira, G., Knox, J., Macgilchrist, F., & Sancho-Gil, J. M. (2019). What's next for Ed-Tech? critical hopes and concerns for the 2020s. *Learning, Media and Technology*, *45*(1), 1–6. doi:10.1080/17439884.2020.1694945

Sriram, A., & Viswanathan, D. V. (2008). Radio, Television and the Internet providing the Right to Education in India. *Asian Journal of Distance Education, 6*(1), 39–52. https://doi.org/https://www.semanticscholar.org/

Chapter 14
Role of Metaverse in the Education Sector

Priya Jindal
Chitkara Business School, Chitkara University, Punjab, India

Ansh Jindal
Chitkara Business School, Chitkara University, Punjab, India

Deepa Sharma
https://orcid.org/0000-0003-4374-917X
Maharishi Markandeshwar University (deemed), Ambala, India

ABSTRACT

Education is widely regarded as a catalyst for transformation. Students are introduced to novel academic and research domains through the integration of technological advancements. The Metaverse inclusion in the education sector has marked a radical break with conventional teaching practices by introducing a new paradigm shift in classroom education. This chapter is about the examination of the possible role of the metaverse in the future of education. Metaverse platforms possess the ability to bridge the gap between the digital and physical worlds by providing students with a safe controlled and diverse interactive learning environment, which advances their interaction. The chapter also covered the educational difficulties brought about by the Metaverse, including protecting students from potential dangers and establishing standards to ensure a high-quality education that sets an example for the world at large.

DOI: 10.4018/979-8-3693-3015-9.ch014

Copyright © 2024, IGI Global. Copying or distributing in print or electronic forms without written permission of IGI Global is prohibited.

INTRODUCTION

Education is an ongoing and continuous process that significantly influences the overall quality of an individual's life. Every nation recognizes the worth of education since it has a direct impact on the advancement of the country. Education serves as a complementary factor in the progress of individuals, societies, and nations. The education system underwent a significant transformation due to the quick advancements in technology and the gains made in learning methods. The advent of technology has revolutionized education with the use of e-learning, which provides ease, personalization, and agility. Education technology is a platform where academic performance is improved, student skills are enhanced and creativity is expressed. For instance, creative design calls for such things as the right infrastructure, and dynamic evolving learning spaces to remain relevant with future changes in curriculum and meet changing student demands. This innovation has greatly increased access to education of superior quality for all. The growth of technology catalyzes a change in thinking since every learner is exposed to an exceptional global standard system of education. Through the integration of education with technology, the right set of circumstances has been opened up regarding accessibility, excellence and knowledge. The metaverse talks about the fully immersive internet that gives us access to virtual and augmented reality while connecting through persistent avatars along with cutting-edge digital technologies.

The phrase 'Metaverse' was introduced in 1982 in Neal Stevenson's book Snow Crash. (El Jaouhari et al., 2023) the characters can go to Stevenson's Metaverse, a virtual world, to get away from the depressingly oppressive real world. During the early 1990s, Sega introduced VR arcade games, which were available for play in various multiple arcades. Following that Sports Vision broadcasted the first NFL game live with these other sports broadcasters soon adopted the practice of superimposing graphics onto real-world imagery. In 2014, Facebook purchased Oculus and Facebook founder Mark Zuckerberg notified that Facebook and Oculus would establish a collaborative collaboration to enhance the Oculus platform and provide more support for a wider range of games. In 2014, XR experienced significant activity as Sony and Samsung declared their intentions to create their virtual headsets, while Google established its first Cardboard device and Google Glass augmented reality (AR) spectacles. The Metaverse, an emerging iteration of the Internet, amalgamates several cutting-edge technologies. Its fusion with the education sector has immense promise (Hines & Netland, 2023).

The chapter highlights the dynamic and ever-changing nature of the metaverse. It identifies three key attributes of the education metaverse: interaction, immersion, and diversity. These traits serve as the foundations of the education metaverse. In the face of various information sources, teachers are facing an uphill struggle in trying to teach the antiquated "chalk and talk" technique to the current generation of tech-savvy kids. Additionally, as the importance of the Fourth Industrial Revolution has grown, education has been seen as the road to Education 4.0. As a result, learning environments have been redesigned with pedagogies fit for the twenty-first century, an organic curriculum has been implemented, new concepts and academic disciplines like artificial intelligence, data science, and big data have emerged, and the most recent educational and learning technologies have been integrated.

The metaverse has been characterized as a step inherent in the evolution of the Internet. Visualize a virtual cosmos where thousands of people join in, get employed and trade, everything they need is taught and communicated to them by their relatives, friends and strangers who are living on VR only (Sangeeta & Tandon 2021). Today's computational devices display serves as passages to augmented 3D virtual legitimacy that imitate global maps reducing the communication gap.

Hence "Metaverse" is the term used for this concept. The ability of the metaverse in higher education is earlier determined as the study goes through the literature together with a comprehensive review of the possible benefits it might offer. Differentiating digital avatars from physical bodies is that they let us retain ourselves as our original selves without actually leaving those identities (Agarwal & Alathur, 2023). The metaverse application in higher education becomes an ideal non-conventional space for students where their interests and learning goals come first. It has the potential to radically change how teaching and learning are done in future. It will introduce a new method of doing things at the college or university level the previous way heavily, where people used to rely on paperwork a lot. It is marked by many positive factors like student-focused instructions, the intrinsic benefits of an individual, and an instructive learning process. A greater proportion of students will be able to access high-quality education by removing the barriers imposed by geographical locations and physical restrictions such as distance and disability (Lim et al., 2021). E-learning facilitates the connection of numerous prospective students to the communication network. Mobile communication and social media networks are being utilized more often to provide self-directed and interactive learning for learners. Universities and academic institutions can now explore several options to accomplish their primary objectives (Kraus, 2022).

REVIEW OF LITERATURE

The literature evaluation encompassed many types of scholarly publications, such as conference papers, book chapters, and research articles. Although the authors found several research works, containing the phrase "Metaverse" and education-related keywords, the author concluded that some of them were not relevant to our analysis. Consequently, this study excluded studies that investigated topics beyond the realms of social science and education, or those which are not directly pertain to the conception of the Metaverse. In recent years, researchers from distinct countries have increasingly focused on the utilization of the metaverse in the field of education. Bag et al., (2023) analyze the perspectives of UAE students on the use of a metaverse for medical-educational purposes, whereas Cheng et al., (2022) explore the intricate factors influencing instructors' preparedness to develop technologically advanced learning settings. Furthermore; they suggest using a system that combines virtual reality and metaverse strategies in the classroom to address the limitations of existing remote methods of hands-on teaching. Amoozad et al., (2023) adopted a constructive training technique to assess viewpoints and interactions in the metaverse with an emphasis on the learner. Tiwari et. al., (2023) concentrates on the creation of the smart education environment use as a base of the metaverse, whereas Hatane et al., (2023) undertake a broad examination of the literature on the application of the metaverse in other industries also. The usefulness of the metaverse platform in higher education during the COVID-19 pandemic is assessed by Mittal et al. (2019) concluded how the utilization of augmented reality affects the motivation of the students in the classroom. By evaluating their ability to develop educational virtual reality (VR) content and metaverse platforms, the researchers also look at how prepared educators are to construct technologically enhanced learning settings. To support a dynamic teaching experience, Jafar and Ahmad (2023) suggest creating an intelligent, student-focused learning environment inside the Metaverse that provides a variety of learning settings. Rana et al. (2022) investigate the opinions and views of the elementary school students. Additionally, they investigate how the metaverse is used in various educational states of affairs such as higher education and industry and they also highlight the issues and the difficulties associated with the implementation of the metaverse in the higher education sector. Pre and Post-test were used to evaluate the impact of metaverse on the knowledge and the skills of the learners. The System Usability Scale (SUS), attendance surveys and knowledge acquisition and retention tests to gauge how user-friendly the VR Metaverse system is. To investigate pedagogical strategies and practices in immersive learning environments, Volpentesta et al. (2023) used theme analysis, data synthesis and mapping research. An analysis of the applications of several new technologies before and during the coronavirus outbreak was conducted by Kumar et al. in 2023 and found that an augmented reality smartphone app was utilized to measure the impact of the software on the student's motivation and excitement for learning.

EVOLUTION AND INCORPORATION OF METAVERSE IN THE EDUCATION SECTOR

A revolutionary journey propelled by technological breakthroughs and the search for creative learning experiences has defined the emergence and integration of the metaverse into the education sector. The journey of the metaverse passes through various stages from early development (2000-2010) to initial integration (2010-2020) and from initial integration to mainstream adoption. In the early 2000s, experimenting began in the virtual background like Second Life (SL) a popular virtual world platform, educators realised the potential of immersion technologies that could revolutionize traditional teaching techniques. Educational institutions began experimenting with virtual classrooms, online courses and simulations to immerse students in interactive learning experiences as AR and VR technologies became more widely accessible in the 2010s. A major defining moment was reached in the mid-2020s when Meta (formerly Facebook) announced a large investment in the expansion of the metaverse, which sparked widespread adoption in the education sector. Renowned educational institutions establishments started incorporating metaverse technologies into their courses, providing learners with immersive learning settings, virtual campuses and cross-border collaborative platforms.

Figure 1. Evolution of Metaverse
Source: Created by author

2000s - 2010s Early Development

- Second Life gains popularity, showcasing potential for virtual environments in education

2010s - Early 2020s Initial Integration

- Google Expeditions launches , offereing virtual trips for classrooms.

Mid 2020s - Present Adoption

- Introduction of the virtual campus and introducing metaverse based learning platforms

CURRENT SCENARIO OF METAVERSE

The Metaverse gained more prominence with Facebook's rebranding of its corporate identity to Meta in October 2021. In addition to Meta, prominent technology companies like as Google, Microsoft, Wipro and Infosys are also allocating substantial financial resources to support this notion (Jafar & Ahmad, 2023). McKinsey & Company, a management consulting company, has made an optimistic prediction that the metaverse economy has the potential to achieve a value of $5 trillion by the year 2030. The metaverse is anticipated to be significantly influenced by e-commerce, as well as gaming, entertainment and education. Presently, enterprises employ the phrase to denote a multitude of sophisticated digital environments (Czok et al., 2023). The Metaverse has transformed and is now referred to as the Multiverse. The Metaverse enables global participation, allowing individuals globally to actively contribute to the expansion of collective interactions (Volpentesta et al., 2023). It's a digital world that's full of possibilities—a new frontier focused on virtual experiences, where anything anyone can imagine can be realized.

METAVERSE AND EDUCATION

The metaverse phenomenon, which is displacing the outmoded conventional teaching techniques to completely transform the education sector 4.0, is being propelled by the Industrial Revolution. In the past few years, the metaverse has gained a lot of attention due to its unique and profound impact across multiple fields. A wide range of technologies are utilized in the metaverse such as big data, artificial intelligence, game designs and the Internet of Things (IoTs). Make a turn for the better in the field of education as a result of the introduction and application of the metaverse in the education sector. Still, the metaverse is in its initial stage of development. Ferrigno (2023) believes that a variety of metaverse-related issues must be addressed to improve academic performance. Zainurin et al., (2023) outlined the most recent challenges and the possibilities related to the metaverse's potential uses in the domain of education comprehensively. One of the integral elements of the Metaverse education system is the Individualized Learning Environment, which involves creating a new and imaginative learning environment for the learners (Kumar et al., 2023). Metaverse – 3D Environment makes it easy to merge traditional and online learning platforms. Metaverse allows the students to create their virtual dummies and enables them to participate in the online learning environment and enjoy the amazing learning experience. Additionally, there is a wide range of opportunities for immersive learning in the metaverse. In this 3D virtual environment, there is a vast array of events and activities including sports and contests that enables the learners to engage effectively. To improve one's understanding of the various concepts, the metaverse possesses the ability to promote the integration and the exchange of ideas from the various domains. Through the use of the metaverse, the users can build a digital environment where virtual meetings, symposiums and debates can be held. The new ways of learning and interaction brought about by the technological developments in the forms of metaverse help teachers and students with new methods and practices to re-skill and reinforce positive attitudes. Such shifting empowers the users with a personalized tech-effective system of services when the core of the metaverse is not organized properly yet. As such, the possibility emerges for academics, educators and digital designers to be just the ones to take the lead.

Fulfilling the potential of the metaverse requires a globally interconnected, immersive, and real-time online environment which provides an innovative way to connect the real world to all digital paces. The incorporation of immersive technologies is core to accounting for students' attention and productivity in the educational system, which motivates to integration of advanced technologies into academic disciplines. It has led to online learning to combine in the manner of acquainted everywhere in the world. Therefore personalizing the teaching process will be one of the initial purposes for a teacher to consider three-dimensional virtual classrooms.

Furthermore, as we move closer to Industry 5.0, large amounts of personal data are continuously being transferred to cloud computing. Therefore, blockchain must enhance authentication processes including security and scalability concerns to improve the quality of online education. Learners can keep up with their teachers, industry partners and peers with integration into the metaverse and related digital technologies that are also developing. It is an effort to increase engagement, promote learning through experience, and introduce students to foreign and multicultural educational systems. It is applied in the realm of education to raise the researcher's and student's academic achievements. This technological advancement provides a suitable solution in the education sector and technology using its methodology. Application of the metaverse in education is demonstrated by virtual laboratories, virtual training and simulation centres and virtual classrooms. Students should have access to a virtual learning environment in the Metaverse that includes interactive objects and multimedia resources to enhance the teaching of lessons. Additionally, Metaverse makes it possible to create customized learning experiences based on users' preferences and requirements. Every student should be able to receive a highly customized learning experience from the Metaverse that is tailored to their unique needs and preferences. Personalized interventions and resources are offered to help the students on their learning pathways based on the analysis of progress, learning preferences and areas of difficulty. utilizing adaptive learning algorithms. Moreover, peer-to-peer learning, group projects and worldwide collaborations are made possible by the collaborative technologies in the metaverse, which encourage the learners to have a feeling of community and collaboration. Through the metaverse, students and teachers should be able to work together on projects in real time, engage in interactive activities and participate in virtual events. Regardless of their location and disability, students ought to be able to access high-quality education from anywhere in the world with access to the Internet.

Even if the metaverse has the potential to provide a dynamic and creative learning environment, developers should pay attention to students, teachers and instructors' safety and security. Metaverse platforms facilitate this through which students can interact with scientific labs and historical sites or engage in e-learning and online classes, among other things. Students will be able to study and experiment with concepts in a safe, immersive environment because there are more immersive situations in which students will find a lot of participatory learning involved. Educationalists are going to appreciate Metaverse as an important development for them as it provides richer encounters for the students and also a more interactive learning atmosphere. The presence of metaverse is going to be highly significant for the education arena thus certainly attracting attention from the education industry. This will lead to an improvement in both engagement and enjoyment during teaching time. Also, while they learn at home, they feel like been taught in a normal classroom making this process seem like a traditional classroom instead of a solitary experience from a distant leadership.

ROLE OF METAVERSE IN ACADEMIC LANDSCAPE

Metaverse possesses the capability to revolutionize the education sector through the utilization of technological advancements such as Virtual reality (VR), augmented reality (AR), and mixed reality (MR). The major role of the metaverse in the academic field is discussed as follows:

1. **Immersive Learning Environment:** Metaverse offers an immersive learning environment to the students. Students can interact with the educational content in the three-dimensional spaces in the immersive learning environment. In contrast to conventional teaching, it enhances the understanding of the students and increases the retention power.
2. **Worldwide Educational Access:** The Metaverse allows students from all across the globe to receive high-quality education without being limited by geography by overcoming physical boundaries. It results in greater access to education. In addition to democratizing education, it encourages diversity and equality.
3. **Customized Learning Environment:** By utilizing the Artificial intelligence algorithm and data analytics, metaverse can create a personalized learning environment to meet the unique requirements, interests and learning styles of the students. Enhancement in the learner's engagement and improvement in the outcomes are brought through a customized learning environment.
4. **Opportunity for Collaborative Learning:** The Metaverse enables the teachers and students to work together in the virtual space i.e. virtual classrooms on

projects, simulations and experiments in real time, no matter where they are in the world.

5. **Experiential Learning:** The metaverse's immersive simulation and virtual field trips provide a chance for the students to experience things such as visiting historical sites or carrying out space exploration, which might not be possible in the real world.

ROLE OF METAVERSE IN VARIOUS FIELDS

Metaverse is not limited only to the education sector. It possesses significant implications across other fields from Digital trade, online shopping, and gaming to Concerts, social media, and Entertainment Events, which are discussed as follows:

1. **Digital Exchange:** The first prerequisite is digital money. Numerous initiatives centred on the metaverse are attempting to set cryptocurrency as the default option on their networks.
2. **Markets/Digital Trade:** Money is the basis of markets. Rana et al. (2022) opined that trading in the Metaverse is its second point, and we can say that the first point simply represents a connection. AI-controlled kiosks aim to replace waiters, cashiers and store clerks. Casual Chat is designed to replace form checkout by taking advantage of advanced card encryption.
3. **Non-fungible Tokens (NFTs) & Digital Assets:** Tokens are the digital version of paper certificates. Martins et al., (2023), highlighted that digital tokens enabled by Blockchain technology function as unfailing provers of ownership and authenticators, seamlessly integrating into the Metaverse. NFTs validate the ownership of distinct items, hence elevating cryptocurrencies such as Bitcoin and Ethereum. Real estate and art are two well-known instances that are already well-prominent in the digital era.
4. **Infrastructure and Environment of Dealing**: The Metaverse's fundamental framework serves as the basis for everyone. Businesses, that make use of this foundation, particularly in the early phases, will have an edge in terms of profitability and bragging rights (Volpentesta et al., 2023). The winners of this race include Decentraland, Sandbox, and other businesses like Meta, formerly known as Facebook. According to Martins et al. (2023), the introduction of virtual worlds and their avatars is the endeavor of this computer decade. Reliable data transfer should be the responsibility of cloud service providers; vitalizing important services should be free of obstacles through network service providers.

5. **Device Independence**: Hardware independence is a need for the metaverse. It must remain accessible to all devices. Its extensive use is the cause of its popularity.
6. **Gaming**: One enduring and powerful cornerstone of the next Metaverse will be gaming. Video games are the source of 3D rendering. Another example of a metaverse is Super Mario. While interacting freely with other players, users can enhance their avatars with virtual materials. Gamers watch films, interact with friends, and play games.
7. **Concerts, social media, and Entertainment Events:** AI has a lot of potential in this concern. A significant amount of user time in the Metaverse is spent having personal experiences. Hyper-personalized forms of social media will also emerge, particularly in the context of virtual reality.
8. **Online Shopping**: The purchasing habits will feel more immersive. A new era of international trade and retail is made possible by 3D visualization. Retailers will almost certainly take advantage of the impending changes to online purchasing.
9. **Workplace**: Metaverse applies to all areas, not just engineers and programmers. Furthermore, since this is a more sophisticated kind of remote employment, more individuals can work from home. Employee knowledge will eventually matter more than their work performance skills.
10. **Artificial Intelligence (AI)**: AI is another thing that the Metaverse will introduce, and if done right, it can boost output. To maximize customer happiness, businesses should think about incorporating AI bots into their operations as they expand (El Jaouhari et al., 2023).
11. **Natural Language Processing (NLP):** NLP is necessary for processes to communicate with AI. Additionally, NLP needs the Semantic Web. Natural language and tone must be understood by artificial algorithms. AI delivers hyper-personalized experiences to consumers in real time, driven by strong natural language processing.

CHALLENGES WHILE INTEGRATING METAVERSE IN THE EDUCATION SECTOR

Taking the metaverse as an incredible educational opportunity for the present time allows for unprecedented level collaboration in the world as well as immersive learning. Although education may benefit from sophisticated technology, there are difficulties in putting technology at the centre of education. Adopting the Metaverse in the educational system entails a set of specific dimensions that require bundling by making proper infrastructural plans and addressing the questions related to online privacy and equality.

1. **Getting into content:** Maximizing the use of metaverse fast internet connectivity gadgets among other technological requirements is the prerequisite. The inadequate infrastructure is one of the reasons which prevent the spread of this amazing technology to a large extent in developing countries.
2. **Expensiveness:** It is costly to introduce the Metaverse in class due to the high initial instalment and maintenance cost of the hardware, software and experimentation. Educational institutions have limited resources and there might be insufficient funding to cover all the costs accordingly.
3. **Content Development:** Courseware preparation for Metaverse entails several skills and technicalities, hence the necessitate for professionals, people with experience and resources that can lead to its fulfilment. This involves designing such interactive experiences by incorporating support to challenge and sculpt the new lifestyles of participants.
4. **Privacy and Data Security:** In a metaverse environment the teacher will be faced with the challenge of keeping the private data and educational information safe. Along with data protection, cyber security standards maintenance should be top on the list of priorities.
5. **Digital Equity and Inclusivity:** Metaverse can be a means to make life-changing education lessons accessible to greater numbers of people. Equitable and inclusive digital capabilities remain an important concern due to disparities in technological capability and digital literacy skills. A crucial task is to make sure that every student participates fairly and focuses on inclusion.
6. **Pedagogical Integration:** Rethinking instructional design techniques and pedagogical approaches is necessary to incorporate Metaverse technologies into current educational frameworks. Special training programs are needed to be designed to train the educators to design and match these Metaverse tools with the learning objectives.

CONCLUSION

The idea of the Metaverse offers a flexible, diversified and ever-changing learning environment that might completely transform the education landscape. Metaverse technology allows a more immersive learning environment, which in turn enhances student engagement and customization, promotes active participation and deepens immersion. Among the many attractive aspects of incorporating metaverse into classroom instructions are the opportunities it presents for interactive and interesting learning experiences that encourage the students to think critically, work together and speak their minds. Learners can acquire substantial knowledge more easily and cultivate metacognitive abilities through the use of the metaverse in the classrooms. Enhance Self-motivation; problem-solving abilities and general academic achievement can all benefit from a classroom learning environment that teachers design with the students in mind. Metaverse implementation is fraught with complexity, spanning infrastructure limitations to privacy and equity concerns; navigating these issues requires strategic planning and careful preparation. Regardless of these obstacles, metaverse provides innovative solutions to enhance the learning process and its results, which might revolutionize the education sector. It will need cooperation between the many stakeholders – including communities, lawmakers, educators and tech developers to resolve these problems and ensure that the metaverse technology is incorporated into education in a morally sound manner.

REFERENCES

Agarwal, A., & Alathur, S. (2023). Metaverse revolution and the digital transformation: intersectional analysis of Industry 5.0. *Transforming Government: People. Process and Policy*, *17*(4), 688–707.

Amoozad Mahdiraji, H., Sharifpour Arabi, H., Beheshti, M., & Vrontis, D. (2023). A mixed-method analysis of Industry 4.0 technologies in value generation for collaborative consumption companies. *Management Decision*. Advance online publication. doi:10.1108/MD-04-2023-0618

Bag, S., Rahman, M. S., Srivastava, G., & Shrivastav, S. K. (2023). Unveiling metaverse potential in supply chain management and overcoming implementation challenges: An empirical study. *Benchmarking*. Advance online publication. doi:10.1108/BIJ-05-2023-0314

Cheng, X., Zhang, S., Fu, S., Liu, W., Guan, C., Mou, J., Ye, Q., & Huang, C. (2022). Exploring the metaverse in the digital economy: An overview and research framework. *Journal of Electronic Business & Digital Economics*, *1*(2), 206–224. doi:10.1108/JEBDE-09-2022-0036

Czok, V., Krug, M., Müller, S., Huwer, J., Kruse, S., Müller, W., & Weitzel, H. (2023). A Framework for Analysis and Development of Augmented Reality Applications in Science and Engineering Teaching. *Education Sciences*, *13*(9), 926. doi:10.3390/educsci13090926

El Jaouhari, A., Arif, J., Samadhiya, A., Kumar, A., Jain, V., & Agrawal, R. (2023). Are Metaverse applications in Quality 4.0 enablers of manufacturing resiliency? An exploratory review under disruption impressions and future research. *The TQM Journal*.

Ferrigno, G., Di Paola, N., Oguntegbe, K. F., & Kraus, S. (2023). Value creation in the metaverse age: A thematic analysis of press releases. *International Journal of Entrepreneurial Behaviour & Research*, *29*(11), 337–363. doi:10.1108/IJEBR-01-2023-0039

Hatane, S. E., Sondak, L., Tarigan, J., Kwistianus, H., & Sany, S. (2023). Eyeballing internal auditors' and the firms' intention to adopt Metaverse technologies: case study in Indonesia. *Journal of Financial Reporting and Accounting*.

Hines, P., & Netland, T. H. (2023). Teaching a Lean masterclass in the metaverse. *International Journal of Lean Six Sigma*, *14*(6), 1121–1143. doi:10.1108/IJLSS-02-2022-0035

Jafar, R. M. S., & Ahmad, W. (2023). Tourist loyalty in the metaverse: The role of immersive tourism experience and cognitive perceptions. *Tourism Review*.

Kraus, S., Kanbach, D. K., Krysta, P. M., Steinhoff, M. M., & Tomini, N. (2022). Facebook and the creation of the metaverse: Radical business model innovation or incremental transformation? *International Journal of Entrepreneurial Behaviour & Research*, *28*(9), 52–77. doi:10.1108/IJEBR-12-2021-0984

Kumar, A., Shankar, A., Shaik, A. S., Jain, G., & Malibari, A. (2023). Risking it all in the metaverse ecosystem: Forecasting resistance towards the enterprise metaverse. *Information Technology & People*. Advance online publication. doi:10.1108/ITP-04-2023-0374

Lim, W. M., Gupta, S., Aggarwal, A., Paul, J., & Sadhna, P. (2021). How do digital natives perceive and react toward online advertising? Implications for SMEs. *Journal of Strategic Marketing*, 1–35. doi:10.1080/0965254X.2021.1941204

Mittal, A., Dhiman, R., & Lamba, P. (2019). Skill mapping for blue-collar employees and organisational performance: A qualitative assessment. *Benchmarking*, *26*(4), 1255–1274. doi:10.1108/BIJ-08-2018-0228

Rana, S., Udunuwara, M., Dewasiri, N. J., Kashif, M., & Rathnasiri, M. S. H. (2022). Is South Asia ready for the next universe–metaverse? Arguments and suggestions for further research. *South Asian Journal of Marketing*, *3*(2), 77–81. doi:10.1108/SAJM-10-2022-141

Sangeeta, & Tandon, U. (2021). Factors influencing adoption of online teaching by school teachers: A study during COVID-19 pandemic. *Journal of Public Affairs, 21*(4), e2503.

Tiwari, C. K., Bhaskar, P., & Pal, A. (2023). Prospects of augmented reality and virtual reality for online education: A scientometric view. *International Journal of Educational Management*, *37*(5), 1042–1066. doi:10.1108/IJEM-10-2022-0407

Volpentesta, T., Spahiu, E., & De Giovanni, P. (2023). A survey on incumbent digital transformation: A paradoxical perspective and research agenda. *European Journal of Innovation Management*, *26*(7), 478–501. doi:10.1108/EJIM-01-2023-0081

Zainurin, M. Z. L., Haji Masri, M., Besar, M. H. A., & Anshari, M. (2023). Towards an understanding of metaverse banking: A conceptual paper. *Journal of Financial Reporting and Accounting*, *21*(1), 178–190. doi:10.1108/JFRA-12-2021-0487

Chapter 15
Unlocking the Future:
The Role of Digital Learning Materials in Fostering 21st-Century Skills Among University Students

Tugra Karademir Coşkun
Sinop University, Turkey

ABSTRACT

In this study, the aim is to determine the effect of the digital learning material development process on university students' 21st-century competencies. Eighty-five university students voluntarily participated in the study, and the research was designed using a sequential exploratory design. Quantitative data were collected through achievement tests, while qualitative data were gathered using an interview form. Achievement tests were administered before and after an eight-week training program, and interviews were conducted at the end of the training sessions. Students were given various tasks during the training process. The obtained quantitative data were subjected to cluster analysis, while the qualitative data underwent content analysis. As a result of the cluster analysis, the group with a low achievement score from the two divided groups reported the development of 21st-century competencies in 12 themes, while the group with a high achievement score reported the development in 15 themes.

DOI: 10.4018/979-8-3693-3015-9.ch015

Copyright © 2024, IGI Global. Copying or distributing in print or electronic forms without written permission of IGI Global is prohibited.

1. INTRODUCTION

The 21st century has brought about significant changes in the way people live, work, and learn. In the digital age, technology has become an essential part of daily life, and education is no exception. Digital learning materials have emerged as an important tool for delivering education in the 21st century. They offer a range of benefits, including flexibility, convenience, and accessibility. Moreover, they can help students develop 21st-century competencies, which are the skills, knowledge, and attitudes required to succeed in the 21st century.

Digital learning materials refer to any educational content that is presented in a digital format (Karademir Coşkun & Alper, 2020). This can include textbooks, lectures, quizzes, interactive activities, videos, and games. Digital learning materials are designed to be accessed and used online, either through a computer or mobile device, and can be accessed anytime, anywhere. Digital teaching materials are one of the learning opportunities that can provide real-world experiences to students both inside and outside the classroom (Beetham & Sharpe, 2013; Wright, 2015). This flexibility and accessibility make digital learning materials an effective way to engage students in learning and provide them with a personalized learning experience (Karademir Coşkun &Alper, 2020).

In the 21st century, the world has experienced an explosion of technological advancement, globalization, and cultural diversity. These changes have greatly impacted education, requiring educators to teach a new set of skills to prepare students for the challenges of the future. These skills are known as 21st-century competencies, and they are essential for students to succeed in today's rapidly changing world. Below are some 21st-century competencies and their definitions as identified by various organizations (Binkley and others, 2012; P21, 2009; MCEETYA, 2008; Wagner 2008; Lonsdale & Anderson, 2012; NEA, 2010):

As seen in Table 1, there are many 21st-century competencies expressed by different institutions and organizations. These competencies are different from traditional academic skills like reading, writing, and math. They focus on skills like critical thinking, problem-solving, communication, creativity, collaboration, digital literacy, and global awareness, etc. The 21st century is characterized by rapid technological advancements and increasing globalization, and students need to be prepared to navigate this changing world. 21st-century competencies equip students with the skills they need to succeed in an ever-changing job market and society. Here are some reasons why 21st-century competencies are important in education:

They prepare students for the future: The world is changing at a faster pace than ever before, and students need to be prepared to adapt to these changes. 21st-century competencies help students develop skills like critical thinking and problem-solving that they will need to succeed in the future.

Table 1. Some 21st-century competencies and their definitions

Competence/skill	Definition
Creativity skill	Creativity is the ability to produce work that is both novel (i.e., original, unexpected) and appropriate (i.e., useful, adaptive concerning task constraints) (Sternberg, 2003).
Innovation skill	"Innovation refers to the intentional introduction and application within a role, group, or organization of ideas, processes, products, or procedures, new to the relevant unit of adoption, designed to significantly benefit the individual, the group, organization or wider society" (Anderson, Potočnik, & Zhou, 2014).
Critical Thinking	"Critical thinking is the process of purposeful, self-regulatory judgment. This process reasons from a set of information and beliefs toward a conclusion, and on the basis of the conclusion, formulating a judgment" (Facione, 1990).
Problem Solving	"Problem-solving involves cognitive processing directed at achieving a goal when no solution method is obvious to the problem solver" (Mayer, 1992).
Decision-making:	"Decision-making is the process of selecting a course of action from a set of alternatives based on the evaluation of relevant information, personal values, and the potential consequences of each option" (Baron, 2000).
Communication	"Communication is a process by which information is exchanged between individuals through a common system of symbols, signs, or behavior. It involves encoding, transmitting, and decoding messages to create shared meaning and understanding" (DeVito, 2015).
Group Work	"Group work is the interaction of individuals in a face-to-face setting, working together to achieve common goals, in which each person is accountable for his or her contribution and influenced by the others" (Johnson, & Johnson, 2009).
Information Literacy / Accessing and Analyzing Information	"Information literacy is the set of integrated abilities encompassing the reflective discovery of information, the understanding of how information is produced and valued, and the use of information in creating new knowledge and participating ethically in communities of learning" (American Library Association, 2000).
ICT (Information and Communication Technology) Literacy:	"ICT literacy is the ability to use digital technology, communication tools, and networks to access, manage, integrate, evaluate, create, and communicate information ethically and effectively" (Educational Testing Service, 2002).
Collaboration skill	"Collaboration is a coordinated, synchronous activity that is the result of a continued attempt to construct and maintain a shared conception of a problem" (Baker, Day, & Salas, 2006).
Leadership:	"Leadership is a process whereby an individual influences a group of individuals to achieve a common goal" (Northouse, 2018).
Adaptation skill	"Adaptation refers to the ability of individuals to adjust their thoughts, emotions, and behaviors to changing environments or novel tasks" (Pulakos, Arad, Donovan, & Plamondon, 2000)
Entrepreneurship	"Entrepreneurship involves the ability to identify, assess, and exploit opportunities for creating new products, services, or processes by marshaling and allocating resources" (Shane, & Venkataraman, 2000).
Effective Speaking and Writing Skills	"Effective speaking and writing skills involve the ability to convey information, ideas, and arguments clearly, concisely, and accurately in spoken and written forms while considering the target audience and context" (Lannon, & Gurak, 2011).

Table 1 continued

Competence/skill	Definition
Curiosity and Imagination skills	"Curiosity and imagination are cognitive processes that drive exploration, questioning, and the generation of new ideas by combining existing knowledge in novel ways. Curiosity motivates individuals to seek out new information and experiences, while imagination allows them to envision alternative possibilities and generate creative solutions" (Craft, 2013).
Media Literacy	"Media literacy is the ability to access, analyze, evaluate, and create media in a variety of forms. It involves understanding the role media play in society and developing the skills to critically engage with media messages" (Hobbs, 1998).
Social and Cross-Cultural Skills	"Social and cross-cultural skills refer to the ability to interact effectively and appropriately with people from diverse cultural backgrounds, demonstrating an understanding of and respect for different values, beliefs, and communication styles" (Matsumoto, & Hwang, 2013).
Production and Accountability	"Production and accountability refer to the ability to set and achieve specific goals while taking responsibility for the outcomes. This skill encompasses planning, organizing, monitoring progress, and adjusting strategies as needed to ensure efficiency and effectiveness in goal attainment" (Drucker, 1999).
Self-direction and Learning to Learn:	"Self-direction is the ability to take charge of one's learning process by setting goals, monitoring progress, and adjusting strategies as needed. Learning to learn is the ability to acquire and apply new knowledge and skills effectively and efficiently, adapting to new situations and changing demands" (Candy, 1991).

They promote lifelong learning: 21st-century competencies are not just about learning specific skills; they are also about learning how to learn. Students who develop these competencies are better equipped to continue learning throughout their lives.

They enhance creativity and innovation: 21st-century competencies encourage students to be creative and innovative, which are essential skills for success in today's world.

They promote collaboration and communication: Collaboration and communication are critical skills in today's globalized world. 21st-century competencies help students learn how to work with others and communicate effectively across cultures.

However, answering the question of how to impart these skills is quite challenging. At this point, digital teaching materials emerge as a solution for developing 21st-century competencies in classroom environments. Firstly, digital learning materials can foster critical thinking and problem-solving skills by offering students interactive and adaptive content. Such materials often include simulations, virtual labs, and game-based learning tools that improve students' independent learning capacity (Hilton, 2016). For example, digital resources can present complex problems and prompt learners to analyze, evaluate, and synthesize information to arrive at a solution (Spector et al., 2014).

Secondly, communication and collaboration skills can be enhanced through digital learning materials that promote teamwork and social interaction. These materials might include online discussion forums, collaborative document editing tools, or project-based learning platforms where students work together to solve real-world challenges (Holland & Muilenburg, 2011). By engaging with peers and instructors online, learners can develop their ability to articulate ideas clearly and listen to diverse perspectives (Ravenscroft et al., 2012).

Moreover, digital learning materials can support the development of creativity by providing a wide range of multimedia tools that enable learners to express their ideas in novel ways (Mishra & Koehler, 2006). For instance, learners can create videos, podcasts, digital stories, or interactive presentations to showcase their understanding of a topic. This process can also help them develop digital literacy (Eshet-Alkalai, 2004), which is an essential 21st-century competency. Finally, digital learning materials can be personalized to better meet individual learners' needs, which is crucial for fostering 21st-century competencies. Adaptive learning technologies can provide real-time feedback, tailor instruction to learners' interests, and adjust the level of challenge to ensure that each student remains engaged and motivated (Pane et al., 2017). Personalized learning experiences can lead to deeper understanding and more effective skill development (Wanner & Palmer, 2015).

Recent studies have shown that digital teaching tools help learners actively learn, construct knowledge, inquire, and explore, and eliminate the physical distance between teachers and learners, even if they are not in the same physical environment (Henderson & Romeo, 2015). Digital teaching tools include various technologies, such as computers, mobile devices, cameras, networks, and projection devices (Huang, Chao & Lin, 2008). When integrated thoughtfully into educational environments, digital tools facilitate communication and interaction between teachers and learners (Chen, Lambert & Guidry, 2010). Well-structured digital teaching tools not only enhance teachers' but also learners' technological knowledge and skills, preparing them for the digital age (Beetham & Sharpe, 2013). Digital technologies can transform students into more active and powerful participants in discussions, enhancing their discursive aspects, fostering liberating thoughts beyond course outcomes, and strengthening their connection with learning activities, thus making education more effective (Henderson & Romeo, 2015).

To adequately prepare students for the 21st century, various in-class and out-of-class learning environments are needed that provide real-life experiences, facilitate access to knowledge, convert and use information in different formats, and promote the generation and dissemination of new knowledge (Karademir Coşkun & Alper, 2020). The diffusion and implementation of educational innovations largely depend on the personal and individual meanings teachers and pre-service teachers assign to these innovations (Fullan, 1991; Becker, 2001, cited in Demirarslan & Usluel, 2005).

With this focus in mind, the motivation for this study is to understand the impact of the digital teaching material development process on 21st-century competencies from the perspective of pre-service teachers.

Purpose

In this study, the aim is to determine the effect of the digital learning material development process on university students' 21st-century competencies. The sub-objectives to be answered in line with the general purpose are given below:

As a result of the cluster analysis, into how many groups are the university students divided according to their digital learning material development success scores.

What is the effect of the digital learning material development process on 21st-century competencies according to the university students in the low achievement group?

What is the effect of the digital learning material development process on 21st-century competencies according to the university students in the high achievement group?

2. METHOD

2.1. Method Research

In this research, the Sequential Exploratory Design from Creswell's (2013) typologies was employed. The mixed methods sequential explanatory design consists of two distinct phases: quantitative followed by qualitative (Creswell et al., 2003). In this design, a researcher first collects and analyzes the quantitative (numeric) data, and the qualitative (text) data are collected and analyzed second in the sequence, helping explain or elaborate on the quantitative results obtained in the first phase (Ivankova, Creswell, and Stick, 2006). In the end, all data provide a deep view of participants and are reported to form a whole. Within the scope of this research, the achievements of the participants were first measured with the achievement test, and then qualitative data were collected through interviews. The interview results of the participants were reported according to their success averages.

2.2. Participants

Eighty-five university students studying in different departments at a state university in the 2022-2023 academic year participated in this research. The students in the research consist of 37.6% male and 62.4% female students. The study group was voluntarily formed from 96 students who took the Instructional Technologies course in the Fall Semester of the 2022-2023 academic year. The participating students comprise 21.2% English Teaching, 24.7% Elementary Mathematics Teaching, 29.4% Classroom Teaching, and 24.7% Turkish Teaching. The students participating in the research had not previously received training in digital teaching material development.

2.3. Data Collection Tools

Achievement test: An achievement test was prepared to measure achievements related to the topics covered during the research process. The test was first prepared by creating an indicator table related to the topics in the attached achievement list. Test items were prepared according to the indicator table, and after receiving expert opinions, the necessary adjustments were made to the test items. To test the comprehensibility, the draft form was read by two university students. After applying the draft form to the university students, the obtained data set was divided into the upper and lower 27% percentile, and validity and reliability calculations were made. Eight items with item discrimination indices below 0.30 (Erkuş, 2012) and one item with a difficulty index value between 0.20 and 0.30 were removed from the test, considering the representation of achievements. Finally, the KR-20 value for the test was calculated to determine its internal consistency, and it was concluded that the reliability coefficient was at the desired level of .70.

Interview form: The research interview is an interview where knowledge is constructed in the interaction between the interviewer and the interviewee (Brinkmann & Kvale, 2018). An interview form was prepared for the purpose of determining the effect of digital teaching materials on 21st-century competencies in the research. The open-ended questions in the interview form focused on questions that would allow for associations with the 18 21st-century competencies listed under the data analysis heading. Interview questions were structured to be non-directive (Turner, 2010) and to include details about the main theme that could be obtained (Taylor, 2005). Investigators who wish to discover what is known about a particular phenomenon or situation from the insiders' perspectives tend to structure their interviews with open-ended questions, which tend to start with words like who, what, where, when, why, and how, and suggest the respondent respond in a more expansive manner (Chenail, 2011). In this research, the questions were prepared open-ended to elaborate on the participants' statements. The interview form was reviewed by two experts, and it was finalized in line with the opinions received.

2.4. Research Process

The research process consisted of the following steps:

1. ***Course training program***: An eight-week course training program, including theoretical and practical applications of digital learning material, was prepared. The details of the program can be found in Table 2.

Table 2. The details of the program

Week	Learning Object	Software	Task
1	Understands visual design principles. Knows visual design elements. Recognizes 21st-century competencies.		
2	Grasps the purpose of using digital concept maps in education. Develops digital concept maps.	Creatly Mindline Mind Map	Prepare a concept map that demonstrates 21st-century competencies.
3	Understands the purpose of using digital puzzles in education. Develops digital puzzles.	Learning Apps Wordmint	Prepare an interactive puzzle that questions 21st-century competency definitions.
4	Understands the purpose of using digital cartoons in education. Develops digital cartoons.	Pixton	Prepare a cartoon that encourages students to think by selecting one of the 21st-century competencies.
5	Understands the purpose of using videos in education. Knows the principles of using green screens. Understands shooting studio standards. Prepares, edits, and publishes educational videos.	Camtasia	Prepare an educational video that describes the features of the five most important 21st-century competencies you see.
6	Understands the purpose of using digital posters in education. Understands the use of infographics in education. Prepares infographics and posters.	Canva	Prepare an infographic summarizing the 21st-century competencies
7	Grasps the purpose of using augmented reality in education. Prepares augmented reality applications.	Assemblr	Prepare an augmented reality application for students to develop one of the 21st-century competencies.
8	Understands the purpose of using animation in education. Develops animations.	Powtoon	Develop a short animation summarizing the entire process.

2. ***Designing Digital Learning Materials:*** Videos for the eight-week course training program were prepared and shared on the learning management system. The course training program was implemented for the participants. Students received 2-hour face-to-face training sessions per week in a computer laboratory. At the end of each week, participants were given practical assignments

related to relevant achievements. Completed assignments were submitted to the instructor through an online platform.

3. At the end of the trainings, an achievement test was administered. Interviews averaging 20 minutes were conducted with participants who were grouped according to their achievement test data. All the data obtained were analyzed and reported.

2.5. Data Analysis

The analysis of the research data began with conducting a K-means clustering analysis to group participants based on their achievement test scores. The K-means algorithm finds K clusters according to a specific standard (clustering is also known as a cluster) and generally adopts the standard of squared error (Zhao & Zhou, 2021). First, the test assumptions were examined (Gagné, 2020). Each cluster had equal variance. Each observation (or data point) was independent of the others. The relationship between the variables was linear, and there was no missing data. Before the analysis, outlier values were cleaned, and multicollinearity values were checked. Subsequently, the dataset was subjected to clustering analysis. As a result of the clustering analysis, interviews conducted to determine the effect of the digital teaching material development process on 21st-century competencies according to the achievement scores of the grouped students were subjected to content analysis.

Qualitative data were subjected to a single cycle of content analysis. In the first cycle, thematic coding was used (Miles, Huberman & Saldana, 2014). "Thematic analysis is a method for identifying, analyzing, and reporting patterns (themes) within data. It minimally organizes and describes your data set in (rich) detail. However, frequently it goes further than this and interprets various aspects of the research topic." (Braun and Clarke, 2006). Themes were created based on the 21st-century competencies obtained from the literature review and included in Table 1. As a result of the analysis, the generated table was sent to two experts, and they were asked to examine the relationship between the expressions and themes. The findings obtained from their opinions were detailed under the "Findings" heading.

2.6. Validity and Reliability of the Research

To address the subjectivity issue encountered in qualitative studies, transferability was prioritized by clearly explaining factors associated with the independent variable (Lincoln & Guba, 1986), and credibility was ensured by supporting the obtained findings with the literature and including direct quotations (Eisenhart & Hove, 1992). To eliminate the emphasis on subjectivity (Arastaman, Fidan & Fidan, 2018), which is seen as a problem in qualitative research, some methods were employed in this study. Prolonged engagement and persistent observation were utilized. Details of the research process (Lincoln & Guba, 1985) were included in the text to ensure transferability. To ensure reflectivity in the data analysis process (Creswell, 2013), notes taken by the researcher were used (member checking - Patton, 2002), and the codes obtained were sent to expert opinion for the calculation of reliability coefficients between encoders (Miles & Huberman, 1994). In addition, detailed descriptions and direct quotations under the heading of findings (Lincoln & Guba, 1985) were provided to ensure credibility.

3. FINDINGS

The detailed findings obtained from the research are provided below:

1. As a result of the cluster analysis, how many groups are the university students divided into according to their digital learning material development success scores?

As a result of the K-means cluster analysis, which aims to minimize the error in clustering students based on their success scores, it has been concluded that students are divided into two groups. The analysis results are presented in Table 3.

Table 3. The K-means cluster analysis

Cluster Number of Case	N	Mean	Distances between Final Cluster Centers
1	52	88,31	12,641
2	33	75,67	

Upon examining the table 3, it is determined that students are divided into two groups according to their success scores because of the K-means clustering analysis. The first group consists of 52 students with a mean success weight average of 88.31, and the second group consists of 33 students with a mean success weight average of 75.61. Considering the success-weighted average scores, the first group of students is named the "high achievement group," while the second group is named the "low achievement group." To measure whether there is a significant difference between the groups, the mean success scores of the students according to their groups were subjected to an independent samples t-test. The results are provided in Table 4.

Table 4. Independent samples t-test score

Group	N	Mean	Std. Deviation	df	t	Sig.
High Achievement Group	52	88,31	3,938	83	13,368	,000
Low High Achievement Group	33	75,67	4,702			

When Table 4 is examined, it can be seen that there is a significant difference between the average success scores of the students divided into clusters as a result of the clustering analysis ($t(83)=13.36; p<.01$). The mean scores of the first group, named the high achievement group, are higher than those of the second group, named the low achievement group. In general, it can be said that the students are divided into two groups based on their achievement groups: high (n=52) and low (n=33).

2. *What is the effect of the digital learning material development process on 21st-century competencies according to the university students in the low achievement group?*

The 21st-century competencies obtained from the interviews with the students in the low achievement group are provided below.

Table 5. Low achievement group's interview analysis result

Competency	Participant	Quotes
Creativity	LAG1	Enhances 3-dimensional thinking and indirectly develops creative thinking
	LAG2	Very effective in developing students' creativity by making abstract concepts concrete
	LAG3	Instructional technologies enable students to adapt to this developing world by providing different perspectives, fostering creative thinking, and other features
	LAG4	Students can think more creatively
Innovation	LAG5	Encourages us to be open to innovation.
	LAG6	A field that strives to bring innovation to education
Critical Thinking	LAG7	Provides positive skills such as critical thinking and problem-solving
Communication	LAG8	Strengthens communication between students and teachers

Table 5 continued

Competency	Participant	Quotes
Information Literacy / Accessing and Analyzing Information	LAG9	In the context of individuals who question and find information on their own, it provides students with an area where they can evaluate themselves
	LAG10	Offers various ways to convey information
ICT Literacy	LAG11	I think the applications we learn to provide children with digital competence will be very useful and contribute to their development in this are
	LAG12	Students gain equipped knowledge in terms of computer usage, learn how to use multiple applications, and become individuals who know technology in the 21st century
Collaboration	LAG13	Instructional technologies help students adapt to this developing world by providing features such as collaboration and collaborative approach.
	LAG14	Facilitates students' collaborative work
Adaptability	LAG15	At the same time, it enables the educator to prepare themselves for the New Age and the world of technology and establish harmony with their students
	LAG16	Instructional technologies and opportunities are essential for students to adapt to this century and the age of technology
Effective Speaking and Writing Skills	LAG17	mportant in terms of developing the ability to express oneself
Media Literacy	LAG18	Instructional technologies contribute to the development of students' creativity and media literacy
Self-Direction and Learning to Learn	LAG19	Enables the student to learn on their own and expands the reach of education to broader audiences
Curiosity and Imagination	LAG20	Captures the student's interest and keeps their curiosity alive
	LAG21	Among its contributions is arousing curiosity
	LAG22	Adds a lot in terms of productivity

Note: "LAG" is the abbreviation for a group name that has a low achievement level.

As a result of the research, it can be seen that the digital teaching material development process mostly improves the creativity of the students in the low achievement group. LAG1 describes the digital teaching material development process as indirectly improving creativity by associating it with 3D thinking, while LAG2 and LAG3's statements directly relate to creativity. Another frequently repeated theme is ICT literacy. This skill is understood from LAG11s "gaining digital proficiency" and LAG12's "acquiring equipped knowledge in terms of computer use" expressions. LAG10 explains another theme, information literacy, by stating that it "offers various ways to convey information," while LAG9 emphasizes "questioning and researching information." According to the students, another benefit of digital teaching materials is innovation skills. LAG5 states that the materials contribute to becoming "open to innovation," while LAG6 expresses that it "brings innovation to education." Another skill, collaboration, is mentioned by LAG14, who says it "... facilitates their work in collaboration..." Another theme frequently repeated and understood from student statements is adaptability. LAG15 and LAG16 state that digital teaching materials "prepare students for this century/age." In addition to these skills, students also mention that digital teaching materials are effective in critical thinking, communication skills, effective speaking and writing skills, media literacy, self-direction, and learning-to-learn skills. It has been determined that the students with low achievement scores did not express opinions on problem-solving, decision-making, group work, citizenship, life and career, personal and social responsibilities, cultural competence and awareness, leadership, entrepreneurship, social and intercultural skills, production.

3. What is the effect of the digital learning material development process on 21st century competencies according to the university students in the high-achievement group?

The 21st-century competencies obtained from the interviews with the students in the high-achievement group are presented below.

Table 6. High achievement group's interview analysis result

Competency	Participant	Quotes
Creativity	HAG1	Enhances creativity and makes individuals more productive
	HAG2	Develops creative thinking skills
	HAG3	Designing and creating new programs not only improves creativity and imagination but also provides convenience and time-saving for users
Innovation	HAG4	The use of instructional technologies is important for teaching students inquiry, innovation, and collaboration skills
Critical Thinking	HAG5	The use of instructional technologies is important for teaching students inquiry, multi-dimensional thinking, innovation, and collaboration skills
	HAG6	This also gives students the ability to think critically and multi-dimensionally
	HAG7	Helps us become individuals who can think critically, inquire, and be active

Table 6 continued

Competency	Participant	Quotes
Problem Solving	HAG8	Problem-solving is necessary for enhancing competencies
	HAG9	Generates problems and finds solutions
	HAG10	Improves problem-solving skills
Communication	HAG11	Students can gain social skills and communicate better
	HAG12	Students' development in communication will be noticeably increased at the end of the process
Group Work	HAG13	Provides learning environments for group work
	HAG14	Develops students' communication skills as it directs group work and involves students in an active role
Information Literacy / Accessing and Analyzing Information	HAG15	Encourages students to think, research, and inquire
	HAG16	Serves as a tool for accessing accurate information and provides digital competency to students
ICT Literacy	HAG17	During the process of using instructional technologies, students develop technology-related skills categorized among 21st-century competencies
	HAG18	Students learn to use technology, one of the 21st-century competencies
Collaboration	HAG19	Students learn to work together, form teams, and make the best use of technology
	HAG20	Facilitates collaboration between students and teachers
	HAG21	The collaboration skill within the group will also increase through the studies
Adaptation	HAG22	It is crucial for acquiring 21st-century creativity skills
	HAG23	It is very beneficial for us to adapt to this lifestyle since we live in a technology era
	HAG24	Learning technology and acquiring this skill provides ease of learning and teaching since everything is connected to technology today
Effective Speaking and Writing Skills	HAG25	Instructional materials support the development of expressing skills
	HAG26	Applications provide opportunities to respect different opinions
Curiosity and Imagination	HAG27	Stimulates curiosity in students
	HAG28	Instructional technologies can guide students in developing their imagination
Curiosity and Imagination	HAG29	Provides students with skills such as digital literacy and media literacy
Production and Accountability	HAG30	Instructional technologies contribute significantly to productivity
	HAG31	With instructional technologies, we use technology to benefit our lives and produce knowledge

Table 6 continued

Competency	Participant	Quotes
Self-direction and Learning to Learn	HAG32	Provides personalized education
	HAG33	Allows for individual learning of students

Note: "HAG" is the abbreviation for a group name that has a high achievement level.

Upon examining Table 6, it is observed that the high achievement group associates the digital teaching material development process with 21st-century competencies more than the low achievement group. As in the other group, creativity and adaptability skills are the most frequently repeated skills in the high achievement group. HAG1 and T HAG2's emphasis on creativity can be understood directly from their expressions, while HAG3 combines creativity and imagination in her explanation. Like the other group, this group also indicates that critical thinking and communication skills improved during the digital teaching material development process.

Differently from the other group, the high achievement group also states that this process affects problem-solving and teamwork skills. Problem-solving skills can be understood from HAG10 and HAG8's emphasis on "developing problem-solving skills," while the same theme is also expressed by HAG9 as "generating problems and finding solution proposals." Similarly, HAG14 mentions that group work skills are developed because it "directs to group work...". Another skill that differs between the two groups is production, accountability, and awareness.

Both groups also mention that they developed various literacies. For example, from HAG17's expression, it can be directly understood that it provides "skills such as media literacy," while HAG18's expression "they learn to use technology" implies an emphasis on ICT literacy. On the other hand, HAG16's definition of it as a "tool for accessing information" and HAG15's emphasis on " ...research and inquiry..." serve as evidence for information literacy. While students in the low achievement group do not express their opinions on this issue, it is observed that HAG30 in the high achievement group states that "it adds a lot in terms of production." In both groups, digital teaching material development processes contribute to the development of innovation, information literacy, ICT literacy, collaboration, effective speaking skills, media literacy, and self-direction and learning-to-learn skills. On the other hand, it has been determined that both groups did not express any opinions regarding the development of decision-making, citizenship, life and career, personal and social responsibilities, cultural competence and awareness, leadership, and entrepreneurship skills.

4. CONCLUSION

In general, it is observed that teacher candidates in both groups agree that the digital teaching material development process improves 21st-century competencies. However, it has been determined that students in the high achievement group establish a stronger connection between digital teaching materials and 21st-century competencies.

During the research process, the top three most frequently repeated skills are creativity, adaptability, and ICT skills. Digital learning materials, such as online courses, digital textbooks, and educational apps, have made learning more accessible and interactive, allowing students to engage with material in ways that were previously impossible. At the same time, they have also opened up new opportunities for creativity in the classroom. One way in which digital learning materials can promote creativity is by providing students with more control over their learning experiences. For example, online courses often allow students to choose the pace at which they progress through the material, which can help them to personalize their learning and explore topics in greater depth. Similarly, educational apps may offer a range of activities or challenges that allow students to approach a concept from different angles, encouraging them to think creatively about how they can solve problems or complete tasks (Salehudin, Degeng, Sulthoni, & Ulfa, 2019). Digital learning materials can also foster creativity by providing students with new tools and resources. For instance, digital textbooks may include interactive multimedia elements, such as videos, animations, and simulations, that can help to bring concepts to life and engage students in a more dynamic way (Jonassen, 2010). It is important to note, however, that the relationship between digital learning materials and creativity is complex and multifaceted. While digital tools and resources can certainly facilitate creativity, they are not a guarantee of it. Creativity is a complex process that depends on a range of factors, including individual motivation, mindset, and the learning environment (Vygotsky, 1978). Therefore, it is essential that educators use digital learning materials in a thoughtful and intentional way and provide students with opportunities to develop their creativity through a range of activities and approaches.

On the other hand, digital teaching materials provide a suitable infrastructure for developing adaptive skills. Adaptive behavior refers to the ways individuals meet their personal needs and deal with the natural and social demands in their environments (Oakland & Harrison, 2008). Digital learning materials provide an ideal platform for learners to develop their adaptivity skills. One reason for this is the ability of these materials to personalize the learning experience for each individual learner. With digital materials, learners can move at their own pace, focus on areas where they need more support, and receive immediate feedback on their progress. This personalized approach to learning can help learners develop adaptive skills by allowing them to engage with the material in a way that suits their individual needs and learning style.

Digital learning materials have many advantages when it comes to developing ICT skills. One advantage is the ability of these materials to provide a platform for learners to practice and develop their technical skills. Another advantage of digital learning materials is their ability to provide access to a wide range of resources and information. Several studies have shown that digital learning materials and ICT-based teaching strategies positively influence students' ICT literacy skills (Fraillon, Ainley, Schulz, Friedman, & Gebhardt, 2013).

In addition to these skills, according to students, the digital instructional material development process has also been effective in enhancing students' abilities such as critical thinking, problem-solving, collaboration and communication, group work, media literacy, information literacy, curiosity, imagination, and self-directed learning. Several studies in the literature support these views. For example, Bridges et al. (2012) found that students in problem-based learning curricula effectively integrated face-to-face and virtual semiotic modes to achieve learning outcomes, emphasizing the importance of blended approaches, and using visual objects to support learning experiences. Kala, Isaramalai, and Pohthong's (2010) study highlights the potential of utilizing technology and constructivist approaches to improve nursing students' knowledge acquisition and problem-solving skills. Hämäläinen & Häkkinen (2010) found that instructional planning using macro-scripts helped promote communication and collaboration skills among students, leading to better learning outcomes. Hobbs & Moore (2013) emphasize the importance of integrating digital media and popular culture into classroom instruction to boost media literacy and engage students in meaningful learning experiences. Song & Hill (2007) suggest that digital learning materials provide the necessary tools and resources to support learner autonomy, motivation, and self-regulation in online learning settings. Lee & Rha (2009) found that well-structured digital learning materials, combined with effective interaction among learners and instructors, promote self-directed learning, leading to improved learning outcomes and satisfaction. Şendağ and Odabaşı (2009) indicate that using digital learning materials in a problem-based learning context can significantly improve students' critical thinking skills while enhancing their content knowledge.

In conclusion, the integration of technology in education plays a crucial role in developing 21st-century competencies among pre-service teachers. As the demands of the modern world continue to evolve, it is essential for teacher candidates to acquire skills such as critical thinking, problem-solving, collaboration, communication, media literacy, information literacy, and self-directed learning. Embracing technological advancements in teaching and learning can significantly contribute to preparing future educators to effectively address the diverse needs of their students. By incorporating digital learning materials, ICT-based teaching strategies, and innovative pedagogical approaches, pre-service teachers can develop the necessary skills to thrive in the 21st-century classroom and foster the same competencies in their students, ultimately shaping a generation of well-equipped learners ready to face the challenges of an ever-changing global society. Teacher attitudes and beliefs towards technology can be a major barrier to technology integration (Hermans, Tondeur, Valcke, & Van Braak, 2006). From this perspective, it is important for teachers and pre-service teachers to view technology as an alternative means to develop students' 21st-century competencies. In fact, the study demonstrates that pre-service teachers have a high level of belief in technology's potential to enhance the development of 21st-century skills.

5. RECOMMENDATIONS

Considering the research findings, the following recommendations can be made for teacher educators, educational institutions, and policymakers:

Teacher education programs should place greater emphasis on the integration of digital learning materials and ICT-based teaching strategies to help pre-service teachers develop 21st-century competencies. This can be achieved through a combination of coursework, practical application, and opportunities for collaboration with peers and experienced educators.

Policymakers should invest in the necessary resources, infrastructure, and support systems to facilitate the integration of digital learning materials and technology in education. This includes providing adequate funding for hardware, software, and professional development opportunities, as well as developing policies that encourage innovation and collaboration in the field of education.

Further research should be conducted to explore the specific ways in which digital learning materials and technology can be used to develop different 21st-century competencies. This can help educators and policymakers make informed decisions about the most effective strategies for promoting these skills among pre-service teachers and their future students.

Educational institutions should establish partnerships with technology companies and other stakeholders to ensure that the digital learning materials and tools available to teachers are relevant, up-to-date, and aligned with the needs of 21st-century learners.

ACKNOWLEDGMENT

Ethical Approval: No ethical approval was required for this study as it did not involve any experiments on animals or humans.

Competing Interests: The authors declare that they have no financial or personal conflicts of interest in relation to this study.

Authors' Contributions: All authors have equally contributed to the design of the research, data collection, and the writing of the paper.

Funding: This study has not been funded by any institution or organization.

Availability of Data and Materials: All data sets used in this study can be accessed by contacting the author

REFERENCES

American Library Association. (2000). *Information literacy competency standards for higher education.* Association of College & Research Libraries.

Anderson, N., Potočnik, K., & Zhou, J. (2014). Innovation and creativity in organizations: A state-of-the-science review, prospective commentary, and guiding framework. *Journal of Management*, *40*(5), 1297–1333. doi:10.1177/0149206314527128

Baker, D. P., Day, R., & Salas, E. (2006). Teamwork as an essential component of high-reliability organizations. *Health Services Research*, *41*(4), 1576–1598. doi:10.1111/j.1475-6773.2006.00566.x PMID:16898980

Baron, J. (2000). *Thinking and deciding*. Cambridge University Press.

Beetham, H., & Sharpe, R. (2007). *Rethinking pedagogy for a digital age: Designing and delivering e-learning*. Routledge. doi:10.4324/9780203961681

Binkley, M., Erstad, O., Herman, J., Raizen, S., Ripley, M., Miller-Ricci, M., & Rumble, M. (2012). Defining twenty-first century skills. In P. Griffin, B. McGaw, & E. Care (Eds.), *Assessment and Teaching of 21st Century Skills* (pp. 17–66). Springer. doi:10.1007/978-94-007-2324-5_2

Bridges, S. M., Whitehill, T., & McGrath, C. (2012). The next generation: Research directions in PBL. In S. Bridges, C. McGrath, & T. Whitehill (Eds.), *Researching problem-based learning in clinical education: The next generation* (pp. 225–232). Springer. doi:10.1007/978-94-007-2515-7_14

Brinkmann, S., & Kvale, S. (2018). *Doing interviews*. SAGE Publications Limited. doi:10.4135/9781529716665

Candy, P. C. (1991). *Self-direction for lifelong learning: A comprehensive guide to theory and practice*. Jossey-Bass.

Chen, P., Lambert, A., & Guidry, K. (2010). Engaging online learners: The impact of web-based learning technology on college student engagement. *Computers & Education, 54*(4), 1222–1232. doi:10.1016/j.compedu.2009.11.008

Chenail, R. J. (2011). Interviewing the Investigator: Strategies for Addressing Instrumentation and Researcher Bias Concerns in Qualitative Research. *The Qualitative Report, 16*(1), 255–262. doi:10.46743/2160-3715/2011.1051

Craft, A. (2013). Childhood, play, and the fostering of creativity. In D. Brooker, M. Blaise, & S. Edwards (Eds.), The SAGE handbook of play and learning in early childhood (pp. 19-30). SAGE Publications.

Creswell, J. W. (2013). *Research Design: Qualitative, Quantitative, and Mixed Methods Approaches* (4th ed.). SAGE Publication.

Creswell, J. W., Plano Clark, V. L., Gutmann, M. L., & Hanson, W. E. (2003). Advanced Mixed Methods Research Designs. In A. Tashakkori & C. Teddlie (Eds.), *Handbook of Mixed Methods in Social and Behavioral Research* (pp. 209–240). Sage.

Demirarslan, Y., & Usluel, K. Y. (2005). Bilgi ve iletişim teknolojilerinin öğrenme öğretme sürecine entegrasyonunda öğretmenlerin durumu. *The Turkish Online Journal of Educational Technology, 4*(3).

DeVito, J. A. (2015). *The interpersonal communication book*. Pearson.

Drucker, P. F. (1999). *Management challenges for the 21st century*. HarperCollins Publishers.

Educational Testing Service. (2002). *Digital transformation: A framework for ICT literacy*. ETS.

Erkuş, A. (2012). *Psikolojide ölçme ve ölçek geliştirme-1: Temel kavramlar ve işlemler*. Pegem Akademi.

Eshet-Alkalai, Y. (2004). Digital literacy: A conceptual framework for survival skills in the digital era. *Journal of Educational Multimedia and Hypermedia, 13*(1), 93–106.

Facione, P. A. (1990). *Critical thinking: A statement of expert consensus for purposes of educational assessment and instruction*. The California Academic Press.

Fraillon, J., Schulz, W., Friedman, T., Ainley, J., & Gebhardt, E. (2015). *International computer and information literacy study: ICILS 2013 technical report*. IEA Secretariat.

Gagné, C. (2020). K-Means Clustering: Concept and Applications. In Data Clustering: Algorithms and Applications (pp. 1-25). CRC Press.

Garrison, D. R., Anderson, T., & Archer, W. (2001). Critical inquiry in a text-based environment: Computer conferencing in higher education model. *The Internet and Higher Education*, *2*(2-3), 87–105. doi:10.1016/S1096-7516(00)00016-6

Hämäläinen, R., & Häkkinen, P. (2010). Teachers' instructional planning for computer-supported collaborative learning: Macro-scripts as a pedagogical method to facilitate collaborative learning. *Teaching and Teacher Education*, *26*(4), 871–877. doi:10.1016/j.tate.2009.10.025

Henderson, M., & Romeo, G. (2015). *Teaching and digital technologies big issues and critical questions*. Cambridge University Press. doi:10.1017/CBO9781316091968

Hermans, R., Tondeur, J., van Braak, J., & Valcke, M. (2008). The impact of primary school teachers' educational beliefs on the classroom use of computers. *Computers & Education*, *51*(4), 1499–1509. doi:10.1016/j.compedu.2008.02.001

Hilton, J. T. (2016). A case study of the application of SAMR and TPACK for reflection on technology integration into two social studies classrooms. *Social Studies Research & Practice*, *11*(1), 1–12.

Hobbs, R. (1998). The seven great debates in the media literacy movement. *Journal of Communication*, *48*(1), 16–32. doi:10.1111/j.1460-2466.1998.tb02734.x

Holland, J., & Muilenburg, L. (2011). Supporting student collaboration: Edmodo in the classroom. In *Proceedings of Society for Information Technology & Teacher Education International Conference* (pp. 3232-3236). Association for the Advancement of Computing in Education (AACE).

Huang, C.-K., Chao, Y.-C., & Lin, C.-Y. (2008). Web 2.0 in and out of the language classroom. In *Proceedings of the 2008 World CALL: Using technologies for language learning* (pp. 39-54). Foukoka, Japan.

Ivankova, N. V., Creswell, J. W., & Stick, S. L. (2006). Using Mixed-Methods Sequential Explanatory Design: From Theory to Practice. *Field Methods*, *18*(1), 3–20. doi:10.1177/1525822X05282260

Johnson, D. W., & Johnson, F. P. (2009). *Joining together: Group theory and group skills*. Pearson.

Jonassen, D. H. (2010). *Learning to solve problems: A handbook for designing problem-solving learning environments*. Routledge. doi:10.4324/9780203847527

Kala, S., Isaramalai, S.-A., & Pohthong, A. (2010). Electronic learning and constructivism: A model for nursing education. *Nurse Education Today*, *30*(1), 61–66. doi:10.1016/j.nedt.2009.06.002 PMID:19573956

Karademir Coşkun, T., & Alper, A. (2020). An ecological approach to technology appropriation. In M. Hicks & R. R. Zhang (Eds.), *Examining the Roles of Teachers and Students in Mastering New Technologies* (pp. 79–106). IGI Global. doi:10.4018/978-1-7998-2104-5.ch004

Lannon, J. M., & Gurak, L. J. (2011). *Technical communication*. Longman Publishing Group.

Lee, K., & Rha, I. (2009). Influence of structure and interaction on student achievement and satisfaction in web-based distance learning. *Journal of Educational Technology & Society*, *12*(4), 372–382.

Lonsdale, M., & Anderson, M. (2012). *Preparing 21st century learners: The case for school community collaborations*. Australian Council for Educational Research.

Matsumoto, D., & Hwang, H. C. (2013). Assessing cross-cultural competence: A review of available tests. *Journal of Cross-Cultural Psychology*, *44*(6), 849–873. doi:10.1177/0022022113492891

Mayer, R. E. (1992). *Thinking, problem-solving, cognition*. W H Freeman/Times Books/Henry Holt & Co.

MCEETYA. (2008). *Melbourne Declaration on Educational Goals for Young Australians*. Ministerial Council on Education, Employment, Training and Youth Affairs.

Miles, M. B., Huberman, A. M., & Saldana, J. (2014). Qualitative Data Analysis: A Methods Sourcebook. *Sage (Atlanta, Ga.)*.

Mishra, P., & Koehler, M. J. (2006). Technological pedagogical content knowledge: A framework for teacher knowledge. *Teachers College Record*, *108*(6), 1017–1054. doi:10.1111/j.1467-9620.2006.00684.x

Morse, J. M. (2007). Enhancing the credibility of qualitative research. *Health Promotion Practice*, *8*(2), 140–144. PMID:17384405

NEA (National Education Association). (2010). *21st century knowledge and skills in educator preparation.* Retrieved from http://www.p21.org/storage/documents/aacte_p21_whitepaper2010.pdf

Northouse, P. G. (2018). *Leadership: Theory and practice*. Sage Publications.

Oakland, T., & Harrison, P. L. (2008). Adaptive behaviors and skills. In *Adaptive Behavior Assessment System-II*. Elsevier. doi:10.1016/B978-012373586-7.00001-1

P21. (2009). *P21 framework definitions*. Retrieved from http://www.p21.org/storage/documents/P21_Framework_Definitions.pdf

Pane, J. F., Steiner, E. D., Baird, M. D., & Hamilton, L. S. (2017). *Informing progress: Insights on personalized learning implementation and effects* (RAND Research Report RR-2041-EDU). RAND Corporation. https://doi.org/ doi:10.7249/RR2041

Patton, M. Q. (2002). *Qualitative research and evaluation methods*. Sage Publications.

Pulakos, E. D., Arad, S., Donovan, M. A., & Plamondon, K. E. (2000). Adaptability in the workplace: Development of a taxonomy of adaptive performance. *The Journal of Applied Psychology*, *85*(4), 612–624. doi:10.1037/0021-9010.85.4.612 PMID:10948805

Ravenscroft, A., Warburton, S., Hatzipanagos, S., & Conole, G. (2012). Designing and evaluating social media for learning: Shaping social networking into social learning? *Journal of Computer Assisted Learning*, *28*(3), 177–182. doi:10.1111/j.1365-2729.2012.00484.x

Salehudin, M., & Degeng, I. N. S. (2019). The Influence of Creative Learning Assisted by Instagram to Improve Middle School Students' Learning Outcomes of Graphic Design Subject. *Journal for the Education of Gifted Young Scientists*, *7*(4), 849–865. doi:10.17478/jegys.626513

Şendağ, S., & Odabaşı, H. F. (2009). Effects of an online problem-based learning course on content knowledge acquisition and critical thinking skills. *Computers & Education*, *53*(1), 132–141. doi:10.1016/j.compedu.2009.01.008

Shane, S., & Venkataraman, S. (2000). The promise of entrepreneurship as a field of research. *Academy of Management Review*, *25*(1), 217–226. doi:10.5465/amr.2000.2791611

Song, L., & Hill, J. R. (2007). A conceptual model for understanding self-directed learning in online environments. *Journal of Interactive Online Learning*, *6*(1), 27–42.

Spector, J. M., Merrill, M. D., Elen, J., & Bishop, M. J. (Eds.). (2014). *Handbook of research on educational communications and technology*. Springer. doi:10.1007/978-1-4614-3185-5

Sternberg, R. J. (2003). *Wisdom, intelligence, and creativity synthesized*. Cambridge University Press. doi:10.1017/CBO9780511509612

Turner, D. W. III. (2010). Qualitative interview design: A practical guide for novice investigators. *The Qualitative Report*, *15*(3), 754–760. doi:10.46743/2160-3715/2010.1178

Vygotsky, L. S. (1978). *Mind in society: The development of higher psychological processes*. Harvard University Press.

Wagner, T. (2008). *The global achievement gap: Why even our best schools don't teach the new survival skills our children need—and what we can do about it*. Basic Books.

Wanner, T., & Palmer, E. (2015). Personalising learning: Exploring student and teacher perceptions about flexible learning and assessment in a flipped university course. *Computers & Education*, *88*, 354–363. doi:10.1016/j.compedu.2015.07.008

Wright, N. (2015). A case for adapting and applying continuance theory to education: Understanding the role of student feedback in motivating teachers to persist with including digital technologies in learning. *Teachers and Teaching*, *21*(4), 459–471. doi:10.1080/13540602.2014.969105

Yulianto, B., Prabowo, H., & Kosala, R. (2016). Comparing the effectiveness of digital contents for improving learning outcomes in computer programming for autodidact students. *Journal of E-Learning and Knowledge Society*, *12*(1). Advance online publication. doi:10.20368/1971-8829/1081

Zhao, Y., & Zhou, X. (2021). K-means clustering algorithm and its improvement research. *Journal of Physics: Conference Series*, *1873*(1), 012074. doi:10.1088/1742-6596/1873/1/012074

Compilation of References

Abdullah, N. A., Ahmad, M. S., & Aziz, A. A. (2017). A new pedagogical framework for enhancing self-regulation and social interactions in learning. *Journal of Educational Technology & Society*, *20*(1), 13–24. https://www.jstor.org/stable/26322208

Abdüsselam, S. M. (2014). Teachers' and students' views on using augmented reality environments in physics education: 11th Grade magnetism topic example. *Egitim ve Ögretim*, *4*(1), 59–74. doi:10.14527/pegegog.2014.004

Abiodun, G., Gbadebo, O., & Tola, O. (2011). Forms of Academic Cheating During Examination among Students with Hearing Impairment in Nigeria: Implication for Counselling Practice. *Eur J Soc*, *26*(2), 276.

Adachi, P. J., & Willoughby, T. (2013). Do video games promote positive youth development? *Journal of Adolescent Research*, *28*(2), 155–165. doi:10.1177/0743558412464522

Adamska, I. (2023). Practical examples of AR in education. Available at https://nsflow.com/blog/examples-of-ar-in-education

Adnan, A. H. M. (2020, September). From interactive teaching to immersive learning: Higher Education 4.0 via 360-degree videos and virtual reality in Malaysia. *IOP Conference Series. Materials Science and Engineering*, *917*(1), 012023. doi:10.1088/1757-899X/917/1/012023

Agarwal, A., & Alathur, S. (2023). Metaverse revolution and the digital transformation: intersectional analysis of Industry 5.0. *Transforming Government: People. Process and Policy*, *17*(4), 688–707.

Aggarwal, A., Chand, P. K., Jhamb, D., & Mittal, A. (2020). Leader–Member Exchange, Work Engagement, and Psychological Withdrawal Behavior: The Mediating Role of Psychological Empowerment. *Frontiers in Psychology*, *11*(423), 423. Advance online publication. doi:10.3389/fpsyg.2020.00423 PMID:32296361

Agrawal, A. K., & Mittal, G. K. (2018). The role of ICT in higher education for the 21st century ICT as a change agent for education. Multidisciplinary Higher Education, Research, Dynamics & Concepts Opportunities & Challenges for Sustainable Development, 1(1), 76–83.

Ahmad RG, Hamed OA (2014). Impact of adopting a newly developed blueprinting method and relating it to item analysis on students' performance. *Med Teach, 36*(1), S55–S61. . doi:10.3109/0142159X.2014.886014

Aiello, P., D'Elia, F., Di Tore, S., & Sibilio, M. (2012). A constructivist approach to virtual reality for experiential learning. *E-Learning and Digital Media*, *9*(3), 317–324. doi:10.2304/elea.2012.9.3.317

Akçayır, M., & Akçayır, G. (2017). Advantages and challenges associated with augmented reality for education: A systematic review of the literature. *Educational Research Review*, *20*, 1–11. doi:10.1016/j.edurev.2016.11.002

Akgun, E., Instanbullu, A., & Avci, S. (2017). Augmented reality in Turkey with researchers' comments for educational use: Problems, solutions, and suggestions. *Journal of Education and Training Studies*, *5*(11), 201–218. doi:10.11114/jets.v5i11.2690

Akkuş, İ. & Özhan, U. (2017). Matematik ve geometri eğitiminde artırılmış gerçeklik uygulamaları. *İnönü Üniversitesi Eğitim Bilimleri Enstitüsü Dergisi, 4*(8), 19-33.

Al Badi, F. K., Alhosani, K. A., Jabeen, F., Stachowicz-Stanusch, A., Shehzad, N., & Amann, W. (2022). Challenges of AI Adoption in the UAE Healthcare. *Vision (Basel)*, *26*(2), 193–207. doi:10.1177/0972262920988398

Alalwan, N., Cheng, L., Al-Samarraie, H., Yousef, R., Alzahrani, A. I., & Sarsam, S. M. (2020). Challenges and prospects of virtual reality and augmented reality utilization among primary school teachers: A developing country perspective. *Studies in Educational Evaluation*, *66*, 100876. doi:10.1016/j.stueduc.2020.100876

Al-Azawi, R. (2018, April). Embedding augmented and virtual reality in educational learning method: present and future. In *2018 9th International Conference on Information and Communication Systems (ICICS)* (pp. 218-222). IEEE. 10.1109/IACS.2018.8355470

Albert, T.C., & Rennella M. (2021, November 11). *Readying students for their careers through project-based learning*. Harvard Business Publishing Education.

Alkhamisi, A. O., Arabia, S. & Monowar, M. M. (2013). Rise of augmented reality: Current and future application areas. *International Journal of Internet and Distributed Systems, 1*(4), 25.

Almaiah, M. A., Al-Khasawneh, A., & Althunibat, A. (2021). The impact of mobile learning on students' learning behaviours and performance: Integrating the technology acceptance model with social cognitive theory. *Interactive Learning Environments*, *29*(1), 1–16. doi:10.1080/10494820.2019.1692486

Alphonso, G. (2023, August 4). Council post: Empowering learners and protecting privacy: Advancing Data Security in EdTech. *Forbes*. https://www.forbes.com/sites/forbestechcouncil/2023/08/02/empowering-learners-and-protecting-privacy-advancing-data-security-in-edtech/?sh=378880db3053

Al-Qahtani, M. F., & Guraya, S. Y. (2019). Comparison of the professionalism behaviours of medical students from four GCC universities with single-gender and Co-educational learning climates. *The Open Nursing Journal, 13*(1), 193–200. doi:10.2174/1874434601913010193

Alqirnas, H. R. (2020). Students' perception of virtual classrooms as an alternative to real classes. *International Journal of Education and Information Technologies, 14*, 153–161. doi:10.46300/9109.2020.14.18

Althunibat, A., Alzyadat, W., Almarashdeh, I., Alsmadi, M., Al Shawabkeh, A. O., Abuhamdah, A., & Alzaqebah, M. (2023). Learning experience of students using the Learning Management System: User's perspective on the use of Moodle in the University of Jordan. *Advances in Human-Computer Interaction, 2023*, 1–11. doi:10.1155/2023/6659245

Altinpulluk, H. (2019). Determining the trends of using augmented reality in education between 2006-2016. *Education and Information Technologies, 24*(2), 1089–1114. doi:10.1007/s10639-018-9806-3

American Association of Colleges for Teacher Education. (2010, March). The clinical preparation of teachers. *Policy Brief.*

American Library Association. (2000). *Information literacy competency standards for higher education.* Association of College & Research Libraries.

Amoozad Mahdiraji, H., Sharifpour Arabi, H., Beheshti, M., & Vrontis, D. (2023). A mixed-method analysis of Industry 4.0 technologies in value generation for collaborative consumption companies. *Management Decision.* Advance online publication. doi:10.1108/MD-04-2023-0618

Anand, A. (2023, April 12). *India's Edtech market expected to grow to $10 billion by 2025.* CNBCTV18. Retrieved March 1, 2024, from https://www.cnbctv18.com/education/india-edtech-market-expected-to-grow-to-10-billion-by-2025-startups-unicorns-16391151.htm

Anderson, N., Potočnik, K., & Zhou, J. (2014). Innovation and creativity in organizations: A state-of-the-science review, prospective commentary, and guiding framework. *Journal of Management, 40*(5), 1297–1333. doi:10.1177/0149206314527128

Antonietti, A., Imperio, E., Rasi, C., & Sacco, M. (2001). Virtual reality and hypermedia in learning to use a turning lathe. *Journal of Computer Assisted Learning, 17*(2), 142–155. doi:10.1046/j.0266-4909.2001.00167.x

Arnett, J. L., Arnett, J. J., Feldman, S. S., & Cauffman, E. (2002). It's wrong, but everybody does it: Academic dishonesty among high school and college students. *Contemporary Educational Psychology, 27*(2), 209–228. doi:10.1006/ceps.2001.1088

Åstedt-Kurki, P., & Heikkinen, R. L. (1994). Two approaches to the study of experiences of health and old age: The thematic interview and the narrative method. *Journal of Advanced Nursing, 20*(3), 418–421. doi:10.1111/j.1365-2648.1994.tb02375.x PMID:7963044

Aydoğan, O., & Karabağ, G. (2020). The effect of history teaching supported by educational computer games on students' chronological thinking and space perception skills. *Uluslararası Sosyal Bilgilerde Yeni Yaklaşımlar Dergisi*, *4*(1), 106–130.

Azuma, R. T. (1997). A survey of augmented reality. *Presence (Cambridge, Mass.)*, *6*(4), 355–385. doi:10.1162/pres.1997.6.4.355

Bacca Acosta, J. L., Baldiris Navarro, S. M., Fabregat Gesa, R., & Graf, S. (2014). Augmented reality trends in education: A systematic review of research and applications. *Journal of Educational Technology & Society*, *17*(4), 133–149.

Bachore, M. M. (2016). The nature, causes and practices of academic dishonesty/cheating in higher education: The case of Hawassa University. *Journal of Education and Practice*, *7*(19), 222–1735.

Bag, S., Rahman, M. S., Srivastava, G., & Shrivastav, S. K. (2023). Unveiling metaverse potential in supply chain management and overcoming implementation challenges: An empirical study. *Benchmarking*. Advance online publication. doi:10.1108/BIJ-05-2023-0314

Baird, J. S. Jr. (1980). Current Trends in College Cheating. *Psychology in the Schools*, *17*(4), 515–522. doi:10.1002/1520-6807(198010)17:4<515::AID-PITS2310170417>3.0.CO;2-3

Baker, D. P., Day, R., & Salas, E. (2006). Teamwork as an essential component of high-reliability organizations. *Health Services Research*, *41*(4), 1576–1598. doi:10.1111/j.1475-6773.2006.00566.x PMID:16898980

Baker, Wentz, R. K., & Woods, M. M. (2009). Using virtual worlds in education: Second Life® as an educational tool. *Teaching of Psychology*, *36*(1), 59–64. doi:10.1080/00986280802529079

Ball, D. L., & Forzani, F. M. (2009). The work of teaching and the challenge for teacher education. *Journal of Teacher Education*, *60*(5), 497–511. doi:10.1177/0022487109348479

Bandura, A. (1986). *Social foundations of thought and action: A social cognitive theory*. Prentice-Hall.

Bányai, F., Griffiths, M. D., Király, O., & Demetrovics, Z. (2019). The psychology of esports: A systematic literature review. *Journal of Gambling Studies*, *35*(2), 351–365. doi:10.1007/s10899-018-9763-1 PMID:29508260

Barata, G., Gama, S., Jorge, J. A., & Gonçalves, D. J. (2014). Relating gaming habits with student performance in a gamified learning experience, *Proceedings of the first ACM SIGCHI annual symposium on Computer-humaninteractioninplay CHI PLAY'14*. 10.1145/2658537.2658692

Baratè. (2019, June). 5G technology for augmented and virtual reality in education. In *Proceedings of the International Conference on Education and New Developments* (Vol. 2019, pp. 512-516). 10.36315/2019v1end116

Barik, N., & Karforma, S. (2012). *Risks and remedies in e-learning system*. arXiv preprint arXiv:1205.2711

Baron, J. (2000). *Thinking and deciding*. Cambridge University Press.

Barriball, L. K., & While, A. (1994) Collecting Data Using a Semi-Structured Interview: A Discussion Paper. *Journal of Advanced Nursing, 19*, 328-335.

Bashandy, H. (2021). Playing, mapping, and power a critical analysis of using minecraft in spatial design. *American Journal of Play, 12*(3), 363–369.

Baştürk, S., & Taştepe, M. (2013). *Bilimsel araştırma yöntemleri* [Scientific research methods]. Vize Yayıncılık.

Baumbusch, J. (2010). Semi-structured interviewing in practice-close research. *Journal for Specialists in Pediatric Nursing, 15*(3), 255–258. doi:10.1111/j.1744-6155.2010.00243.x PMID:20618640

Beck, D. (2019). Augmented and virtual reality in education: Immersive learning research. *Journal of Educational Computing Research, 57*(7), 1619–1625. doi:10.1177/0735633119854035

Becker, H. J. (1994). How exemplary computer-using teachers differ from other teachers: Implications for realizing the potential of computers in schools. *Journal of Research on Computing in Education, 26*(3), 291–321. doi:10.1080/08886504.1994.10782093

Beetham, H., & Sharpe, R. (2007). *Rethinking pedagogy for a digital age: Designing and delivering e-learning*. Routledge. doi:10.4324/9780203961681

Begum, M., & Uddin, M. S. (2020). Digital Image Watermarking Techniques: A Review. *Information (Basel), 11*(2), 110. doi:10.3390/info11020110

Beins, B. C. (2017). *Research method: a tool for life*. Cambridge University Press.

Bernacki, M. L., Greene, J. A., & Crompton, H. (2020). Mobile technology, learning, and achievement: Advances in understanding and measuring the role of mobile technology in education. *Contemporary Educational Psychology, 60*, 101827. doi:10.1016/j.cedpsych.2019.101827

Best 8 Principles of Gamified Learning. (2023, June 26). Future Education Magazine. https://futureeducationmagazine.com/8-principles-of-gamified-learning/

Bi, T., & Song, S. (2011). *Problems and solutions of educational game development* [Conference presentation]. 2011 International Conference on Consumer Electronics, Xianning, China.

Billinghurst, M. (2002). Augmented reality in education. *New horizoKuo-Ting Huangns for learning, 12*(5), 1-5.

Billinghurst, M., & Kato, H. & Poupyrev, I. (2001). The magicbook-moving seamlessly between reality and virtuality. *IEEE Computer Graphics and Applications, 21*(3), 6–8.

Binkley, M., Erstad, O., Herman, J., Raizen, S., Ripley, M., Miller-Ricci, M., & Rumble, M. (2012). Defining twenty-first century skills. In P. Griffin, B. McGaw, & E. Care (Eds.), *Assessment and Teaching of 21st Century Skills* (pp. 17–66). Springer. doi:10.1007/978-94-007-2324-5_2

Biswas, P., Orero, P., Swaminathan, M., Krishnaswamy, K., & Robinson, P. (2021, May). Adaptive accessible AR/VR systems. In *Extended Abstracts of the 2021 CHI Conference on Human Factors in Computing Systems* (pp. 1-7). Academic Press.

Blanco-Herrera, J. A., Gentile, D. A., & Rokkum, J. N. (2019). Video games can increase creativity, but with caveats. *Creativity Research Journal*, *31*(2), 119–131. doi:10.1080/10400419.2019.1594524

Blumberg, F. C., & Altschuler, E. (2011). From the playroom to the classroom: Children's views of video game play and academic learning. *Child Development Perspectives*, *5*(2), 99–103. doi:10.1111/j.1750-8606.2011.00163.x

Bolick, C., Adams, R., & Willox, L. (2019). The marginalization of elementary social studies in teacher education. *Social Studies Research & Practice*, *14*(3), 31–44.

Boot, W. R., Kramer, A. F., Simons, D. J., Fabiani, M., & Gratton, G. (2008). The effects of video game playing on attention, memory, and executive control. *Acta Psychologica*, *129*(3), 387–398. doi:10.1016/j.actpsy.2008.09.005 PMID:18929349

Bowden, J. L.-H., Tickle, L., & Naumann, K. (2021). The four pillars of tertiary student engagement and success: A holistic measurement approach. *Studies in Higher Education*, *46*(6), 1207–1224. doi:10.1080/03075079.2019.1672647

Bower, M., Howe, C., McCredie, N., Robinson, A., & Grover, D. (2014). Augmented Reality in education–cases, places and potentials. *Educational Media International*, *51*(1), 1–15. doi:10.1080/09523987.2014.889400

Bridges, S. M., Whitehill, T., & McGrath, C. (2012). The next generation: Research directions in PBL. In S. Bridges, C. McGrath, & T. Whitehill (Eds.), *Researching problem-based learning in clinical education: The next generation* (pp. 225–232). Springer. doi:10.1007/978-94-007-2515-7_14

Brier, D. J., & Lebbin, V. K. (2004). Teaching information literacy using the short story. *RSR. Reference Services Review*, *32*(4), 383–387. doi:10.1108/00907320410569734

Brinkmann, S., & Kvale, S. (2018). *Doing interviews*. SAGE Publications Limited. doi:10.4135/9781529716665

Calabuig-Moreno, González-Serrano, M. H., Fombona, J., & García-Tascón, M. (2020). The emergence of technology in physical education: A general bibliometric analysis with a focus on virtual and augmented reality. *Sustainability (Basel)*, *12*(7), 2728. doi:10.3390/su12072728

California State University. (2008). History, the History of Computers, and the History of Computers in Education. History of computers in Education. https://home.csulb.edu/~murdock/histofcs.html

Çalışkan, H., & Biter, M. (2019). Values education with educational in social studies courses: An action research. *Journal of Interdisciplinary Education: Theory and Practice*, *1*(1), 1–28.

Candy, P. C. (1991). *Self-direction for lifelong learning: A comprehensive guide to theory and practice*. Jossey-Bass.

Can, T. & Şimşek, İ. (2016). Eğitimde yeni teknolojiler: Sanal gerçeklik. Eğitim Teknolojileri Okumaları, 2016. The Turkish Online Journal of Educational Technology (TOJET), 21. *Bölüm, 351*, 363.

Carbonell, C., Avarvarei, B. V., Chelariu, E. L., Draghia, L., & Avarvarei, S. C. (2017). Mapreading skill development with 3d technologies. *The Journal of Geography, 116*(5), 197–205. doi:10.1080/00221341.2016.1248857

Carbonell, C., Gunalp, P., Saorin, J. L., & Hess-Medler, S. (2020). Think spatially with game engine. *ISPRS International Journal of Geo-Information, 9*(03), 159. doi:10.3390/ijgi9030159

Carbonell-Carrera, C., Jaeger, A. J., Saorín, J. L., Melián, D., & de la Torre-Cantero, J. (2021). Minecraft as a block building approach for developing spatial skills. *Entertainment Computing, 38*, 1–7. doi:10.1016/j.entcom.2021.100427

Cavas, B, Capar, S., Cavas, L, & Yahsi, Ö. (2021). Turkish STEM Teachers' Opinions About Scientist-Teacher-Student Partnership. *Journal of Turkish Science Education, 18*(4).

Checa-Romero, M., & Pascual Gómez, I. (2018). Minecraft and machinima in action: Development of creativity in the classroom. *Technology, Pedagogy and Education, 27*(5), 625–637. doi:10.1080/1475939X.2018.1537933

Chen, P., Liu, X., Cheng, W., & Huang, R. (2017). A review of using Augmented Reality in Education from 2011 to 2016. *Innovations in smart learning*, 13-18.

Chenail, R. J. (2011). Interviewing the Investigator: Strategies for Addressing Instrumentation and Researcher Bias Concerns in Qualitative Research. *The Qualitative Report, 16*(1), 255–262. doi:10.46743/2160-3715/2011.1051

Chenail, R. J. (2011). Ten Steps for Conceptualizing and Conducting Qualitative Research Studies in a Pragmatically Curious Manner. *The Qualitative Report, 16*(6), 1715–1732.

Cheng, X., Zhang, S., Fu, S., Liu, W., Guan, C., Mou, J., Ye, Q., & Huang, C. (2022). Exploring the metaverse in the digital economy: An overview and research framework. *Journal of Electronic Business & Digital Economics, 1*(2), 206–224. doi:10.1108/JEBDE-09-2022-0036

Chen, P., Lambert, A., & Guidry, K. (2010). Engaging online learners: The impact of web-based learning technology on college student engagement. *Computers & Education, 54*(4), 1222–1232. doi:10.1016/j.compedu.2009.11.008

Childs, E., Mohammad, F., Stevens, L., Burbelo, H., Awoke, A., Rewkowski, N., & Manocha, D. (2021). An overview of enhancing distance learning through augmented and virtual reality technologies. arXiv preprint arXiv:2101.11000.

Choi, D. H., Dailey-Hebert, A., & Estes, J. S. (Eds.). (2020). *Current and prospective applications of virtual reality in higher education*. IGI Global. doi:10.4018/978-1-7998-4960-5

Choo, A., Karamnejad, M., & May, A. (2013). *Maintaining long distance togetherness Synchronous communication with Minecraft and Skype* [Conference presentation]. 2013 IEEE International Games Innovation Conference, Vancouver, Canada.

Choudhury, P. K. (2022, August 26). *The art of storytelling in science and research*. Researcher. Life. https://researcher.life/blog/article/storytelling-in-science-and-research

Cicek, I., Bernik, A., & Tomicic, I. (2021). Student thoughts on virtual reality in higher education—A survey questionnaire. *Information (Basel)*, *12*(4), 151. doi:10.3390/info12040151

Cilliers, E. J. (2017). The challenge of teaching generation Z. PEOPLE. *The International Journal of Social Sciences (Islamabad)*.

Cintang, N., Setyowati, D. L., & Handayani, S. S. D. (2018). The Obstacles and Strategy of Project Based Learning Implementation in Elementary School. *Journal of Education and Learning*, *12*(1), 7–15. doi:10.11591/edulearn.v12i1.7045

Cizek, G. J. (2003). *Detecting and preventing classroom cheating: Promoting integrity in assessment*. Corwin Press.

Clark, D. B., Virk, S. S., Barnes, J., & Adams, D. M. (2016). Self-explanation and digital games: Adaptively increasing abstraction. *Computers & Education*, *103*, 28–43. doi:10.1016/j.compedu.2016.09.010

Codish, D., & Ravid, G. (2014). Personality based gamification-educational gamification for extroverts and introverts. *CHAIS Conference for the Study of Innovation and Learning Technologies, 1*. https://www.openu.ac.il/innovation/ chais2014/download/E2-2.pdf

Committee on Support for Thinking Spatially. (2006). *Learning to think spatially*. National Academies Press.

Connolly, T. M., Boyle, E. A., MacArthur, E., Hainey, T., & Boyle, J. M. (2012). A systematic literature review of empirical evidence on computer games and serious games. *Computers & Education*, *59*(2), 661–686. doi:10.1016/j.compedu.2012.03.004

Corporate Author. (2023b, June 16). Top 10 startups in EdTech in India - tracxn. Retrieved March 1, 2024, from https://tracxn.com/d/explore/edtech-startups-in-india/__fpQpYpejRQUpr2Den-JxfLl7qv4ORAU4R34IA5folf0/companies

Çoruh, L. (2011). *Sanat tarihi dersinde bir öğrenme modeli olarak sanal gerçeklik uygulamasının etkililiğinin değerlendirilmesi: Erciyes Üniversitesi Mimarlık ve Güzel Sanatlar Fakülteleri örneği uygulaması (Yayımlanmamış Doktora Tezi)*. Gazi Üniversitesi Eğitim Bilimleri Enstitüsü.

Cowling, M. A., Crawford, J., Vallis, C., Middleton, R., & Sim, K. (2022). The EdTech difference: Digitalisation, digital pedagogy, and technology enhanced learning. *Journal of University Teaching & Learning Practice*, *19*(2), 1–13. doi:10.53761/1.19.2.1

Cox, E. (2019). *Narrative Medicine: The Importance of Storytelling in Health Care*. US News & World Report. https://health.usnews.com/health-care/for-better/articles/narrative-medicine-the-importance-of-storytelling-in-health-care

Craft, A. (2013). Childhood, play, and the fostering of creativity. In D. Brooker, M. Blaise, & S. Edwards (Eds.), The SAGE handbook of play and learning in early childhood (pp. 19-30). SAGE Publications.

Craig, A. B., Sherman, W. R., & Will, J. D. (2009). *Developing Virtual Reality Applications: Foundations of Effective Design*. Elsevier.

Creswell, J. W. (2013). *Research Design: Qualitative, Quantitative, and Mixed Methods Approaches* (4th ed.). SAGE Publication.

Creswell, J. W. (2021). *Araştırma deseni nitel, nicel ve karma yöntem yaklaşımları*. Nobel Akademik.

Creswell, J. W., Plano Clark, V. L., Gutmann, M. L., & Hanson, W. E. (2003). Advanced Mixed Methods Research Designs. In A. Tashakkori & C. Teddlie (Eds.), *Handbook of Mixed Methods in Social and Behavioral Research* (pp. 209–240). Sage.

Cridland, E. K., Jones, S. C., Caputi, P., & Magee, C. A. (2015). Qualitative research with families living with autism spectrum disorder: Recommendations for conducting semistructured interviews. *Journal of Intellectual & Developmental Disability*, *40*(1), 78–91. doi:10.3109/13668250.2014.964191

Criollo-C, S., Altamirano-Suarez, E., Jaramillo-Villacís, L., Vidal-Pacheco, K., Guerrero-Arias, A., & Luján-Mora, S. (2022). Sustainable teaching and learning through a mobile application: A case study. *Sustainability (Basel)*, *14*(11), 6663. doi:10.3390/su14116663

Criollo-C, S., Guerrero-Arias, A., Jaramillo-Alc'azar, ´. A., & Luj'an-Mora, S. (2021). Mobile learning technologies for education: Benefits and pending issues. *Applied Sciences (Basel, Switzerland)*, *11*(9), 4111. doi:10.3390/app11094111

Crompton, H. (2013). A historical overview of m-learning: Toward learner-centered education. In *Handbook of mobile learning* (pp. 3–14). Routledge.

Cuban, L. (1986). *Teachers and machines: The classroom use of technology since 1920*. Teachers college press.

Curran, K., Middleton, G., & Doherty, C. (2011). Cheating in exams with technology. *International Journal of Cyber Ethics in Education*, *1*(2), 54–62. doi:10.4018/ijcee.2011040105

Czetwertyński, S. (2017). Importance of copyrights in online society. *Managerial Economics.*, *18*(2), 147. doi:10.7494/manage.2017.18.2.147

Czok, V., Krug, M., Müller, S., Huwer, J., Kruse, S., Müller, W., & Weitzel, H. (2023). A Framework for Analysis and Development of Augmented Reality Applications in Science and Engineering Teaching. *Education Sciences*, *13*(9), 926. doi:10.3390/educsci13090926 da Cruz, F. C., Stefenon, S. F., Furtado, R. G., Dela Rocca, G. A., & Silva Ferreira, F. C. (2018). Financial feasibility study for radio installation link on the mobile telephone network. *Revista Geintec-Gestao Inovacao E Tecnologias, 8*(3), 4447-4460.

da Silva, L. M., Dias, L. P., Barbosa, J. L., Rigo, S. J., dos Anjos, J., Geyer, C. F., & Leithardt, V. R. (2022). Learning analytics and collaborative groups of learners in distance education: A systematic mapping study. *Informatics in Education, 21*(1), 113–146.

Dalim, C. S. C., Kolivand, H., Kadhim, H., Sunar, M. S., & Billinghurst, M. (2017). Factors influencing the acceptance of augmented reality in education: A review of the literature. *Journal of Computational Science, 13*(11), 581–589. doi:10.3844/jcssp.2017.581.589

Damala, A., Marchal, I., & Houlier, P. (2007, October). Merging augmented reality-based features in mobile multimedia museum guides. In *Anticipating the Future of the Cultural Past, CIPA Conference 2007, 1-6 October 2007,* (pp. 259-264). Academic Press.

Davenport, T., & Kalakota, R. (2019). The potential for artificial intelligence in healthcare. *Future Healthcare Journal, 6*(2), 94–98. doi:10.7861/futurehosp.6-2-94 PMID:31363513

Davis, F., Drinan, F., & Gallant, B. (2009). *Cheating in Schools: What We Know And What We Can Do*. Wiley. doi:10.1002/9781444310252

De Cecco, J. P. (1968). *The psychology of learning and instruction: educational psychology.* Prentice-Hall.

Dearmer, A. (2023, August 16). *Unlocking Blended Learning: Strategies, Benefits & Tools.* Appsembler. https://appsembler.com/blog/unlocking-blended-learning-strategies-benefits-tools/#:~:text=Incorporating%20Varied%20Instructional%20Strategies%3A%20In

Dearnley, C. (2005). A reflection on the use of semi-structured interviews. *Nurse Researcher, 13*(1), 19–28. doi:10.7748/nr2005.07.13.1.19.c5997 PMID:16220838

Delello, J. A., McWhorter, R. R., & Camp, K. M. (2015). Integrating augmented reality in higher education: A multidisciplinary study of student perceptions. *Journal of Educational Multimedia and Hypermedia, 24*(3), 209–233.

Demirarslan, Y., & Usluel, K. Y. (2005). Bilgi ve iletişim teknolojilerinin öğrenme öğretme sürecine entegrasyonunda öğretmenlerin durumu. *The Turkish Online Journal of Educational Technology, 4*(3).

Demitriadou, Stavroulia, K.-E., & Lanitis, A. (2020). Comparative evaluation of virtual and augmented reality for teaching mathematics in primary education. *Education and Information Technologies, 25*(1), 381–401. doi:10.1007/s10639-019-09973-5

Denecke, K. (2015). Ethical issues of social media usage in healthcare. *Yearbook of Medical Informatics, 24*(01), 137–147. doi:10.15265/IY-2015-001 PMID:26293861

Denzin, N. K. (1978). Triangulation: A case for methodological evaluation and combination. *Sociological Methods*, 339-357.

DePape, A. M., Barnes, M., & Petryschuk, J. (2019). Students' experiences in higher education with virtual and augmented reality: A qualitative systematic review. *Innovative Practice in Higher Education, 3*(3).

DeVito, J. A. (2015). *The interpersonal communication book.* Pearson.

Dezuanni, M., O'Mara, J., & Beavis, C. (2015). 'Redstone is like electricity': Children's performative representations in and around Minecraft. *E-Learning and Digital Media, 12*(2), 147–163. doi:10.1177/2042753014568176

Dias, R., & Torkamani, A. (2019). Artificial intelligence in clinical and genomic diagnostics. *Genome Medicine, 11*(1), 70. doi:10.1186/s13073-019-0689-8 PMID:31744524

Diego, A. (2017). Friends with benefits: Causes and effects of learners 'cheating practices during examination. *IAFOR J Educ, 5*(2), 121–138. doi:10.22492/ije.5.2.06

Dien, J. (2023). Editorial: Generative artificial intelligence as a plagiarism problem. *Biological Psychology, 181*, 108621. doi:10.1016/j.biopsycho.2023.108621 PMID:37356702

Doğan, E. & Koç, H. (2017). The impact of instruction through digital games on students' academic achievement in teaching earthquakes in a social science class. *Uluslararası Türk Eğitim Bilimleri Dergisi, 5*(8).

Doğanay, H. (2017). *Coğrafya bilim alanları sözlüğü* [Dictionary of geography science fields]. PEGEM Akademi.

Domínguez, A., Saenz-de-Navarrete, J., de-Marcos, L., Fernández-Sanz, L., Pagés, C., & Martínez-Herráiz, J.-J. (2013). Gamifying learning experiences: Practical implications and outcomes. *Computers & Education, 63*(1), 380–392. doi:10.1016/j.compedu.2012.12.020

Drucker, P. (2000). *Yeni Gerçekler, Çev. Birtane Karanakçı.* Türkiye İş Bankası Kültür Yayınları.

Drucker, P. F. (1999). *Management challenges for the 21st century.* HarperCollins Publishers.

Duan, G., Han, M., Zhao, W., Dong, T., & Xu, T. (2018). Augmented reality technology and its game application research. *2018 3rd Int. Conf. Autom. Mech. Control Comput. Eng.,* 701–705.

Duncan, M., Cunningham, A., & Eyre, E. (2019), A combined movement and story-telling intervention enhances motor competence and language ability in preschoolers to a greater extent than movement or storytelling alone. European Physical Education Review, 25(1), 221-235.

Dusu, P. B., Gotan, A., Mohammed, J. D., & Gambo, B. (2016). Management of re-occurring cases of examination malpractice in plateau state college of health technology, Pankshin. *Nigeria J Educ Pract, 7*(6), 38–43.

Educational Testing Service. (2002). *Digital transformation: A framework for ICT literacy.* ETS.

Egbert, J., & Borysenko, N. (2019). Standards, engagement, and Minecraft: Optimizing experiences in language teacher education. *Teaching and Teacher Education, 85*, 115–124. doi:10.1016/j.tate.2019.06.015

Eitel, A., Krey, O., Sodian, B., & Dörfler, T. (2017). Learning from virtual agents: Empowering students for science learning by coupling them with virtual characters. *Computers & Education, 106*, 46–58.

El Jaouhari, A., Arif, J., Samadhiya, A., Kumar, A., Jain, V., & Agrawal, R. (2023). Are Metaverse applications in Quality 4.0 enablers of manufacturing resiliency? An exploratory review under disruption impressions and future research. *The TQM Journal.*

Elmqaddem, & … . (2019). Augmented reality and virtual reality in education. Myth or reality? *International Journal of Emerging Technologies in Learning, 14*(3), 234. doi:10.3991/ijet.v14i03.9289

Emerson, T. (1993). Mastering The Art Of VR: On Becoming The HIT Lab Cybrarian. *The Electronic Library, 11*(6), 385–391. doi:10.1108/eb045261

Ennis, R. H. (1987). *A taxonomy of critical thinking dispositions and abilities.* Academic Press.

Erkuş, A. (2003). *Psikometri üzerine yazılar* [Articles on psychometrics]. Türk Psikologlar Derneği Yayınları.

Erkuş, A. (2012). *Psikolojide ölçme ve ölçek geliştirme-1: Temel kavramlar ve işlemler.* Pegem Akademi.

Erol, F. Z., & Akpınar, E. (2021). A review on experimental studies on the ability to perceive space carried out in the field of social studies education. *International Journal of Social Science Research, 10*(1), 1–16.

Eryalçın, B. (1994). Hayalle Gerçeğin Dansı Sanal Gerçeklik. *Bilim ve Teknik, 27*(323), 20–27.

Eshet-Alkalai, Y. (2004). Digital literacy: A conceptual framework for survival skills in the digital era. *Journal of Educational Multimedia and Hypermedia, 13*(1), 93–106.

Etlican, G. (2012). X ve Y Kuşaklarının Online Eğitim Teknolojilerine Karşı Tutumlarının Karşılaştırılması [Tezi. Bahçeşehir Üniversitesi Sosyal Bilimler Ens. İstanbul].

Facione, P. A. (1990). *Critical thinking: A statement of expert consensus for purposes of educational assessment and instruction.* The California Academic Press.

Feng, J., Spence, I., & Pratt, J. (2007). Playing an action video game reduces gender differences in spatial cognition. *Psychological Science, 18*(10), 850–855. doi:10.1111/j.1467-9280.2007.01990.x PMID:17894600

Ferrigno, G., Di Paola, N., Oguntegbe, K. F., & Kraus, S. (2023). Value creation in the metaverse age: A thematic analysis of press releases. *International Journal of Entrepreneurial Behaviour & Research, 29*(11), 337–363. doi:10.1108/IJEBR-01-2023-0039

Fetzner, M., Hirt, E. R., & Bläsi, B. (2021). Learning to create in immersive virtual reality: Effectiveness of a VR drawing intervention in supporting creativity and spatial skills. *Educational Technology Research and Development, 69*(1), 75–96.

Fishman, B. J., Konstantopoulos, S., Kubitskey, B. W., Vath, R., Park, G., Johnson, H., & Edelson, D. C. (2013). Comparing the impact of online and face-to-face professional development in the context of curriculum implementation. *Journal of Teacher Education*, *64*(5), 426–438. Advance online publication. doi:10.1177/0022487113494413

Fitchett, P. G., & Heafner, T. L. (2010). A national perspective on the effects of high-stakes testing and standardization on elementary social studies marginalization. *Theory and Research in Social Education*, *38*(1), 114–130. doi:10.1080/00933104.2010.10473418

Fitria, T. N. (2023). Augmented Reality (AR) and Virtual Reality (VR) Technology in Education: Media of Teaching and Learning: A Review. *International Journal of Computer and Information System*, *4*(1), 14–25.

Flores, N., Paiva, A. C., & Cruz, N. (2020). Teaching software engineering topics through pedagogical game design patterns: An empirical study. *Information (Basel)*, *11*(3), 153. doi:10.3390/info11030153

Forkuor, J. B., Amarteifio, J., Attoh, D. O., & Buari, M. A. (2019). Students' perception of cheating and the best time to cheat during examinations. *The Urban Review*, *51*(3), 424–443. doi:10.1007/s11256-018-0491-8

Fraillon, J., Schulz, W., Friedman, T., Ainley, J., & Gebhardt, E. (2015). *International computer and information literacy study: ICILS 2013 technical report*. IEA Secretariat.

Fredricks, J. A., Blumenfeld, P. C., & Paris, A. H. (2004). School engagement: Potential of the concept, state of the evidence. *Review of Educational Research*, *74*(1), 59–109. doi:10.3102/00346543074001059

Frizzo Stefenon, S., Kasburg, C., Nied, A., Rodrigues Klaar, A. C., Silva Ferreira, F. C., & Waldrigues Branco, N. (2020). Hybrid deep learning for power generation forecasting in active solar trackers. *IET Generation, Transmission & Distribution*, *14*(23), 5667–5674. doi:10.1049/iet-gtd.2020.0814

Gagné, C. (2020). K-Means Clustering: Concept and Applications. In Data Clustering: Algorithms and Applications (pp. 1-25). CRC Press.

Garrison, D. R., Anderson, T., & Archer, W. (2001). Critical inquiry in a text-based environment: Computer conferencing in higher education model. *The Internet and Higher Education*, *2*(2-3), 87–105. doi:10.1016/S1096-7516(00)00016-6

Gauquier, E., & Schneider, J. (2013). Minecraft programs in the library. *Young Adult Library Services*, *11*(2), 17–19.

Gee, J. P. (2007). *Good video games good learning: Collected essays on video games, learning, and literacy*. Peter Lang. doi:10.3726/978-1-4539-1162-4

Gilchrist, A. (2016). *Industry 4.0: the industrial internet of things*. Apress. doi:10.1007/978-1-4842-2047-4

Gomez, D. (2001). Putting the shame back in student cheating. *Education Digest*, *67*(4), 1–6.

González, C., Barreda, G., Ortega, M., Ampuero, C., & Norambuena, M. (2021). Geografía y Minecraft: Potencialidades de una herramienta para la enseñanza a partir de un videojuego de mundo abierto. *Informes Científicos Técnicos*, *13*(1), 30–53. doi:10.22305/ict-unpa.v13.n1.788

Granic, I., Lobel, A., & Engels, R. C. (2014). The benefits of playing video games. *The American Psychologist*, *69*(1), 66–78. doi:10.1037/a0034857 PMID:24295515

Green, C. S., & Bavelier, D. (2006). Effect of action video games on the spatial distribution of visuospatial attention. *Journal of Experimental Psychology. Human Perception and Performance*, *32*(6), 1465–1478. doi:10.1037/0096-1523.32.6.1465 PMID:17154785

Green, C. S., & Bavelier, D. (2012). Learning, attentional control, and action video games. *Current Biology*, *22*(6), R197–R206. doi:10.1016/j.cub.2012.02.012 PMID:22440805

Grijalva, T., Nowell, C., & Kerkvliet, J. (2006). Academic Honesty and Online Courses. *College Student Journal*, *40*(1), 180–185.

Gros, B. (2017). Game dimensions and pedagogical dimension in serious games. In Handbook of Research on Serious Games for Educational Applications (pp. 402-417). IGI Global. doi:10.4018/978-1-5225-0513-6.ch019

Grusec, J. E. (1992). Social learning theory and developmental psychology: The legacies of Robert Sears and Albert Bandura. *Developmental Psychology*, *28*(5), 776–786. doi:10.1037/0012-1649.28.5.776

Guba, E. G., & Lincoln, Y. S. (1982). Epistemological and methodological bases of naturalistic inquiry. *Educational Communication and Technology*, *30*(4), 233–252. doi:10.1007/BF02765185

Gudoniene, D., & Rutkauskiene, D. (2019). Virtual and augmented reality in education. *Baltic Journal of Modern Computing*, *7*(2), 293–300. doi:10.22364/bjmc.2019.7.2.07

Güneş, G., Ayantaş, T., Güneş, C., Güleryüz, O., & Arıkan, A. (2021). Review of theses on the use of technology in social studies education. *Türkiye Sosyal Araştırmalar dergisi, 25*(3), 859-890.

Gupta, S., Sharma, P., Chaudhary, S., Kumar, V., Singh, S. P., Lourens, M., & Beri, N. (2024). Study on the Beneficial Impacts and Ethical Dimensions of Generative AI in Software Product Management. *International Journal of Intelligent Systems and Applications in Engineering*, *12*(8s), 251–264.

Gurevych, R., Silveistr, A., Mokliuk, M., Shaposhnikova, I., Gordiichuk, G., & Saiapina, S. (2021). Using augmented reality technology in higher education institutions. *Postmodern Openings*, *12*(2), 109–132. doi:10.18662/po/12.2/299

Hagendorff, T. (2020). The Ethics of AI Ethics: An Evaluation of Guidelines. *Minds and Machines*, *30*(1), 99–120. doi:10.1007/s11023-020-09517-8

Haines, V. J., Diekhoff, G. M., LaBeff, E. E., & Clark, R. E. (1986). College Cheating: Immaturity, Lack of Commitment, and the Neutralizing Attitude. *Research in Higher Education*, *25*(4), 342–354. doi:10.1007/BF00992130

Haleem, A., Javaid, M., Qadri, M. A., & Suman, R. (2022). Understanding the role of digital technologies in education: A review. *Sustainable Operations and Computers*, *3*, 275–285. doi:10.1016/j.susoc.2022.05.004

Hämäläinen, R., & Häkkinen, P. (2010). Teachers' instructional planning for computer-supported collaborative learning: Macro-scripts as a pedagogical method to facilitate collaborative learning. *Teaching and Teacher Education*, *26*(4), 871–877. doi:10.1016/j.tate.2009.10.025

Hamzah, Ambiyar, A., Rizal, F., Simatupang, W., Irfan, D., & Refdinal, R. (2021). Development of Augmented Reality Application for Learning Computer Network Device. *International Journal of Interactive Mobile Technologies*, *15*(12), 47. doi:10.3991/ijim.v15i12.21993

Hantono, B. S., Nugroho, L. E., & Santosa, P. I. (2018, July). Meta-review of augmented reality in education. In *2018 10th international conference on information technology and electrical engineering (ICITEE)* (pp. 312-315). IEEE. 10.1109/ICITEED.2018.8534888

Hardin, M., & Greer, J. D. (2009). The influence of gender-role socialization, media use and sports participation on perceptions of gender-appropriate sports. *Journal of Sport Behavior*, *32*(2), 207–226.

Harmon, O. R., & Lambrinos, J. (2008). Are online exams an invitation to cheat? *The Journal of Economic Education*, *39*(2), 116–125. doi:10.3200/JECE.39.2.116-125

Hatane, S. E., Sondak, L., Tarigan, J., Kwistianus, H., & Sany, S. (2023). Eyeballing internal auditors' and the firms' intention to adopt Metaverse technologies: case study in Indonesia. *Journal of Financial Reporting and Accounting*.

Henderson, M., & Romeo, G. (2015). *Teaching and digital technologies big issues and critical questions*. Cambridge University Press. doi:10.1017/CBO9781316091968

Hensley, L. C., Kirkpatrick, K. M., & Burgoon, J. M. (2013). Relation of gender, course enrollment, and grades to distinct forms of academic dishonesty. *Teaching in Higher Education*, *18*(8), 895–907. doi:10.1080/13562517.2013.827641

Hermans, R., Tondeur, J., van Braak, J., & Valcke, M. (2008). The impact of primary school teachers' educational beliefs on the classroom use of computers. *Computers & Education*, *51*(4), 1499–1509. doi:10.1016/j.compedu.2008.02.001

Hill, V. (2015). Digital citizenship through game design in Minecraft. *New Library World*, *116*(7-8), 369–382. doi:10.1108/NLW-09-2014-0112

Hilton, J. T. (2016). A case study of the application of SAMR and TPACK for reflection on technology integration into two social studies classrooms. *Social Studies Research & Practice*, *11*(1), 1–12.

Hines, P., & Netland, T. H. (2023). Teaching a Lean masterclass in the metaverse. *International Journal of Lean Six Sigma, 14*(6), 1121–1143. doi:10.1108/IJLSS-02-2022-0035

Hinojosa, J., & Barreto, E. (2017). Virtual reality in mathematics education: A study on the effects of immersive VR on students' mathematical achievement and spatial ability. In *Proceedings of the 49th Annual Southeast Regional Conference* (pp. 273-278). ACM. https://doi.org/10.1145/3077286.3077330

Hobbs, R. (1998). The seven great debates in the media literacy movement. *Journal of Communication, 48*(1), 16–32. doi:10.1111/j.1460-2466.1998.tb02734.x

Hodgson, P., Lee, V. W., Chan, J. C., Fong, A., Tang, C. S., Chan, L., & Wong, C. (2019). Immersive virtual reality (IVR) in higher education: Development and implementation. *Augmented reality and virtual reality: The power of AR and VR for business*, 161-173.

Holden, O. L., Norris, M. E., & Kuhlmeier, V. A. (2021). "Academic integrity in online assessment: A research review." *Frontiers in Education. Frontiers.*

Holland, J., & Muilenburg, L. (2011). Supporting student collaboration: Edmodo in the classroom. In *Proceedings of Society for Information Technology & Teacher Education International Conference* (pp. 3232-3236). Association for the Advancement of Computing in Education (AACE).

Holloway, I., & Wheeler, S. (1996). *Qualitative research for nurses*. Blackwell Science.

Huang, C.-K., Chao, Y.-C., & Lin, C.-Y. (2008). Web 2.0 in and out of the language classroom. In *Proceedings of the 2008 World CALL: Using technologies for language learning* (pp. 39-54). Foukoka, Japan.

Huang, K. T., Ball, C., Francis, J., Ratan, R., Boumis, J., & Fordham, J. (2019). Augmented versus virtual reality in education: An exploratory study examining science knowledge retention when using augmented reality/virtual reality mobile applications. *Cyberpsychology, Behavior, and Social Networking, 22*(2), 105–110. doi:10.1089/cyber.2018.0150 PMID:30657334

Hu-Au. (2017). Virtual reality in education: A tool for learning in the experience age. *International Journal of Innovation in Education, 4*(4), 215–226. doi:10.1504/IJIIE.2017.091481

Hughes, J. M., & McCabe, D. L. (2006). Understanding Academic Misconduct. *Canadian Journal of Higher Education, 36*(1), 49–63. doi:10.47678/cjhe.v36i1.183525

Hurix, C. A. (2024, January 23). *Top eleven education solution providers in India - Hurix Digital*. Digital Engineering & Technology | Elearning Solutions | Digital Content Solutions. Retrieved March 1, 2024, from https://www.hurix.com/top-edtech-companies-in-india-edtech-excellence-2/

Iahad, N. A., & Ahmad, N. (2015). Gamification in online collaborative learning for programming courses: A literature review. *ARPN Journal of Engineering and Applied Sciences, 10*(23), 1–3.

Iatsyshyn. (2020a). *Application of augmented reality technologies for preparation of specialists of new technological era*. Academic Press.

Iatsyshyn. (2020b). *Application of augmented reality technologies for education projects preparation*. Academic Press.

IBEF. (2023, February). *Growth and expansion of India's Edtech Industry: IBEF*. India Brand Equity Foundation. Retrieved March 1, 2024, from https://www.ibef.org/research/case-study/growth-and-expansion-of-india-s-edtech-industry

Iberahim, H., Hussein, N., Samat, N., Noordin, F., & Daud, N. (2013). Academic dishonesty: Why business students participate in these practices? *Procedia: Social and Behavioral Sciences*, *90*, 152–156. doi:10.1016/j.sbspro.2013.07.076

İbili, E. ve Şahin, S. (2015). Investigation Of The Effects On Computer Attitudes And Computer Self-Efficacy To Use Of Augmented Reality In Geometry Teaching, Necatibey Faculty of Education Electronic Journal of Science &. *The Mathematics Educator*, *9*(1), 332–350.

Ibrahim, H. A. H. (2014). Quality assurance and accreditation in education. *Open Journal of Education*, *2*(2), 106–110. doi:10.12966/oje.06.06.2014

Importance of Storytelling for Tech Jobs & Career Growth. (2022, April 21). Stoodnt.com. https://stoodnt.com/blog/storytelling-tech-jobs-career/

Israel, M., & Hay, I. (2006). *Research Ethics for Social Scientists*. SAGE Publications, Ltd. doi:10.4135/9781849209779

Ivankova, N. V., Creswell, J. W., & Stick, S. L. (2006). Using Mixed-Methods Sequential Explanatory Design: From Theory to Practice. *Field Methods*, *18*(1), 3–20. doi:10.1177/1525822X05282260

Ivanova, M. ve Ivanov, G. (2011). Enhancement of learning and teaching in computer graphics through marker augmented reality technology. *International Journal on New Computer Architectures and Their Applications*, *1*(1), 176–184.

Jafar, R. M. S., & Ahmad, W. (2023). Tourist loyalty in the metaverse: The role of immersive tourism experience and cognitive perceptions. *Tourism Review*.

Jain, S., Lall, M., & Singh, A. (2020). Teachers' voices on the impact of covid-19 on school education: Are Ed-tech companies really the Panacea? *Contemporary Education Dialogue*, *18*(1), 58–89. doi:10.1177/0973184920976433

Jamali, S., Shiratuddin, M. F., & Wong, K. (2014). An overview of mobile-augmented reality in higher education. *International Journal on Recent Trends In Engineering & Technology*, *11*(1), 229–238.

Jantjies, M., Moodley, T., & Maart, R. (2018, December). Experiential learning through virtual and augmented reality in higher education. In *Proceedings of the 2018 international conference on education technology management* (pp. 42-45). 10.1145/3300942.3300956

Javornik, A. (2016). Augmented reality: Research agenda for studying the impact of its media characteristics on consumer behaviour. *Journal of Retailing and Consumer Services*, *30*, 252–261. doi:10.1016/j.jretconser.2016.02.004

Jereb, E., Urh, M., Jerebic, J., & Šprajc, P. (2018). Gender differences and the awareness of plagiarism in higher education. *Social Psychology of Education, 21*(2), 409–426. doi:10.1007/s11218-017-9421-y

Johnson, D. W., & Johnson, F. P. (2009). *Joining together: Group theory and group skills*. Pearson.

Johnson, L., Adams Becker, S., Cummins, M., Estrada, V., Freeman, A., & Ludgate, H. (2018). *NMC/CoSN Horizon Report: 2018 Higher Education Edition*. The New Media Consortium.

Johnson, L., Adams Becker, S., Estrada, V., & Freeman, A. (2015). *NMC/CoSN Horizon Report: 2015 K-* (12th ed.). The New Media Consortium.

Jonassen, D. H. (2010). *Learning to solve problems: A handbook for designing problem-solving learning environments*. Routledge. doi:10.4324/9780203847527

Joseph Evanick. (2023, November 21). Ethical dilemmas in student data privacy: Navigating edtech safeguards. eLearning Industry. https://elearningindustry.com/ethical-dilemmas-in-student-data-privacy-navigating-edtech-safeguards

Junco, R. (2014). Beyond screen time: What minecraft teaches kids. *Atlantic (Boston, Mass.)*.

Jung, T., Chung, N., & Leue, M. C. (2015). The determinants of recommendations to use augmented reality technologies: The case of a Korean theme park. *Tourism Management, 49*, 75–86. doi:10.1016/j.tourman.2015.02.013

K, P. (2018, November 4). *School textbooks to turn smarter with QR codes from this year*. The New Indian Express. Retrieved March 1, 2024, from https://www.newindianexpress.com/cities/bengaluru/2018/Oct/29/school-textbooks-to-turn-smarter-with-qr-codes-from-this-year-1891393.html

Kafai, Y. B. (2006). Playing and making games for learning. *Games and Culture, 1*(1), 36–40. doi:10.1177/1555412005281767

Kafai, Y. B., & Burke, Q. (2015). Constructionist gaming: Understanding the benefits of making games for learning. *Educational Psychologist, 50*(4), 313–334. doi:10.1080/00461520.2015.1124022 PMID:27019536

Kagan, S., & Kagan, M. (1994). Cooperative Learning. Academic Press.

Kala, S., Isaramalai, S.-A., & Pohthong, A. (2010). Electronic learning and constructivism: A model for nursing education. *Nurse Education Today, 30*(1), 61–66. doi:10.1016/j.nedt.2009.06.002 PMID:19573956

Kalemkuş, J., & Kalemkuş, F. (2023). Effect of the use of augmented reality applications on academic achievement of student in science education: Meta analysis review. *Interactive Learning Environments, 31*(9), 6017–6034. doi:10.1080/10494820.2022.2027458

Kallio, H., Pietilä, A. M., Johnson, M., & Kangasniemi, M. (2016). Systematic methodological review: Developing a framework for a qualitative semi-structured interview guide. *Journal of Advanced Nursing*, *72*(12), 2954–2965. doi:10.1111/jan.13031 PMID:27221824

Kamińska, D., Zwoliński, G., Laska-Leśniewicz, A., Raposo, R., Vairinhos, M., Pereira, E., Urem, F., Ljubić Hinić, M., Haamer, R. E., & Anbarjafari, G. (2023). Augmented reality: Current and new trends in education. *Electronics (Basel)*, *12*(16), 3531. doi:10.3390/electronics12163531

Kaplan, A., & Haenlein, M. (2020). Rulers of the world, unite! The challenges and opportunities of artificial intelligence. *Business Horizons*, *63*(1), 37–50. doi:10.1016/j.bushor.2019.09.003

Kaplan, Cruit, J., Endsley, M., Beers, S. M., Sawyer, B. D., & Hancock, P. A. (2021). The effects of virtual reality, augmented reality, and mixed reality as training enhancement methods: A meta-analysis. *Human Factors*, *63*(4), 706–726. doi:10.1177/0018720820904229 PMID:32091937

Kapp, K. M. (2012). *The gamification of learning and ınstruction: game-based methods and strategies for training and education*. John Wiley & Sons.

Karademir Coşkun, T., & Alper, A. (2020). An ecological approach to technology appropriation. In M. Hicks & R. R. Zhang (Eds.), *Examining the Roles of Teachers and Students in Mastering New Technologies* (pp. 79–106). IGI Global. doi:10.4018/978-1-7998-2104-5.ch004

Karakaş, M., & Özerbaş, M. (2020). Fizik dersinde artırılmış gerçeklik uygulamalarının öğrencilerin akademik başarılarına etkisi. *Eğitim Teknolojisi Kuram ve Uygulama*, *10*(2), 452–468. doi:10.17943/etku.691179

Karamustafaoğlu, O., & Kılıç, M. F. (2020). Investıgatıon of natıonal scıentıfıc studıes about educatıonal games. *Atatürk Üniversitesi Kazım Karabekir Eğitim Fakültesi Dergisi*, (40), 1–25.

Kastens, K. A., & Ishikawa, T. (2006). Spatial thinking in the geosciences and cognitive sciences: A cross-disciplinary look at the intersection of the two fields. *Special Papers-Geological Society of America*, *413*, 53. doi:10.1130/2006.2413(05)

Katju, M. (2011). Plagiarism and social sciences. *Economic and Political Weekly*, 45–48.

Kaur, B., & Singh, J. P. (2023). *Empowering Research Communities: Implementing ETDs as Catalysts for Knowledge Sharing at Chitkara University Punjab*. Academic Press.

Kayabaşı, Y. (2005). Sanal gerçeklik ve eğitim amaçlı kullanılması. *The Turkish Online Journal of Educational Technology*, *4*(3), 151–166.

Kayisolu, N. B., & Temel, C. (2017). An Examination of Attitudes towards Cheating in Exams by Physical Education and Sports High School Students. *Universal Journal of Educational Research*, *5*(8), 1396–1402. doi:10.13189/ujer.2017.050813

Kesim. (2012). Augmented reality in education: current technologies and the potential for education. *Procedia-social and behavioural sciences*, *47*, 297-302.

Khan. (2020). Corona virus pandemic paving ways to next generation of learning and teaching: futuristic cloud based educational model. Available at SSRN 3669832. doi:10.2139/ssrn.3669832

Khurshid, F., Bibi, M., & Bibi, M. (2020). Effectiveness of educational videos and games for the concepts clarity and understanding of social studies subject: An intervention study. *Pakistan Journal of Education*, *37*(2), 61–78. doi:10.30971/pje.v37i2.1310

Kılıç, S. (2013). Sampling methods. *Journal of Mood Disorders*, *3*(1), 44–46. doi:10.5455/jmood.20130325011730

Kim, C., Yoon, H. C., Kim, D. H., & Do, Y. R. (2018). Spectroscopic influence of virtual reality and augmented reality display devices on the human nonvisual characteristics and melatonin suppression response. *IEEE Photonics Journal*, *10*(4), 1–11. doi:10.1109/JPHOT.2021.3107852

Kim, M., & Shin, J. (2016). The pedagogical benefits of SimCity in urban geography education. *The Journal of Geography*, *115*(2), 39–50. doi:10.1080/00221341.2015.1061585

Kırıkkaya, E. B. (2018). Güneş sistemi ve ötesi ünitesinde artırılmış gerçeklik teknolojisi kullanılmasının öğrenci akademik başarısına etkisi. *Kastamonu Eğitim Dergisi*, *26*(1), 181–189. doi:10.24106/kefdergi.375861

Kiryakova. (2018). The potential of augmented reality to transform education into smart education. *TEM Journal*, *7*(3), 556.

Klausmeier, H. J. (1992). Concept learning and concept teaching. *Educational Psychologist*, *27*(3), 267–286. doi:10.1207/s15326985ep2703_1

Klimova, B., & Polakova, P. (2020). Students' perceptions of an EFL vocabulary learning mobile application. *Education Sciences*, *10*(2), 37. doi:10.3390/educsci10020037

Klopfer, E., & Squire, K. (2008). Environmental Detectives—The development of an augmented reality platform for environmental simulations. *Educational Technology Research and Development*, *56*(2), 203–228. doi:10.1007/s11423-007-9037-6

Kobets, V., Liubchenko, V., Popovych, I., & Koval, S. (2021). Institutional Aspects of Integrated Quality Assurance of Engineering Study Programs at HEI Using ICT. In *Design, Simulation, Manufacturing: The Innovation Exchange* (pp. 301–310). Springer International Publishing. doi:10.1007/978-3-030-77719-7_30

Kocoń, J., Cichecki, I., Kaszyca, O., Kochanek, M., Szydło, D., Baran, J., Bielaniewicz, J., Gruza, M., Janz, A., Kanclerz, K., Kocoń, A., Koptyra, B., Mieleszczenko-Kowszewicz, W., Miłkowski, P., Oleksy, M., Piasecki, M., Radliński, Ł., Wojtasik, K., Woźniak, S., & Kazienko, P. (2023). ChatGPT: Jack of all trades, master of none. *Information Fusion*, *99*, 101861. doi:10.1016/j.inffus.2023.101861

Koka, V. (2018). *Sosyal bilgiler dersinde kullanılan bilgisayar destekli eğitsel oyunların öğrencilerin ders başarısına olan etkisi* [The effect of computer aıded educatıonal games used ın socıal scıences course] (Unpublished master thesis), İnönü Üniversitesi Eğitim Bilimleri Enstitüsü, Malatya.

Kolo, K. (2021). 9 AR Platforms Bring Augmented Reality Content in the Classroom. Available at https://www.thevrara.com/blog2/2021/10/26/9-desktop-ar-platforms-to-bring-ar-content-in-the-classroom

Koretz, D. M. (2008). *Measuring up*. Harvard University Press. doi:10.4159/9780674039728

Köstlbauer, J. (2018). The strange attraction of simulation realism, authenticity, virtuality. In Playing with the Past: Digital Games and the Simulation of History (pp. 169-183). Bloomsbury Academic.

Kraus, S., Kanbach, D. K., Krysta, P. M., Steinhoff, M. M., & Tomini, N. (2022). Facebook and the creation of the metaverse: Radical business model innovation or incremental transformation? *International Journal of Entrepreneurial Behaviour & Research*, *28*(9), 52–77. doi:10.1108/IJEBR-12-2021-0984

Krauss, S. E., Hamzah, A., Omar, Z., Suandi, T., Ismail, I. A., Zahari, M. Z., & Nor, Z. M. (2009). Preliminary investigation and interview guide development for studying how Malaysian farmers' form their mental models of farming. *The Qualitative Report*, *14*(2), 245.

Krüger, J. M., Buchholz, A., & Bodemer, D. (2019, December). Augmented reality in education: three unique characteristics from a user's perspective. In Proc. 27th Int. Conf. on Comput. in Educ (pp. 412-422). Academic Press.

Krüger. (2019, December). Augmented reality in education: three unique characteristics from a user's perspective. In *Proc. 27th Int. Conf. on Comput. In Educ* (pp. 412-422). Academic Press.

Küçük, S., Kapakin, S., & Goktas, Y. (2015). Medical faculty students' views on anatomy learning via mobile augmented reality technology. *Journal of Higher Education and Science*, *5*(3), 316–323. doi:10.5961/jhes.2015.133

Kugelman, A., Shaoul, J., Ben-Ami, R., Shoenfeld, Y., & Wientroub, S. (2018). Use of augmented reality technology in orthopedic surgery. *Acta Orthopaedica*, *89*(5), 503–507. PMID:29790397

Kulshrestha, D., Tiwari, M. K., Shalender, K., & Sharma, S. (2022). Consumer Acatalepsy Towards Buying Behaviour for Need-Based Goods for Sustainability During the COVID-19 Pandemic. *Indian Journal of Marketing*, *52*(10), 50–63. doi:10.17010/ijom/2022/v52/i10/172347

Kumar, P. P., Thallapalli, R., Akshay, R., Sai, K. S., Sai, K. S., & Srujan, G. S. (2022, May). State-of-the-Art: Implementation of Augmented Reality and Virtual Reality with the Integration of 5G in the Classroom. In AIP Conference Proceedings (Vol. 2418, No. 1). AIP Publishing.

Kumar, V., Sharma, D., & Chauhan, S. (2023). Role of Customer Experience-Driven Business Innovation Framework for the Modern Enterprises. In Innovation, Strategy, and Transformation Frameworks for the Modern Enterprise (pp. 310-326). IGI Global. doi:10.4018/979-8-3693-0458-7.ch013

Kumar, A., Shankar, A., Shaik, A. S., Jain, G., & Malibari, A. (2023). Risking it all in the metaverse ecosystem: Forecasting resistance towards the enterprise metaverse. *Information Technology & People*. Advance online publication. doi:10.1108/ITP-04-2023-0374

Lang, J. M. (2013). *Cheating Lessons: Learning From Academic Dishonesty*. Harvard University Press. doi:10.4159/harvard.9780674726239

Lannon, J. M., & Gurak, L. J. (2011). *Technical communication*. Longman Publishing Group.

Lata Dangwal, K. (2017). Blended Learning: An Innovative Approach. *Universal Journal of Educational Research*, *5*(1), 129–136. doi:10.13189/ujer.2017.050116

Lawshe, C. H. (1975). A quantitative approach to content validity. *Personnel Psychology*, *28*(4), 563–575. doi:10.1111/j.1744-6570.1975.tb01393.x

Learning, E. (n.d.). Appsembler. https://appsembler.com/glossary/what-is-experiential-learning/

Learning, S. (2022, June 15). 12 Project Based Learning (PBL) Examples. Creative Learning Systems. https://www.smartlablearning.com/project-based-learning-examples/

Lee, K., & Rha, I. (2009). Influence of structure and interaction on student achievement and satisfaction in web-based distance learning. *Journal of Educational Technology & Society*, *12*(4), 372–382.

Liagkou, Salmas, D., & Stylios, C. (2019). Realizing virtual reality learning environment for industry 4.0. *Procedia CIRP*, *79*, 712–717. doi:10.1016/j.procir.2019.02.025

Liarokapis, F., & Anderson, E. F. (2010). *Using augmented reality as a medium to assist teaching in higher education*. Academic Press.

Lim, W. M., Gupta, S., Aggarwal, A., Paul, J., & Sadhna, P. (2021). How do digital natives perceive and react toward online advertising? Implications for SMEs. *Journal of Strategic Marketing*, 1–35. doi:10.1080/0965254X.2021.1941204

Lonsdale, M., & Anderson, M. (2012). *Preparing 21st century learners: The case for school community collaborations*. Australian Council for Educational Research.

López Belmonte, J., Moreno-Guerrero, A. J., López Núñez, J. A., & Pozo Sánchez, S. (2019). Analysis of the productive, structural, and dynamic development of augmented reality in higher education research on the web of science. *Applied Sciences (Basel, Switzerland)*, *9*(24), 5306. doi:10.3390/app9245306

Lucander, H., & Christersson, C. (2020). Engagement for quality development in higher education: A process for quality assurance of assessment. *Quality in Higher Education*, *26*(2), 135–155. doi:10.1080/13538322.2020.1761008

Lund, B., & Wang, T. (2019). Effect of virtual reality on learning motivation and academic performance: What value may virtual reality have on library instruction? *Kansas Library Association College and University Libraries Section Proceedings*, *9*(1), 4. doi:10.4148/2160-942X.1073

Maguth, B. M., List, J. S., & Wunderle, M. (2015). Teaching social studies with video games. *Social Studies*, *106*(1), 32–36. doi:10.1080/00377996.2014.961996

Mahmoudi, S., Jafari, E., Nasrabadi, H. A., & Liaghatdar, M. J. (2012). Holistic education: An approach *for 21 century. International Education Studies, 5*(2), 178–186. doi:10.5539/ies.v5n3p178

Mandal, A. (2023). How surgeons are using AI to diagnose a brain tumour. Available at: https://www.financialexpress.com/healthcare/news-healthcare/how-surgeons-are-using-ai-to-diagnose-brain-tumor-bkg/3271108/

Manohar, S., Mittal, A., & Marwah, S. (2020). Service innovation, corporate reputation and word-of-mouth in the banking sector: A test on multigroup-moderated mediation effect. *Benchmarking, 27*(1), 406–429. doi:10.1108/BIJ-05-2019-0217

Manwani, K. (2022, April). *An empirical study on using storytelling as a learning tool for online and offline education.* http://Journalppw.com

Marcon, N., & Faulkner, J. (2016). Exploring minecraft as a pedagogy to motivate girls' literacy practices in the secondary English classroom. *Engineers Australia, 51*(1), 63–69.

Marshall, S. (2014). Exploring the ethical implications of moocs. *Distance Education, 35*(2), 250–262. doi:10.1080/01587919.2014.917706

Martín-Gutiérrez, J., Fabiani, P., Benesova, W., Meneses, M. D., & Mora, C. E. (2015). Augmented reality to promote collaborative and autonomous learning in higher education. *Computers in Human Behavior, 51*, 752–761. doi:10.1016/j.chb.2014.11.093

Mathewson, J. H. (1999). Visual-spatial thinking: An aspect of science overlooked by educators. *Science Education, 83*(1), 33–54. doi:10.1002/(SICI)1098-237X(199901)83:1<33::AID-SCE2>3.0.CO;2-Z

Matsumoto, D., & Hwang, H. C. (2013). Assessing cross-cultural competence: A review of available tests. *Journal of Cross-Cultural Psychology, 44*(6), 849–873. doi:10.1177/0022022113492891

Mavoa, J., Carter, M., & Gibbs, M. (2018). Children and minecraft: A survey of children's digital play. *New Media & Society, 20*(9), 3283–3303. doi:10.1177/1461444817745320

Mayer, R. E. (1992). *Thinking, problem-solving, cognition.* W H Freeman/Times Books/Henry Holt & Co.

McCabe, D. L., Treviño, L. K., & Butterfield, K. D. (2001). Cheating in academic institutions: A decade of research. *Ethics & Behavior, 11*(3), 219–232. doi:10.1207/S15327019EB1103_2

McDury, J., & Alterio, M. (2001). Achieving Reflective Learning using storytelling pathways. *Innovations in Education and Teaching International, 38*(1), 63–73. doi:10.1080/147032901300002864

MCEETYA. (2008). *Melbourne Declaration on Educational Goals for Young Australians.* Ministerial Council on Education, Employment, Training and Youth Affairs.

McGonigal, J. (2011). *Reality is broken: Why games make us better and how they can change the world.* Penguin.

McGrath. J. E. (1995). Methodology matters: Doing research in the behavioral and social sciences. In Readings in Human–Computer Interaction (pp. 152–169). Elsevier. doi:10.1016/B978-0-08-051574-8.50019-4

McGraw, K. L., & Westerman, D. L. (2017). Innovations in Augmented Reality: Pedagogical Shifts for Mobile Learning. *TechTrends*, *61*(1), 5–12.

McGurgan, P., Calvert, K. L., Narula, K., Celenza, A., Nathan, E. A., & Jorm, C. (2020). Medical students' opinions on professional behaviours: The Professionalism of Medical Students' (PoMS) study. *Medical Teacher*, *42*(3), 340–350. doi:10.1080/0142159X.2019.1687862 PMID:31738619

McLellan, H. (1996). Virtual realities. In Handbook of research for educational communications and technology. Macmillan Library Reference.

MEB. (2004). İlköğretim sosyal bilgiler dersi 4-5. sınıflar öğretim program [Elementary social studies curriculum for 4th and 5th grades]. Talim ve Terbiye Başkanlığı, Ankara: MEB.

MEB. (2018). Sosyal bilgiler dersi (4, 5, 6 ve 7. sınıflar) öğretim program [Social studies curriculum for 4th, 5th, 6th and 7th grades]. Ankara.

MEB. (2021). *5. Sınıf sosyal bilgiler ders kitabı* [5th grade social studies textbook]. Millî Eğitim Bakanlığı.

Mendes, A. S., Silva, L. A., Blas, H. S. S., de La Iglesia, D. H., Encinas, F. G., Leithardt, V. R. Q., & González, G. V. (2021). Physical movement helps learning: teaching using tracking objects with depth camera. In Trends and Applications in Information Systems and Technologies: Volume 4 9 (pp. 183-193). Springer International Publishing. doi:10.1007/978-3-030-72654-6_18

Merriam, S. B. (1998). *Qualitative research and case study applications in education*. Jossey-Bass Publishers.

Mhlanga, D., & Moloi, T. (2020). COVID-19 and the digital transformation of education: What are we learning on 4IR in South Africa? *Education Sciences*, *10*(7), 180. doi:10.3390/educsci10070180

Miles, M. B., & Huberman, A. M. (1994). Qualitative data analysis: An expanded sourcebook. Thousand Oaks.

Miles, M. B., Huberman, A. M., & Saldana, J. (2014). Qualitative Data Analysis: A Methods Sourcebook. *Sage (Atlanta, Ga.)*.

Miller, Y., & Izsak, R. (2017). Students' involvement in academic dishonesty and their attitudes towards copying in exams and academic papers. *Sociology and Anthropology (Alhambra, Calif.)*, *5*(3), 225–232. doi:10.13189/sa.2017.050306

Mishra, P., & Koehler, M. J. (2006). Technological pedagogical content knowledge: A framework for teacher knowledge. *Teachers College Record*, *108*(6), 1017–1054. doi:10.1111/j.1467-9620.2006.00684.x

Mittal, A., Aggarwal, A., & Mittal, R. (2020). Predicting university students' adoption of mobile news applications: The role of perceived hedonic value and news motivation. *International Journal of E-Services and Mobile Applications, 12*(4), 42–59. doi:10.4018/IJESMA.2020100103

Mittal, A., Dhiman, R., & Lamba, P. (2019). Skill mapping for blue-collar employees and organisational performance: A qualitative assessment. *Benchmarking, 26*(4), 1255–1274. doi:10.1108/BIJ-08-2018-0228

Mittal, A., Mantri, A., Tandon, U., & Dwivedi, Y. K. (2022). A unified perspective on the adoption of online teaching in higher education during the COVID-19 pandemic. *Information Discovery and Delivery, 50*(2), 117–132. doi:10.1108/IDD-09-2020-0114

Mix, K. S., Levine, S. C., Cheng, Y.-L., Young, C. J., Hambrick, D. Z., & Konstantopoulos, S. (2017). The latent structure of spatial skills and mathematics: Further evidence from wave 2. *Journal of Cognition and Development, 4*, 465–492. doi:10.1080/15248372.2017.1346658

Mohit Sharma. (2020). Impact of COVID-19 on online education sector and edtech companies. *PalArch's Journal of Archaeology of Egypt / Egyptology, 17*(12), 1278-1288. Retrieved from https://archives.palarch.nl/index.php/jae/article/view/6802

Moon, K., & Blackman, D. (2014). A Guide to Understanding Social Science Research for Natural Scientists. *Conservation Biology, 28*(5), 1167–1177. doi:10.1111/cobi.12326

Mørch, A. I., Eie, S., & Mifsud, L. (2018). Tradeoffs in combining domain-specific and generic skills' practice in minecraft in social studies in teacher education. *Cultures of Participation in the Digital Age, 2101*(6), 44–52.

Morin, J. É., Olsson, C., & Atikcan, E. Ö. (2021). *Research methods in the social sciences: An az of key concepts.* Oxford University Press. doi:10.1093/hepl/9780198850298.001.0001

Morse, J. M. (2007). Enhancing the credibility of qualitative research. *Health Promotion Practice, 8*(2), 140–144. PMID:17384405

Muzyleva, I., Yazykova, L., Gorlach, A., & Gorlach, Y. (2021, June). Augmented and Virtual Reality Technologies in Education. In *2021 1st International Conference on Technology Enhanced Learning in Higher Education (TELE)* (pp. 99-103). IEEE. 10.1109/TELE52840.2021.9482568

Nabokova, L. S., &Zagidullina, F. R. (2019). Outlooks of applying augmented and virtual reality technologies in higher education. *Professional education in the modern world, 9*(2), 2710-2719.

NEA (National Education Association). (2010). *21st century knowledge and skills in educator preparation.* Retrieved from http://www.p21.org/storage/documents/aacte_p21_whitepaper2010.pdf

Neffati, O. S., Setiawan, R., Jayanthi, P., Vanithamani, S., Sharma, D. K., Regin, R., ... Sengan, S. (2021). An educational tool for enhanced mobile e-Learning for technical higher education using mobile devices for augmented reality. *Microprocessors and Microsystems, 83*, 104030. doi:10.1016/j.micpro.2021.104030

Nesenbergs, K., Abolins, V., Ormanis, J., & Mednis, A. (2020). Use of augmented and virtual reality in remote higher education: A systematic umbrella review. *Education Sciences*, *11*(1), 8. doi:10.3390/educsci11010008

Newzoo. (2020). *The Impact of Coronavirus on Games and Esports: Our First Thoughts*. Retreived 13 June 2023 from https://newzoo.com/news/impact-of-coronavirus-on-games-and-esports-our-first-thoughts/

Nguyen, V. T., Jung, K., & Dang, T. (2019, December). Creating virtual reality and augmented reality development in classroom: Is it a hype? In *2019 IEEE International Conference on Artificial Intelligence and Virtual Reality (AIVR)* (pp. 212-2125). IEEE. 10.1109/AIVR46125.2019.00045

Nietfeld, J. L. (2019). Predicting transfer from a game-based learning environment. *Computers & Education*, 146.

Ninno Muniz, R., Frizzo Stefenon, S., Gouvêa Buratto, W., Nied, A., Meyer, L. H., Finardi, E. C., & Ramati Pereira da Rocha, B. (2020). Tools for measuring energy sustainability: A comparative review. *Energies*, *13*(9), 2366. doi:10.3390/en13092366

NIU. (2023). *Academic Dishonesty Definition and Types*. https://www.niu.edu/academic-integrity/faculty/types/index.shtml

Northouse, P. G. (2018). *Leadership: Theory and practice*. Sage Publications.

Oakland, T., & Harrison, P. L. (2008). Adaptive behaviors and skills. In *Adaptive Behavior Assessment System-II*. Elsevier. doi:10.1016/B978-012373586-7.00001-1

Oberdörfer, S., Birnstiel, S., Latoschik, M. E., & Grafe, S. (2021, June). Mutual benefits: Interdisciplinary education of pre-service teachers and hci students in vr/ar learning environment design. *Frontiers in Education*, *6*, 693012. doi:10.3389/feduc.2021.693012

Orok, E., Adeniyi, F., Williams, T., Dosunmu, O., Ikpe, F., Orakwe, C., & Kukoyi, O. (2023). Causes and mitigation of academic dishonesty among healthcare students in a Nigerian university. *International Journal for Educational Integrity*, *19*(1), 13. doi:10.1007/s40979-023-00135-2

Öztürk, T., & Yeşiltaş, E. (2015). The effect of computer supported instruction on students achievements in civics topics of social studies lesson. *E-International Journal of Educational Research*, *6*(2), 86–101.

P21. (2009). *P21 framework definitions*. Retrieved from http://www.p21.org/storage/documents/P21_Framework_Definitions.pdf

Pane, J. F., Steiner, E. D., Baird, M. D., & Hamilton, L. S. (2017). *Informing progress: Insights on personalized learning implementation and effects* (RAND Research Report RR-2041-EDU). RAND Corporation. https://doi.org/ doi:10.7249/RR2041

Pantelidis, V. S. (2010). Reasons to use virtual reality in education and training courses and a model to determine when to use virtual reality. *Themes in Science and Technology Education*, *2*(1-2), 59–70.

Pan, X., Zheng, M., Xu, X., & Campbell, A. G. (2021). Knowing your student: Targeted teaching decision support through asymmetric mixed reality collaborative learning. *IEEE Access : Practical Innovations, Open Solutions*, *9*, 164742–164751. doi:10.1109/ACCESS.2021.3134589

Papanastasiou, Drigas, A., Skianis, C., Lytras, M., & Papanastasiou, E. (2019). Virtual and augmented reality effects on K-12, higher and tertiary education students' twenty-first century skills. *Virtual Reality (Waltham Cross)*, *23*(4), 425–436. doi:10.1007/s10055-018-0363-2

Paszkiewicz, Salach, M., Dymora, P., Bolanowski, M., Budzik, G., & Kubiak, P. (2021). Methodology of implementing virtual reality in education for industry 4.0. *Sustainability (Basel)*, *13*(9), 5049. doi:10.3390/su13095049

Patel, N. V. (2003). A holistic approach to learning and teaching interaction: Factors in the development of critical learners. *International Journal of Educational Management*, *17*(6), 272–284. doi:10.1108/09513540310487604

Patton, M. Q. (2002). *Qualitative research and evaluation methods*. Sage Publications.

Pavela, G. (1978). Judicial review of academic decision-making after, *Horowitz. School Law Journal*, *55*, 55–75.

Penn, M., & Umesh, R. (2019). The use of virtual learning environments and achievement in physics content tests. *Proceedings of the International Conference on Education and New Developments* (Vol. 1). https://eric.ed.gov/?id=EJ1236608

Peppler, K., Danish, J., Zaitlen, B., Glosson, D., Jacobs, A., & Phelps, D. (2010). BeeSim: Leveraging wearable computers in participatory simulations with young children. *Proceedings of the Ninth International Conference on Interaction Design and Children (IDC 2010)*, (pp. 246–249). ACM. 10.1145/1810543.1810582

Perini, S., Oliveira, M., Margoudi, M., & Taisch, M. (2018). The use of digital game based learning in manufacturing education–a case study. *Learning and Collaboration Technologies. Learning and Teaching: 5th International Conference, LCT 2018, Held as Part of HCI International 2018, Las Vegas, NV, USA, July 15-20, 2018 Proceedings*, *5*(Part II), 185–199.

Phakamach, P., Senarith, P., & Wachirawongpaisarn, S. (2022). The metaverse in education: The future of immersive teaching & learning. *RICE Journal of Creative Entrepreneurship and Management*, *3*(2), 75–88.

Philippe, Souchet, A. D., Lameras, P., Petridis, P., Caporal, J., Coldeboeuf, G., & Duzan, H. (2020). Multimodal teaching, learning and training in virtual reality: A review and case study. *Virtual Reality & Intelligent Hardware*, *2*(5), 421–442. doi:10.1016/j.vrih.2020.07.008

Piovesan, S. D., Passerino, L. M., & Pereira, A. S. (2012). Virtual reality as a tool in the education. *IADIS International conference on cognition and exploratory learning in digital age*, 295-298.

Poláková, P., & Klímová, B. (2019). Mobile technology and Generation Z in the English language classroom—A preliminary study. *Education Sciences*, *9*(3), 203. doi:10.3390/educsci9030203

Pramoth, A. (2022, November 18). Modern trends in education pros and cons. *The Times of India*. https://timesofindia.indiatimes.com/readersblog/modern-trends-in-education-pros-and-cons/modern-trends-in-education-pros-and-cons-46765/

Pulakos, E. D., Arad, S., Donovan, M. A., & Plamondon, K. E. (2000). Adaptability in the workplace: Development of a taxonomy of adaptive performance. *The Journal of Applied Psychology*, *85*(4), 612–624. doi:10.1037/0021-9010.85.4.612 PMID:10948805

R, V., Dimri, A., Chhetri, V., Fyler, T., & Prabhu, A. (2024, February 5). *Byju's valuation down 99%: India's Edtech Decacorn seeking $200m at $225M valuation, what exactly happened? - TFN*. Tech Funding News. Retrieved March 1, 2024, from https://techfundingnews.com/byjus-valuation-down-99-indias-edtech-decacorn-seeking-200m-at-225m-valuation-what-exactly-happened/#:~:text=However%2C%20the%20same%20year%20witnessed,its%20peak%20of%20%2422%20billion

Rader, E., Love, R., Reano, D., Dousay, T. A., & Wingerter, N. (2021). Pandemic minecrafting: An analysis of the perceptions of and lessons learned from a gamified virtual geology field camp. *Geoscience Communication*, *4*(4), 475–492. doi:10.5194/gc-4-475-2021

Radosavljevic, S., Radosavljevic, V., & Grgurovic, B. (2020). The potential of implementing augmented reality into vocational higher education through mobile learning. *Interactive Learning Environments*, *28*(4), 404–418. doi:10.1080/10494820.2018.1528286

Raja. (2021). Conceptual Origins, Technological Advancements, and Impacts of Using Virtual Reality Technology in Education. *Webology, 18*(2).

Raja, M., & Lakshmi Priya, G. G. (2022). Using virtual reality and augmented reality with ICT tools for enhancing quality in the changing academic environment in COVID-19 pandemic: An empirical study. In *InTechnologies, artificial Intelligence and the Future of learning post-COVID-19* (pp. 467–482). Springer. doi:10.1007/978-3-030-93921-2_26

Raju, G. V. (2020). Art of Storytelling: A Critical Perspective on English Language Teaching. *Journal of Emerging Technologies and Innovative Research.*

Rana, S., Udunuwara, M., Dewasiri, N. J., Kashif, M., & Rathnasiri, M. S. H. (2022). Is South Asia ready for the next universe–metaverse? Arguments and suggestions for further research. *South Asian Journal of Marketing*, *3*(2), 77–81. doi:10.1108/SAJM-10-2022-141

Ravenscroft, A., Warburton, S., Hatzipanagos, S., & Conole, G. (2012). Designing and evaluating social media for learning: Shaping social networking into social learning? *Journal of Computer Assisted Learning*, *28*(3), 177–182. doi:10.1111/j.1365-2729.2012.00484.x

Reich, J. (2020). *Failure to disrupt: why technology alone can't transform education*. Harvard University Press.

Robin, B. R. (2008). Digital storytelling: A powerful technology tool for the 21st century classroom. *Theory into Practice*, *47*(3), 220–228. doi:10.1080/00405840802153916

Ross, T. (2019). Top 10 Augmented Reality Tools for the Classroom. Available at https://www.ebsco.com/blogs/ebscopost/top-10-augmented-reality-tools-classroom

Sala, G., & Gobet, F. (2019). Cognitive training does not enhance general cognition. *Trends in Cognitive Sciences, 23*(1), 9–20. doi:10.1016/j.tics.2018.10.004 PMID:30471868

Salah, Abidi, M., Mian, S., Krid, M., Alkhalefah, H., & Abdo, A. (2019). Virtual reality-based engineering education to enhance manufacturing sustainability in industry 4.0. *Sustainability (Basel), 11*(5), 1477. doi:10.3390/su11051477

Saldana, J. (2009). *The Coding Manual for Qualitative Researchers*. Sage Publications.

Salehudin, M., & Degeng, I. N. S. (2019). The Influence of Creative Learning Assisted by Instagram to Improve Middle School Students' Learning Outcomes of Graphic Design Subject. *Journal for the Education of Gifted Young Scientists, 7*(4), 849–865. doi:10.17478/jegys.626513

Salimovna, F. D., & Salimovna, Y. N. (2019). Security issues in E-Learning system. *2019 International Conference on Information Science and Communications Technologies (ICISCT)*. IEEE.

Saluja, S. (2022). Identity theft fraud-major loophole for FinTech industry in India. *Journal of Financial Crime.*

Saluja, S., Aggarwal, A., & Mittal, A. (2021). Understanding the fraud theories and advancing with integrity model. *Journal of Financial Crime.*

Sanchez-Mena, A., & Marti-Parreño, J. (2017). Drivers and barriers to adopting gamification: Teachers' perspectives. *Electronic Journal of e-Learning, 5*(15), 434–443.

Sangeeta, & Tandon, U. (2021). Factors influencing adoption of online teaching by school teachers: A study during COVID-19 pandemic. *Journal of Public Affairs, 21*(4), e2503.

Sangeeta, T., & Tandon, U. (2021). Factors influencing adoption of online teaching by school teachers: A study during COVID-19 pandemic. *Journal of Public Affairs, 21*(4), e2503. doi:10.1002/pa.2503 PMID:33173442

Sanır, F. (2000). *Coğrafya terimleri sözlüğü* [Dictionary of geography terms]. Gazi Kitapevi.

Sarigoz, O. (2019). Augmented reality, virtual reality and digital games: A research on teacher candidates. *Educational Policy Analysis and Strategic Research, 14*(3), 41–63. doi:10.29329/epasr.2019.208.3

Sarma, A., & Jaybhave, S. (2024, January 24). *Edtech in India: Boom, Bust, or bubble?* Edtech in India: Boom, bust, or bubble? Retrieved March 1, 2024, from https://www.orfonline.org/expert-speak/edtech-in-india-boom-bust-or-bubble#:~:text=The%20country%20had%20emerged%20decisively,4.73%20billion%20in%202021%20alone

Saunders, R., & Katula Mwila, N. (2023, September 16). *How can you use gamification to enhance student engagement in higher education?* [Review of How can you use gamification to enhance student engagement in higher education?]. Linkedin. www.linkedin.com

Saxena, K. (2023). Future Prospects of Augmented Reality in the Education Industry. Available at https://www.codingninjas.com/studio/library/augmented-reality-in-education-industry

Scavarelli, A., Arya, A., & Teather, R. J. (2019). Circles: exploring multi-platform accessible, socially scalable VR in the classroom. In 2019 IEEE Games, Entertainment, Media Conference (GEM) (pp. 1-4). IEEE. 10.1109/GEM.2019.8897532

Scavarelli, A., Arya, A., & Teather, R. J. (2021). Virtual reality and augmented reality in social learning spaces: A literature review. *Virtual Reality (Waltham Cross)*, *25*(1), 257–277. doi:10.1007/s10055-020-00444-8

Scheitle, C. P. (2011). Google's Insights for Search: A Note Evaluating the Use of Search Engine Data in Social Research. *Social Science Quarterly*, *92*(1), 285–295. doi:10.1111/j.1540-6237.2011.00768.x

Schug, M. C., Todd, R. J., & Beery, R. (1982). *Why kids don't like social studies*. National Council for the Social Studies.

Seidametova, Z. S., Abduramanov, Z. S., & Seydametov, G. S. (2021, July). Using augmented reality for architecture artifacts visualizations. *CEUR Workshop Proceedings*.

Selwyn, N., Hillman, T., Eynon, R., Ferreira, G., Knox, J., Macgilchrist, F., & Sancho-Gil, J. M. (2019). What's next for Ed-Tech? critical hopes and concerns for the 2020s. *Learning, Media and Technology*, *45*(1), 1–6. doi:10.1080/17439884.2020.1694945

Sena, C. C. R. G., & Jordãob, B. G. F. (2021). Challenges in the teaching of cartography during the COVID-19 pandemic: use of minecraft in the remote classroom setting. *Proceedings of the ICA*, (4). 10.5194/ica-proc-4-99-2021

Şendağ, S., & Odabaşı, H. F. (2009). Effects of an online problem-based learning course on content knowledge acquisition and critical thinking skills. *Computers & Education*, *53*(1), 132–141. doi:10.1016/j.compedu.2009.01.008

Seyfried, M., & Pohlenz, P. (2020). Assessing quality assurance in higher education: quality managers' perceptions of effectiveness. Academic Press.

Shaheen, M. Y. (2021). Applications of Artificial Intelligence (AI) in healthcare. *RE:view*. Advance online publication. doi:10.14293/S2199-1006.1.SOR-.PPVRY8K.v1

Shalender, K. (2023). *Skill development for society 5.0: A focus on the new-age skilling process. Innovations and Sustainability in Society 5.0*. Nova Science Publisher.

Shalender, K., & Shankar, S. (2023). *Building Innovation Culture for the Automobile Industry: Insights from the Indian Passenger Vehicle Market. Constructive Discontent in Execution*. Apple Academic Press.

Shalender, K., & Yadav, R. K. (2019). Strategic Flexibility, Manager Personality, and Firm Performance: The Case of Indian Automobile Industry. *Global Journal of Flexible Systems Managment*, *20*(1), 77–90. doi:10.1007/s40171-018-0204-x

Shalimov, A. (2023). Augmented reality in education: How to apply it to your EdTech Business. Available at https://easternpeak.com/blog/augmented-reality-in-education/

Shane, S., & Venkataraman, S. (2000). The promise of entrepreneurship as a field of research. *Academy of Management Review*, *25*(1), 217–226. doi:10.5465/amr.2000.2791611

Sharma, R., Mehta, K., & Vyas, V. (2023). Investigating academic dishonesty among business school students using fraud triangle theory and role of technology. *Journal of Education for Business*, *99*(2), 69–78. doi:10.1080/08832323.2023.2260925

Sharples, M., Arnedillo-Sánchez, I., Milrad, M., & Vavoula, G. (2009). Mobile learning. Small Screens, Big Ideas: Theories and Applications of Mobile Learning. Academic Press.

Sharples, M., Taylor, J., & Vavoula, G. (2007). A theory of learning for the mobile age. In The Sage Handbook of E-learning Research (pp. 221-247). Sage Publications.

Shepard, R. N., & Metzler, J. (1971). Mental rotation of three-dimensional objects. *Science*, *171*(3972), 701–703. doi:10.1126/science.171.3972.701 PMID:5540314

Shirke, A. (2021, October 7). *What is Pedagogy? Importance of pedagogy in teaching and learning process*. Www.iitms.co.in

Short, D. (2012). Teaching scientific concepts using a virtual world: Minecraft. *Teaching Science*, *58*(3), 55-58.

Simon, F., Luca, P., Alexis, C., Ryan-Rhys, G., Tommaso, S., Thomas, L., Philipp, P., & Julius, B. (2023). Mathematical Capabilities of ChatGPT. *37th Conference on Neural Information Processing Systems (NeurIPS 2023) Track on Datasets and Benchmarks*, 1–46. https://ghosts.friederrr.org

Sinha, S. (2021). Augmented Reality (AR) In Education: A Staggering Insight Into The Future. Available at https://elearningindustry.com/augmented-reality-in-education-staggering-insight-into-future

Sirin, S. R. (2005). Socioeconomic status and academic achievement: A meta-analytic review of research. *Review of Educational Research*, *75*(3), 417–453. doi:10.3102/00346543075003417

Smeyers, P. (2018). *International handbook of philosophy of education*. Springer. doi:10.1007/978-3-319-72761-5

Smiderle, R., Rigo, S. J., Marques, L., de Miranda Coelho, J. A. P., & Jaques, P. (2020). *The impact of gamification on students' learning, engagement and behavior based on their personality traits* [Review of The impact of gamification on students' learning, engagement and behavior based on their personality traits]. doi:10.1186/s40561-019-0098-x

Sms, S. (2021). Recognizing mental rotation and spatial visualization skills in Minecraft in-game practices. *Proceedings of the International Conference on Future of Education, 4*(1), 47-57.

Sohail, R. (2020). *Utilizing social cognitive theory to explore knowledge gaps in school health education: A phenomenological study*. California State University. https://scholarworks.calstate.edu/downloads/9019s503g

Song, L., & Hill, J. R. (2007). A conceptual model for understanding self-directed learning in online environments. *Journal of Interactive Online Learning, 6*(1), 27–42.

Sopcak, P. (2020). Academic integrity and the pandemic. *Canadian Perspectives on Academic Integrity, 3*(2), 41–42.

Sorby, S. A. (2009). Educational research in developing 3-D spatial skills for engineering students. *International Journal of Science Education, 31*(3), 459–480. doi:10.1080/09500690802595839

Sousa, M. J., & Rocha, Á. (2019). Leadership styles and skills developed through game-based learning. *Journal of Business Research, 94*, 360–366. doi:10.1016/j.jbusres.2018.01.057

Spector, J. M., Merrill, M. D., Elen, J., & Bishop, M. J. (Eds.). (2014). *Handbook of research on educational communications and technology*. Springer. doi:10.1007/978-1-4614-3185-5

Spires, H. A., & Lester, J. C. (2016). Game-based learning: Creating a multidisciplinary community of inquiry. *On the Horizon, 24*(1), 88–93. doi:10.1108/OTH-08-2015-0052

Spychalski, B. (2023). Holistic Education for Sustainable Development: A Study of Shaping the Pro-Quality Attitude of Students in the Polish Educational System. *Sustainability (Basel), 15*(10), 8073. doi:10.3390/su15108073

Squire, K. D. (2008). Video game–based learning: An emerging paradigm for instruction. *Performance Improvement Quarterly, 21*(2), 7–36. doi:10.1002/piq.20020

Srikanthan, G., & Dalrymple, J. F. (2002). Developing a holistic model for quality in higher education. *Quality in Higher Education, 8*(3), 215–224. doi:10.1080/1353832022000031656

Sriram, A., & Viswanathan, D. V. (2008). Radio, Television and the Internet providing the Right to Education in India. *Asian Journal of Distance Education, 6*(1), 39–52. https://doi.org/https://www.semanticscholar.org/

Statica. (2023). *Video gaming worldwide*. Statista. Retreived june 2023 from https://www.statista.com/topics/1680/gaming/#topicOverview

Steele, P., Burleigh, C., Bailey, L., & Kroposki, M. (2020). Studio thinking framework in higher education: Exploring options for shaping immersive experiences across virtual reality/augmented reality curricula. *Journal of Educational Technology Systems, 48*(3), 416–439. doi:10.1177/0047239519884897

Stefenon, S. F., Bruns, R., Sartori, A., Meyer, L. H., Ovejero, R. G., & Leithardt, V. R. Q. (2022b). Analysis of the ultrasonic signal in polymeric contaminated insulators through ensemble learning methods. *IEEE Access : Practical Innovations, Open Solutions*, *10*, 33980–33991. doi:10.1109/ACCESS.2022.3161506

Stefenon, S. F., Ribeiro, M. H. D. M., Nied, A., Mariani, V. C., Coelho, L. D. S., Leithardt, V. R. Q., & Seman, L. O. (2021). Hybrid wavelet stacking ensemble model for insulators contamination forecasting. *IEEE Access : Practical Innovations, Open Solutions*, *9*, 66387–66397. doi:10.1109/ACCESS.2021.3076410

Stefenon, S. F., Ribeiro, M. H. D. M., Nied, A., Yow, K. C., Mariani, V. C., dos Santos Coelho, L., & Seman, L. O. (2022d). Time series forecasting using ensemble learning methods for emergency prevention in hydroelectric power plants with dam. *Electric Power Systems Research*, *202*, 107584. doi:10.1016/j.epsr.2021.107584

Stefenon, S. F., Seman, L. O., Neto, N. F. S., Meyer, L. H., Nied, A., & Yow, K. C. (2022). Echo state network applied for classification of medium voltage insulators. *International Journal of Electrical Power & Energy Systems*, *134*, 107336. doi:10.1016/j.ijepes.2021.107336

Stefenon, S. F., Singh, G., Yow, K. C., & Cimatti, A. (2022c). Semi-ProtoPNet deep neural network for the classification of defective power grid distribution structures. *Sensors (Basel)*, *22*(13), 4859. doi:10.3390/s22134859 PMID:35808353

Sternberg, R. J. (2003). *Wisdom, intelligence, and creativity synthesized.* Cambridge University Press. doi:10.1017/CBO9780511509612

Storytelling - benefits and tips. (n.d.). Teaching English. https://www.teachingenglish.org.uk/professional-development/teachers/managing-resources/articles/storytelling-benefits-and-tips

Sudhakar, M. (2023). *Enhancing Plagiarism Detection: The Role of Artificial Intelligence in Upholding Academic Integrity*. Library Philosophy & Practice.

Sung, H. Y., & Hwang, G. J. (2013). A collaborative game-based learning approach to improving students' learning performance in science courses. *Computers & Education*, *63*, 43–51. doi:10.1016/j.compedu.2012.11.019

Sun, J. C. Y., Ye, S. L., Yu, S. J., & Chiu, T. K. (2023). Effects of Wearable Hybrid AR/VR Learning Material on High School Students' Situational Interest, Engagement, and Learning Performance: The Case of a Physics Laboratory Learning Environment. *Journal of Science Education and Technology*, *32*(1), 1–12. doi:10.1007/s10956-022-10001-4

Sviridova, E., Yastrebova, E., Bakirova, G., & Rebrina, F. (2023, October). Immersive technologies as an innovative tool to increase academic success and motivation in higher education. [). Frontiers.]. *Frontiers in Education*, *8*, 1192760. doi:10.3389/feduc.2023.1192760

Sweller, J., van Merriënboer, J. J. G., & Paas, F. (2019). Cognitive architecture and instructional design: 20 years later. *Educational Psychology Review*, *31*(2), 261–292. doi:10.1007/s10648-019-09465-5

Syed-Abdul, S., Malwade, S., Nursetyo, A. A., Sood, M., Bhatia, M., Barsasella, D., Liu, M. F., Chang, C.-C., Srinivasan, K., M, R., & Li, Y. C. J. (2019). Virtual reality among the elderly: A usefulness and acceptance study from Taiwan. *BMC Geriatrics*, *19*(1), 1–10. doi:10.1186/s12877-019-1218-8 PMID:31426766

T.C. (2019, May 22). *Successful project-based learning*. Harvard Business Publishing Education.

Taba, H. (1967). *Teachers' handbook for elementary social studies*. Addison-Wesley.

Tan, Y., Xu, W., Li, S., & Chen, K. (2022). Augmented and Virtual Reality (AR/VR) for Education and Training in the AEC Industry: A Systematic Review of Research and Applications. *Buildings*, *12*(10), 1529. doi:10.3390/buildings12101529

Tao, H., Chongmin, L., Zain, J. M., & Abdalla, A. N. (2014). Robust Image Watermarking Theories and Techniques: A Review. *Journal of Applied Research and Technology*, *12*(1), 122–138. doi:10.1016/S1665-6423(14)71612-8

Tashko, R., & Elena, R. (2015). Augmented reality as a teaching tool in higher education. *International Journal of Cognitive Research in Science. Engineering and Education*, *3*(1), 7–15.

Tepe, T., & Kaleci, D. & Tüzün, H. (2016). Eğitim teknolojilerinde yeni eğilimler: Sanal gerçeklik uygulamaları. *10th International Computer and Instructional Technologies Symposium (ICITS)*, 547-555.

TEQSA. (2021). *What is academic Integrity.* https://www.teqsa.gov.au/students/understanding-academic-integrity/what-academic-integrity

The Benefits of Experiential Learning for Students. (n.d.). Retrieved February 27, 2024, from https://www.envisionexperience.com/blog/the-benefits-of-experiential-learning#

Tiwari, C. K., Bhaskar, P., & Pal, A. (2023). Prospects of augmented reality and virtual reality for online education: A scientometric view. *International Journal of Educational Management*, *37*(5), 1042–1066. doi:10.1108/IJEM-10-2022-0407

Tomlinson, C. A. (2001). *How to differentiate instruction in mixed-ability classrooms*. Ascd.

Tong, D. H., Uyen, B. P., & Ngan, L. K. (2022). The effectiveness of blended learning on students' academic achievement, self-study skills and learning attitudes: A quasi-experiment study in teaching the conventions for coordinates in the plane. *Heliyon*, *8*(12), e12657. doi:10.1016/j.heliyon.2022.e12657 PMID:36643330

Traxler, J. (2007). Defining, discussing, and evaluating mobile learning: The moving finger writes and having writ..... *International Review of Research in Open and Distance Learning*, *8*(2), 1–12. doi:10.19173/irrodl.v8i2.346

Trilling, B., & Fadel, C. (2012). *21st century skills: Learning for life in our times*. John Wiley & Sons.

Turner, D. W. (2010). Qualitative interview design: A practical guide for novice investigators. *The qualitative report, 15*(3), 754.

Turner, D. W. III. (2010). Qualitative interview design: A practical guide for novice investigators. *The Qualitative Report, 15*(3), 754–760. doi:10.46743/2160-3715/2010.1178

Tvarozek, J., & Brza, T. (2014). Engaging students in online courses through interactive badges. *2014 International Conference on-Learning*. https://pdfs.semanticscholar.org/fe68/5176c8d4bf7f6507f3870815f56a65097c89.pdf

Ubaka, C., Gbenga, F., Sunday, N., & Ndidiamaka, E. (2013). Academic dishonesty among Nigeria pharmacy students: A comparison with United Kingdom. *African Journal of Pharmacy and Pharmacology, 7*(27), 1934–1941. doi:10.5897/AJPP2013.3587

Udeozor, C., Toyoda, R., Russo Abegão, F., & Glassey, J. (2022). Digital games in engineering education: Systematic review and future trends. *European Journal of Engineering Education, 48*(2), 321–339. doi:10.1080/03043797.2022.2093168

Uppot, Laguna, B., McCarthy, C. J., De Novi, G., Phelps, A., Siegel, E., & Courtier, J. (2019). Implementing virtual and augmented reality tools for radiology education and training, communication, and clinical care. *Radiology, 291*(3), 570–580. doi:10.1148/radiol.2019182210 PMID:30990383

Vasilevsk. (2020). Analysing construction student experiences of mobile mixed reality enhanced learning in virtual and augmented reality environments. *Research in Learning Technology, 28*(0), 28. doi:10.25304/rlt.v28.2329

Veneziano, L., & Hooper, J. (1997). A method for quantifying content validity of health-related questionnaires. *American Journal of Health Behavior, 21*(1), 67–70.

Verganti, R., Vendraminelli, L., & Iansiti, M. (2020). Innovation and Design in the Age of Artificial Intelligence. *Journal of Product Innovation Management, 37*(3), 212–227. doi:10.1111/jpim.12523

Videnov, K., Stoykova, V., & Kazlacheva, Z. (2018). Application of augmented reality in higher education. ARTTE Applied Researches in Technics. *Technologies and Education, 6*(1), 1–9.

Vieira, J. C., Sartori, A., Stefenon, S. F., Perez, F. L., De Jesus, G. S., & Leithardt, V. R. Q. (2022). Low-cost CNN for automatic violence recognition on embedded system. *IEEE Access : Practical Innovations, Open Solutions, 10*, 25190–25202. doi:10.1109/ACCESS.2022.3155123

Volpentesta, T., Spahiu, E., & De Giovanni, P. (2023). A survey on incumbent digital transformation: A paradoxical perspective and research agenda. *European Journal of Innovation Management, 26*(7), 478–501. doi:10.1108/EJIM-01-2023-0081

Vygotsky, L. S. (1978). *Mind in society: The development of higher psychological processes*. Harvard University Press.

Wagner, T. (2008). *The global achievement gap: Why even our best schools don't teach the new survival skills our children need—and what we can do about it*. Basic Books.

Wai, J., Lubinski, D., & Benbow, C. P. (2009). Spatial ability for STEM domains: Aligning over 50 years of cumulative psychological knowledge solidifies its importance. *Journal of Educational Psychology, 101*(4), 817–835. doi:10.1037/a0016127

Waller, V. (2011). Not just information: Who searches for what on the search engine Google? *Journal of the American Society for Information Science and Technology, 62*(4), 761–775. doi:10.1002/asi.21492

Wanner, T., & Palmer, E. (2015). Personalising learning: Exploring student and teacher perceptions about flexible learning and assessment in a flipped university course. *Computers & Education, 88*, 354–363. doi:10.1016/j.compedu.2015.07.008

Wawak, S., Teixeira Domingues, J. P., & Sampaio, P. (2023). Quality 4.0 in higher education: Reinventing academic-industry-government collaboration during disruptive times. *The TQM Journal*. Advance online publication. doi:10.1108/TQM-07-2023-0219

Wei, C. Y., Kuah, Y. C., Ng, C. P., & Lau, W. K. (2021). Augmented Reality (AR) as an enhancement teaching tool: Are educators ready for it? *Contemporary Educational Technology, 13*(3), ep303. doi:10.30935/cedtech/10866

Whiting, L. S. (2008). Semi-structured interviews: Guidance for novice researchers. *Nursing Standard, 22*(23), 35–40. doi:10.7748/ns2008.02.22.23.35.c6420 PMID:18323051

Whitley, B. E., & Keith-Spiegel, P. (2002). *Academic dishonesty. An educators guide*. Lawrence Erlbaum Associates Publishers.

Williams, J., & Harvey, L. (2015). Quality assurance in higher education. The Palgrave international handbook of higher education policy and governance, 506-525.

Wolbers, T., & Hegarty, M. (2010). What determines our navigational abilities? *Trends in Cognitive Sciences, 14*(3), 138–146. doi:10.1016/j.tics.2010.01.001 PMID:20138795

Wood, D. (2010). *Rethinking the power of maps*. Guilford Press.

Wright, N. (2015). A case for adapting and applying continuance theory to education: Understanding the role of student feedback in motivating teachers to persist with including digital technologies in learning. *Teachers and Teaching, 21*(4), 459–471. doi:10.1080/13540602.2014.969105

Wu, T., He, S., Liu, J., Sun, S., Liu, K., Han, Q.-L., & Tang, Y. (2023). A Brief Overview of ChatGPT: The History, Status Quo and Potential Future Development. *IEEE/CAA Journal of Automatica Sinica, 10*(5), 1122–1136. doi:10.1109/JAS.2023.123618

Wu, H. K., Lee, S. W. Y., Chang, H. Y., & Liang, J.-C. (2013). Current Status, Opportunities And Challenges Of Augmented Reality In Education. *Computers & Education, 62*, 41–49. doi:10.1016/j.compedu.2012.10.024

Yamanaka, G. (2019). *Geo-Fencing in Wireless LANs with Camera for Location-Based Access Control. 2019 16th IEEE Annual Consumer Communications & Networking Conference*. CCNC. doi:10.1109/CCNC.2019.8651877

Yang, F. C. O., Lai, H. M., & Wang, Y. W. (2023). Effect of augmented reality-based virtual educational robotics on programming students' enjoyment of learning, computational thinking skills, and academic achievement. *Computers & Education*, *195*, 104721. doi:10.1016/j.compedu.2022.104721

Yeşiltaş, E., & Cantürk, A. (2022). Trends of researches on the use of games in social studies education: 1971 – 2021. *Journal of History School*, *15*(61), 4434–4466.

Young, G. W., Stehle, S., Walsh, B. Y., & Tiri, E. (2020). Exploring virtual reality in the higher education classroom: Using VR to build knowledge and understanding. *Journal of Universal Computer Science*, *26*(8), 904–928. doi:10.3897/jucs.2020.049

Yulianto, B., Prabowo, H., & Kosala, R. (2016). Comparing the effectiveness of digital contents for improving learning outcomes in computer programming for autodidact students. *Journal of E-Learning and Knowledge Society*, *12*(1). Advance online publication. doi:10.20368/1971-8829/1081

Yurdugül, H. (2005). Ölçek geliştirme çalışmalarında kapsam geçerliği için kapsam geçerlik indekslerinin kullanılması [Using content validity indices for content validity in scale development studies]. XIV. Ulusal Eğitim Bilimleri Kongresi. Pamukkale Üniversitesi.

Zainurin, M. Z. L., Haji Masri, M., Besar, M. H. A., & Anshari, M. (2023). Towards an understanding of metaverse banking: A conceptual paper. *Journal of Financial Reporting and Accounting*, *21*(1), 178–190. doi:10.1108/JFRA-12-2021-0487

Zhai, X., Chu, X., Chai, C. S., Jong, M. S. Y., Istenic, A., Spector, M., & Li, Y. (2021). A Review of Artificial Intelligence (AI) in Education from 2010 to 2020. *Complexity*, *2021*, 1–18. doi:10.1155/2021/8812542

Zhang, R., Zhou, J., Hai, T., Zhang, S., Iwendi, M., Biamba, C., & Anumbe, N. (2022). Quality assurance awareness in higher education in China: big data challenges. *Journal of Cloud Computing*, *11*(1), 1-9.

Zhang, Y. (2009). Digital Watermarking Technology: A Review. *Proceedings of the ETP International Conference on Future Computer and Communication*, 250–252.

Zhao, Y., & Zhou, X. (2021). K-means clustering algorithm and its improvement research. *Journal of Physics: Conference Series*, *1873*(1), 012074. doi:10.1088/1742-6596/1873/1/012074

Zheng, M., & Spires, H. A. (2014). Fifth graders' flow experience in a digital game-based science learning environment. *International Journal of Virtual and Personal Learning Environments*, *5*(2), 69–86. doi:10.4018/ijvple.2014040106

Zhou, X., Tang, L., Lin, D., & Han, W. (2020). Virtual & augmented reality for biological microscope in experiment education. *Virtual Reality & Intelligent Hardware*, *2*(4), 316–329. doi:10.1016/j.vrih.2020.07.004

About the Contributors

Rashmi Aggarwal is working as Professor and Assistant Dean (Under-Graduation) at Chitkara Business School, Chitkara University, Punjab, India.

Rajni Bala is presently working as an assistant professor in Chitkara Business School, Chitkara University, Punjab, India. She is having 15.2 years of teaching experience. She has worked with NIT, Kurukshetra, Maharishi Markandeshwar deemed to be University, Mullana and Mukand Lal National Group. She is having 25 research publications in her account indexed in Scopus and UGC care. She has presented a number of papers in various national and international conferences. She is having 4 patents and 3 copyrights in her account. She has delivered workshops on Writing Literature Review, Statistical Tools on Excel, Innovative technologies in education, etc.

* * *

Yogi Agravat is a seasoned professional who has excelled in various facets of his career, boasting a rich background in both industry and academia. After pursuing studies at renowned institutions, he embarked on an entrepreneurial journey, leveraging his expertise to deliver engaging and impactful teaching experiences. Specializing in Marketing and Entrepreneurship, his teaching approach is grounded in practical insights and real-world applications, equipping students with the necessary skills for success in these fields. As a dedicated mentor and expert in their domain, he brings valuable expertise to the classroom, guiding aspiring business professionals towards excellence.

Garima Arora is a Research Scholar in Maharishi Markandeshwar (Deemed to be University), Mullana, Ambala. She has 4.5 years of teaching experience. She has published papers in journals and a chapter in a reputed book.

Ansh Jindal is pursuing MBA finance from Chitkara Business School, Chitkara University, Punjab, India.

Hüseyin Kocasaraç works at the General Directorate of Innovation and Educational Technologies at the Ministry of National Education. He has studied innovative education, innovative teachers, and digital education. Kocasaraç holds a Doctorate of Education focusing in Curriculum and Instruction from the University of Yıldız Teknik in Turkey.

Imroz Mansuri is an academician having industry as well as academic experience. He has worked with some renowned corporates such as Adani, HDFC Bank, and Anand Rathi. He holds tremendous experience in Stock Exchange, Mutual funds, Structured Products, Investment Banking and Global Financial Markets. He also holds an Editorial position with the International Engineering Journal for Research & Development. His problem-solving approach surely becomes a guiding point for the students of Narayana Business School.

Handson Fingi Mlotshwa is the Director of ICT Programs at the Matthew Goniwe School of Leadership & Governance. He is also a Fellow of the Cambridge HP partnership for education. Handson holds a Master of Education focusing in educational technology from the University of the Witwatersrand in South Africa.

Neena Nanda is a distinguished educator and leader in the field of Educational Leadership & Management. Recognized for her outstanding contributions, she has received accolades such as the "Women Excellence Award 2021" and "Best Professor in Business Information & Analytics." With expertise in quantitative data analysis and employer branding, Dr. Nanda has pioneered statistical models to measure and predict online engagement in the digital landscape. Holding key roles in academia, she mentors Ph.D. candidates and instructs on Statistics for Decision Making, Operations Research, and Research Methodology. Dr. Nanda's dedication to student growth and her prolific research contributions have established her as a thought leader in her field. She also offers consultancy services to SMEs, leveraging her expertise in data analysis and strategic planning to enhance operational efficiency and competitiveness.

Geetanjali Pinto, an esteemed professional in the fields of Finance, Accounts, Audits, Taxation, and Company law matters, boasts over 24 years of diverse experience. Throughout her career, Dr. Pinto has excelled in various roles within industry and academia, leaving a lasting impact due to her professional attitude and meticulous approach. Presently, Dr. Pinto holds the position of Associate Professor & Head of Department – PGDM Finance at SIES School of Business Studies in Mumbai. Her journey in academia has been characterized by a deep commitment to teaching and research excellence. In the realm of research, Dr. Pinto is renowned for her specialization in corporate finance and her adept use of panel data econometric tools for data analysis. Her scholarly contributions extend to numerous articles presented at conferences and published across ABDC, Web of Science, Scopus Indexed and UGC-approved journals. Dr. Pinto's unwavering dedication to excellence and her extensive expertise have earned her respect in both academia and industry circles. She continues to inspire and empower the next generation of finance professionals through her teaching, research, and leadership.

Sabyasachi Pramanik is a professional IEEE member. He obtained a PhD in Computer Science and Engineering from Sri Satya Sai University of Technology and Medical Sciences, Bhopal, India. Presently, he is an Associate Professor, Department of Computer Science and Engineering, Haldia Institute of Technology, India. He has many publications in various reputed international conferences, journals, and book chapters (Indexed by SCIE, Scopus, ESCI, etc). He is doing research in the fields of Artificial Intelligence, Data Privacy, Cybersecurity, Network Security, and Machine Learning. He also serves on the editorial boards of several international journals. He is a reviewer of journal articles from IEEE, Springer, Elsevier, Inderscience, IET and IGI Global. He has reviewed many conference papers, has been a keynote speaker, session chair, and technical program committee member at many international conferences. He has authored a book on Wireless Sensor Network. He has edited 8 books from IGI Global, CRC Press, Springer and Wiley Publications.

Bhavna Raina has 15+ years' experience in industry and academics in the field of Human Resources. She has certifications in Behavioural Event Interview from Aon Hewitt, Personal Profile Analyst from Thomas International, Master Trainer and Assessor from Management & Entrepreneurship And Professional Skills Council(Govt. of India) and is also a POSH trainer. She has done Certification in Fundamentals of Business from Harvard Business School and certification in labour laws from XLRI. She has published many articles in Scopus and UGC care journals on topics related to Human Resources and Organisation Behaviour.

Yogita Rawat is working as Head of Department at Department of Digital Marketing & Transformation, ITM Business School, Navi Mumbai, Kharghar. Her area of interests are majorly in Digital Marketing & Analytics.

Shefali Saluja is working as an Assistant Professor in Chitkara University holding Doctoral degree in Corporate Governance. She has conducted research on "Detection and Prevention of Corporate Frauds" in her PhD studies. She has total 12 years of work experience. Shefali has been an expert in the field of Ethics and Governance. Her current job position includes various teaching and administrative related responsibilities in Chitkara university. She is managing NAAC Accreditation and AACSB Internal accreditation process for Chitkara Business School. Shefali has been continuously invited in many teaching opportunities nationally and internationally. Shefali has written 19 research papers that are published, 6 submitted and 3 granted patents, 14 copyrights in multidisciplinary research areas. She is the member of Association of Certified Fraud Examiners (ACFE), USA and has been doing volunteer work for them since 2021.

Kumar Shalender is a Post-Doctoral Fellow of the Global Institute of Flexible Systems Management and a Doctor of Philosophy in Strategic Management. He has more than 14-year experience in the domain of Business Policy, Strategic Management, and Business Model Development and a total of 70 Publications including presentations at international/national conferences and book chapters to his credit. His current research areas include the field of Metaverse, Blockchain Technology, and Sustainable Development with a special focus on sustainable cities and mobility ecosystems in India.

Deepa Sharma has done Ph.D., MBA in Human Resource Management, currently working as Assistant Professor at MMIM, Maharishi Markandeshwar (Deemed to be University), NAAC Accredited Grade 'A++' University, Mullana, Ambala (Haryana). She has more than 7 years of experience in academics. She has written 45+ research papers for various Scopus and UGC listed referred National & International Journals.

Shivangi Shukla Bhavsar is an Associate Professor at Narayana Business School, Ahmedabad, Gujarat. She has specialization in Marketing and has more than 11 years of teaching and research experience. An academician by passion, an author and a researcher. She bags many publications in various national as well as international journals. She has won many awards as best Research paper presenter at various global conferences. She organically transforms the attitude of students in the most positive manner.

Amandeep Singh holds a Doctorate in Management specializing in Marketing and he is also UGC-NET qualified. He holds more than 16 years of teaching experience. His main area of research is Consumer Sciences and Business Innovations. Currently, he is working as Professor at Chitkara Business School, Chitkara University, Punjab, India. He has published 48 research papers in various journals and conferences which are indexed in Scopus, Web of Science and Google Scholar. He has edited 7 books published by IGI Global, De Gruyter and Wiley. He has also chaired many National and International Conferences. He is on the editorial board of 3 International Journals. He was awarded the Best Teacher in 2008. He is also part of the Board of Studies of various B-Schools and leading universities in Northern India.

Babita Singla is a professor at Chitkara Business School, Chitkara University, Punjab, India. She has a Ph.D. in management and is UGC-NET qualified. She has over 13 years of experience in teaching, research, and administration. Her areas of expertise are marketing, e-commerce, omnichannel, and retail. In her career, she has been involved in important academic and research assignments such as being the guest editor of reputed journal, organizing and conducting international and national-level conferences, faculty development programs, and providing guidance for research projects along the way. She has research publications in reputable international and national journals such as Scopus, SCI, etc., and has presented research papers at various national and international conferences. In the short span of 13 years of her career in academia and administration, she has authored and edited several books on retailing, supply chain management, branding, customer relationship management, and product management, covering the course content of various universities across the nation. She has successfully delivered guest sessions at international and national universities.

Rajit Verma is a confident, extrovertd, flexible and energetic person with good communication skills. He has Proven strength in problem solving and coordination with strong analytical skills. He is a diligent and tenacious worker with a deep sense of ethics and integrity and strong Interpersonal skills. He has 15 years of teaching experience in the university teaching. He is PhD in the area of Finance and Financial econometrics from Kurukshetra University in 2018. He pursued MBA (Finance) from Kurukshetra University in 2009. His key area of research is Artificial Neural Networks and machine learning in security market, portfolio management, investment analysis, Block chains and cryptograph. He has many achievements and has conferred many national and international research awards. He has more than 25 Scopus/SCI publications and also he has 25+ patents to his name.

Prachi Yadav is currently pursuing PGDM in Digital Marketing at ITM Business School, Navi Mumbai, Kharghar. She is also an active member of various student's forums & clubs at ITM Business School.

Index

21st-century competencies 229-230, 232-235, 237, 239, 241, 243-246

A

Academic Dishonesty 157-164
Academic Honesty 56, 59, 158
Academic Integrity 57, 60, 157-158, 160, 162-164, 192
AI algorithms 76, 80-82, 97
AI systems 77-79, 82
AR technologies 14, 43-44, 70, 98, 109, 111, 205
AR tools 4, 6-8, 11-15, 205
Artificial Intelligence (AI) 2, 67, 76, 78, 80-82, 87, 97, 106, 110, 188-189, 191-193, 199, 204, 206, 209, 212, 217, 220
Augmented Reality (AR) 1-2, 11-12, 15, 26, 40-41, 43-44, 46, 50-52, 66-67, 69-76, 78, 82, 86-90, 92-93, 95-98, 106, 109-113, 196, 199, 205-206, 208-209, 211, 216, 218, 222

B

Blended Learning 57, 168-169, 171-173

C

Chat GPT 189
Collaborative Projects 19, 28, 206
computer-generated environment 107, 109
course administration 198, 203
Covid19 outbreak 57
critical thinking 15, 24, 68, 71, 81-82, 91, 125, 162, 168, 170, 230, 232, 241, 243, 245
cultural factors 20, 22-24, 27-29, 34, 38
culturally responsive 32, 34
curriculum design 21-22, 29, 38, 77
curriculum requirements 43-44
cutting-edge instruments 87, 89

D

Data Breach 59-60, 63
development process 229, 234, 237, 240, 243-245
digital domain 211-212
digital education 198, 203
digital games 123-124, 126, 143-146
digital information 63, 69, 72, 109
Digital Learning Material 229, 234
digital literacy 12, 73, 79-80, 92, 164, 230, 233
Digital materials 244
digital platforms 57, 59
digital teaching 230, 232-235, 237, 240-241, 243-244
digital tools 2, 52, 59, 122, 173, 233, 244

E

E-Content 56, 60, 62
EdTech tools 196-198, 203, 206-207, 211-212

Educational Organisations 11, 13-14
educational practices 20, 32, 34, 87, 112, 196-197, 210
Educational Technology (EdTech) 58, 196-198, 207-208, 210-212
Effective Teaching 22, 24, 29, 31, 126, 179
E-Learning 14, 56-63, 157-158, 162, 197, 216-217, 222
Experiential Learning 19, 21, 25, 28, 36, 71, 73, 168-169, 180-181, 183, 205
Explanatory Mixed-Method 122

G

Gamification 98, 124, 168-169, 174, 176, 199, 211

H

hands-on experiences 20, 28, 92

I

ICT literacy 240, 243, 245
ICT skills 244-245
ICT-based teaching 245-246
immersive experiences 67-73, 81, 90, 96-97
Immersive Learning 3, 66, 70-72, 74, 81, 86, 89, 95, 97-98, 106, 111, 197, 199, 205, 218-220, 224-225
Immersive Technologies 67-69, 72-74, 76, 78-82, 221
intellectual property 193
Interactive Learning Tools (ILT) 196, 199, 204

L

Learning Experience 3, 90, 109, 112, 160, 173, 197, 199, 204-206, 209, 220-221, 230, 244

M

Massive Open Online Courses (MOOCs) 196, 210-211
material development 229, 234-235, 237, 240, 243-245
Metaverse 215-226
Minecraft 122, 125-129, 133, 135, 138, 140, 142-146
Mobile Environment 106

O

observational learning 19-20, 23-24, 27-29, 31, 36-38
Online Data 63
Online Learning Platforms 196, 199, 206, 220

P

pedagogical transformation 168-170
Postgraduate Education 19, 21-24, 28, 31, 34, 38
post-test achievement 127, 134, 138
predictive analytics 2, 199, 204, 207
pre-service teachers 233-234, 245-246
professional development 37-38, 41, 47, 49, 52, 73-74, 77, 88, 200, 210-212, 246
Project Based Learning 177

R

Research Ethics 191-192

S

Science Research 188-192
SCT framework 20, 30, 32, 34, 38
Search Engines 189-190
Sequential Exploratory Design 229, 234
simulated environment 4-5, 8-9, 42, 51, 96
Social Cognitive Theory 19-20, 22-23, 27-28, 111
social interaction 123, 125, 172, 174, 233
social media 26, 217, 223
Social Science Research 188-192
Social Studies 122, 124-127, 129-131, 133, 136-137, 142-146

spatial perception 122, 125-131, 135, 140-146
Spatial Perception Skills 122, 126-129, 131, 135, 140-146
Stakeholders 1, 3, 7-9, 20, 22, 80, 189-191, 208, 210, 212, 226, 246
Storytelling 12, 95, 123, 145, 168-169, 178-180

T

Teaching and learning 25-27, 38, 40-41, 44-46, 48-52, 56, 58, 91-92, 108-109, 196-198, 203-204, 206-208, 211-212, 217, 245
technological competency 211-212
Technology-Enhanced Education 19, 28, 32
traditional classroom 57, 66, 81, 88, 94, 118, 171, 222
Transformative Power 69, 110, 196, 198

U

University Students 229, 234-235

V

virtual environments 66, 70-71, 73, 78, 81, 90, 110
virtual landscape 158
Virtual Reality (VR) 6, 40-48, 50-52, 66-78, 82, 86-90, 92-98, 107-109, 111-113, 118, 170, 197, 205, 207, 209, 218, 222

Publishing Tomorrow's Research Today

Uncover Current Insights and Future Trends in

Education

with IGI Global's Cutting-Edge Recommended Books

Print Only, E-Book Only, or Print + E-Book.

Order direct through IGI Global's Online Bookstore at **www.igi-global.com** or through your preferred provider.

ISBN: 9781668493007
© 2023; 234 pp.
List Price: US$ **215**

ISBN: 9798369300749
© 2024; 383 pp.
List Price: US$ **230**

ISBN: 9781668486467
© 2023; 471 pp.
List Price: US$ **215**

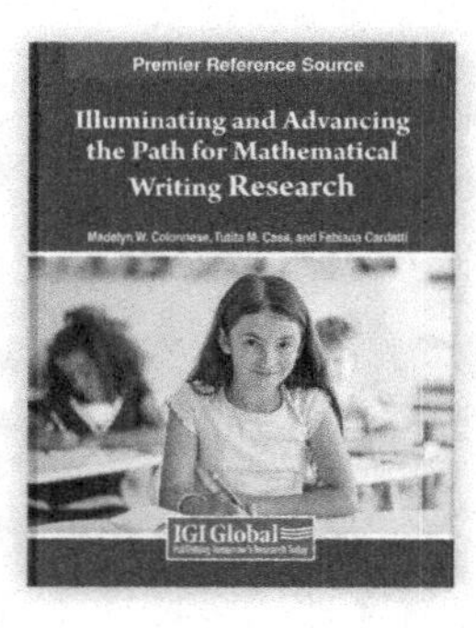

ISBN: 9781668465387
© 2024; 389 pp.
List Price: US$ **215**

ISBN: 9781668475836
© 2024; 359 pp.
List Price: US$ **215**

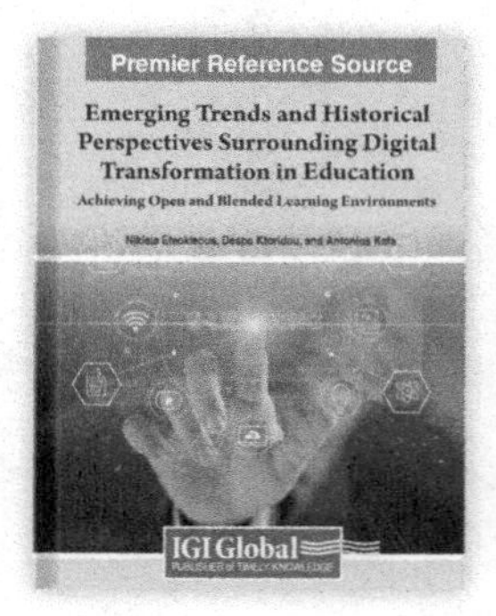

ISBN: 9781668444238
© 2023; 334 pp.
List Price: US$ **240**

Do you want to stay current on the latest research trends, product announcements, news, and special offers?
Join IGI Global's mailing list to receive customized recommendations, exclusive discounts, and more.
Sign up at: www.igi-global.com/newsletters.

Scan the QR Code here to view more related titles in Education.

www.igi-global.com Sign up at www.igi-global.com/newsletters facebook.com/igiglobal twitter.com/igiglobal linkedin.com/igiglobal

Ensure Quality Research is Introduced to the Academic Community

Become a Reviewer for IGI Global Authored Book Projects

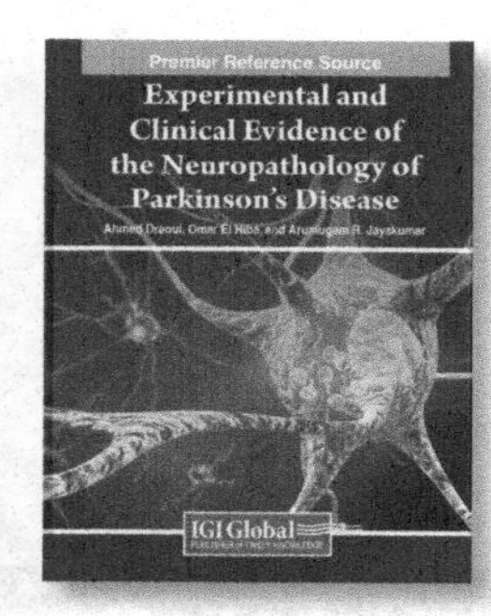

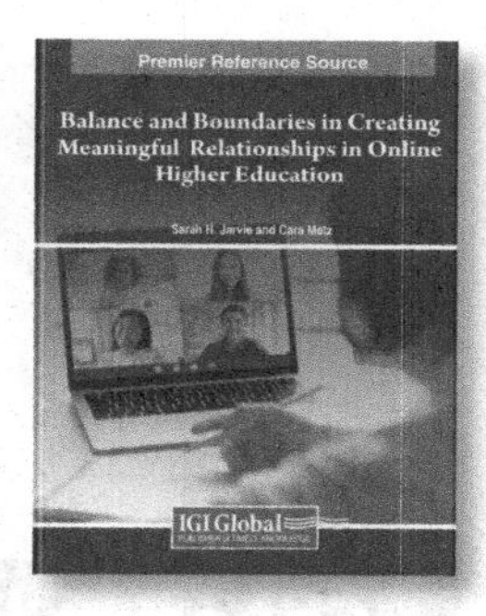

The overall success of an authored book project is dependent on quality and timely manuscript evaluations.

Applications and Inquiries may be sent to:
development@igi-global.com

Applicants must have a doctorate (or equivalent degree) as well as publishing, research, and reviewing experience. Authored Book Evaluators are appointed for one-year terms and are expected to complete at least three evaluations per term. Upon successful completion of this term, evaluators can be considered for an additional term.

If you have a colleague that may be interested in this opportunity, we encourage you to share this information with them.

www.igi-global.com

Publishing Tomorrow's Research Today

IGI Global's Open Access Journal Program

Including Nearly 200 Peer-Reviewed, Gold (Full) Open Access Journals across IGI Global's Three Academic Subject Areas: Business & Management; Scientific, Technical, and Medical (STM); and Education

Consider Submitting Your Manuscript to One of These Nearly 200 Open Access Journals for to Increase Their Discoverability & Citation Impact

Web of Science Impact Factor 6.5

Web of Science Impact Factor 4.7

Web of Science Impact Factor 3.2

Web of Science Impact Factor 2.6

JOURNAL OF
Database Management
IGI PUBLISHING

Choosing IGI Global's Open Access Journal Program Can Greatly Increase the Reach of Your Research

Higher Usage
Open access papers are 2-3 times more likely to be read than non-open access papers.

Higher Download Rates
Open access papers benefit from 89% higher download rates than non-open access papers.

Higher Citation Rates
Open access papers are 47% more likely to be cited than non-open access papers.

Submitting an article to a journal offers an invaluable opportunity for you to share your work with the broader academic community, fostering knowledge dissemination and constructive feedback.

Submit an Article and Browse the IGI Global Call for Papers Pages

We can work with you to find the journal most well-suited for your next research manuscript.
For open access publishing support, contact: journaleditor@igi-global.com

Publishing Tomorrow's Research Today

IGI Global

e-Book Collection

Including Essential Reference Books Within Three Fundamental Academic Areas

Business & Management
Scientific, Technical, & Medical (STM)
Education

- Acquisition options include Perpetual, Subscription, and Read & Publish
- No Additional Charge for Multi-User Licensing
- No Maintenance, Hosting, or Archiving Fees
- Continually Enhanced Accessibility Compliance Features (WCAG)

Over **150,000+** Chapters	Contributions From **200,000+** Scholars Worldwide	More Than **1,000,000+** Citations	Majority of e-Books Indexed in Web of Science & Scopus	Consists of Tomorrow's Research Available Today!

Recommended Titles from our e-Book Collection

Innovation Capabilities and Entrepreneurial Opportunities of Smart Working
ISBN: 9781799887973

Advanced Applications of Generative AI and Natural Language Processing Models
ISBN: 9798369305027

Using Influencer Marketing as a Digital Business Strategy
ISBN: 9798369305515

Human-Centered Approaches in Industry 5.0
ISBN: 9798369326473

Modeling and Monitoring Extreme Hydrometeorological Events
ISBN: 9781668487716

Data-Driven Intelligent Business Sustainability
ISBN: 9798369300497

Information Logistics for Organizational Empowerment and Effective Supply Chain Management
ISBN: 9798369301593

Data Envelopment Analysis (DEA) Methods for Maximizing Efficiency
ISBN: 9798369302552

Request More Information, or Recommend the IGI Global e-Book Collection to Your Institution's Librarian

For More Information or to Request a Free Trial, Contact IGI Global's e-Collections Team: eresources@igi-global.com | 1-866-342-6657 ext. 100 | 717-533-8845 ext. 100

Are You Ready to Publish Your Research?

IGI Global
Publishing Tomorrow's Research Today

IGI Global offers book authorship and editorship opportunities across three major subject areas, including Business, STM, and Education.

Benefits of Publishing with IGI Global:

- Free one-on-one editorial and promotional support.
- Expedited publishing timelines that can take your book from start to finish in less than one (1) year.
- Choose from a variety of formats, including Edited and Authored References, Handbooks of Research, Encyclopedias, and Research Insights.
- Utilize IGI Global's eEditorial Discovery® submission system in support of conducting the submission and double-blind peer review process.
- IGI Global maintains a strict adherence to ethical practices due in part to our full membership with the Committee on Publication Ethics (COPE).
- Indexing potential in prestigious indices such as Scopus®, Web of Science™, PsycINFO®, and ERIC – Education Resources Information Center.
- Ability to connect your ORCID iD to your IGI Global publications.
- Earn honorariums and royalties on your full book publications as well as complimentary content and exclusive discounts.

Join Your Colleagues from Prestigious Institutions, Including:

Learn More at: www.igi-global.com/publish

or by Contacting the Acquisitions Department at: acquisition@igi-global.com

Individual Article & Chapter Downloads

US$ 37.50/each

Easily Identify, Acquire, and Utilize Published Peer-Reviewed Findings in Support of Your Current Research

- Browse Over ***170,000+ Articles & Chapters***
- ***Accurate & Advanced*** Search
- Affordably Acquire ***International Research***
- ***Instantly Access*** Your Content
- Benefit from the ***InfoSci® Platform Features***

"*It really provides an excellent entry into the research literature of the field. It presents a manageable number of highly relevant sources on topics of interest to a wide range of researchers. The sources are scholarly, but also accessible to 'practitioners'.*"

- Ms. Lisa Stimatz, MLS, University of North Carolina at Chapel Hill, USA

Printed in the United States
by Baker & Taylor Publisher Services